THE CATHOLIC UNIVERSIT

PATRISTIC STUDI

VOL. XXVII

THE VOCABULARY OF HEGESIPPUS

A STUDY IN LATIN LEXICOGRAPHY

A Dissertation

SUBMITTED TO THE FACULTY OF THE GRADUATE SCHOOL OF ARTS AND SCIENCES
OF THE CATHOLIC UNIVERSITY OF AMERICA IN PARTIAL FULFILLMENT
OF THE REQUIREMENTS FOR THE DEGREE OF DOCTOR OF PHILOSOPHY

BY

WILLIAM FRANCIS DWYER, S.S., M.A.

THE CATHOLIC UNIVERSITY OF AMERICA
WASHINGTON, D. C.
1931

TO MY FATHER AND MOTHER

TABLE OF CONTENTS

PART I
LATE LATIN

I. VOCABULARY

SELECT BIBLIOGRAPHY

I. EDITIONS OF HEGESIPPUS AND JOSEPHUS.

Editio princeps, J. Ascensius, Aegesippi historiographi fidelissimi ac disertissimi et ınter christianos antiquissimi historia de bello Iudaico. Sceptri sublatione. Iudaeorum dispersione. Et Hierosolymitano excidio. A divo Ambrosio Mediolanen. Antistite e Graeca Latina facta. Cum eiusdem anacephaleosi et tabellis congruentiarum cum Iosephi libri etiam de gestis Machabaeorum, Paris, 1510.

A. Gallandi, Bibliotheca veterum Patrum, VII, Venice, 1765-1781, pp. 653-771.

Benedictine edition (second reprint), Venice, 1781-1782, II, Appendix (with special pagination). The original Benedictine edition of St. Ambrose (J. du Frische and N. le Noury, Sancti Ambrosii Opera Omnia, 2 vols., fol., Paris, 1686-1690) does not contain the so-called Hegesippus.

Migne PP. L., XV, Sancti Ambrosii Opera Omnia, Paris, 1845, col. 1961-2224. (The Migne edition takes over Gallandi).

C. F. Weber and J. Caesar, Hegesippus qui dicitur sive Egesippus de bello Iudaico recognitus, Marburg, 1864.

P. Ballerini, Sancti Ambrosii Opera Omnia, VI, Milan, 1875-1883, pp. 1-276. (Ballerini takes over the Weber-Caesar edition).

V. Ussani, Iosippi (Hegesippi qui dicitur) historiae liber I, c. I-XXX, in: Memorie del Reale Istıtuto Veneto di Scienze, Lettere ed Arti, vol. XXIX, No. 4 and No. 5, Venice, 1922-1923. (The complete text of Hegesippus, edited by Ussani for the Corpus Scriptorum Ecclesiasticorum Latinorum, has been announced as being in press).

H. St. J. Thackeray, Josephus, 8 vols., Loeb Classical Library, New York. (The Jewish War appears in vols. II and III, 1927-1928).

II. WORKS ON HEGESIPPUS.

A. Works concerned with the Linguistic and Stylistic Aspect.

Hey, O., Aus dem kaiserlichen Kanzleistil, in: Archiv für lateinische Lexikographie und Grammatik 15 (1908), pp. 55-62.

Ihm, M., Studia Ambrosiana, in: Jahrbücher fur klassische Philologie, Supplementband 17, Leipzig, 1890, pp. 1-124.

Landgraf, G., Die Hegesippus-Frage, in: Archiv für lateinische Lexikographie und Grammatik 12 (1902), pp. 465-472.

Rönsch, H., Die lexikalischen Eigentumlichkeiten der Latinität des sogen. Hegesippus, in: Romanische Forschungen (1883), I, pp. 256-321; re-edited in: Collectanea Philologia, Bremen, 1891, pp. 32-89.

Vogel, F., 'Ομοιότητες Sallustianae, in: Acta seminarii philol. Erlangensis
    I (1878), pp. 348-365.
————, Review of Rönsch's Die lexikalischen Eigentümlichkeiten der
    Latinität des sogen. Hegesippus, in: Romanische Forschungen
    (1883), I, pp. 415-417.
Weyman, C., Sprachliches und Stilistiches zu Florus und Ambrosius, in:
    Archiv für lateinische Lexikographie und Grammatik 14 (1906),
    pp. 41-61.

            B.   Works concerned chiefly with the Historical Aspect.

Caesar, J., Review of Vogel's De Hegesippo, qui dicitur, Iosephi interprete,
    in: Neue Jahrbücher für Philologie und Pädogogik, Leipzig, 1882,
    pp. 65-75.
Jülicher, A., Review of Wittig's Der Ambrosiaster Hilarius, in: Theolo-
    gische Literaturzeitung 31 (1906), No. 20, pp. 550-551.
Kalinka, E., Ad Josephum latinum, in: Wiener Studien 16 (1894), III,
    pp. 78-120, 254-313.
Klebs, E., Das lateinische Geschichtswerk über den judischen Krieg, in:
    Festschrift zum 50 jährigen Doktorjubiläum Ludwig Friedländer
    dargebracht, Leipzig, 1895, pp. 210-241.
Koch, H., Review of Scholz's Die Hegesippus-Ambrosius Frage, in:
    Deutsche Literaturzeitung, 31 (1910), p. 3091.
Morin, D., L'Opuscule perdu du soi-disant Hégésippe sur les Machabées,
    Revue Bénédictine, vol. XXXI (1914), pp. 83-91.
Niese, B., Review of Vogel's De Hegesippo, qui dicitur, Iosephi interprete,
    in: Deutsche Literaturzeitung 2 (1881), pp. 1265-1266.
Scholz, O., Die Hegesippus-Ambrosius Frage, in: Kirchengeschichtliche
    Abhandlungen, Breslau, 1909, pp. 149-195.
————, Die Hegesippus-Ambrosius Frage, Diss. Breslau, 1913.
Schürer, E., Review of Vogel's De Hegesippo, qui dicitur, Iosephi inter-
    prete, in: Theologische Literaturzeitung 6 (1881), No. 23, pp. 544-
    546.
Stiglmayr, J., Ambrosius und Pseudo-Hegesippus, in: Zeitschrift für kath.
    Theol. 38 (1914), pp. 102-112.
Traube, L, Zum lateinischen Josephus, in: Rheinisches Museum für
    Philologie 39 (1884), pp. 477-478.
Ussani, V., La Questione e la Critica del così detto Egesippo, in: Studi
    italiani di Filologia classica, XIV, Florence, 1906, pp. 245-361.
Vogel, F., De Hegesippo, qui dicitur, Iosephi interprete, Erlangen, 1881.
————, Ambrosius und der Übersetzer des Josephus, in: Zeitschrift für
    die österreich. Gymnasien (1883), XXXIV, pp. 241-249.
————, Review of Ussani's La Questione e la Critica del così detto
    Egesippo, in: Philologische Wochenschrift, 1907, No. 21, pp. 654-
    655.

Weyman, C., Review of Scholz's Die Hegesippus-Ambrosius Frage, in: Historisches Jahrbuch der Goerres-gesellschaft, 1909, p. 881.

——, Review of Ussani's La Questione e la Critica del cosÌ detto Egesippo, in: Wochenschrift fur klass. Philologie 27 (1907), pp. 749-751.

Wilmart, A., Review of Scholz's Die Hegesippus-Ambrosius Frage, in: Literarische Rundschau fur das katholische Deutschland, Jahrg. 37 (1911), p. 180.

Wittig, J., Der Ambrosiaster Hilarius, in: Kirchengeschichtliche Abhandlungen, Breslau, 4 (1906), pp. 46-66.

III. Works on Language and Style.[1]

Adams, Sister Miriam Annunciata, The Latinity of the Letters of Saint Ambrose, Washington, 1927.

Barry, Sister Mary Finbarr, The Vocabulary of the Moral-Ascetical Works of Saint Ambrose. A Study in Latin Lexicography. Washington, 1926.

Buck, Sister Mary Joseph Aloysius, S. Ambrosii de Helia et Ieiunio: A Commentary, with an Introduction and Translation, Washington, 1929.

Cooper, F. T., Word Formation in the Roman Sermo Plebeius, New York, 1895.

Goelzer, H., Étude lexicographique et grammaticale de la latinité de Saint Jérome, Paris, 1884.

——, Le Latin de Saint Avit, Paris, 1909.

Krebs-Schmalz, Antibarbarus der lateinischen Sprache, 2 vols., 7th ed., Basel, 1905-1907.

Mannix, Sister Dolorosa, Sancti Ambrosii Oratio de Obitu Theodosii: Text, Translation, Introduction and Commentary, Washington, 1925.

McGuire, M. R. P., S. Ambrosii de Nabuthae: A Commentary, with an Introduction and Translation, Washington, 1927.

Parsons, Sister Wilfrid, A Study of the Vocabulary and Rhetoric of the Letters of St. Augustine, Washington, 1923.

Rönsch, H., Itala und Vulgata, 2nd ed., Marburg, 1875.

Stolz-Schmalz, Lateinische Grammatik, 5th ed., Munich, 1928.

IV. Lexica.

Benoist-Goelzer, Nouveau Dictionnaire Latin-Français, 10th ed. (no date), 9th ed., Paris, 1922.

Forcellini-Corradini-Perin, Lexicon Totius Latinitatis, Padua, 1864-1887.

---

[1] A more complete list may be found in several of the earlier volumes of the Patristic Studies. I have confined myself here to those works which have been useful from the point of view of vocabulary, especially the vocabulary of Ambrose.

Fügner, F., Lexicon Livianum, vol. I (a-bustum), Leipzig, 1897.

Georges, K. E., Ausfuhrliches Lateinisch-Deutsches Handwörterbuch, 2
    vols., Hanover and Leipzig, 1913-1918.

————, Lexicon der lateinischen Wortformen, Leipzig, 1890.

Lewis and Short, Harper's Latin Dictionary, New York, 1907.

Merguet, H., Handlexikon zu Cicero, Leipzig, 1905.

————, Lexikon zu den Reden des Cicero, 4 vols., Jena, 1877-1884.

————, Lexikon zu den philosophischen Schriften Cicero's, 3 vols., Jena,
    1887-1894.

Meusel, H., Lexicon Caesarianum, 3 vols., 1887-1893.

Neue-Wagener, Formenlehre der lateinischen Sprache, 4 vols., 3rd ed.,
    Leipzig, 1892-1905.

Thesaurus Linguae Latinae, vols. I-IV, V (to dolor), VI (to germen),
    Leipzig, 1900 ff. (T. L. L.).

Walde, A, Lateinisches Etymologisches Wörterbuch, 2nd ed., Heidelberg,
    1910.

V. OTHER WORKS.

Bardenhewer, O., Geschichte der Altkirchlichen Literatur, III, Freiburg-
    i-B., 1912, pp. 505-506.

Jordan, H., Geschichte der altchristlichen Literatur, Leipzig, 1911.

Schanz, M., Römische Literaturgeschichte, VI, 1, 2nd ed., Munich, 1914,
    pp. 109 ff.

Schürer, E., Geschichte des jüdischen Volkes in Zeitalter Jesu Christi,
    Leipzig, 1901.

Teuffel-Kroll-Skutsch, Geschichte der römischen Literatur, III, 6th ed.,
    Leipzig-Berlin, 1913, pp. 325-326.

PREFACE

The *De Bello Iudaico* or *De Excidio Urbis Hierosolymitanae* is
a free rendering or paraphrase in Latin of the Περὶ τοῦ Ἰουδαικοῦ
πολέμου of Flavius Josephus by an anonymous author, the so-called
Hegesippus. Whereas the Greek original of Josephus is in seven
books, the Latin adaptation is in five books, the first four of which
are taken from the corresponding ones of the work of Josephus,
and the fifth is an epitome of the fifth, sixth, and seventh books
of the Greek work. Hegesippus freely adds to the original, sometimes from the later books of the Ἰουδαικὴ Ἀρχαιολογία of Josephus,
sometimes from the Roman historians.

The *De Bello Iudaico* has come down to us in the manuscript
tradition of Ambrose. This association of the name of Ambrose
with the work has led scholars to investigate the question of the
identification of Hegesippus with Ambrose. While the manuscript
evidence certainly favors Ambrosian authorship, yet this manuscript evidence is by no means absolutely conclusive.

A number of scholars, therefore, have appealed to internal criti-
cism in an effort to solve the question. One group, which includes
Vogel, Klebs, Wittig, Scholz, and Morin, has concerned itself chiefly
with the historical side. A second group, among whom may be
mentioned Rönsch, Ihm, Landgraf, Weyman, Ussani, and Hey, has
appealed to the evidence of the language, syntax, and style of the
De Bello Iudaico. Of this latter group, Rönsch,[1] however, is the
only one who has made an extensive investigation of the language
of Hegesippus. But, except for a few words, he has confined his
attention to Late Latin.

My purpose in this study is to examine the general vocabulary
of Hegesippus, paying special attention to Late Latin words and
meanings, because it is here particularly that the problem of authorship, if it can be solved on a linguistic basis, must be attacked.

So far as the research of Ronsch is concerned, thanks to the
help of more adequate tools and to a number of special studies
on Ambrose since his time, I have been able to make a more

---

[1] Rönsch, Collectanea Philologia, pp. 32-89.

exhaustive study of the field covered by Rönsch, in part supplementing, and in part superseding portions of his work.

When I began this work, the edition of Hegesippus that is to be published by Professor Ussani in the *Corpus Scriptorum Ecclesiasticorum Latinorum* was already announced as being in press. I had hoped to have this text within a few months. But, unfortunately, this text has not yet appeared. Hence, for the first thirty chapters of Book I the text published by Ussani in the *Memorie del Reale Istituto Veneto di Scienze, Lettere ed Arti*, vol. XXIX, No. 4 (1922) and No. 5 (1923), has been utilized. Otherwise, I have had to rely on the text established by Weber-Caesar. A careful comparison of Ussani's text with that of Weber-Caesar convinces me that my treatment of vocabulary will not have to be essentially modified in the light of Ussani's complete text when it appears. So far as vocabulary is concerned, I have found the differences of a quite minor nature.

In my exposition of the vocabulary of Hegesippus I have followed as my model, so far as was practicable, Goelzer's excellent treatment of vocabulary in his work, *Le Latin de Saint Avit*. In my opinion it is one of the most thorough and satisfactory studies on Late Latin vocabulary that has so far been made.

In my investigation of the vocabulary of Hegesippus I have employed the *Thesaurus Linguae Latinae* so far as possible. Otherwise, I have relied on the dictionaries of Georges and Benoist-Goelzer and on the various monographs treating in whole or in part of Late Latin vocabulary.

In citing Latin authors I have followed the system employed by the *Index Librorum Scriptorum Inscriptionum* to the *Thesaurus Linguae Latinae*.

All references to the Jewish War of Flavius Josephus are made to the Greek text established by H. St. J. Thackeray for his edition in the Loeb Classical Library. Thackeray's text " is based on that of Niese, but is the outcome of a careful and independent investigation of the MS. evidence collected in his (Niese's) great edition." [2]

The study has been divided into two parts. Part I treats of Late Latin under the two headings of Vocabulary and Semantics.

---

[2] Cf. Loeb Classical Library, Josephus, vol. II, Introd. p. xxvii.

In the section on Vocabulary are grouped the words which are found in authors from Apuleius on. In the section on Semantics only those words are discussed whose meanings are found in writers from Apuleius on. Words and meanings special to Hegesippus are marked with an asterisk (*). In Part II are grouped all other words under the four following categories: a) Rare Classical—words occurring for the first time either in form or in meaning in the classical prose writers and then, but rarely; b) Early—words found first in the ante-classical writers and only rarely, if at all, in classical authors; c) Poetic—words used for the first time either in form or in meaning by the classical poets; d) words occurring for the first time either in form or in meaning in the prose and poetry from Livy to Suetonius.

I wish to express my gratitude to Professor Roy J. Deferrari for suggesting the subject of this study and for reading the manuscript. My very special thanks are due to Dr. Martin R. P. McGuire, under whose constant direction this volume has been brought to completion. Further indebtedness is acknowledged to Brother Giles, C. F. X., Ph. D., for a careful reading of the manuscript, and to Reverend Clement Hrdlicka, O. S. B., M. A., for many valuable suggestions in preparing this work.

PART I

LATE LATIN

I. VOCABULARY

The Late Latin words in any author are always interesting and significant. In order, therefore, to observe 1) the influence which Hegesippus himself exercised on the Latin language by coining new words, and 2) the employment of Late Latin words by Hegesippus in common with other Late Latin writers, the Late Latin words in his work have been grouped into a separate chapter.

In arranging the Late Latin words of Hegesippus in the morphological divisions I have given along with each Latin word its English equivalent, the Late authors who use it, the places where it is to be found in Hegesippus, and at least one quotation from the text to illustrate the meaning. Words which have been used apparently by Hegesippus alone or seemingly first by Hegesippus and then by writers subsequent to him have been marked with an asterisk (*).

A. NOUNS

1. Nouns in *-tor, -sor.*

appetitor, *one who strives for something* (Itala; Iren.; Amm.; Hier.; Ps. Ambros.; Aug.; Lampr.; Cassian.; et al), 2, 9, 1: appetitor salutis; 4, 7.

ascensor, *one who ascends* (Itala; Ambros.; Hier.; Vulg.; Greg. Tur.), 5, 41: cum se iactent . . . ascensores aetherios.

commentator,[1] *a contriver* (Apul.; Tert.; Hil.; Filastr.; Hier.; et al), 1, 44, 8: quem commentatorem arguis parricidii.

confessor,—Cf. Semantics.

*excisor,—Cf. Semantics.

excitator, *one who rouses, an agitator* (Prud.; Iul. apud Aug.), 2, 10, 4: excitatores belli; 3, 5, 3; 4, 7.

*excitor, *an agitator* (Heg.), 3, 26, 4: belli excitores; 5, 31.

---

[1] T.L L. III 1862, 25 ff. cites Char. gramm. I 123, 10 as speaking of the use of this word by Plin. mai.

1

exspectator, *a spectator* (Paul. Nol.; and Eccl.), 5, 2: et ideo exspectatores malebant esse Romani quam percussores.

exspoliator, *a plunderer* (Ambros.; Salv.; Ps. Aug.), 2, 1, 1: expoliatorem publicum.

incentor, *an inciter* (Amm.; Hier.; Vulg.; Rufin.; Paul. Nol.; Oros.), 1, 12, 4: flagitii incentores; 5, 16; 5, 17; 5, 41.

incitator, *an instigator* (Fronto; Amm.; Tert.; Cypr.; Hier.; Prud.; Aug.), 1, 40, 10: illos incitatores adulescentium.

instaurator, *a restorer* (Amm.; Ambros.; Hier.; Aug.; Inscr.), 5, 53, 1: piorum instaurator secretorum.

peccator, *a sinner* (Tert.; Cypr.; Lact.; Arnob.; Ambros.; and Late), 5, 22: si mihi Saul utpote peccatori occurrerit.

persecutor, *a religious persecutor* (Lact.; Hil.; Ambros.; Hier.; Rufin.; and Eccl.), 3, 2 (bis): (Petrus) captus a persecutoribus; 5, 22.

perturbator, *a disturber* (Ambros.; Sulp. Sev.; Aug.), 1, 40, 10: perturbatores regiae domus; 3, 26, 4; 4, 4, 5; 4, 6, 6.

praereptor, *a usurper* (Hier.; Paul. Nol.), 2, 1, 2: praereptorem imperii.

praesumptor,—Cf. Semantics.

prosecutor, *an attendant, companion* (Veget.; Cod. Th.; Cod. Iust.; Cassiod.), 4, 23, 3: paucis virorum prosecutoribus.

protector, *a protector, guardian* (Tert.; Hier.; Vulg.), 1, 44, 7: hic erat protector meus; 1, 44, 8.

repulsor, *one who drives back or repels* (Ambros.), 1, 40, 1: sine repulsore.

sepultor, *one who buries* (Aug.; Rufin.), 5, 21, 3 (bis): ne mors praeveniret et sepultor deesset.

stimulator, *an instigator* (Claud.; Claud. Mam.), 1, 29, 1: quibus stimulator accessit Lysanias.

triumphator, *a conqueror* (Apul.; Ambros.; C. I. L.), 1, 33: Augustus Caesar actiaci triumphator certaminis; 2, 9; 3, 24; 5, 51, 2.

usurpator, *a usurper* (Symm.; Amm.; Ambros.), 2, 13, 2: usurpatoris insolentiam.

2. Nouns in *-tas*.

impossibilitas,—Cf. Semantics.

indemnitas, *indemnity* (Amm.; Dig.), 3, 3, 5: ad dominorum indemnitatem.

longaevitas, *length, duration* (Ambros.; Hier.; Aug.), 3, 2: vitae longaevitatem.

possibilitas, *possibility, power, ability to do a thing* (Arnob.; Pallad.; Amm.; Ambros.; Hier.; Rufin.; Aug.; Vulg.; et al), 2, 12, 1: ultra humanam possibilitatem; 5, 15.

pusillitas, *smallness, littleness* (Tert.; Lact.; Ambros.; Hier.), 5, 37, 2: pusillitatem hominis.

sollemnitas, *solemnity, festival* (Gell.; Tert.; Auson.; Ambros.; Hier.; Rufin.; Aug.; Solin.; et al), 1, 16, 5: sacrificiorum sollemnitati; 1, 16, 6; 1, 36, 1; 2, 9; 2, 10, 5; 2, 13, 1 (bis); 4, 6, 5; 4, 6, 9; 4, 7; 5, 2; 5, 31; 5, 44, 1; 5, 49, 4.

formality, usage (Ict.), 2, 13, 1: quia abrogaverat legitimae successionis sollemnitatem.

trinitas, *the Holy Trinity* (Tert.; Hil.; Ambros.; Hier.; Rufin.; Aug.; et al), 5, 9, 4: trinitatis cognitio.

validitas, *strength* (Ps. Apul.; Ambros.; Gloss. Philox.), 1, 35, 6: validitatem operis; 5, 42, 3.

3. Nouns in *-tio, -sio.*

abominatio, *an abomination* (Itala; Hier.; Vulg.; Aug.; et al), 5, 31: abominatio desolationis..

annuntiatio, *an announcement, prophecy* (Tert.; Lact.; Herm.; Arnob.; Eucher.; Ambros.; Ambrosiast.; Aug.; et al), 5, 2: prophetarum annuntiationes.

benedictio, *a blessing* (Itala; and very frequent in Late Latin), 4, 17: tanti prophetae benedictionibus.

causatio, *a pretext, excuse* (Tert.; Itala; Symm.; Ambros.; Hier.; Aug.; et al), 1, 30, 5: ut nulla Siloni superesset causatio.

circumcisio, *circumcision* (Itala; Tert.; Iren.; Lact.; Filastr.; Ambros.; et al), 2, 10, 7: pollicens usque ad circumcisionem quoque se Iudaeum futurum.

circumventio, *a circumventing, fraud* (Itala; Ulp.; Hermog.; Cypr.; Arnob.; Firm.; Vulg.; and frequent in Late Latin), 5, 43, 2: falsis circumventionibus.

comminutio,[2] *a crushing, smashing* (Hier.; Claud. Mam.; Anon. in Job I, p. 54), 3, 11, 3: in machinamenti comminutione.

compassio, *pity, compassion* (Tert.; Hil.; Ambros.; Hier.; and Late), 3, 2: quadam misericordiae compassione; 5, 53, 1.

constipatio, *a dense crowd* (Paneg.; Ambros.; Ps. Ambros.; Vopisc.; Hier.; Aug.; Rufin.; Amm.; Schol. Hor.; et al), 3, 14: tantam hominum constipationem.

contextio, *a composing, context* (Symm.; Avell.; Aug.; et al), 4, 7: ex contextione sermonum; 5, 44, 1.

coruscatio, *a flashing, lightning* (Itala; Iren.; Hil.; Serv.; Ambros.; Ambrosiast.; Vulg.; Vopisc.; Aug.; et al), 4, 9, 1: terribiles coruscationes.

desolatio, *desolation* (Itala; Hil.; Hier.; Vulg.; Ps. Ambros.; Rufin.; et al), 5, 31: abominatio desolationis.

devoratio, *food* (Itala; Lact.; Vulg.; Lib. iubil.), 5, 2: escae volatilium et devoratio canum.

devotatio,—Cf. Semantics.

dilectio,—Cf. Semantics.

dispersio, *a dispersion, scattering* (Itala; Tert.; Hil.; Serv.; Hier.; Vulg.; Rufin.; et al), 1, 21, 1: reliquorum dispersione bellum confectum, 4, 23, 1.

exagitatio, *a disturbance* (Ambros.; Aug.; Th. Prisc.; Acro; Cass. Fel.; Muscio), 1, 32, 6; 5, 53, 1: curarum humanarum . . . exagitatio.

excitatio, *a rousing up* (Arnob.; Chalcid.; Petr. Chrys.), 3, 3, 4: excitationes tubarum.

incursatio, *an attack* (Cypr.; Non.), 5, 51, 2: quorum conperta incursatione Titus Antiochiam contendit.

instauratio, *restoration, rebuilding* (Veget.; Hier.; Vulg.; Aug.; Eumen.; Paul.), 3, 3, 5: instaurationi murorum.

interfusio, *a flowing between* (Lact.; Ambros.), 3, 26, 1: sine ulla interfusione progreditur (Iordanes).

interminatio, *a threatening* (Cypr.; Rufin.; Donat.; Cassian.; Cod. Th.; Cassiod.), 5, 44, 1: gravioribus interminationibus territus.

---

[2] This word is used also in the sense of " a melting " in Jerome, and in the sense of " a weakening " in Augustine.

minitatio, *a threatening, menace* (Avien.; Ambros.), 1, 26, 4: minitatione vindictae.

obiectio, *a reproach, upbraiding* (Tert.; Ambros.; Ps. Ambros.; Hier.; Vulg.; Rufin.; Mart. Cap.), 2, 9: gravior obiectionum invidia.

oblatio, *a giving, a bestowing* (Apul.; Cael. Aur.; Leo; Cod. Iust.), 1, 14, 2: pecuniae oblatione.

an offer, proposal (Ulp.), 2, 9, 1: qua oblatione victi; 3, 18, 2.

opitulatio, *help, assistance* (Itala; Iren.; Ulp.; Arnob.; Hier.; Vulg.; Aug.; Iul. apud Aug.; Oros.; Fulg.; Cod. Iust.; et al), 2, 13, 8: non immerito eos divina deseruit opitulatio.

ostensio, *a manifestation* (Apul.; Tert.; Iren.; Aquil.; Hil.; Ambros.; Hier.; Vulg.), 5, 27: ostensionem gloriae.

passio, *suffering* (Tert.; Ps. Apul.; Arnob.; Prud.; Cael. Aur.; Th. Prisc.; Cass. Fel.), 1, 30, 13: passioni maerorem distulit; 1, 45, 9 (bis); 2, 18; 3, 2 (bis); 5, 18, 3.

a passion, feeling (Ambros.; Hier.; Rufin.; Aug.), 1, 1, 7: iustae passionis affectu superabatur; 1, 17, 1; 1, 37, 7; 2, 18; 4, 25, 2; 5, 2; 5, 24, 3; 5, 40; 5, 53, 2.

a physical disturbance (Apul.), 1, 32, 6: habent suam noxam passiones elementorum.

*praesuasio, *the act of speaking beforehand in some one's behalf* (Heg.), 5, 22: ille tamen servavit ultimam matrem ad praesuasionem regiae voluntatis.

protectio, *protection* (Ps. Quint.; Tert.; Ambros.; Hier.; Vulg.; Aug.), 1, 32, 6: protectio dei.

*refractio [3] (= refragium), *opposition, resistance* (Heg.), 5, 27: sine refractione fretum scinditur.

reparatio, *repair, renewal* (Veget.; Hier.; Rufin.; Prud.; Oros.; C. I. L.), 5, 26, 1: per inopiam silvarum reparationis subsidia non suppeditabant; 5, 32.

*repressio, *a signal for a retreat* (Heg.), 3, 3, 4: ut agnoscerent excitationes tubarum et repressiones (Cf. Joseph. B. I. 2, 20, 7: σάλπιγγος προκλήσεις τε καὶ ἀνακλήσεις).

resultatio, *reverberation, echo* (Ambros.; Cassiod.), 4, 17; caelestis oraculi resultatio.

---

[3] Forcellini cites *refractio* for Boeth. de Syllog. categ. 2 p. 595 in the meaning of " conversion "—a philosophical term (ἀνάκλασις).

resurrectio, *rising from the dead* (Tert.; Ambros.; Lact.; Hier.; Vulg.; Sulp. Sev.; Rufin.; Aug.), 3, 6, 4; 5, 9, 4: testes sunt passionis eius ac resurrectionis; 5, 22.

sanctıficatio,—Cf. Semantics.

transactio, *agreement, transaction* (Ict.), 1, 13, 3: transactio huiusmodi.

4. Nouns in -*tus*.

coalitus,—Cf. Semantics.

incolatus, *residence in a place, dwelling* (Itala; Tert.; Modest.; Ambros.; Hıer.; Cod. Th.; Inscr.), 1, 24, 2: cuius incolatus Iudaeorum exercitus appellabatur; 2, 18; 3, 24; 5, 53, 1.

5. Nouns in -*tura*.

ruptura,—Cf. Semantics.

6. Nouns in -*ia*.

honorificentia, *honor* (Spart.; Arnob.; Symm.; Ambros.; Hier.; Vulg.; Rufin.; Aug.; Vopisc.; Capit.; C. I. L.), 2, 1, 3: ea vobis honorificentia servetur.

inobedientia, *disobedience* (Tert.; Hil.; Ambros.; Hier.; Vulg.; Rufin.; Aug.; Paul. Nol.; et al), 5, 42, 6: inobedientiae metum; 5, 46.

praescientia, *foreknowledge, prescience* (Tert.; Ambros.; Hier.; Vulg.; Aug.; Mart. Cap.; Vict. Vit.; Boeth.), 1, 1, 10: praescientia quadam animi.

7. Nouns in -*men*.

*stipamen, *a crowd, throng, press* (Heg.), 2, 6, 3; turbae stipamine; 5, 3, 1.

8. Nouns in -*ium*.

refragium, *hindrance* (Ambros.), 4, 26, 3: subsidium sibi quaerendum . . . aut refragium Vitellio.

9. Nouns in -*o* (*onis*).

binio, *a coin* (Origo Rom. chron.; Isid.), 5, 24, 3: biniones aureos.

10. Nouns in -*crum*, -*culum*.

lavacrum,—Cf. Semantics.

habitaculum, *a dwelling place* (Gell.; Tert.; Pallad.; Amm.; Ambros.; Hier.; Vulg.; Aug.; Prud.; Avit.), 1, 35, 1: addidit ... gemina habitacula maximi ambitus; 3, 16; 3, 20, 3; 4, 18; 5, 2; 5, 27; 5, 53, 1.

signaculum, *a mark, sign* (Tert.; Ambros.; Hier.; Rufin.; Prud.; Aug.), 1, 39: vestri amoris intemeratum signaculum.

11. Nouns in *-tudo, -edo*.

inquietudo, *restlessness* (Ambros.; Lact.; Sol.; Hier.; Rufin.; Aug.; Oros.; Ruric.; Cael. Aur.; Ennod.; Marc. Emp.; Cod. Iust.), 1, 9, 2: inquietudo morum; 1, 11, 2; 1, 20; 2, 9.

putredo, *rottenness, putridity* (Apul.; Veget.; Ambros.; Aug.; Vulg.; Prud.; Macr.; Cael. Aur.; Ven. Fort.; Avit.), 5, 2: resolutorum putredo viscerum.

12. Diminutives.

infantulus, *an infant* (Apul.; Ambros.; Hier.; Nazar.; Aug.), 5, 40: habebat mulier infantulum quem genuerat.

13. Compound Nouns.

aquaeductus, *an aqueduct* (Fronto; Veget.; Arnob.; Hier.; Vulg.; Sidon.; et al.), 5, 53, 2: (mulier) quae filios quinque in aquaeductu abscondit.

arcuballista, *a ballista furnished with a bow* (Veget.), 2, 15, 8: arcuballistae arietes ceteraque instrumenta.

fideiussor, *one who gives security for anyone, a surety* (Labeo; Digest.; Ambros.; Ps. Cypr.; Firm.; Priscill.; Ambrosiast.; Vulg.; et al), 5, 22: ego fideiussor tuus; 5, 31.

14. Greek Nouns.

allophylus (ἀλλόφυλος), *a foreigner, stranger* (Itala; Tert.; Lucif.; Ambros.; et al), 5, 16: inrogatum ab allophylis proelium.

angelus (ἄγγελος), *a good angel* (Tert.; Arnob.; Lact.; Chalcid.; Ambros.; Hier.; Aug.; et al), 1, 32, 6: circumfusi angelorum legionibus; 3, 16; 5, 2; 5, 16 (bis); 5, 41; 5, 53, 1.

apostolus (ἀπόστολος), *an Apostle of Christ* (Tert.; Gaudent.; Ambros.; Hier.; Vulg.; Prud.; Aug.; Avit.; et al), 3, 2(ter): sanctus apostolus (Petrus); 5, 9, 4.

*aristocratia (ἀριστοκρατία), *aristocracy* (Heg.), 2, 13, 1: quibus temporibus et aristocratia fuit et monarchia iudicum (Cf. Joseph. A. I. 20, 10(8) : ἀριστοκρατικὴ).

*atelia (ἀτέλεια), *exemption from taxes* (Heg.), 1, 24, 3: ateliam quoque contulit (Cf. Joseph. B. I. 1, 9, 5: αὐτὸν . . . ἐδωρήσατο καὶ ἀτελείᾳ).

baptismus (βαπτισμός), *Baptism* (Itala; and frequent in Late Latin), 2, 12, 2: baptismum propter purificationem animae et corporis instituerat.

baptista (βαπτιστής), *the Baptist,* cognomen of John, the precursor of Christ (Itala; Iuvenc.; Ambros.; Vulg.; and frequent in Eccl. writers), 2, 12, 2(bis): occisus erat ante mortem Iesu baptista Iohannes vir sanctus.

byssus (βύσσος), *linen made from a fine kind of flax* (Apul.; Hier.; Vulg.; and Late), 5, 9, 2 (bis): byssoque intextum et purpura.

*charadra [4] (χαράδρα, χαράδρη), *a deep gully, ravine* (Heg.), 1, 30, 9: saxum inminens charadris (Cf. Joseph. B. I. 1, 16, 4: ταῖς χαράδραις).

daemonium (δαιμόνιον), *an evil spirit* (Apul.; Min. Fel.; Tert.; and frequent in Late Latin), 1, 8: lenta tabe daemonium exsaturetur.

democratia (δημοκρατία), *a democracy* (Serv.; Hier.), 2, 13, 1: usque ad hoc tempus democratia tenuit.

epitaphium (ἐπιτάφιον),—cf. Semantics.

gazophylacium (γαζοφυλάκιον), *treasure room in the Temple at Jerusalem* (Vulg.; Eucher.; Greg. M.), 5, 48: Phineas custos gazophylacii.

holocaustum (ὁλόκαυστον), *a whole burnt offering* (Ambros.; Hier.; Vulg.; Prud.; Aug.; et al), 5, 40: si . . . aversamini holocaustum meum, manducabo quod reliquum est; 5, 41.

hyacinthus (ὑάκινθος), *violet-blue silk* (Vulg.), 5, 9, 2(bis): peripetasma . . . cocco et hyacintho byssoque intextum et purpura.

leopardus (λεοπάρδαλος), *a leopard* (Spart.; Vopisc.; Lampr.), 5, 15: ut unusquisque cedat potentiori . . . leopardo caprea.

manganum (μάγγανον), *a war-machine* (Neorid. apud Aug. ep. 8), 4, 20: manganum quoddam sibi de ligno paravit.

martyr (μάρτυρ), *a martyr* (Tert.; Ambros.; Prud.; and Eccl.), 5, 22: patimur nos quod passi martyres sunt.

---

[4] T.L.L. III 595, 81 cites Weber-Caesar reading *catarractis.*

*melamborium (μελαμβόριον), the black north wind (Heg.), 3, 20,·
2: flatus . . . quem Melamborium . . . navigantes vocant
(Cf. Joseph. B. I. 3, 9, 3: μελαμβόριον ὑπὸ τῶν ταύτῃ πλοϊζομένων
καλεῖται).

metropolis (μητρόπολις), chief city (Spart.; Hier.; Cod. Th.; Cod.
Iust.), 3, 5, 2: urbs ea Syriae . . . prima ideoque metropolis
habetur; 4, 7.

monarchia (μοναρχία), monarchy (Tert.; Lact.; Hier.; Capit.),
2, 13, 1: quibus temporibus et aristocratia fuit et monarchia
iudicum.

neocorus (νεωκόρος), an overseer of the Temple (Firm.; C. I. L.),
1, 17, 2: neocoris iussit mundare templi interiora.

neomenia (νεομηνία), the new moon (Tert.; Vulg.), 5, 22: neo-
meniis et omnibus sanctis festae celebritatis diebus.

paradisus (παράδεισος), a park (Gell.; Aug.), 4, 17: diversis . . .
floribus paradisi.

patriarcha (πατριάρχης), a patriarch (Tert.; Cypr.; Ambros.;
Hier.; Vulg.; Paul. Nol.; Aug.; Prud.), 5, 15 (bis): Iacob
. . . patriarcha.

pentecoste (πεντηκοστή), Pentecost (Tert.; Ambros.; Hier.; Vulg.;
Aug.; et al), 5, 44, 1: in ipsa Pentecostes sollemnitate.

propheta (προφήτης), a prophet (Apul.; Tert.; Lact.; Ambros.;
Hier.; Vulg.; Aug.; and Eccl.), 2, 12, 1: secundum prophetarum scripta; 3, 16; 4, 17; 5, 2(ter).

psalmus (ψαλμός), a psalm (Tert.; Lact.; Ambros.; Vulg.; Aug.;
Avit.; Ennod.), 5, 2: suavitatem psalmorum.

pseudopropheta (ψευδοπροφήτης), a false prophet (Tert.; Vulg.),
2, 7, 1: Aegyptius pseudopropheta; 5, 43, 2.

sabbatum (σάββατον), the Sabbath (Ambros.; Hier.; Vulg.; Aug.;
Schol. Iuv.; Avit.), 1, 1, 2: belli sabbato adoriendi auctor
fuit; 1, 16, 4; 2, 9; 2, 14, 5; 5, 53, 1.

scenopegia⁵ (ἡ σκηνοπηγία), the Jewish Feast of Tabernacles
(Vulg.; Gloss.), 1, 5: scenopegia Iudaeorum in terris ex lege
celebrabantur; 5, 44, 1.

---

⁵ Hegesippus treats this word as a neuter plural. In the Vulgate and
Glossaries it is considered a feminine singular. Josephus uses σκηνοποιέω
instead of a noun form.

stolus [6] (στόλος), *a fleet equipped for an expedition* (Heg.), 2, 9:
ubi est stolus navium? (Cf. Joseph. B. I. 2, 16, 4: ποῦ μὲν ὁ
στόλος ὑμῖν διαληψόμενος τὰς 'Ρωμαίων θαλάσσας;).

synagoga (συναγωγή), *synagogue of the Jews* (Tert.; Arnob.;
Ambros.; Hier.; Aug.; Schol. Iuv.), 2, 12, 1: principes syna-
gogae; 5, 51, 3.

tenon (τένων), *a tendon, muscle* (Cael. Aur.; Cass. Fel.), 4, 1, 1:
quasi tenontem quendam cervicis medio attollens.

thymiaterium [7] (θυμιατήριον), *a censer* (Vulg. 2, Par. 4, 22), 5, 9,
4(bis): intus thymiaterium, intus mensa.

xenodochium (ξενοδοχεῖον), *a hospice for strangers* (Hier.; Cod.
Iust.), 1, 1, 8: fertur ea pecunia Hyrcanus instituisse primus
xenodochia, quibus adventum susciperet pauperum peregri-
norum.

15. Hebrew Nouns.

cherubin [8] (plur.), *Cherubim* (Vulg.; Prud.; Ven. Fort.; Isid.),
1, 17, 2: inspexit . . . tabulas testamenti superque eas
Cherubin.

pascha, *the Pasch, Feast of the Passover* (Tert.; Symm.; Amm.;
Ambros.; Hier.; Vulg.; Aug.; et al), 2, 1, 2: paschae celebritate; 5, 44, 1.

16. Hybrids.

fundibalus (funda—βάλλω),—Cf. Semantics.

17. Miscellaneous Nouns.

caupulus, *a kind of small ship* (Gell.; Isid.; Lex Burg.), 2, 9: iam
non caupulis Germanorum repletur.

---

[6] This word is found also in Cod. Th. 13, 5, 7 in the sense of " a maritime
expedition."

[7] The form *thymiamaterium* is found in the Vulg. Jer. 52, 19; Ambros. ep.
5(4), 3; 66, 6; Heg. 1, 17, 2; 5, 2.

[8] T.L.L. Suppl. II, 389 doubts whether the ending -*bin* is genuine. This
word is usually masculine, but T.L.L. cites the word as neuter for this
passage.

B. ADJECTIVES

1. Adjectives in -bilis.

acceptabilis, *acceptable, pleasing* (Itala; Tert; Ambros.; and Late), 5, 53, 1: civitas . . . acceptabilis deo.

*deplorabilis, *mournful, pathetic* (Heg.), 5, 53, 1: epilogum quendam deplorabilem.

despicabilis, *contemptible, despicable* (Pacian.; Amm.; Schol. Verg.; Ambros.; Ps. Ambros.; Ps. Hier.; Ps. Rufin.; Paul. Nol.; Sulp. Sev.; et al), 5, 28: quem . . . despicabilem putaverat; 5, 30.

inaccessibilis, *inaccessible* (Tert.; Cypr.; Ambros.; Hier.; Vulg.; Rufin.; Novat.; Porphyr.; Claud. Mam.; et al), 2, 9(bis): incolas . . . insuperabiles et inaccessibiles.

incorruptibilis, *incorruptible* (Tert.; Lact.; Firm.; Ambros.; Arnob.; Hier.; Rufin.; Aug.; Avit.; et al), 1, 44, 8: incorruptibilia elementorum testimonia.

*inexitiabilis, *not fatal, not ruinous* (Heg.), 4, 14: qua via inexitiabile sibi id foret non reperiebant.

inhabitabilis, *inhabitable* (Arnob.), 2, 9: inhabitabili parte.

insensibilis, *senseless, that cannot feel* (Lact.; Ambros.; Hier.), 5, 2: simulacrorum insensibilium; 5, 53, 1.

irreconciliabilis, *irreconcilable* (Act. Niceph. mart.), 1, 40, 8: insimulatis irreconciliabilis (Herodes).

possibilis, *possible* (Ict.; Paul.; Prisc.; Lact.; Ambros.; Vulg.; Rufin.; Cael. Aur.), 5, 15: non quid utile sit sed quid possibile.

solubilis, *that may be loosed* (Lact.; Min. Fel.; Amm.; Prud.; Cass. Fel.), 3, 6, 4: solubilis terra; 5, 26, 3.

*triumphabilis, *triumphal* (Heg.), 3, 24: amictus adoreis triumphabilibus.

veniabilis, *venial, pardonable* (Ambros.; Prud.; Aug.; Claud. Mam.; Sidon.; Isid.; Salv.), 1, 43, 6: veniabilis erroris correctio; 1, 44, 7; 2, 15, 2; 4, 4, 2; 5, 48.

2. Adjectives in -alis.

bestialis, *bestial, beast-like* (Filastr.; Ambros.; Rufin.; Prud.; Aug.; Ps. Aug.; Leo M.; et al), 4, 9, 4: bestialem . . . immanitatem.

carnalis, *corporal, temporal, earthly* (Itala; Tert.; Hier.; Vulg.; Aug.; Avit.; Cassian.; Claud. Mam.; et al), 5, 16: arma quae sunt non carnalia; 5, 53, 1.

*excidialis, *pertaining to destruction* (Heg.), 5, 42, 5: diem excidialem.

imperialis, *royal, imperial* (Ambros.; Aug.; Capit.; Aur. Vict.; Ict.), 1, 39: vestem et cultum imperialem; 4, 21.

orientalis, *eastern* (Gell.; Iustin.; Capit.; Treb. Poll.; Vopisc.; Hier.; Vulg.; Aug.; Avit.), 4, 29, 2; 5, 39, 1: usque ad porticum orientalem; 5, 44, 1; 5, 45.

paschalis, *belonging to the Pasch* (Ambros.; Hier.; Aug.; Sedul.; Cassian.; Ennod.; Avit.; Cod. Th.), 5, 5: paschalis . . . celebritatis; 5, 49, 4.

praesidialis, *belonging to the governor of a province* (Amm.; Lampr.; Symm.), 2, 1, 2: praesidiale iudicium.

ruralis, *rural, belonging to the country* (Amm.; Macrob.; Ambros.; Calp.; Sid.; Avit.), 3, 3, 4: ruralibus cultoribus.

3. Adjectives in -*is*.

infirmis, *weak* (Itala; Herm.; Amm.; Ambros.; Hier.; Aug.; Gloss. Amplon.), 3. 8, 2: diffidentes infirmibus munimentis.

*tribulis,[9] *tribal* (Heg.), 2, 17: tribule collegium.

4. Adjectives in -*arius, -orius*.

a) in -*arius*.

*ferentarius,[10] *preliminary,* i. e., fought with lighter troops (Heg.), 3, 9, 4: in ferentariis proeliis.

b) in -*orius*.

perfunctorius,[11] *careless, negligent* (Optat.; Gaudent.; Ambros.; Chalc.; Novell.; Petr. Chrys.), 2, 9, 1 (bis): non perfunctoria bellorum materia; 5, 44, 1.

purgatorius, *cleansing* (Macr.; Symm.; Aug.), 5, 41: purgatorius ignis.

---

[9] As a substantive this word is found in Ter.; Cic.; Hor.; Liv.; Mart.

[10] As a substantive this word is found in Cato; Sall.; Tac.; Veg.; Ambros.; Heg.

[11] Landgraf in the Archiv XII, p. 407 calls attention to the use of this word along with a negative by Ambrose and Hegesippus.

5. Adjectives in -*anus*.

biduanus, *of two days* (Chiron.; Cassian.; Avit.; Isid.; Canon. Migne), 5, 24, 2: post biduanum ieiunium.

metropolitanus, *metropolitan* (Zosim.; Cod. Iust.; Isid.), 4, 26, 3: de ipsa urbe metropolitana.

6. Adjectives in -*aneus*.

momentaneus, *momentary* (Tert.; Ambros.; Hier.; Vulg.; Rufin.; Fulg.; Avit.; Cod. Iust.), 4, 25, 2: momentanei bellatores.

spontaneus, *voluntary* (Arnob.; Veget.; Ambros.; Hier.; Macr.; Rufin.; Aug.; Avit.; et al), 2, 1, 1: spontaneum successorem; 3, 16; 3, 26, 2; 4, 7; 4, 23, 1; 4, 27.

7. Adjectives in -*inus*.

serpentinus, *belonging to a serpent* (Ambros.; Apul.; Aug.; Cypr.; Iust.; Hier.; Vict. Vit.), 5, 18, 2: serpentini generis.

8. Adjectives in -*ensis*.

portuensis, *belonging to a port* (Cod. Th.; C. I. L.), 4, 27 (bis): index faucium portuensium.

9. Adjectives in -*ulentus*.

*cinerulentus, *sprinkled with ashes* (Heg.), 5, 53, 1: cinerulenta canitie.

10. Participles as Adjectives.

praeeminens, *eminent* (Claud. Mam.), 1, 35, 4: opportunitate et gratia loci praeminens; 5, 22, 2.

redundans, *overflowing, excessive* (Tert.; Ambros.; Cael. Aur.), 4, 17: ut profectus redundantior sit; 4, 32; 5, 16.

11. Compound Adjectives.

extramuranus, *without the walls* (Lampr.; Ambros.), 1, 17, 2: extramurani populi; 4, 25, 2.

*impinguis, *productive* (Heg.), 3, 26, 2: inpinguis arva opimat.

inaccessibilis,—Cf. Adjectives in -bilis.

incapax, *incapable* (Hier.; Rufin.; Prud.; Aug.; Ps. Rufin.; Salv.; Paul. Nol.; et al), 5, 24, 2: incapaces affectuum.

incoinquinatus, *undefiled, unpolluted* (Ambros.; Vulg.; Aug.;
Anon. in Job), 1, 31, 3 : templum a gentilibus incoinquinatum.

incorruptibilis,—Cf. Adjectives in -bilis.   °

*inexcruciatus, *not put to the torture* (Heg.), 5, 22 : denique ne
Matthian quidem inexcruciatum necavit.

inexitiabilis,—Cf. Adjectives in -bilis.

inexoratus, *unasked* (Arnob.), 1, 23 : inexoratam coniunctionem.

inexpressus, *obscure, vague* (Schol. Lucan.), 5, 45 : quid deberetur
reverentiae sacerdotibus . . . non inexpressum reliquit.

*inexustus, *unburned* (Heg.), 5, 42, 2 : si (aedificia) inexusta
reservarentur.

insensibilis,—Cf. Adjectives in -bilis.

invelatus,—Cf. Semantics.

irreconciliabilis,—Cf. Adjectives in -bilis.

septennis,[12] *of seven years* (Lact.; Capit.), 1, 29, 9 : septennem
puerum.

superfluus, *useless, needless* (Capit.; Vopisc.; Ambros.; Vulg.;
Aur. Vict.; Eutr.; Claud. Mam.), Praef. : ne quis vacuum
fide et superfluum putet; 2, 2, 2; 2, 9 (bis).

12. Greek Adjectives.

heptamyxos (ἑπτάμυξος), *seven-branched* (Ambros.), 5, 9, 4 : lu-
cerna . . . quae . . . est in gratiae plenitudine heptamyxo.

propheticus (προφητικός), *prophetical, of a prophet* (Tert.; Lact.;
Ambros.; Hier.; Vulg.; Prud.; Aug.; Avit.; et al), Praef. :
propheticus sermo; 3, 16; 5, 16; 5, 31.

tetragonus (τετράγωνος), *four-sided* (Auson.; Boeth.; Grom. vet.),
5, 44, 2 (bis) : tetragonum templum.

C. Verbs

1. Verbs derived from Nouns.

crapulari,[13] *to be inebriated* (Itala; Ambros.; Vulg.; Rufin.; Ps.
Orig.; Greg. Tur.; Cassian.), 4, 29, 2 : Vitellius quasi crapu-
latus.

evaginare, *to unsheathe* (Hyg.; Iustin.; Veget.; Vulg.; Mythog.),
1, 28, 3 : evaginatis gladiis; 4, 30.

---

[12] The form *septuennis* is found in Plaut.; Prud.
[13] Most often (as here) used in the perfect, passive participle.

feriari, *to rest, cease from work* (Ambros.; Macr.; Max. Taur.;
  Faust. Rei.; Ennod.; Aug.; Sidon.; Dionys. Exig.), 1, 11, 2:
  ubi a domesticis proeliis feriatum (est); 2, 15, 4; 3, 21, 1;
  4, 22, 1; 5, 1, 2; 5, 1, 3; 5, 18, 2; 5, 24, 2.
remediare, *to cure, heal* (Scrib.; Hyg.; Gargil. Mart.; Tert.;
  Herm.; Plin. Val.), 2, 12, 1: ad remediandos et sanandos eos.
viare, *to go, travel* (Apul.; Sol.; Ambros.; Vulg.; Sulp. Sev.;
  Ennod.; Amm.; Avit.; Cassian.), 2, 9: Romanis supra nubes
  viantibus; 4, 27; 4, 33; 5, 46.

2. Verbs derived from Adjectives.

humiliare, *to humiliate, humble* (Tert.; Cypr.; Amm.; Ambros.;
  Hier.; Vulg.; Rufin.; Aug.; Sidon.; Ennod.), 1, 32, 7: hu-
  miliati Arabes a rege.
ieiunare, *to fast* (Itala; Tert.; Filastr.; Th. Prisc.; Ambros.;
  Hier.; Aug.; Cass. Fel.; Sidon.), 5, 40: quod ausa esset ipsis
  ieiunantibus edere.
intimare,—Cf. Semantics.
opimare, *to fertilize, make fruitful* (Apul.; Auson.), 3, 26, 2;
  4, 27: solum opimat.
placidare, *to calm* (Ambros.), 4, 27: placidatur a fragoribus.
sequestrare, *to surrender, put aside* (Veget.; Treb. Poll.; Ambros.;
  Vulg.; Macr.; Aug.; Cassian.; Claud. Mam.; Sidon.; Ennod.;
  Avit.), 1, 33: sequestravi regni insignia; 1, 40, 9; 2, 9, 1;
  2, 9, 2; 5, 4, 3.

3. Verbs in *-tare.*

eructuare (= eructare), *to vomit forth* (Itala; Hier.; Aug.), 4,
  29, 2: Vitellium . . . semper eructuantem epulis; 4, 32.

4. Verbs in *-scere.*

efferascere, *to become savage, fierce.* (Amm.), 1, 37, 7: efferasse
  postea atque in multorum necem praesentium odio fertur ex-
  asperatus.

5. Compound Verbs.

a) Compounded with a Preposition or a Prefix.

ablevare, *to take away* (Ambros.), 5, 2: quae sola solet ablevare
  miserias.
*adopperiri, *to await* (Heg.), 3, 18, 3: alieni nutus sortem adopperiri.

attaminare, *to touch, defile* (Itala; Ps. Tert.; Porphyr.; Capit.; Iustin.; Ambros.; Serv.; Aur. Vict.; Aug.; Cassian.; Eugipp.; Ps. Aug.; Cod. Th.), 1, 44, 5: ne igitur contigeris nec attaminaveris quem scelere petisti.

commacerare, *to weaken terribly* (Ambros), 5, 27: languore commaceratos; 5, 40; 5, 45.

compati, *to feel pity* (Ps. Quint.; Ambrosiast.; Ambros.; Hier.; Aug.; and Late), 1, 42, 9: et sedulo conpatiebatur; 1, 44, 8; 3, 3, 4; 5, 18, 3.

conterminare, *to border upon* (Amm.), 4, 27: ın hespero ipsa Aegyptus aridis Libyae conterminat.

cooperari, *to unite, to work with* (Herm.; Vulg.; Rufin.; Gennad.; et al), 4, 9, 2: cooperatus est illis caeli fragor.

*defurere,[14] *to relax one's anger* (Heg.), 4, 9, 5: post ubi defurere visi (sunt).

depraedari, *to plunder* (Apul.; Ulp.; Itala; Filastr.; Dares; Ambros.; Vulg.; Rufin.; Aug.; and Late), 4, 22, 2: ad depraedandi licentiam.

innodare, *to fasten with a knot* (Amm.; Ambros.; Sedul.), 5, 49, 2: perpetuis vinculis innodatus.

intaminare, *to sully, contaminate* (Gloss. Philox.), 2, 10, 4: ne templum intaminarent.

obviare,—Cf. Semantics.

offuscare, *to vilify, degrade* (Tert.; Ambros.; Rufin.; Salv.), 1, 1, 10: in quo actus eıus offuscaretur.

praefigurare, *to prefigure* (Cypr.; Lact.; Ambros.; Hier.; Rufin.; Aug.), 5, 49, 1: quod metuebat animus oculi praefigurabantur.[15]

praevarıcare, *to transgress* (Tert.; Aug.; Prosp.; Not. Tir.), 3, 17: non praevaricabo legem tuam.

*recongerere, *to put together, compile* (Heg.), 1, 40, 10: dolo recongesta.

redoperire, *to uncover* (Ambros.), 5, 40: redoperuit ambusta membra.

*refrigere (= refringere), *to check* (Heg.), 1, 1, 9: impetum non refrigebant (Cf. Plin. ep. 9, 26, 7: ingeniorum impetus refringendos).

---

[14] This word is found in Hier. in Gal. 5, 17 p. 502 meaning "to be mad."
[15] The word is used here in a middle sense.

renitere, *to shine back, flash* (Prisc.; Ambros.), 5, 46: non
 aquarum rutilo decepti renitentium.

subintrare, *to steal into, enter by stealth* (Itala; Tert.; Ambros.;
 Hier.; Aug.; Rufin.), 3, 13: Romani subintraverunt.

subiugare, *to subjugate, subject* (Lact.; Auson.; Firm.; Iul. Val.;
 Hier.; Aug.; Rufin.; Salv.; Cassian.; Sidon.; Ennod.; Avit.),
 3, 1, 2: quarum gentium bella non viderant, subiugatarum
 tropaea celebraverant.

b) Compounded from an Adverb and a Verb.

benedicere, *to bless* (Apul.; Tert.; Cypr.; Lact.; Ambros.; Hier.;
 Vulg.; Aug.; et al), 4, 17: ex illa . . . benedicti solis infusione; 5, 53, 1.

c) Compounded from a Noun and a Verb.

maestificare, *to sadden, make sorrowful* (Ambros.; Aug.; Mart.
 Cap.; Sidon.), 1, 36, 2: caveret ne in aliquo mulieris animum
 maestificaret.

sanctificare, *to consecrate, sanctify* (Tert.; Cypr.; Ambros.; Hier.;
 Vulg.; Aug.; Avit.), 4, 17: fontis sanctificati.

vivificare, *to vivify* (Tert.; Ambros.; Hier.; Vulg.; Prud.; Aug.;
 Min. Fel.; Avien.), 5, 46: ut anima in corpore omnia vivificat
 sua; 5, 53, 1.

6. Hybrids.

prophetare, *to predict, foretell* (Tert.; Ambros.; Hier.; Vulg.;
 Aug.; Prud.; Avit.; C. I. L.), 2, 12 1: alia innumerabilia de
 eo . . . prophetaverunt; 5, 31.

D. Adverbs

1. Adverbs in -*e*.

imperatorie,[16] *like a ruler, imperiously* (Heg.), 1, 40, 4: at ille
 fiilios . . . partim imperatorie terruit, partim affectu paterno
 hortatus est (Cf. Joseph. B. I. 1, 24, 4: ὡς βασιλεύς).

inoffense, *without hindrance* (Gell.; Itin. Alex.; Ambros.; Chalcid.;
 Oros.; Th. Prisc.; Cassiod.), 1, 12, 2: regnandi ius mulier
 inoffense exercuit.

nimie, *excessively, very much* (Spart.; Capit.; Pallad.; Cael. Aur.;
 Cass. Fel.; Avit.), 1, 41, 2: nimie cupidus opum.

---

[16] This word is cited for Treb. Poll. Claud. 6, 2 meaning "like a general."

2. Adverbs in *-ter*.

aequanimiter, *calmly* (Tert.; Hil.; Zeno; Amm.; Comm.; Ambros.; Ps. Ambros.; Hier.; Serv.; and Late), 1, 13, 3: Hyrcanus aequanimiter in domum Aristoboli concessit; 2, 9, 1.

competenter, *becomingly, suitably* (Apul.; Ulp.; Paul.; Edict. imp. Constant.; Ps. Apul.; Ps. Cypr.; Prob.; Ambros.; and very frequent in Late Latin), 1, 46, 2: conpetenter atque magnifice funus curatum.

invisibiliter, *invisibly* (Tert.; Ambros.; Hier.; Paul. Nol.; Sulp. Sev.; Aug.; Cod. Th.), 5, 53, 1: et hoc invisibiliter singulis anima sua conferat.

irrationabiliter, *irrationally* (Tert.; Amm.; Lact.; Charis.; Hier.; Sulp. Sev.; Cael. Aur.; Hil.; Aug.; Prisc.; et al), 5, 37, 2: docuit in proelio neminem inrationabiliter insultare oportere.

iugiter, *continually* (Apul.; Veget.; Amm.; Ambros.; Hier.; Vulg.; Aug.; Ruric.; Ennod.; Claud. Mam.; Avit.), 3, 26, 1: quod ita iugiter plena est aquarum; 5, 44, 1; 5, 53, 1.

rationabiliter, *reasonably* (Apul.; Ps. Apul.; Amm.; Lact.; Chalcid.; Cypr.; Ambros.; Hier.; Aug.; Isid.; Avit.), 1, 31, 3: humanissime milites suscepit, rationabiliter duces.

3. Adverbs in *-o*.

clanculo, *secretly* (Apul.; Tert.; Sol.; Zeno; Amm.; Ambros.; Aug.; et al), 4, 20: in suburbanum rus clanculo concessit (Nero); 4, 23, 1.

maturato, *hastily* (Schol. Verg.), 1, 44, 3: rescripsit Herodes maturato eum contendere oporteret.

superfluo, *uselessly, needlessly* (Mart. Cap.; Ambros.; Hier.; Serv.; Aug.; Salv.; Cod. Iust.; Boeth.), 3, 26, 2; haut superfluo quidam aestimaverunt.

SUMMARY

In the list of one hundred and twenty-eight Late Latin nouns found in Hegesippus thirty-seven end in the suffix *-io*, twenty-four in *-tor* (*-sor*), eight in *-tas*, three in *-ia*, two each in *-tus* and *-culum*, one each in *-tura*, *-men*, *-ium*, *-crum*, *-tudo*, *-edo*, and *-o*. Thirty-six Greek nouns have been noted, also two Hebrew nouns, one hybrid, one diminutive, three compounds, and one miscellaneous noun.

Of this group of Late nouns eight are special to Hegesippus alone—*excitor, praesuasio, repressio, stipamen, aristocratia, atelia, charadra, melamborium.* The last four mentioned either have been transliterated from the Greek text of Josephus or show the influence of that text.

Two other nouns in this Late Latin group which seem to have been used first by Hegesippus are quoted for writers of a much later period. The word *excisor* is cited for the Glossarium Philoxenianum and for Adamanus (VII saec.), and *refractio* for Boethius.

Fifty-four Late Latin adjectives have been listed for Hegesippus. Sixteen are compound adjectives. Thirteen have the suffix in *-bilis*, eight in *-alis*, two each in *-orius, -aneus, -anus, -is,* and one each in *-arius, -inus, -ensis, -ulentus.* Three Greek adjectives and two present participles used adjectivally complete the list of Late Latin adjectives.

Ten of these fifty-four Late Latin adjectives seem to be special to Hegesippus—*deplorabilis, inexitiabilis, triumphabilis, excidialis, tribulis, ferentarius, cinerulentus, impinguis, inexcruciatus, inexustus.* It is worthy of note that four out of the ten adjectives ascribed to Hegesippus are compounded with *in-*(negative). This fondness for the *in-*prefix is common to other writers of the time, especially Ambrose and Jerome.

Of the thirty-nine Late Latin verbs which have been gathered from Hegesippus twenty-one are compounded with a preposition or a particle, three are compounded from a noun and a verb, one from an adverb and a verb. There are eleven derivatives—five from nouns and six from adjectives. One frequentative, one inchoative, and one hybrid complete the list of Late Latin verbs in Hegesippus.

Three of the twenty-one Late verbs compounded with a preposition or a particle appear to be special to Hegesippus—*adopperiri, recongerere,* and *refrigere.*[17]

The total number of Late Latin adverbs in Hegesippus is twelve. Those ending in *-ter* are six in number, while there are three each with suffixes in *-e* and *-o.* None of these adverbs have been coined by Hegesippus.

---

[17] If the reading of the text is to be accepted.

II. SEMANTICS

It is my purpose to note 1) those semantic changes which are to be found in Hegesippus in common with Late Latin authors from Apuleius on; 2) those meanings which seem to be proper or special to Hegesippus alone. These latter will be marked with an asterisk (*).

In order that a bird's-eye view of each change may be had I have cited in each case the Latin word, its English equivalent, the Late authors who use it, the places where it is found in Hegesippus, and at least one citation from the text so that the new meaning may be illustrated to the reader. Very often the citation may not seem to be adequate to render the exact shade of meaning clear, but lack of space prevents citing at great length. In addition I have appended either the fundamental or the most closely related meaning in which the Latin word is to be found in Classical or Silver Latin, along with a list of the authors in whom this fundamental or most closely related meaning occurs.

Several words (*coalitus, confessor, devotatio, dilectio, epitaphium, excisor, fundibalus, impossibilitas, intimare, invelatus, lavacrum, obviare, praesumptor, ruptura, sanctificatio, tetragonum*) which are all of Late origin are included in the Semantics because they have undergone a decided change of meaning since their introduction into the language.

In my presentation of the semantic changes I have grouped the words into the five categories outlined by Goelzer in his treatment of Semantics in his study on the Latinity of St. Avitus.[1]

1. Etymological reaction.

The tendency to employ in their proper or original meaning words which are found in the literary language of the Classical Age only in a metaphorical sense is characteristic of the Late Latinity. This so-called etymological reaction does not denote a semantic change in the strict sense. For purposes of convenience, however, it is usually included in a section of Semantics.

[1] Le Latin de Saint Avit, pp. 559 ff.

a) Nouns.

alluvio, *an inundation* (Apul.; Avien.; Ambros.; Vulg.; Inscr.; et al), 3, 11, 2: aquae alluvione; 4, 16, 2;—*alluvial land* (Cic.; Ict.).

commotio, *earthquake* (Vulg.; Hier.; Hil.; Ps. Rufin.; Leo M.), 1, 32, 6: nec vos insensibilium commotiones perterreant;—*perturbation of mind* (Cic.; rare in Silver and Late Latin).

confessor, *a confessor* (in the profane sense) (Ruric.), 1, 40, 9: confessor ausi parricidalis;—*a confessor of the faith* (Tert.; and frequent in Late Latin).

deiectio, *a destruction, a throwing down* (Paneg.; Pallad.), 5, 13: ad murorum deiectionem;—*an ejection, a turning out of possession* (Cic.; Ulp.; Cod. Iust.).

diffusio, *a spreading out, an extending* (Mart. Cap.; Aug.; Ps. Aug.; Oros.; Sigism.; Avit.; Verec.; Cassiod.; Boeth.), 4, 27: diffusio maris;—*cheerfulness* (Sen. phil.; Aug.; Cael. Aur.).

donaria (plur.), *sacred gifts* (Sol.; Itin. Alex.; Paneg.; Vopisc.; Firm.; Hier.; Vulg.; and Late), 5, 46: integra omnia reservavit donaria; 5, 51, 3;—*the place where sacred gifts are deposited,* i. e., altar, temple (Verg.; Ov.; Val. Fl.; Lucan.; Apul.).

egressio, *a going out* (Apul.; Hier.; Vulg.; Macr.; and Eccl.), 5, 6: aliorum egressionem voluntariam; 5, 17;—*a digression in speaking* (Quint.; Fortunat.).

flagrantia, *heat* (Gell.; Apul.; Arnob.; Sol.; Macr.; Iul. Val.; Ambros.; Mart. Cap.; Cypr.; Aug.), 3, 19: aestatis flagrantia;—*ardor, vehement desire* (Plaut.; Cic.; Gell.; and Late).

fortitudo, *physical strength* (Itala; Herm.; Arnob.; Lact.; Filastr.; Hier.; Vulg.; et al), 2, 18 (bis): corporis fortitudine;—*bravery, courage, fortitude* (Ter.; Pacuv.; Afran.; Rhet. Her.; Cic.; Caes.; et al).

fulcrum, *a prop, support* (Ambros.; Vulg.; Cypr. Gall.; Ennod.; Carm. Epigr.), 5, 20, 1: materies quae fulcra cuniculo dabat;—*a post or foot of a couch* (Lucil.; Varr.; Verg.; Prop.; Ov.; Plin. mai.; Stat.; Iuv.; Suet.; and Late).

incisio, *a cut, incision* (Ambros.), 1, 15, 3: per eas incisiones distillat humor;—*a division of a sentence* (Cic.).

interruptio, *a breaking, an interrupting* (Hier.; Mart. Cap.; Macr.), 4, 18: cuius attactu . . . interruptio proditur;— *a sudden break in the thought or expression* (Quint.).

praedicator, *one who makes a thing publicly known* (Apul.), 1, 40, 9: non me negabo ultorem, qui me ultionis exactae praedicatorem parabam;—*a praiser, eulogist* (Cic.; Plin. min.).

praesumptor, *a usurper, preoccupier* (Cassiod.), 4, 33: praesumtores constituendi imperii;—*a bold, presumptuous person* (Tert.; Cypr.; Amm.; Hier.; Aug.; Leo M.).

regressio, *a return* (Fronto; Apul.; Hier.; Aug.), 1, 18: hoc regressionis eius pretium fuit; 2, 13, 1;—*regression,* i. e., a figure of speech (Quint.; Rufinian.).

relator, *a narrator, relater* (Tert.; Ambros.; Sidon.; Ven. Fort.), Praef.: relator egregius;—*a proposer in public deliberations* (Balb. apud Cic. Att. 8, 15, litt. A, 2).

vernaculi (plur.), *household slaves* (Capit.; Apul.), 5, 16: vernaculorum validam manum;—*buffoons, jesters* (Mart.; Suet.).

voracitas, *greediness, voracity* (Apul.; Aug.; Eutr.), 5, 2: bestiarum voracitatem;—*voracity* (transf. sense) (Plin. mai.; Salv.).

b) Adjectives.

inaestimabilis, *innumerable, that cannot be estimated* (Lact.; Amm.; Chalc.), 5, 25, 1: numerum . . . inaestimabilem; 5, 44, 1;—*inestimable* (Liv.; Sen. phil.; Val. Max.; Lact.).

inexstinguibilis, *inextinguishable* (Tert.; Arnob.; Lact.; Ambros.; Hier.; Vulg.; Aug.; Rufin.), 2, 10, 5: ne quando ignis deficeret, quem oportebat inextinguibilem perseverare;—*indelible* (Varr. fr.; Scrib.; Arnob.).

insolubilis, *that cannot be loosed,* i. e., indestructible (Macr.), 1, 35, 6: insolubile maneat opus et mari et vetustati;—*that can not be paid* (Sen. phil.); *that cannot be refuted* (Quint.).

sedulus (se (sine) dolo), *sincere* (Ambros.), 1, 42, 9: his indiciis sedulae caritatis; 3, 16; 3, 22, 1; 4, 4, 2; 5, 18, 3; 5, 22, 1;—*solicitous* (Cic.; Hor.; Ov.; Sen. phil.).

c) Verbs.

*incidere, *to cut off, to cut away* (Heg.), 4, 23, 3: plerisque incidebat manus;—*to cut off* (fig.) (Liv.; Sen. phil.).

initiare, *to begin, commence* (Tert.; Firm.; Pallad.; Cod. Iust.),
2, 14, 5: posita sabbati celebritate quod veteri cultu et sollemni
observatione initiabant;—*to consecrate to religious rites* (Cic.;
Liv.; Plin. mai.; Apul.).

perurgere, *to press upon greatly* (Treb. Poll.; Spart.; Amm.;
Vulg.; Aur. Vict.), 1, 40, 10: cum insidiantium catervis
perurgeretur; 2, 15, 6; 4, 4, 6; 4, 6, 7;—*to urge strongly by
words* (Suet.; Rufin.).

scaturire, *to stream, flow, gush out* (Apul.; Ampel.; Pallad.), 1,
35, 3: fontes scaturiunt; 3, 26, 1; 5, 16;—*to be full of*
(Colum.; Sen. phil.); *to possess* (Cael. in Cic. ep.; Aug.).

As might be expected in the case of an historian, this category
is not large in Hegesippus. Eighteen nouns, four adjectives, and
three verbs make up the list of words which I note for Hegesippus
in common with other Late writers. There is only one instance
of etymological reaction that can be assigned to Hegesippus alone—
the use of the verb *incidere* in its proper meaning.

2. Change from the material to the mental or moral meaning.

A language has relatively few words. Yet, despite the paucity
of terms, it is able to express many objects and actions. This is
accomplished principally by the use of Figures of Speech, and may
be a conscious or unconscious process, but usually the latter.
Metaphor and Metonomy play the principal rôle by transferring
the meaning of a word from the material to the mental or moral
sphere, from the literal to the figurative, by interchanging the
subjective and objective sense, etc.

a) Nouns.

clavis, *a key* (Fronto; Tert.; and Late), 5, 53, 1: has illis claves
refundimus novo sanguinis testamento;—*a key* (Plaut.; Cato;
Titin.; Varr.; Cic.; Sall.; Poetical, Silver and Late).

*coalitus, *a union* (Heg.), 4, 4, 1: multorum coalitu . . . etiam
mitiorum studia . . . corrumpebantur;—*a joining together*
(Ambros.); *communion, fellowship* (Arnob.).

color, *a pretext, excuse* (Marcell. dig.; Marcian. dig.; Tert.;
Symm.; Rufin.; Sulp. Sev.; et al), 1, 41, 9: color ullus acer-

bissimae necis; — *a tint, hue, fashion* (Cic.; Poetical, Silver and Late).

conciliabulum, *an assembly place* (Hier.), 1, 40, 1: quoddam versutiarum conciliabulum;—*an assembly place* (Plaut.; Fronto; Paneg.; Tert.; Heg.; Hier.).

conexio, *a connection, union* (Paul. Fest.; Pomp.; Ps. Apul.; and Late), 1, 43, 3: magnum vinculum connexionis;—*a series, order* (Cic.; Aug.; Ps. Ambros.).

contemplatio,[2] *consideration, regard* (Apul.; Paul.; Ulp.; Papin.; Ict.; Tert.; Iust.; Amm.; Itala; Ambros.; et al), 1, 40, 12: naturae contemplatione; 2, 9; 3, 8, 2; 5, 24, 4;—*a viewing, surveying* (Cic.; Silver and Late).

contuitus,[3] *consideration* (Donat.; Ambros.; Aug.; Ps. Aug.; Mart. Cap.; Claud. Mam.; Amm.), 1, 3: morum eius contuitu; 1, 12, 4; 1, 38, 6; 1, 44, 3; 5, 22, 1 (bis); 5, 46;—*a view* (Curt.; Plin. mai.; and Late).

deiectio, *an abject condition* (Mar. Victorin.; Hier.; Vulg.; Aug.; Cassian.; Greg. M.), 5, 49, 1: in hanc humilem et plebeiam deiectionem; — *an ejection, a turning out of possession* (Cic.; Ulp.; Cod. Iust.).

examinatio, *an examination* (Ulp.; Veget.; Mart. Cap.; Cypr.; Arnob.; Rufin.; Gaud.), 4, 7: in pace veritatis examinatio (est); — *poise, equilibrium* (Vitr.).

femores (plur.), *the loins* (Itala; Vulg.; Cypr.; Hier.; Aug.; Rufin.; et al), Praef.: a femoribus Iudae; — *the thighs* (Plaut.; Cic.; Caes.; Poetical, Silver and Late).

figura, *an example, type, allegory* (Tert.; Itala; Barnab.; Lact.; Filastr.; Priscill.; Ambros.; et al), 1, 40, 2: qui figuras maiorum vitiis suis obtentui ducunt; 5, 9, 3; 5, 44, 1; — *a form, shape* (Ter.; Acc.; Varr.; Cic.; Poetical, Silver and Late).

fulcrum, *aid, help* (Ambros.; Hier.; Carm. Epigr.; Gild.), 2, 9, 1: orientis spolia non ad fulcrum dominationis quaesita; — *a*

---

[2] This word when used in the ablative singular with this meaning has the force of a preposition. The same holds true of *contuitus* and *intuitus*, which are mentioned later in this list. Cf. T.L.L. IV 648, 80 ff.

[3] Cf. footnote to *contemplatio* above.

prop, support (Ambros.; Vulg.; and Late); *a bed-post* (Lucil.; Varr.; Poetical, Silver and Late).

intuitus,[4] *consideration, respect* (Treb. Poll.; Capit.; Ulp.; Veget.), 2, 6, 2: morum eius intuitu (found only in the ablative singular in this meaning); — *a view* (Varr.; Vulg.; Salv.) (used in various cases in this meaning).

invectio, *an attack with words, invective* (Schol. Gronov. Cic. Verr.; Ambros.; Hier.; Rufin.; Fulg.; Iulian. apud Aug.), 5, 7, 2: invectionis auctoritate; — *an importation of goods* (Cic.); *an entrance* (Cic.).

naevus, *a blemish, fault* (Symm.; Ambros.; Aug.; Avit.; Cassiod.), 4, 33: ne qui naevus deesset rebus secundis; — *a bodily blemish* (Cic.; Hor.; Ov.; Sen. rhet.; Sen. phil.).

petitus, *a request, desire* (Gell.; Apul.; Cypr.), 1, 40, 5: petitu Herodis; — *an inclining towards* (Lucr.).

prolapsio, *an error, mistake* (Amm.; Ambros.; Aug.; Innoc. pap.), 1, 39: quibus auctor prolapsionis est; 1, 40, 12; 4, 2; 4, 30; — *a falling* (Cic.; Suet.; Chalc.).

*retinaculum, *a check* (Heg.), 2, 9: qui ferociae suae retinaculum Rhenum putabant; — *a rope, cable* (Verg.; Hor.; Ov.; Vitr.).

*saeptum, *an enclosure* (Heg.), 5, 53, 1: ut saepto virtutis tegamur; — *an enclosure, wall* (Varr.; Cic.; Lucr.; Verg.; Colum.; Ov.; Cels.; Mart.; Avit.).

subiectio, *subjection, subjugation* (Ambros.; Hier.; Aug.; Oros.), 3, 2: subiectiones gentium; 5, 15 (bis); — *a placing under* (Cic.; Quint.; Gell.).

b) Adjectives.

*invelatus, *unconcealed, undisguised* (Heg.), 1, 37, 4: promtum ad libidines et invelatas; — *unveiled, uncovered* (Ambros.; Mart. Cap.).

profundus, *deep, profound* (Aug.), 4, 9, 2: profundiora seniorum ingenia;—*deep, vast* (Cic.; Liv.; Sen. phil.).

spiritalis, *spiritual* (Tert.; Iren.; Cypr.; Ambros.; Hier.; Vulg.; Rufin.; Prud.; Aug.), 3, 17: repletus cibo gratiae spiritalis;— *belonging to the air or to breathing* (Vitr.; Arnob.; Lact.).

*vilis, *common, general* (Heg.), 1, 45, 6: contemtus quoque in dies vilior;—*common, abundant* (Verg.).

---

[4] Cf. footnote to *contemplatio* above.

c) Verbs.

acervare, *to increase* (Ambros.; Mart. Cap.; Prosp.), 1, 45, 5:
(aegritudinem) . . . senectus suis incommoditatibus acervabat;—*to heap or pile up* (Liv.; Silver and Late).

adolere, *to stir up, enkindle* (Paneg.; Avien.; Ambros.; Prud.),
5, 3, 1: Titus bellum adolebat; — *to burn* (Ov.; Colum.; Gell.;
and Late).

affingere [5] (= fingere), *to feign, forge* (Apul.; Arnob.; Aur. Vict.;
Ps. Ascon.; Paul. Nol.), 1, 37, 4: affectati adulterii afficto a
suis crimine; 1, 44, 7; 2, 5, 1; 2, 13, 6; 4, 6, 2; 5, 5; 5, 51,
3;—*to make up, frame* (Lucr.; Cic.; Caes.; Silver and Late).

arere, *to be dried up* (Vulg.; Symm.; Sidon.; Hier.; Paul. Nol.;
et al), 5, 2: fides aret et sepulta est pietas;—*to be dry*
(Plaut.; Cato; Verg.; Ov.; Hor.; Silver and Late).

artare, *to vex, afflict* (Ambrosiast.; Vulg.; Vict. Vit.; Coripp.;
Ennod.; Gild.; Greg. Tur.), 3, 1, 3: Nero artabatur futuris
scelerum suorum poenis;—*to hem in* (Plaut.; Lucr.; Liv.;
Colum.; Vell.; Silver and Late).

astruere, *to affirm, show* (Papin. dig.; Iren.; Porphyr.; Hil.; Zeno;
Lucif.; Ambros.; and Late), 1, 15, 2: regnum sibi iure dela-
tum adstruere; 1, 30, 1; 2, 10, 3; 3, 21, 1; 4, 10, 1; 5, 44, 1;—
to add to (Ov.; Sen. rhet.; Vell.; Sen. phil.; Silver and Late).

circumfremere, *to boast loudly* (Amm.; Hier.; Aug.; Prud.; Ps.
Quint.), 1, 40, 10: huiusmodi oratione circumfremens; — *to
go around with noise* (Sen. phil.; Amm.; Hier.; Aug.).

*circumvagari, *to wander about* (Heg.), 4, 5: hactenus circumvagari licuerit, . . . dum . . . circa alias urbes stilum occu-
pamus; — *to wander about* (Vitr.; Ps. Aug.; Heg.).

coacervare, *to increase* (Lact.; Ambros.; Hier.), 1, 40, 5: maes-
titiam tamen coacervarunt; 2, 12, 1; 4, 6, 1; — *to heap up*
(Cic.; Caes.; Liv.; Silver and Late).

compungere, *to feel remorse* (Tert.; Ambros.; and very frequent
in Late Latin), 4, 30: conpuncti sunt plerique . . . Vitelli
poenitentia; — *to prick, sting* (Plaut.; Cic.; Lucr.; Val.
Max.; Silver and Late).

---

[5] Weber-Caesar reads for Hegesippus 5, 51, 3 " afflicto " instead of the
correct " afficto."

convalescere, *to become valid* (Lab. dig.; Afric.; Gaius; Tert. dig.; Ulp.; Ict.), 2, 12, 3: unde patrio more convaluit neminem fieri principem sacerdotem, nisi qui esset ex sanguine Aaron; — *to gain strength* (Cato; Varr.; Cic.; Silver and Late).

deferre, *to pay deference to* (Capit.; Vulg.; Nepotian.; Ambros.; Avell.; Schol. Iuv.; Schol. Hor.; Claud. Don.), 1, 26, 3; 2, 2, 2: qui ultra privatum modum quasi regis filio detulerant; 2, 8, 4; 4, 6, 1 (bis); — *to hand over, to transfer* (Ter.; Cic.; Silver and Late).

demulcere, *to soften, allure* (Gell.; Tert.; Iuvenc.; Ambros.; Ps. Ambros.; et al), 4, 18, 1: illa demulcent animum; 5, 27; — *to stroke caressingly* (Ter.; Liv.; Gell.; Tert.; Lact.; et al).

derelinquere (= praecedere), *to excel, surpass* (Ruric.), 2, 8, 3: (Albinus) ut supergressus nequitiam superiorum, ita a successore Floro . . . longo sed proximo intervallo praeteritus ac derelictus; — *to leave behind* (Plaut.; Cic.; Sen. rhet.; Plin. mai.; Apul.; and Late).

dimittere, *to renounce, desert* (Paul.; Hier.; Vulg.; Eugraph.; Pass. Thom.), 2, 15, 8: societatem (Romanorum) dimisissent; — *to send away* (Early, Classical, Poetic, Silver and Late).

dirigere, *to establish, confirm* (Tert.; Vulg.; Cael. Aur.; Dionys. Exig.), 1, 15, 3: direxit Magni intentionem . . . nuntius; — *to direct, set in a straight line* (Cato; Varr.; Cic.; Poetical, Silver and Late).

discutere, *to examine, inquire* (Itala; Tert.; Hier.; Rufin.; and frequent in Late Latin), 1, 41, 9: sed nemo discutiebat, nemo examinare audebat; 1, 44, 7; 5, 39, 2; — *to shatter, dash to pieces* (Lucil.; Cic.; Plin. mai.; Sil.; and Late).

distendere, *to disturb, distress, harass* (Itala; Ambrosiast.; Cassian.; Victorin.; Pomer.; Salv.), 3, 1, 1: distendebatur animi sollicitudine; — *to stretch out* (Plaut.; Ov.; Liv.; Silver and Late).

evacuare, *to make void, render useless* (Tert.; Cypr.; Itala apud Aug.; Ps. Cypr.; Ambros.; Aug.; Vulg.; Cod. Iust.; et al), 1, 28, 6: evacuavit invidiam adversum se directae legationis; 1, 41, 6; 3, 11, 2; 3, 14; 3, 18, 1; 5, 20, 1; 5, 44, 1; — *to empty out, evacuate* (Plin. mai.; Cael. Aur.).

*imprimere (= premere), *to press, urge* (Heg.), 4, 26, 2: cessit imprimentibus; — *to stamp, impress, engrave* (Cic.; Poetical, Silver and Late).

incandescere, *to kindle itself* (Claud. in Rufin.; Symm.), 1, 37, 7: tantus incanduit fervor cupiditatis; 3, 4, 3; — *to glow, kindle* (Catull.; Verg.; Ov.; Plin. min.; Frontin.; Sol.; Claud.).

inequitare, *to insult, outrage* (Arnob.; Macr.; Ambros.), 5, 5: Simoni inequitabat Iohannes; — *to ride upon* (Flor.; Apul.; Arnob.).

*inniti (= niti), *to strive* (Heg.), 5, 1, 3: alii quasi ad victoriam vehementius innitebantur ut turbatos delerent; 5, 11, 2; — *to lean upon, rest upon* (Caes.; Nep.; Liv.; Ov.; Sen phil.; Plin. mai.; Tac.; Apul.).

*intexere, *to contrive* (Heg.), 5, 7, 1: nec mirum si Iudaei dolos intexant; — *to interweave* (Verg.; Ov.; Petron.; Plin. mai.; Curt.; Hier.; Ps. Cypr.; Ambros.).

intimare, *to announce, make known* (Spart.; Mart. Cap; Ambros.; Aug.; Sol.), 1, 21, 1: (Gabinius) militibus intimavit (eos) fuga lapsos; 1, 41, 6; — *to cause to enter, to put into* (Apul.; Tert.; Sol.; Chalc.; et al).

*involvere, *to overwhelm* (Heg.), 2, 15, 5: donec complures ac paene universos iudaicae gentis ruina involveret; 5, 16; — *to overwhelm* (Verg.; Sol.; Tac.; Vulg.).

*meare, *to find its way* (Heg.), 2, 16, 2: ut ne ad uxores quidem suas conatus istiusmodi tractatus mearet; — *to go, pass* (Lucr.; Ov.; Curt.; Plin. mai.; Sen. phil.; Lucan.; Mart. Cap.).

*obtendere, *to draw before, spread before* (Heg.), 2, 13, 6: quo insidiarum velamen obtenderetur; — *to draw before* (Verg.; Curt.; Suet.; Sol.).

obtexere, *to put forth as an excuse* (Ambros.), 3, 2: haec et alia Petrus obtexere, sed plebs lacrimis quaerere, ne se relinqueret; — *to weave over* (Plin. mai.).

obviare, *to oppose* (Macr.; Dig.), 1, 6, 1: ne quis conatibus eius obviare auderet; 4, 6, 4; — *to meet someone* (Veget.; Ambros.; Hier.; Vulg.; Rufin.; et al).

*occurrere, *to meet a situation* (Heg.), 5, 21, 3: sed ubi occurrere nequeunt, tunc de muro defunctorum reliquias in profunda praecipitia deiciebant; — *to meet a person* (Caes.; Liv.; Curt.; Plin. min.).

praestringere, *to touch, move* (Amm.), 1, 28, 6: ne sermone quidem ullo praestrictus; 1, 30, 9; — *to touch lightly* (Suet.; Avien.).

*superfluere,[6] *to overwhelm* (Heg.), 1, 41, 10: naturae gratiam superfluere iniquitates; — *to overflow* (Itala).

*vadari, *to be a pledge of* (Heg.), 1, 32, 6: nunc mihi trepidatio vestra vadatur praerogativam victoriae; — *to bind over by bail* (Plaut.; Cic.; Hor.; Ov.; Liv.).

For Hegesippus in common with other Late writers I have noted in this category seventeen nouns, two adjectives, and twenty-four verbs. Three nouns, two adjectives, and ten verbs are cited in metaphorical meanings special to Hegesippus alone.

3. Interchange of concrete and abstract terms.

The use of abstract nouns with concrete meanings, while frequent in Early and Classical Latin, became especially so in Late Latin.[7] The use of concrete nouns with abstract meanings, although seldom found in Early and Classical Latin, became more frequent in Late Latin.[8]

a) Abstract to concrete.

commercia (plur.), *resources, supplies* (Hil.; Hier.; Ps. Rufin.; Val. Clem.; Avien.; Dares; Cypr. Gall.; Novell.), 4, 27: et populi innumerabiles eorundem locorum ad usum sui expetunt totius orbis commercia; — commercium (sing.), *intercourse, communication* (Plaut.; Classical, Poetical, Silver and Late).

defectus, *a sloping part of a mountain* (Amm.), 3, 9, 5: in defectu montis; — *an ending, a going down* (Plin. mai.; and Late).

devotio, *zeal, piety, faith* (Tert.; Nemes.; Paneg.; Capit.; Lact.; Ambros.; et al), 1, 16, 6: pro veritate devotionis et fidei; 1, 45, 7; 2, 12, 1; 5, 41; — *a devoting, a consecrating* (Cic.; Nep.; Silver and Late).

---

[6] Used transitively in both Hegesippus and the Itala.

[7] Cf. Stolz-Schmalz, p. 792.

[8] Cf. ibid.

firmitudo (= firmamentum), *support, prop* (Ambros.), 4, 26, 1:
cum belli incentivum sit ignavia imperatoris et contra firmitudo pacis in hoste virtus; — *strength, vigor* (Plaut.; Cic.;
Caecin. in Cic. ep.; Caes.; Tac.; Amm.).

*fragores (plur.), *the waves or surge of the sea* (Heg.), 4, 27:
totius portus. . . sinus placidatur a fragoribus; — *a sound,
crash* (Lucr.; Cic.; Poetical, Silver and Late).

furiae (plur.), *punishment, torments* (Comm.; Rufin.), 2, 5, 2:
praecipitibus furiis actum (Pilatum) intellegi datur; — *the
Furies, avenging spirits* (Enn.; Varr.; Cic.; Poetical, Silver
and Late).

generatio, *a family* (Itala; Vulg.; Hil.; Filastr.; et al), Praef.:
generationis eius successio; 1, 30, 9; 1, 42, 6; 2, 1, 2; 2, 17;
4, 17; — *a begetting, a generating* (Plin. mai.; Lact.;
Candid.; Hil.; Ambros.; and Late).

germanitas, *brothers or sisters* (Apul.; Cypr.; Arnob.; Zeno; Mart.
Cap.; Salv.; Ennod.), 1, 17, 3: Antigonus cum feminei sexus
germanitate . . . deducti; 1, 38, 6; 1, 40, 1; — *relationship
between brothers and sisters* (Cic.; Liv.; Apul.; and Late).

*hereditas, *descendants* (Heg.), 5, 15 (bis): ibi hereditas eorum
. . . tamen haerere desiderabat; — *an inheritance* (Cic.; Nep.;
Iust.).

humanitas, *mankind* (Apul.; Min. Fel.; Arnob.; Hier.), 1, 24, 2:
quae necessaria forent usui humanitatis; — *human nature*
(Cic.; Sen. rhet.).

indulgentia, *a remission of punishment or penalty* (Capit.; Eumen.;
Amm.; Vulg.; Aug.; et al), 1, 40, 11: ab eodem poscere sibi
indulgentiam; — *gentleness, mildness* (Cic.; Verg.; Liv.; Sen.
phil.; Val. Max.; Auson.; and Late).

ingressus, *a way into a place, an entrance* (Non.; Hier.; Prud.;
Ambros.), 1, 30, 9: ipse in ingressu stetit; 2, 15, 1; 4, 27
(quater); 5, 34, 2; — *a going into a place* (Vell.; Plin. min.;
Spart.; Auson.).

iustitiae (plur.), *precepts, ordinances* (Hier.; Vulg.), 1, 1, 2:
temerantes usum patrium et iustitias legis; — *justice, equity*
(Ter.; Cic.; Nep.; Curt.; Plin. min.).

lectio, *that which is read, a reading* (Tert.; Arnob.; Serv.; Amm.;
Hier.; Aug.; Cod. Th.; Cod. Iust.), 5, 44, 1: quod . . . liquido

significatum (esse) lectio docet; — *a perusal* (Cic.; Sen. phil.; Quint.; Gell.).

*obsequia (plur.), *ministrations, services* (Heg.), 1, 16, 6: nec obsequia vatum impedita (sunt); — obsequium (sing.), *service* (Veget.; Capit.; Vulg.).

officium, *an officer, official* (Tert.; Lact.; Treb. Poll.), 5, 2: ita quodam furore occiderant pietatis officia; — *an official duty* (Caes.; Ov.; Sen. phil.; Plin. min.; Quint.; Suet.; Spart.; et al).

sanctificatio, *a sanctuary* (Vulg), 1, 17, 2: illa abscondita ante sanctificationum mysteria retecta (sunt) gentibus; — *sanctification* (Ambros.; Hil.; Hier.; Vulg.; Rufin.; Aug.).

virtus, *military forces* (Vulg.), 3, 5, 3: Agrippa rex cum omni virtute sua expectabat Vespasianum; 3, 9, 3; 4, 25, 3; 5, 2; — *military courage* (Cic.; Caes.; Sall.; Nep.; Liv.; Tac.).

b) Concrete to abstract.

*Hesperus, *the West* (Heg.), 4, 27: in Hespero ipsa Aegyptus aridis Libyae conterminat; — *the evening star* (Varr.; Cic.; Sen. phil.; Plin. mai.; et al).

*lavacrum, *washing* (Heg.), 3, 10: quod abundaret ad lavacrum vestimentorum; — *water for bathing, for washing* (C. I. L.; Apul.; Min. Fel.; Auson.; Claud.; Cael. Aur.).

Hegesippus in common with other Late writers uses fourteen abstract nouns with concrete meanings. I have noted only three other nouns that are special to Hegesippus in this respect.

Only two concrete nouns with abstract meanings have been found for Hegesippus alone, and none for Hegesippus in common with other Late writers.

4. Restriction of meaning.

In this category are found words which originally had a very general or extensive meaning applicable to many related objects or actions. In the process of time these words came to be used in a particular or restricted sense applicable to one specific object or action.

a) Nouns.

absolutio, *a freeing of captives, slaves, etc.* (Amm.; Zacch.; Cod. Th.; Ennod.; Lex Visig.; Cassiod.; Dict.), 1, 24, 2: Mithridate . . . non solum suae absolutionis interprete sed etiam fortitudinis praedicatore; — *an acquittal before judges* (Cic.; Silver and Late).

accersitor (arcessitor), *an accuser* (Amm.; Ambros.), 1, 40, 12: flagitiorum accersitore pariter ac teste; — *one who calls* (Plin. min.; Apul.; Heg.).

advocatus, *Christ, our Advocate* (Itala; Tert.; Clem.; Cypr.; Pacian.; Ambros.), 5, 2: cum tuis vocibus advocatum tuum (Christum) exterminares; — *a legal assistant* (Plaut.; Ter.; Cic.; Silver and Late).

arca, *the Ark of the Covenant* (Tert.; Itin. Theod.; Filastr.; Hier.; Vulg.; Aug.; Paul. Petr.), 5, 16: capta etiam arca dei; — *a chest, box* (Plaut.; Cato; Varr.; Cic.; Poetical, Silver and Late).

aroma, *a spice for perfuming* (Ambros.; Hier.; Vulg.; Prud.; Aug.), 1, 46, 2: (servi et liberti) regiae domus adspargebant aromata, ut suavi odore tota fragraret via; — *a spice, condiment* (Cels.; Colum.; Ps. Apul.; Diosc.; Galen.; Cael. Aur.; et al).
   incense for sacrifice (Apul.; Vulg.; Paul. Nol.; Aug.; Mart. Cap.; et al), 1, 17, 2: multitudinem aromatum dispersa; 5, 48; — as above.

auxiliator, *Christ, our Helper* (Itala; Ambros.; Vulg.; Hier.; Ps. Rufin.; Ps. Cypr.; et al), 5, 2: cum tuis infestationibus auxiliatorem tuum (Christum) interficeres; 5, 15; — *a helper* (Petron.; Stat.; Quint.; Tac.; Apul.; and Late).

beati (plur.), *the blessed in Heaven* (Hier.; Aug.; and Late), 5, 53, 1: sanctorumque habitaculis fruitur et beatorum consortiis gaudet; — *the dead* (Cic.; Aug.; Mart. Cap.; et al).

captivitas, *the Jewish Captivity* (Iren.; Filastr.; Ambros.; Vulg.; Aug.; Sulp. Sev.; et al), Praef.; 2, 13, 1 (bis): usque ad tempora captivitatis; 5, 16; — *captivity* (Sen. rhet.; Sen. phil.; Petron.; Quint.; Frontin.; Tac.; Flor.; and Late).

cilicium, *sack-cloth, a penitential garment* (Itala; Ps. Ambros.; Hier.; Vulg.; Rufin.; Aug.; and Late), 5, 16: cilicio se sicut scuto induit; — *a covering made from the hair of Cilician goats and worn by soldiers and sailors* (Sisenn. fr.; Cic.; Varr.; Vitr.; Liv.; Colum.; Plin. mai.; Suet.; Ulp.; and Late).

cinis, *penitential ashes* (Itala; Hier.; Vulg.; Aug.; Ps. Ambros.; Rufin.; Sulp. Sev.; Optat.; et al), 5, 16: pro galea cinere caput texit; — *ashes of the hearth* (Plaut.; Varr.; Verg.; Poetical, Silver and Late).

commentum, *a ruse, plan, project* (Iust.; Flor.; Ulp.), 1, 40, 9: scripsit . . . libellos, quibus commentum sceleris . . . confiteretur; 3, 10; 3, 11, 2; 4, 11; 4, 22, 1; 5, 24, 3; — *a notion, fancy* (Plaut.; Ter.; Cic.; Varr.; Poetical, Silver and Late).

commotio, *anger* (Iul. Val.; Amm.; Ambros.; Aug.; Leo M.; Avit.; et al), 1, 29, 10: iustae commotionis dolor; 1, 40, 9; 1, 40, 10; 1, 41, 7; 1, 44, 5; 1, 45, 2; 1, 45, 4; 2, 12, 2; 2, 16, 1; 3, 8, 2; 3, 21, 2; — *an agitation of mind* (Cic.; Quint.; Firm.; and Late).

conflictus, *a fight* (de singulis personis) (Gell.; Mar. Victorin.; Ennod.; Prud.; Aug.; et al), 5, 53, 1: hinc frequenter inter eos conflictus fuere; — *a collision, a striking together* (Cic.; Plin. mai.; Apul.; and Late).

a battle (Iul. Val.; Itin. Alex.; Capit.; Ruf. Fest.; Amm.; and Late), 1, 30, 7: conflictu habito cessit cornu Herodis sinistrum; 1, 32, 6; 2, 10, 4; 5, 53, 1; — as above.

creator, *God, the Creator* (Tert.; and frequent in Late Latin), 5, 9, 2: (deus) qui caelo et aeri . . . quasi creator elementorum dominaretur; — *one who produces or begets* (Cic.; Ov.; Sen. phil.; Lucan.; et al).

*decessio, *a removal from office* (Heg.; cf. also Spart. Did. 7, 11), 1, 41, 4: qui dicerent . . . compositas regi insidias dolore decessionis; — *a departure, a going away* (Cic.; Iord.).

diluvium, *the Deluge under Noah* (Tert.; Victorin.; Iren.; Comm.; Optat.; Ambros.; Hier.; Rufin.; et al), 5, 41: cum se iactent (Iudaei) diluvii superstites; — *a flood, deluge* (Varr.?; Verg.; Mela; Plin. min.; Val. Fl.; Flor.; Apul.; and Late).

discessio, *departure of the soul* (Ps. Apul.; Hil.), 5, 53, 1: infusione animae mortuus resurgit, discessione vivus exanimatur; — *a departure* (Tac.; Don.; Auson.; Heg.; Vulg.; Sulp. Sev.; and Late).

3

discipulus, *a follower of Christ* (Tert.; Lact.; Hier.; Vulg.; Aug.),
2, 12, 1 (bis): qui (Iesus) apparuerit discipulis suis post
triduum mortis suae; — *a scholar, pupil, disciple* (Plaut.;
Varr.; Cic.; Ov.; Silver and Late).

dispositio,[9] *the divine plan* (Itala; Tert.; and frequent in Late
Latin), 1, 8: profunda quadam dispositione domini; — *an
arrangement* (Rhet. Her.; Cic.; Silver and Late).

dominus, *the Lord God* (Min. Fel.; Tert.; and frequent in the
Church Fathers), 1, 8: quadam dispositione domini; 3, 16;
5, 2; — *the master* (frequent in all Latinity).

evangelium, *the Gospel* (Ambros.; Hier.; Vulg.; Aug.; and the
Church Fathers), 2, 5, 3: praedicator evangelii; 3, 14; 5, 44,
1; — *good news* (Cic. Att. 2, 31: written as Greek—εὐαγγέλια.

fides, *Christian faith* (Min. Fel.; Tert.; and Late), Praef.: fidei
intentione; 1, 16, 6; 2, 12, 1; passim; — *faith, confidence,
promise* (Cic.; Caes.; Sall.; Early, Poetical, Silver and Late).

fovea, *a pit for concealing soldiers, a trench* (Amm.; Vulg.; Salv.),
1, 11, 2 (bis): foveis ingentibus ductis; — *a pit, ditch* (Lucr.;
Verg.; Hor.; Liv.; Silver and Late).

fragilitas, *frailty of mind* (Arnob.; Lact.; Firm.; Filastr.; Hier.;
Rufin.; Aug.; Salon.; Sid.; et al), 5, 53, 1: anima . . .
hominem . . . ultra mortalem provehat fragilitatem, ut cog-
nitionem sapiat secretorum caelestium; — *weakness, frailty in
general* (Cic.; Sen. rhet.; Silver and Late).

gentes (plur.), *gentiles, pagans* (Itala; Vulg.; Comm.; Sedul.;
Tert.; Aug.; Nicet.; et al), 1, 35, 3: ut homini templum
sacraret usumque gentium in Iudaeum induceret; 2, 8, 1; 2,
10, 2 (bis); 4, 7; 5, 2; 5, 16; 5, 53, 1; — *foreigners,* i. e.,
non-citizens (Cic.; Bell. Hisp.; Vitr.; Val. Max.; Tac.; et al).

gentiles (plur.), *gentiles, pagans* (Tert.; Itala; Cypr.; Eucher.;
Ambros.; Hier.; et al), 1, 31, 3: templum a gentilibus incoinquinatum reservaret; 2, 8, 1 (ter); 2, 10, 3; 2, 11, 3 (bis);
2, 12, 1; 2, 16, 2; 2, 17 (ter); 3, 2; 5, 34; 5, 53, 1 (sexies);—
foreigners (Auson.; Comm.; Cassiod.; Cod. Th.).

gratia, *divine grace* (Cypr.; Ambros.; Hier.; Vulg.; Aug.; Avit.;
et al), 2, 5, 2: Christum . . . profudentem . . . misericordiae suae gratiam; 2, 9; 3, 17 (bis); 4, 17; 5, 9, 4 (bis);

---

[9] Used first in this sense of the pagan gods by Apuleius.

5, 19; 5, 31; 5, 53, 1 (bis) ; — *favor, esteem* (Plaut.; Cic.; Caes.; and throughout all Latinity).

impossibilitas, *powerlessness* (Rufin. interpr. Jos. Antiq. 3, 10), 5, 21, 3 : congestio cadaverum spem ademerat, impossibilitatem incusserat ;—*impossibility* (Apul.; Tert.; Hier.; Rufin.; Cassian.; Salv.; Petr. Chrys.).

*incommoditas, *an ailment, sickness* (Heg.), 1, 45, 5 : (aegritudinem) imbecilla senectus suis incommoditatıbus acervabat cotidie; 1, 45, 9; 1, 45, 11;—*an inconvenience* (Plaut.; Ter.; Cic.; Liv.; Arnob.).

*infideles (subst.), *infidels,* i. e., non-Jews (Heg.), 5, 30 : quia de templo fuerant exterminandi deo infideles;—infidelis (adj.), *faithless, unreliable* (Plaut.; Cic.; Plin. mai.; Plin. min.; et al).

infidelitas, *lack of faith, unbelief* (Ambros.; Hier.; Vulg.; Rufin.; Aug.; Interpr. Orig.; Anon.; Claud. Mam.), 4, 5 : ut veritatem sequerentur qui per angustias infidelitatis imagines non sequebantur; 5, 16 ;—*faithlessness* (Cic.; Caes.).

*interpellatio,[10] *sollicitation* (Heg.), 2, 4 : (Paulina) temtata ducis interpellationibus nec inflexa ;—*an interruption in speaking* (Cic.; Quint.).

*irrigua (plur.), *irrigation* (Heg.), 5, 16 : ut hortorum inriguis non desit aquarum abundantıa; 2, 9 (sing.) ;—*overflowings* (Plin. mai).

iustus, *a just or virtuous man according to divine law* (Ambros.; Vulg.), 3, 16 (bis) : lex divina quae perpetuam iustis promisit immortalitatem ; — *an upright, honorable man* (Nep.; Hor.; Ov.).

lex, *the Mosaic Law* (Ambros.; Vulg.; Aug.; et al), Praef.: reverentia sacrae legis ; passim ;—*a law* (Cic.; Poetical, Silver and Late).

*media (plur.), *midriff, abdomen* (Heg.), 5, 18, 2 : turgescentibus mediis;—medium (sing.), *the middle* (Plaut.; Cic.; Verg.; Liv.; Tac.).

*mysticus (= mystes),[11] *a priest of the Jewish law* (Heg.), 5, 34, 2 : ut solis mysticis pateat secretorum cognitio;—mysticus

---

[10] Cf. Paul. dig. 47, 11, 1: qui mulierem puellamve interpellaverit.

[11] Cf. mystes, *a priest of divine worship*: Ov.; Auson.; Fulg.; Sid.; et al.

(subst.), *a title of a pantomime* (Plin. mai.) ; mysticus (adj.), *mystic, belonging to secret rites* (Verg.; Tibull.; Stat.; Mart.; Lact.; Amm.).

nationes (plur.), *unbelievers, pagans, gentiles* (Tert.; Ambros.; Vulg.), 3, 13: ut donarentur eorum (Iudaeorum) supplicia nationibus;—natio (sing.), *a race, nation, class* (Cic.; Caes.; Nep.; Tac.; Silver and Late).

observantia, *observance of religious duties, ceremonies* (Ambros.; Vulg.; Aug.; Rufin.; Cod. Th.; Avit.), 1, 16, 6: ad cultus sacri observantiam; — *reverence, respect* (Cic.; Planc. in Cic. ep.; Liv.; Plin. mai.).

operatio, *a good work, Christian charity* (Tert.; Lact.; Prud.), 5, 2: ubi nunc istae operationes sanctorum?;—*a work, labor* (Vitr.; Plin. mai.; Ambros.; Vulg.; and Late).

oratio, *prayer* (Tert.; Ambros.; Hier.; Rufin.; and Eccl.), 3, 2: celebrata oratione; 5, 2; 5, 16 (sexies);—*an address, speech* (Cic.; Caes.; Nep.; Liv.; Quint.; et al).

paradisus, *the abode of the blessed, heaven* (Tert.; Ambros.; Aug.; and Eccl.), 3, 16: ad illam regionem paradisi ubi pias animas deus sacravit; 3, 17 (bis) ; 5, 18, 3; 5, 53, 1;—*a park* (Gell.; Aug.).

the Garden of Eden (Ambros.; Hier.; and Eccl.), 3, 17: Adam latebat, quia praeceptum dei praevaricatus est, exclusus est de paradiso;—as above.

passio, *the Passion of Christ* (Lact.; Hier.; Sulp. Sev.; Aug.; et al), 5, 9, 4 (bis): duodecim apostoli testes sunt passionis eius; — *suffering* (Ps. Apul.; Tert.; Prud.; Arnob.; et al).

peccatum, *sin* (collectively) (Ambros.; Hier.; Rufin.; Aug.), 5, 9, 3: ut tolleret peccatum mundi; — *a fault, error* (Ter.; Cic.; Verg.; Hor.; et al).

perfidia, *a turning from the true religion, disloyalty to God* (Ambros.; Hier.; Rufin.; Avit.), Praef.: consortem se enim perfidiae Iudaeorum . . . exhibuit; 2, 12, 1; 5, 2 (bis);—*treachery* (Plaut.; Cic.; Tac.; Suet.).

pietas, *love and duty towards God* (Lact.; Cypr.; Ambros.; Vulg.; Aug.; et al), 1, 1, 2: perseveravit in viro . . . pietatis vigor; 1, 17, 1; 1, 35, 1; passim; — *reverence for gods, country, parents* (very frequent throughout all Latinity).

praedicator, *a preacher* (Tert.; Hil.; Hier.; Vulg.; Aug.; Sulp.
Sev.), 2, 5, 3: praedicator evangelii; — *a eulogist* (Cic.; Plin.
min.).

praevaricator, *a sinner, transgressor* (Itala; Tert.; Cypr.; Lact.;
Hil.; Ambros.; Hier.; Vulg.; Aug.; et al), 2, 5, 3: quasi legis
exsequutor praevaricatorem legis condemnavit; — *one who vio-
lates his duty, a sham defender or accuser* (Cic.; Plin. min.;
Ict.).

princeps sacerdotum, *the Jewish high priest* (Vulg.), 1, 17, 2:
quod soli principi sacerdotum . . . patebat; 2, 10, 1; 2, 10, 4;
2, 12, 3; 2, 13, 1; — princeps, *a prince, ruler* (Ov.; Plin. mai.;
Tac.).

principatus sacerdotii, *the Jewish high priesthood* (Vulg.), 1, 17,
2: Hyrcano quoque principatum sacerdotii dedit; 2, 12, 3; —
principatus, *the chief place in the state or army* (Cic.; Caes.;
Nep.; Vell.; Tac.; Suet.).

sacerdos, *a Jewish priest* (Vulg.), 1, 1, 2: quod factum Mattathias
sacerdos perpeti nequivit; 1, 17, 1; passim; — *a priest* (Cic.;
Verg.; Ov.; Liv.; Plin. mai.).

summus sacerdos,[12] *the Jewish high priest* (Vulg.), 2, 12, 3: a
principio Aaron summus sacerdos fuit; — sacerdos, *a priest*
(as above).

sacerdotium, *the Jewish priesthood* (Vulg.), 1, 17, 2; 1, 19, 4:
Hyrcano . . . sacerdotii honor remansit; 1, 29, 1; 1, 29, 7;
passim; — *a priesthood* (Cic.; Liv.; Vitr.; Plin. mai.).

summum sacerdotium,[13] *the Jewish high priesthood* (Vulg.; Sulp.
Sev.), 1, 24, 3: Hyrcano etiam summum sacerdotium . . .
firmavit; 1, 36, 2; 2, 12, 3; 2, 13, 2; — sacerdotium, *a priesthood* (as above).

salus, *eternal salvation* (Tert.; Cypr.; Ambros.; Vulg.; Aug.; et
al), 2, 5, 2 (bis): Christum dominum ad salutem humani
generis advenientem; 2, 12, 2; 5, 2 (bis); — *safety, welfare*
(Plaut.; Ter.; Cato; Cic.; Nep.; Poetical, Silver and Late).

salutaris, *the Saviour* (of Christ) (Lact.; Vulg.), 5, 2: cum tuis
manibus salutarem tuum crucifigeres; — *the saviour* (of Juppi-
ter) (Cic.).

---

[12] Cf. Lactantius: sacerdotes maximi.
[13] Cf. Lactantius: sacerdotium maximum.

scriptura, *Holy Scriptures* (Tert.; Ambros.; Hier.; Vulg.; Aug.; Chalc.; et al), Praef.: scriptura sacra; 1, 44, 8; 2, 9; 3, 17 (bis); 5, 15; 5, 16; — *a writing, composition* (Ter.; Cic.; Nep.; Liv.; Suet.).

spiritus, *an evil spirit* (Lact.; Ambros.; Sedul.), 5, 2: qui a deo recessit et improbum contradictionis spiritum sequitur; — *the spirit, soul, mind* (Verg.; Ov.; Vell.; Val. Max.).

spiritus sanctus, *the Holy Ghost* (Auson.; Veget.; Ambros.; Vulg.; Aug.; Cod. Iust.), 5, 9, 3: hoc significante spiritu sancto; 5, 9, 4; — spiritus, *the soul, spirit, mind* (as above).

stibium, *a sulphuret of antimony,* used by women to color eyebrows and lashes black (Ambros.; Hier.; Vulg.; Cypr.; Commod.), 4, 25, 2: stibio oculos depingebant; — *antimony* (Cels.; Plin. mai.; Scrib.).

stola, *a vestment of the Jewish priest* (Ambros.; Vulg.), 1, 17, 1: amicti sacerdotalibus stolis; 5, 2; — *a garment for a man* (Enn.; Vulg.); *a long, upper garment* (Varr.; Cic.).

*superstitio, *the Samaritan religion* (Heg.), 3, 14: ut cessaret superstitio et vera religio succederet; — *a religion contrary to the accepted one* (Quint.; Tac.; Iust.; Ict.; Ambros.).

tabernaculum, *the Jewish tabernacle in the Temple at Jerusalem* (Vulg.; Ambros.), 1, 17, 2: vidit tabernaculum secundum quod soli principi sacerdotum . . . patebat; 5, 9, 3; 5, 53, 1;— *a tent in which to observe the auspices previous to holding the comitia* (Cic.; Liv.).

templum, *the Temple at Jerusalem* (Ambros.; Vulg.; Aug.; Avit.), Praef.: ad incendium templi; 1, 1, 2; 1, 17, 2; 2, 9; 2, 12, 1 (bis); 2, 13, 1; passim; — *a temple of a god* (Cic.; Caes.; Bell. Alex.; Verg.; Hor.; et al).

tabulae testamenti, *the Decalogue* (Vulg.), 1, 17, 2: intus inspexit lucernam . . . et tabulas testamenti; — testamentum, *a will, testament* (Cic.; Nep.; Hor.; Plin. min.; Quint.; Silver and Late).

virga, *the rod of Aaron* (Vulg.), 5, 2: virga sacerdotalis floruit; 5, 9, 4; 5, 16 (bis); — *a magic wand* (Verg.; Ov.).

b) Adjectives.

genitalis, *parental* (Ennod.; Ven. Fort.), 5, 40: pietatis genitalis usu obliterato; — *native, natal* (Vell.; Iuvenc.; and Late).

natural (referring to parents who bore a person) (Ambros.;
Prud.; Ven. Fort.; C.I.L.), 1, 44, 8: qui non sunt patrum
genitalium parricidae; — *native, natal* (as above).

gentilis, *gentile, pagan* (Tert.; Cypr. Gall.; Iren.; Cypr.; and
Late), 3, 19: urbem gentilibus refertam inhabitantibus; 5,
51, 3 (bis); 5, 53, 1; — *foreign, barbarian* (Amm.; Comm.;
Claud.; Ennod.; et al).

c) Verbs.

adiudicare, *to condemn* (Vulg.; Hier.; Aug.; Sidon.), 1, 32, 2;
1, 44, 8: et ego sine te a patre adiudicor; 1, 45, 2; 2, 12, 1;
3, 2; 3, 17; 3, 18, 2; 4, 4, 5; 5, 22, 1; 5, 27; 5, 49, 3; — *to
award, adjudge* (Early, Classical, Poetical, Silver and Late).

adsciscere, *to inflict upon one's self* (death) (Herm.; Schol. Germ.;
Cod. Iust.; Iren.; C. I. L.), 1, 29, 8: Phaselus adscitae sibi
mortis celeritate contumeliam praevertit; — *to inflict upon
one's self* (evil) (Stat.; Amm.).

convertere, *to turn to penance* (Itala; Tert.; Herm.; Ps. Cypr.;
Lact.; Hil.; Ps. Hil.; Ambros.; et al), 5, 16: convertimini
aliquando, aliquando resipiscite; — *to turn* (frequent in all
Latinity).

dealbare, *to paint or powder the face* (Schol. Pers.; Hier.; Itala;
Aug.; Rufin.; Querol.), 4, 25, 2: vultum dealbare; — *to
whiten over, to whitewash* (Cic.; Vitr.; Suet.; C.I.L.; and
Late).

*decurrere, *to swim down* (Heg.), 4, 15, 2: si quis forte secundo
amne decurrens evasurus aestimaretur; 5, 46; — *to traverse*
(Pacuv.; Lucr.; Cic.; Caes.; Poetical, Silver and Late).

depingere, *to daub with rouge or paint* (Hier.; Vulg.; Comm.;
Ennod.; Apon.), 4, 25, 2: stibio oculos depingebant; — *to
paint, draw* (Nep.; Prop.; Vitr.; Plin. mai.; Quint.; Silver
and Late).

deponere, *to destroy* (Itala; Iavol.; Tert.; Ulp.; Paul.; C.I.L.;
and Late), 5, 36, 1: depositis omnibus (aedificiis) . . . latior
facta est via; — *to lay or put down* (frequent throughout all
Latinity).

*laxare,[14] *to unbridle a horse* (Heg.), 5, 36, 1: si quis bellatorum

---

[14] Cf. Apuleius: canes laxare.

equum pabulo laxaverat; — *to loosen, slacken* (Nep.; Verg.; Liv.; Ov.; Curt.; Silver and Late).

orare, *to pray* (Christian sense) (Lact.; Ambros.; Vulg.), 5, 9, 4: oraculo monitus oravit et meruit mortis dilationem; 5, 16 (bis); — *to pray* (pagan sense) (Verg.; Hor.).

redimere, *to redeem from sin* (Ambros.; Vulg.; Aug.; Avit.), 5, 9, 4: qua mundum redemit (Christus); — *to buy back, set free* (Plaut.; Ter.; Cic.; Nep.; Verg.; Ov.; Liv.; et al).

resurgere, *to rise from the grave* (Lact.; Vulg.), 5, 53, 1: infusione animae mortuus resurgit; — *to rise again* (Verg.; Ov.; Prop.; Liv.; Silver and Late).

resuscitare, *to raise from the dead* (Tert.; Ambros.; Lact.; Hier.; Vulg.; Prud.; et al), 3, 2 (sexies): quod mortuos resuscitaret; 5, 41; — *to revive, resuscitate* (Ov.; Paul. dig.; Vulg.).

suscitare, *to raise from the dead* (Lact.; Ambros.; Aug.), 5, 2 (ter): suscitare et tu Iesus Nave; — *to raise or rouse from sleep, etc.* (Plaut.; Varr.; Cic.).

Hegesippus in common with other Late writers uses fifty-eight nouns, two adjectives, and eleven verbs in this restricted sense.

For Hegesippus alone I note eight nouns and two verbs with a special restricted meaning.

5. Generalization or extension of meaning.

This is by far the largest category in any semantic group. Words in this class originally had a very special or particular meaning, but through various causes the meanings of these words became extended to objects or actions not in the same sphere as the object or action designated in the original meaning. Literary and historical influences are perhaps the chief causes for this extension of meaning.

a) Nouns.

absolutio, *pardon, excuse* (Ambros.; Avit.), 1, 40, 10: ut . . . et ultioni potius quam absolutioni intenderit; — *an acquittal* (Cic.; Silver and Late).

adsertio, *an assertion, confirmation, affirmation* (Min. Fel.; Tert.; Ambros.; and frequent in Late Latin), 1, 25, 2: non verborum referens vicem sed rerum assertionem; 1, 38, 5; 3, 18, 1; — *a formal declaration that one is a freeman or a slave* (Quint.; Suet.; Traian.; Ulp.; and Late).

*adulter, *a usurper, unlawful occupant* (Heg.), 2, 1, 2: quum . . . ipse adulter regni fuerit; — *an adulterer* (Cic.; Verg.; Hor.; Sen. rhet.; Tac.; et al).

*aestiva (plur.), *things belonging to the summer* (here used of trees, plants, etc.) (Heg.), 3, 26, 2: aestiva hibernis mixta; — *summer pastures for cattle* (Varr.; Verg.; Plin. mai.; Stat.; Arnob.); *a summer camp* (Cic.; Liv.; Curt.; et al).

aggressio, *a beginning* (Gell.), 3, 24: proelii aggressione; — *a hostile attack* (Cic.(fig.); Apul.; and Late).

allegatio, *an excuse, allegation* (Tryph.; Ulp.; Paul.; Hermog.; Apul.; Tert.; and often in Late Latin), 1, 15, 1: allegationibus . . . non muneribus ut ante niti coepere; 1, 28, 7; 1, 44, 7; — *a despatching or sending to anyone* (Cic.).

apex, *a character, a letter* (Gell.; Apul.; Auson.; Amm.; Ambros.; Hier.; et al), 1, 25, 2: inscriptos cordis apices gero; 1, 44, 8; 5, 34, 2; — *a sign over a long vowel* (Quint.; Ter. Scaur.; Isid.).

arbitra, *mistress* (Gell.; Amm.; Symm.; Ambros.), 1, 43, 2: matrem Antipatri . . . universorum arbitram flagitiorum; — *a witness* (Hor.); *a judge* (Sen. ep.).

caespes, *a tomb* (Hier.; Sidon.; Ennod.; Inscr.), 5, 22: et insepulta adhuc velut quodam corporis mei cespite tegam; — *a sod, turf* (Cic.; Caes.; Poetical, Silver and Late).

caro, *the body, the flesh* (as opposed to the spirit, soul) (Itala; Tert.; and frequent in Late Latin), 5, 9, 3: quae succingere debeat carnis intemperantiam; 5, 44, 2; 5, 53, 1; — *meat, flesh* (Early, Classical, Poetical, Silver and Late).

*circumscriptio, *a mockery* (Heg.), 4, 6, 5: illis ludibrio erat circumscriptio veteris sollemnitatis; — *a deception, fraud* (Cic.; Sen. phil.; Quint.; Paul.; Tert.; Arnob.; Ambros.).

collatio, *a conferring, a giving* (Tert.; Arnob.; Cod. Th.; Fulg.; Fulg. Rusp.; Cod. Iust.), 1, 37, 3: sacerdotii conlationem; 2, 10, 2; — *a comparison* (Rhet. Her.; Cic.; Quint.; Silver and Late).

commotio, *a sedition, tumult* (Oros.; Mart. Cap.; Cod. Iust.), 3, 22, 1: ut aegra partium eius a commotionis et discordiae furore resipiscerent; — *an agitation of mind* (Cic.; Quint.; and Late).

comperendinatio, *a delay of any kind* (Itin. Alex.; Symm.; Ambros.; Rufin.; Zacch.; Macr.; Avell.; et al), 5, 53, 1: quis . . . de comperendinatione vivendi cogitans audeat ad caelum levare oculos?; — *a judicial delay to the third day* (Sen. phil.; Plin. min.; Tac.; Gell.; Symm.; Ps. Ascon.).

conciliabulum, *an assemblage of persons* (Fulg.; Avell.; Pass. Cypr.), 4, 7: fugite . . . coetus parricidales . . . deserite latronum conciliabula; 5, 16; — *an assembly place* (Plaut.; Fronto; Tert.; and rare in Late Latin).

*conspirati (plur.), *an assembled multitude*[15] (Heg.), 2, 18: ac si forte conspirati adessent; — *conspirators* (Suet.; Aug.; Oros.).

copula, *a matrimonial connection* (Tert.; Ambros.; Hier.; Gennad.; Aug.; Ps. Ambros.; Mart. Cap.; Ennod.; Cassian.; et al), 1, 38, 3: ius copulae nuptialis; 1, 40, 5; 1, 42, 3; 1, 42, 6; — *a rope, thong* (Plaut.; Nep.; Caes.).

correptio, *reproof* (Itala; Tert.; Cypr.; Iren.; Ambros.; Vulg.; and Late), 5, 7, 2: animadversio . . . procedere debeat . . . usque ad correptionem; — *a shortening* (Vitr.; Quint.); *a laying hold of* (Gell.; Rufin.; Cod. Iust.).

corruptio, *a seducing of women* (Rufin.; Aug.; Cassiod.), 1, 37, 6: indubiam corruptionem (mulieris); — *a corrupt condition* (Cic.; and Late).

*decemprimus, *a decurion, a commander of ten men* (Heg.; cf. Joseph. B. I. 4, 1, 5: δεκαδάρχης), 4, 1, 5: illic decemprimus cecidit Ebutius multis ante bellis probatus; — *a senator in the Italian cities or colonies* (Cic.; Liv.; C.I.L.; Firm.; Sort. Sangall.; et al).

despectus, *contempt, disgust* (active sense) (Ps. Quint.; Apul.; Ps. Apul.; Itala; Ps. Rufin.; Aug.; et al), 5, 50: insolentia quadam propriae fortitudinis et in ceteros despectu superbo; — *low esteem, disregard* (passive sense) (Rhet. Her.; Tac.; Suet.; and Late).

destitutio, *desertion, defection* (Tert.; Decl. in Catil.; Ambros.;

---

[15] Cf. Weber-Caesar edition, p. 167, footnote, for this meaning. This meaning is not given in the T.L.L.

Oros.; Ennod.), 3, 5, 3: destitutionis (Sepphoritanorum) commoti dolore; — *a deception, disappointment* (Cic.).

*devotatio (= devotio), *devotion, sacrifice* (Heg.), 5, 2: ubi est illa devotatio patrum?; — *a curse, imprecation* (Itala; Vulg.; Aug.).

dilectio, *love of friends* (Arnob.; Claud. Don.; Vulg.; Aug.; Sidon.; Avit.; et al), 1, 29, 9: paternae immemorem dilectionis; 1, 39; 1, 41, 10; 5, 53, 1; — *Christian charity* (Tert.; and frequent in Late Latin).

discessio, *defection, desertion, sedition* (Rufin.; Iord.; Vulg.; Aug.), 2, 6, 2: erupit in seditiones graves, latrocinia, discessiones eorum insolentia; 2, 6, 4; 2, 9; 3, 3, 7; 3, 3, 8; 3, 8, 2; — *a going over to anyone in voting* (Cic.; Hirt.; Sen. phil.; Plin. min.; Tac.; Suet.).

dispositio, *government, administration* (Paneg.; Capit.; Lampr.; and very frequent in Late Latin), 1, 22, 2: lusae sunt dispositiones Caesaris; 1, 29, 3; 1, 42, 8; — *an arrangement* (Rhet. Her.; Cic.; Silver and Late).

dissimulatio, *carelessness, negligence* (Veget.; Aug.; Iul. apud Aug.; Mart. Cap.; Cod. Th.; et al), 5, 16: prophetae dissimulatione famem adolevisse; — *a disregarding* (Quint.; Tac.; Plin. min.; Suet.; Papin.; Ulp.; Tert.; and Late).

dissolutio, *licentiousness* (Spart.; Treb.; Schol. Iuv.; Ambros.; Ps. Ambros.; Hier.; Aug.; Zacch.; Salv.; Pomer.; Apon.; Greg. M.), 4, 25, 2: (pumicare genas, vellicare barbulam) et in hac dissolutione saevitiam crudelitatis exercere intolerabilem; 5, 7, 1; — *inactivity, idleness* (Cic.; Sen. phil.; Iul. Val.; Arnob.).

draco, *a cohort's standard* (Veget.; Treb. Poll.; Prud.; Amm.; Nemes.; Claud.; Vopisc.), 5, 16: adversus regem Aegyptiorum exercitumque et dracones eius; — *a serpent, dragon* (Cic.; Rhet. Her.; Suet.).

*epilogus, *an apostrophe* (Heg.), 1, 45, 1: itaque conversus ad oratorum versutias velut epilogo quodam excitabat ab inferis peremtorum animas; — *a conclusion, peroration* (Cic.; Quint.; Lact.; Mart. Cap.).

epitaphium, *burial*,[16] *funeral* (Heg.), 1, 45, 10: quo praeclarissime

---

[16] For this meaning, cf. Rönsch, Collectanea Philologia, p. 38.

suum epitaphium celebraretur (Cf. Joseph. B. I. 1, 33, 6:
δύναμαι δὲ πενθεῖσθαι δι' ἑτέρων καὶ λαμπρὸν ἐπιτάφιον ἔχειν) ; — an
epitaph (C.I.L. 10, 2066; de Rossi Inscr. Chr., tom. 1, p. 310,
No. 710).

excessus, *a trance, stupor, ecstasy* (Vulg.; Aug.; Cassian.), 1, 37, 7:
in excessu mentis; 5, 43, 2; 5, 44, 1; — *a departure from life*
(Cic.; Val. Max.; Suet.).

*excisor, *a destroyer* (Heg.), 5, 11, 2: arietem excisorem urbium;—
a cutter-out, a hewer (Gloss. Cyrill.) ; *a wood-cutter* (Ada-
man.).

fasces (plur.), *power, rule, dominion* (Tert.; Anthol.; Aur. Vict.;
Rufin.; Claud.), 2, 9, 1: populos Romanis fascibus ascrip-
tos; — *consular power* (Lucr.; Cic.; Caes.; Bell. Hisp.; Verg.;
Hor.; Silver and Late).

honor, *dignity* (Sidon.; Avit.; Carm. Epigr.; Inscr.; Greg.
Tur.), 5, 22, 2: habent et sacerdotia suos fasces, qui elevantur
non umeris, sed moribus; — *consular power* (as above).

fibra, *a vein, blood vessel* (Lact.; Ambros.), 4, 6, 7: fiibraeque
patentis vulneris vestibus . . . farciebantur; — *a filament of
the entrails* (Cic.; Verg.; Tibull.; Ov.; Lucan.; Silver and
Late).

firmamentum, *authority* (Filastr.; Cod. Th.), 1, 46, 1: ut . . . ei
(Caesari) arbitrium et firmamentum omnium dispositionum
suarum reservaret; — *a support, prop* (Afran.; Cic.; Liv.;
Sen. phil.; Silver and Late).

*fluentum, *a ditch with water* (Heg.), 4, 27: distinctam (regionem) cernas fluentis; — *a river, stream* (Lucr.; Verg.;
Homer.; Sil.; Apul.; and Late).

functio, *payment of taxes, tribute* (C.I.L.; Frg. Vat.; Cod. Th.;
Cod. Iust.; Novell.; Aur. Vict.; Symm.; Cassiod.; Ps. Aug.;
et al), 1, 19, 4: quo functio regionum non vacillaret; 2, 9,
1; — *a performance of a public office* (Cic.; Frg. Vat.; Cod.
Th.; and Late).

* fundibalus, *a weapon that has been hurled by a hurling machine* [17]
(Heg.), 5, 44, 1: fundibalo ictus in eadem voce amisit

---

[17] The T.L.L. VI, 1556, 45-47, gives this meaning. However, the word as
used here in Hegesippus might refer to the machine itself.

spiritum; — *a machine for throwing weapons* (Itala; Veget.; Ambros.; Vulg.).

generatio, *a begetting, a creating of the things of nature* (Chalc.; Vulg.; Lib. gener. chron.), 5, 9, 2: ut duo (signa) ex colore, duo ex generatione colligas; — *a begetting of men* (Plin. mai.; Lact.; Candid.; and Late).

gigantes (plur.), *giants,* i. e., the Philistines (Ambros.; Vulg.; Avit.; et al), 5, 19: noster quoque David cum pugnaret adversum gigantes; — *giants,* i. e., the fabled sons of Earth and Tartarus (Cic.; Ov.; Hor.; Sil.; Val. Fl.; Mart.).

hebdomas, *seven days, each division of seven days of the month* (Gell.; Hier.; Aug.; Vulg.; et al), 4, 4, 3: cum supersit hebdomadis sacrae dies; — *the fourth week of a sickness* (Cic.).

*hiberna (plur.), *things belonging to winter* (here used of trees, plants, etc.) (Heg.), 3, 26, 2: illic aestiva hibernis mixta; — *winters* (Verg.); *winter quarters* (Cic.; Caes.; Liv.; et al).

inaequalitas, *unwholesomeness* (Ambros.; Cael. Aur.), 1, 9, 4: morum inaequalitas; — *inequality, unevenness* (Varr.; Colum.; Plin. mai.; Quint.).

indigentia, *want, lack, failure* (Ambros.; Vulg.; Aug.; Rufin.), 1, 18; 4, 4, 1; 5, 14, 3; 5, 21, 2: indigentia cibi; — *necessity, indigence* (Cic.; Sen. ep.; Chalc.).

*indulgentia, *opportunity* (Heg.), 4, 13, 2: latrocinii saevitia bellum acerbabat sine venia deditionis aut susceptionis indulgentia (Cf. Joseph. B. I. 4, 7, 2: φθάνεσθαι δὲ τὰς ἀμύνας); — *indulgence, complaisance* (Cic.; Verg.; Liv.; Sen. phil.; Val. Max.; and Late).

infulae (plur.), *the insignia of an office* (Spart.; Ict.), 1, 13, 2: infulas regni induit; 1, 41, 3; 2, 13, 5; — *fillets worn as a sign of religious consecration* (Cic.; Caes.; Verg.; Liv.; Silver).

*interpositio, *a halt, respite, intermission* (Heg.), 1, 30, 7: refectis cibo et stativa interpositione militibus; — *an insertion* (Quint.; Aug.); *an introduction of persons into a discourse* (Cic.).

lacus, *a deep pit* (Ambros.; Vulg.; Prud.; et al), 3, 15, 4 (ter): Iosephus in lacu quodam delitescebat; — *a bin for grain* (Colum.); *a pit for lime* (Vitr.).

monilia (plur.), *jewels, gems* (Apul.), 2, 9: offerunt vestes, monilia, elephantos quoque; — *a necklace, collar* (Cic.; Verg.; Ov.;
Amm.; Macr.).

nepos, *a nephew* (Hier.; Eutr.; C.I.L.; Oros.; Ven. Fort.), 1, 40,
2: Pheroram et Salomen alienos a nepotibus fecerat; 1, 42, 4;
1, 42, 6; 4, 31; — *a grandson* (Plaut.; Cic.; Sall.; Hor.; Liv.;
Silver and Late).

neptis, *a niece* (Spart.; Ambros.), 1, 38, 3: Salomes filia neptis
Herodis; — *a granddaughter* (Afran.; Cic.; Sall.; Cels.;
Suet.).

*obsequium, *deference, respect* (Heg.), 1, 46, 2: magno obsequio
per tantum spatii deductus; — *service* (Capit.; Veget.; Vulg.).

*pabulum, *a growing thing used as food, a shrub* (Heg.), 5, 36, 2:
ut vagandi et quaerendi radices arborum pabulorumque liberior
fieret excursus; — *fodder for animals* (Caes.; Verg.; Ov.;
Sen. phil.; Tac.).

parvulus, *a small child* (Iust.; Vulg.), 1, 42, 3: sine lacrimis aspi-
cere non posse parvulos hos; 2, 11, 4; 3, 15, 3; 5, 40 (ter); —
the young of animals (Caes.).

*penetralia (plur.), *intestines* (Heg.), 1, 44, 8: in interiora penetralia descendant fidiculae quaestionum; — *a temple sanctuary*
(Liv.; Fest.; Mart.; Tac.).

periculum, *ruin, destruction* (Arnob.), 1, 37, 2: cuius periculum
pro mercede adulterii postulavisset; 1, 40, 10; 1, 45, 3 (bis);
5, 24, 3; — *danger* (Plaut.; Cic.; Poetical, Silver and Late).

*placiditas, *calm weather* (Heg.), 4, 27: placiditas maxima (erat)
quavis tempestate; — *mildness, gentleness* (Varr.; Gell.;
Lact.; Amm.; Ambros.; Cassian.).

platea, *a plaza, a place* (Vulg.; Vict. Vit.), 5, 51, 3: tetragonum
plateam maximamque partem aedificiorum cremari; — *a city
street* (Ter.; Caes.).

pluvia, *a shower of anything* (Claud.; Aug.), 5, 15: quando caelestis escae pluviis alimoniam servitutis extremae praeferebatis; —
rain (Cic.; Verg.; Colum.; Liv.; Sen. phil.).

pontifex, *the Jewish high priest* (Vulg.), 1, 43, 7: Mariamne filia
pontificis; — *a Roman high priest* (Cato; Varr.; Cic.; Poetical, Silver and Late).

*posteriora (plur.), *the rear of an army, city, etc.* (Heg.), 2, 15,

6: invadunt posteriora agminis (Cf. Joseph. B. I. 2, 19, 7: κατὰ τῶν ὑστάτων) ; 4, 1, 1; — *posteriors* (Tert.; Ambros.; Vulg.; Lampr.).

* *second place* (Heg.), 1, 17, 1: ne in posterioribus ponerent officium religionis quam salutis praesidium (Cf. Joseph. B. I. 1, 7, 5: τῆς πρὸς τὸ θεῖον θεραπείας ἐν δευτέρῳ τὴν σωτηρίαν τιθέμε- νοι) ; 1, 40, 1; — *posteriors* (as above).

* *later books, sequel* (Heg.), 1, 35, 3: nobis quid veritas habeat in posterioribus aperiendum videtur (Cf. Joseph. B. I. 1, 21, 3: τὸ δ' ἀκριβὲς ἐν τοῖς ἑξῆς δηλώσομεν) ; — *posteriors* (as above).

*potestas, *a person in authority,* i. e., God (Heg.), 5, 53, 1: quo- modo tamen poterimus declinare indignationem tantae po- testatis? ; — *a person in authority* (Cic.; Verg.; Amm.).

potestates (plur.), *heavenly powers* (Vulg.), 5, 41; 5, 46: quod coelestes potestates vobis pugnaverint; — *high officials of state* (Plin. mai.; Suet.; Ambros.).

praesul, *governor, ruler* (Sol.; Auson.; Ambros.; Sid.; Pallad.), 1, 25, 4: Phaselum . . . praesulem Hierosolymis et ducem militiae constituit; 1, 41, 8; 1, 43, 6; 1, 44, 8; 3, 2; 4, 6, 9; 5, 2; 5, 32; — *a leader of the dance* (Cic.).

praesumptio, *boldness, daring* (Tert.; Apul.; Ambros.; Hier.; Rufin.; Ps. Cypr.), 1, 32, 6: incauta semper nimia prae- sumtio; 1, 38, 3; 3, 11, 3; 4, 4, 2; — *a supposition, a presump- tion* (Sen. phil.; Spart.; Iust.).

praevaricatio, *a transgression of law* (Itala; Cypr.; Herm. Past.; Hier.; Aug.), 4, 7: paternorum statutorum praevaricatio; — *a violation of duty* (Cic.; Plin. ep.).

processus, *lapse or process of time* (Arnob.; Lact.; Firm.; Amm.; Prud.; Cod. Th.; Porphyr.), 1, 42, 2: processu temporis; 4, 4, 1; 4, 9, 5; — *course, progress, advance of anything* (Cic.; Verg.; Sulp. Sev.).

profectus, *improvement of the sick* (Cael. Aur.), 1, 45, 9: Asphalti- tes lacus plerisque medicabilis sine ullo profectu aegrum tene- bant; — *increase, growth* (Varr.; Vell.; Sen. phil.; Quint.; Ambros.; Hier.).

*puerulus, *a slave* (Heg), 1, 44, 7: sed hostem induxi . . . qui excitaret puerulos; — *a young slave* (Sen. phil.).

a boy (Heg.), 5, 45: bibit puerulus; — *a little boy* (Val. Max.; Apul.).

reatus, *a charge of which one stands accused* (Apul.), 3, 24: reatum huiusmodi non reformido; — *the condition of an accused person* (Mart.; Iust.; Ict.) ; *sin* (Tert.; Hier.; Vulg.; Prud.).

repromissio, *a promise* (Tert.; Ambros.; Vulg.; Hil.; Hier.; Rufin.; Oros.), 4, 18: usque in terram repromissionis; — *a counter-promise* (Cic.).

*ruptura, *a breach in a wall* (Heg.), 3, 11, 1: ut muri latus cederet cavatumque in rupturis fenestram daret; — *a fracture or break of a limb or vein* (Gell.; Veget.).

sacramentum, *a mystery, a secret thing* (Tert.; Lact.; Ambros.; Hier.; Vulg.; Rufin.; Aug.), 1, 31, 3: si quid sacramentorum divulgaretur; 2, 9; 5, 9, 3; 5, 9, 4; 5, 18, 3; 5, 22; 5, 48; — *a military oath* (Cic.; Caes.; Liv.; Tac.; et al) ; *an oath of any kind* (Hor.; Plin. min.; Eutr.; Iust.).

sedulitas, *friendliness, kindness, courtesy* (Ambros.), 1, 20: re-munerandae sedulitatis eius gratia; 1, 25, 1; 1, 34, 2; 1, 38, 2; 1, 38, 3; 2, 4; — *zeal, earnestness* (Cic.; Hor.; Plin. mai.; Plin. min.; Fronto).

servulus (= servus), *a slave* (Ambros.), 1, 29, 6: ipse cum servulis insequentes barbaros fudit; 1, 30, 15; 1, 43, 3; 1, 45, 3; 3, 13; 3, 17; — *a young slave* (Plaut.; Ter.; Cic.; Plin. mai.).

sobrietas, *prudence, circumspection* (Amm.), Praef.: sermonum sobrietati; 1, 37, 7; 3, 21, 2; — *moderation in drinking* (Sen. phil.; Val. Max.).

stilus, *testament, will* (Amm.), 2, 1, 3: quem potissimum sibi cu-piant succedere ultimo scribant stilo; — *writing, composition* (Ter.; Cic.; Tac.; Plin. min.; Suet.; Gell.).

suggestio, *a hint, intimation, suggestion* (Vopisc.; Ambros.; Hier.; C.I.L.; Aug.; Avit.; Symm.; Ennod.; Rufin.; Cassian.), 1, 2: ut cito pravis suggestionibus extorqueatur; 1, 41, 4; 2, 12, 2;— *suggestion,* i. e., a rhetorical figure (Quint.).

*susceptio, *a retaliation, a taking up of arms in defence* (Heg.), 4, 13, 2: latrocinii saevitia bellum acerbabant sine venia dedi-tionis aut susceptionis indulgentia (Cf. Joseph. B. I. 4, 7, 2: φθάνεσθαι δὲ τὰς ἀμύνας) ; — *an undertaking* (Cic.; Gell.).

*tetragonum, *a public square* (Heg.), 5, 51, 3: tetragonum plateam maximamque partem aedificiorum cremari; — *a square, a four-sided figure* (Censor.; Mart. Cap.; Gromat.; Auson.; Isid.).

tractatus, *a discussion, consultation* (Veget.; Ict.; Cypr.), 2, 16, 2: conatus istiusmodi tractatus; 4, 4, 3; 4, 29, 1; 5, 42, 4; — *management, treatment, handling* (Cic.; Liv.; Plin. mai.; Quint.; Plin. min.; Gell.).

usurpatio, *usurpation, a using unlawfully* (Cod. Iust.), 2, 1, 2 (bis): cum usurpatione temeraria iamdudum intra Iudaeam inconsulto Caesare regem exercuisset; — *a making use, an employment* (Cic.; Liv.; Plin. mai.; Val. Max.; Gell.).

*vates, *a Jewish priest* (Heg.), 1, 16, 6: nec . . . obsequia vatum inpedita; — *a prophet* (Christian sense) (Ambros.; Prud.; Paul. Nol.); *a soothsayer* (pagan sense) (Plaut.; Cic.; Verg.; Ov.; et al).

vestigium, *a foot* (Ambros.), 1, 44, 6: sese ad vestigia deiciens patris; 1, 45, 9; 3, 2; 4, 15, 2; 4, 23, 2; 5, 22; 5, 25, 2; 5, 27; — *the sole of the foot* (Cic.; Catull.; Verg.; Ov.; Plin. mai.; Lact.).

viaticum, *resources, means* (Quadrig. apud Gell.), 5, 29: illi desperatione salutis omne effundebant virtutis viaticum nec reservabant; — *provision for a journey* (Plaut.; Cic.; Plin. min.; Ict.).

vivacitas, *activity* (Arnob.; Ambros.; Aug.), 1, 43, 3: consilii vivacitate; — *length of life* (Plin. mai.; Quint.; Plin. min.; Val. Max.; Apul.).

b) Adjectives.

diffidens, *anxious about, distrustful of* (Itin. Alex.; Mart. Cap.; Symm.), 5, 20, 3: diffidentes Iudaeos munitionum sola niti temeritate; — *suspicious, mistrustful* (Suet.).

*excitatus (= exercitatus), *disciplined, exercised* (Heg.), 5, 4, 3: Romani ipso usu veteri et diversorum generum proeliis excitati; — *aroused, animated* (Cic.; Liv.; Plin. mai.; Quint.).

*finitimus, *menaced by, near to* (of persons) (Heg.), 5, 37, 2: si vinceretur excidio finitimus; — *near to, imminent* (of things) (Cic.; Ov.; Claud.; Arator; Pass. Petr.).

genitalis, *natural* (Calp.; Cassiod.; Eustath.), 3, 9, 5: saepto geni-

4

tali abscondita (civitas) ; — *generative, productive* (Lucr.;
Poetical, Silver and Late).

*inaequalis, *sick* (Heg.), 1, 5: accidit ut fratrem adveniens inae-
qualem offenderet (Cf. Ambros. Hex. 3, 10, 43: inaequalitas =
sickness) ; — *uneven, unequal, changeable* (Cic.; Liv.; Hor.;
Ov.; Sen. rhet.; Plin. min.; Suet.; Gell.).

incuratus, *uncared for, neglected* (Vopisc.), 4, 33: nec tamen in-
curatum Iudaeae bellum reliquit; — *uncured* (Hor.).

positus, *residing, stationed, being* (of persons) (Tert.; Cypr.;
Ambros.; Paulin.; Arnob.; Vict. Vit.; Greg. Tur.), 1, 16, 5:
ante aram positi feriebantur; 1, 29, 11; 1, 32, 6; 1, 34, 1; 1, 36,
1; 1, 37, 7; 1, 40, 10; 1, 43, 4; 1, 44, 1; 1, 44, 8; 3, 3, 6;
3, 13; 3, 17; 3, 18; 4, 9, 1; 4, 24; 4, 25, 2; 4, 26, 1; 4, 29, 2;
4, 31 (bis) ; 5, 16; 5, 27; 5, 33, 1; 5, 46; — *situated, lying* (of
places, things) (Cic.; Liv.).

prolixus, *long, extended, protracted* (of time) (Ict.; Apul.; Iul.
Val.; Boeth.), 4, 29, 1: prolixae navigationis revocatus formi-
dine; 5, 1, 4; — *long, stretched out* (in extent) (Lucr.;
Colum.; Suet.; Gell.; Hier.).

visibilis, *visible, that can be seen* (passive) (Apul.; Ambros.;
Vulg.; Prud.; Aug.), 3, 26, 1: visibili per terras atque aperto
flumine; — *that can see, seeing* (active) (Plin. mai.).

c) Verbs.

adnuntiare (= praenuntiare), *to foretell, proclaim* (Tert.; Lact.;
Itala; Ambros.; Hier.; Vulg.; Aug.; Sulp. Sev.; Oros.), 1, 6,
4: quae futura erant adnuntiasse historia vetus prodidit; 2, 7,
1; 2, 12, 1; 5, 31; — *to make known, declare* (Sen. phil.;
Curt.; Plin. mai.; Stat.; Suet.; Frontin.; Apul.; and Late).

adserere, *to say, affirm* (Ps. Quint.; Apul.; Tert.; C.I.L.; Cypr.;
Lact.; Ambros.; et al), 1, 6, 1: ut credibile duceret, quod pro
vero asserebatur; 1, 30, 4; 1, 31, 3; 1, 38, 3; 1, 40, 8; 1, 41, 7;
1, 41, 9; 1, 41, 11; 1, 43, 1; 1, 44, 7; 1, 45, 10; 2, 1, 3; 2, 2, 2;
2, 9 (bis) ; 2, 14; 3, 17; 3, 24; 3, 25, 3; 4, 6, 9; 4, 11; 5, 2;
5, 25, 1; 5, 27; 5, 31; 5, 42, 3; 5, 44, 1; 5, 49, 4; — *to declare
a slave to be free by laying hands upon him* (Plaut.; Ter.;
Varr.; Cic.; Liv.; Silver and Late).

adstipulari, *to favor, to be favorable* (Ambros.; Oros.; Cod. Iust.;

Greg. Tur.), 1, 10, 2: adstipulantibus ad misericordiam rebus
adversis; 1, 38, 5; 1, 39; 1, 41, 2; 1, 42, 4; — *to agree with*
(Liv.; Plin. mai.; and Late).

*alligare [18] (= allegare), *to relate, mention* (Heg.), 1, 29, 8: addi-
disse alligatur in ultimis suis cum iam exhalaret spiritum (Cf.
Joseph. B. I. 1, 30, 10: φασὶ γοῦν) ; — *to bind to* (Varr.; Cic.;
Colum.; Sen. phil.).

appetere, *to accuse* (Firm.; Amm.; Canon. interpr. Migne), 1, 38,
6; 4, 7: bonus iudex . . . est fallenti infestior quam adpeti-
tus; — *to attack, assail* (Plaut.; Pacuv.; Cic.; Caes.; Liv.;
Silver and Late).

celebrare, *to sollemnize* (of Christian worship) (Tert.; Lact.;
Optat.; Ambros.; Hier.; Filastr.; Aug.; et al), 3, 2: celebrata
oratione; — *to keep a festival* (Early, Classical, Poetical, Silver and Late).

collidere, *to fight* (Lucif.; Faustin.; Cypr. Gall.), 5, 53, 1: postea
inter se armis colliderent; — *to batter, beat* (Cic.; Lucr.;
Colum.; Ov.; Lucan.; Petron.; Plin. mai.; Itala; and Late).

comperendinare, *to delay, defer* (Min. Fel.; Itin. Alex.; Ambros.;
Hier.; Zacch.; Petr. Chrys.), 1, 10, 1: pugna in manibus nec
comperendinata; 2, 15, 5; — *to defer a trial* (Cic.; and Late).

consignare, *to hand over, consign* (Rufin.; Cassian.; and Late),
1, 29, 7: ut Phaselus et Hyrcanus in potestatem eius consigna-
rentur; — *to seal, sign* (Plaut.; Cic.; Quint.; Gell.; and Late).

contestari, *to confirm by testimony, to prove* (Min. Fel.; Tert.;
Itala; and Late), 2, 13, 4: velut contestaturus pacti iniquita-
tem; — *to call a witness* (Cic.; Caes.; Sen. phil.; and Late).

to say, affirm solemnly (Dict.; Amm.; Ambrosiast.; Maximin.;
Vulg.; Sulp. Sev.; Oros.; et al), 5, 34, 2: Titus . . . invitum
se deduci ad excidium urbis . . . contestabatur; — *to call a
witness* (as above).

*convenire, *to be more fit, suitable* (Heg.), 5, 15: fuerat . . .
humani ingenii contendere pertinaciter . . . licet convenerit
Romanos . . . armis non provocari; — *to be fit, suitable*
(Plaut.; Ter.; Cic.; Silver and Late).

to address, accost (Apul.; Ps. Quint.; Ps. Cypr.; Vopisc.;
Lampr.; Iul. Val.; Firm.; Hil.; Amm.; Ambros.; Hier.; et

---

[18] The T.L.L. I, 1669, 23, cites Hegesippus 1, 29, 8 s. v. allegare.

al), 1, 13, 2: Hyrcanus matrem lacrimis conveniebat; 1, 25, 4; 1, 28, 7; 1, 29, 5; 1, 41, 3; 3, 18, 1; 4, 23, 3; 4, 28, 1; 5, 15; 5, 16 (bis); 5, 22; 5, 27; — *to meet* (Enn.; Plaut.; Ter.; Cic.; Liv.; Silver and Late).

    to affect, reach (Ps. Quint.; Symm.; Iord.), 3, 18, 2: ut se nemo subtrahat, cum sors conveniat universos; — *to meet* (as above).

corripere, *to punish, correct* (Itala; Hier.; Aug.; Eugipp.; Lex Visig.; Salon.), 5, 44, 1: corripi flagellis hominem iubens; — *to accuse someone before a judge* (Tac.; Paneg.; Rufin.; Sid.; Cod. Th.).

crispare, *to become wavy* (Tract. in Luc.; Ambros.; Hier.; Aug.; Vict. Vit.; Avit.; Drac.), 3, 26, 1: crispantibus aquis; — *to curl, crisp* (of the hair) (Sen. phil.; Plin. mai.; and Late).

crudescere, *to be indigestible* (Rufin.; Macr.), 5, 24, 2: post biduanum ieiunium si quid avidius sumpseris, statim crudescit; — *to grow worse* (Verg.; Stat.; Tac.; Auson.; Symm.; Lact.; et al).

*defenerare (= obstringere), *to pledge, bind* (Heg.), 1, 32, 1: Antonius Cleopatrae amori defoeneratus inserviebat; — *to involve in debt* (Plaut.; Cic.; Apul.; Schol. Cic. Bob.; Ambros.; Aug.).

*demetere, *to cut down, to destroy anything* (Heg.), 5, 38: proxima quaeque demetunt; — *to cut down, to harvest fruits, grain* (Cato; Cic.; Catull.; Verg.; Colum.; Liv.; Silver and Late).

*depasci, *to eat* (of men) (Heg.), 5, 18, 2: plerique . . . egrediebantur urbem ut . . . radices depascerentur; — *to eat* (of animals) (Lucr.; Paneg. in Mess.; Plin. mai.; Iuv.; Paul.; Sol.; Itala; Ambros.; et al).

deputare, *to hand over, allot, assign, destine* (Tert.; Lampr.; Firm.; Iren.; Pallad.; and Late), 2, 11, 1: ut nulli quem praedae studio deputassent neci parcendum existimarent; 5, 21, 2; 5, 35, 1; — *to esteem, consider* (Plaut.; Ter.; Caecil.; Acc.; Cic.; Tert.; and Late).

derelinquere, *to leave remaining* (Itala; Tert.; Hil.; Hier.; Vulg.; et al), 1, 28, 6: nomen (regis) solum Hyrcano ad speciem honoris dereliquisse; 2, 1, 1; — *to forsake* (Plaut.; Cic.; Sall.; Silver and Late).

derogare, *to dishonor a person* (Ambros.; Rufin.; Theod. Mops. in

Gal.), 4, 26, 1: si honorare nolumus (Vespasianum), non
derogemus; — *to detract from something* (Cic.; Caes.; Liv.;
Silver and Late).

*detegere (= arguere), *to accuse* (Heg.), 1, 40, 6: ancilla disposi-
tionis initae, ut ad Parthos confugeret, familiarium confes-
sionibus detegebatur; — *to discover, reveal, betray* (Liv.; Ov.;
Silver and Late).

*diloricare, *to strip the leather corselet from and to kill a person*
(Heg.), 1, 6, 2: qui Antigonum diloricarent; 4, 25, 2; — *to
tear open one's dress* (Cic.; Apul.; Ambros.; Heg.).

dirigere (= ducere), *to lead* (Greg. Tur.), 1, 6, 1: quod pompam
armatorum dırexerit; 3, 16; — *to lead away somewhere* (Sil.;
Tert.; and Late).

*se effundere, *to unburden one's self* (Heg.), 1, 41, 3: Alexander
. . . effudit sese mercenario Antipatri; — *to give one's self up
to, to yield* (Cic.; Liv.; Curt.; Sen. rhet.; Tac.).

*egredi, *to disobey* (Heg.), 5, 6: egrediuntur plerique praescrip-
tum; — *to overstep, exceed* (Vell.; Sen. rhet.; Plin. min.;
Tac.; Fronto).

evolvere, *to elapse, pass* (of time) (Vulg.; Aug.), 1, 43, 3: cur-
ricula evoluta temporum; — *to unroll, unfold* (Cic.; Verg.;
Ov.; Liv.).

*expectare (= spectare), *to watch* (Heg.), 5, 34: gentıles cum
formidine templum expectabant; — *to await, expect* (Cato;
Cic.; Caes.; Poetical, Silver and Late).

fervere, *to increase, flourish, spread abroad* (Cypr.; Arnob.; Amm.;
Prud.; Aug.; Cod. Th.; Eucher.; Avit.; Facund.), 1, 40, 8:
fervebant calumniae; — *to ramble, to go to and fro* (Acc.;
Lucr.; Ov.; Lucan.; Val. Fl.; Sılver and Late).

figurare, *to symbolize* (Tert.; Novatian.; Lact.; Hier.; Pelag.;
Aug.; Cassian.; Eustath.; Greg. M.), 5, 9, 2: cocco . . . ig-
neum caelum figuratur; — *to imagine, fancy* (Sen. rhet.; Sen.
phil.; Curt.; Colum.; Ps. Quint.; and Late).

*fovere (= observare), *to comply with* (Heg.), 5, 24, 4: ut praeceptum foverent; — *to favor, support* (Cic.; Poetical, Silver
and Late).

fulcire, *to provide, equip, adorn* (Apul.; Tert.; Porphyr.; Avien.;
Amm.; Prud.; Ven. Fort.; Anthol.; Ambros.; Hier.; et al),

1, 38, 4: omni ornatu cultuque regio fulciebatur; 2, 1, 2;
4, 16, 2; — *to strengthen, support* (Cic.; Prop.; Liv.; Silver
and Late).

*imminere (= intendere), *to turn one's attention to* (Heg.), 1, 16,
4: nisi imminere suos aggerendis terrarum tumulis imperavis-
set; — *to strive eagerly after, to be intent on* (Cic.; Liv.;
Curt.).

incubare, *to hold back unlawfully* (Ict.), 1, 25, 6: ut Hyrcanum et
Antipatrum incubare alienis, quae sibi et fratribus suis per
scelus erepta forent, questu gravissimo coacerbaret; — *to
guard, to watch over jealously* (Cic.; Verg.; Liv.; Sen. phil.;
Mart.; Quint.).

inculcare (= conculcare), *to trample upon, walk upon* (Itala;
Tert.; Iren.; Cpyr.; Min. Fel.; Gloss. Cyrill.), 5, 25, 2: terra
ipsa inculcata; — *to force upon* (Cic.; Sen. phil.).

inhalare, *to breathe the odor or fragrance from something* (Ambros.), 4, 17: inhalantes floribus paradisi; 5, 25, 2; — *to
breathe the smell of food* (Cic.).

*inhorrescere (= horrescere),[19] *to bristle* (of weapons) (Heg.), 5,
19: inhorrescere super eum telorum vis plurima (coepit); —
to send forth sharp points (Pacuv. fr.; Verg.; Sen. rhet.;
Sen. poet.; Curt.; Plin. mai.).

*inserere, *to pierce with a weapon* (Heg.), 3, 26, 3: iaculo insertus . . . vitam deponeret; 5, 50; — *to ingraft, implant*
(Colum.; Hier.; Porphyr.).

insinuare, *to say, make known, communicate* (Itala; Iul. Val.;
Capit.; Ambros.; Dar.; Hier.; Macr.; Aug.; Spart.; Vict.
Vit.; Musc.), 1, 6, 2; 1, 14, 1: ut insinuari faceret Aristobolo;
1, 20; 1, 29, 9; 1, 41, 3; 2, 12, 2; 4, 16, 1; 4, 23, 3; 4, 28, 1;
5, 11, 1; 5, 16; 5, 19; 5, 22, 1; 5, 35, 1; 5, 47, 1; — *to penetrate thoroughly, to make one's way into* (Lucr.; Cic.; Plin.
mai.; Suet.).

*insuere [20] (= configere), *to pierce* (Heg.), 4, 15, 2: insuebatur
sagittis ac subito resupinus interiebat; — *to sew into, to em-
broider* (Varr.; Verg.; Ov.; Colum.).

---

[19] Cf. Ennius and Vergil: horrescere, *to bristle* (of weapons).

[20] Cf. Hegesippus 3, 26, 3: sagittae iaculo insertus; 5, 50: iaculo insertus.

internecare, *to destroy* (Amm.; Ambros.; Prud.), 4, 17: internecare solitus sata; — *to kill* (Plaut.).

intersecare, *to divide, intersect* (Macr.; Amm.; Avien.), 3, 5, 2:
fluvius eam medius intersecat; 3, 26, 1; 4, 16, 2; — *to cut
apart* (Vitr.; Stat.; Amm.).

*intexere, *to join together* (Heg.), 3, 3, 4: clypeos intexerent; —
to interweave, interlace (Verg.; Ov.; Petron.; Curt.; Plin.
mai.; Hier.; Ps. Cypr.).

to intersperse, scatter (Heg.,) 5, 52, 2: ne quis elaberetur in-
textis castellum custodiis circumvallarunt; — *to interweave,
interlace* (as above).

licitari, *to expose or offer for sale* (Amm.; Ambros.), 1, 37, 2:
qui formam suam venalem offerret et pulchritudine licitaretur;
— *to offer a price, to bid* (Plaut.; Curt.).

militare, *to serve, be of service to* (of inanimate objects) (Tert.),
2, 9: cuius nova gratia et naturalis fecunditas Romanis
militat; — *to serve, be of service to* (of animate objects)
(Hor.; Ov.; Apul.).

*mutuare [21] (= mutare), *to sell, exchange* (Heg.), 5, 39, 2: si
quis (paleas) repererat, grandi pretio mutuabat; — *to borrow*
(Caecil.; Vitr.; Plin. mai.; Tert.).

*nectere, *to bind* (of persons) (Heg.), 1, 39: ut eos uno osculo
caritatis invicem sibi necteret; — *to join, bind, fasten together*
(of things) (Cic.; Verg.; Hor.; Ov.; Liv.; Val. Max.; Tac.).

*obtendere (= offerre), *to offer, give* (Heg.), 1, 44, 7: arbitrabar
quod et illos mihi redderet, moerorem auferret, pietatem ob-
tenderet; — *to place before* (Verg.; Curt.; Suet.; Sol.).

operari, *to work, cause, do, exercise* (Ambros.; Vulg.; Hier.; Lact.;
Aug.), 3, 17; 4, 6, 4; 5, 53, 1: quum excedit corpore, mortem
operatur; — *to labor, toil, be occupied with* (Verg.; Hor.;
Ov.; Liv.; Quint.; Tac.; et al).

to be active, effectual (Lampr.; Hier.; Rufin.; Capit.; Cod.
Iust.; Prisc.), 5, 21, 3: ubi hostis deerat, fames operabatur; —
to toil, labor, be occupied with (as above).

*perstringere (= stringere),[22] *to touch, border* (Heg.), 1, 35, 4:

---

[21] If the reading of the text is to be accepted.
[22] Cf. Ovid and Curtius: stringere, *to touch, border.*

utraque ex parte perstringitur importuoso litore; — *to graze against* (Cic.; Verg.; Curt.).

*perstrmgere (= praestringere),[23] *to touch, move, affect* (Heg.), 1, 37, 3: perstrictum illum splendore imaginum et Sossii praecipue testimonio; 1, 37, 5; 1, 40, 3; 2, 4; 5, 37, 2; — *to seize* (Liv.; Val. Max.).

*praeesse (= prodesse), *to be of benefit to, to profit* (Heg.), 1, 41, 6: sacramento interposito fidem fecit, sed adulescentibus nihil praefuit; — *to be set over, to rule over* (Cic.; Sall.; Caes.; Nep.; et al).

*praeicere, *to push forward* (Heg.), 4, 1, 4: plerique praeicientes se lapsis aedibus occupabantur (Cf. Joseph. B. I. 4, 1, 4: πρόσω βιαζομένων) ; — *to set before, place in front* (Ter. Scaur.).

praeiudicare, *to be prejudicial, injurious* (Macer.; Tert.; Ambros.; Hier.; Aug.; Fulg. Rusp.; Avit.), 2, 12, 1: non tamen veritati praeiudicat; — *to judge beforehand* (Cic.).

*praelibare, *to start* (Heg.), 3, 24: licet praelibare bellum, . . . dum adiumenta veniunt; — *to foretaste* (Stat.; Fulg. cont. Verg.).

praestringere, *to touch or strike in passing* (Amm.), 4, 27: ne praestringat tenuis carina cautes; — *to touch lightly* (Suet.; Avien.).

praesumere, *to trust, be confident* (Vulg.; Aug.), 1, 15, 1: praesumebat de Scauri redemtione; 1, 40, 9; 2, 9; 3, 3, 4; 4, 29, 2; 5, 46; — *to presume, take for granted* (Val. Max.; Tac.; Iust.; Aur. Vict.; Aug.).

to dare, venture (Vulg.; Hier.; Rufin.; Auct. inc. pan. Const.; Sulp. Sev.; Fest. Ruf.), 1, 42, 5: praesumsit orare; 2, 1, 2; 3, 8, 3; 4, 22, 1; — *to presume, take for granted* (as above).

praevaricari, *to transgress, violate* (Ambros.; Hier.; Vulg.; Rufin.), 1, 32, 6: praevaricati sunt legem omnium hominum; 3, 17; 4, 4, 3; — *to commit irregularities in a judicial procedure* (Cic.).

*procumbere (= occumbere),[24] *to die* (Heg.), 5, 24, 1: pro patria, dum salutaria suadet, procumbere; — *to fall down* (Caes.; Verg.; Ov.; Liv.; Silver and Late).

---

[23] Cf. Amm. 16, 10, 13; 29, 6, 9: praestringere, *to touch, move, affect.*
[24] Cf. Cicero Att. 3, 15, 4: occumbere, *to die.*

*proludere (= praeludere),[25] *to prelude* (trans.) (Heg.), 3, 24:
cedendo atque insequendo bellum proludit; — *to rehearse,
practice beforehand* (intrans.) (Verg.; Ov.; Flor.; Anthol.).

propinquare, *to be near* (Ambros.; Aug.; Rufin.), 5, 21, 4: iam
non propinquantibus silvis; — *to draw near, approach* (Sall.
fr.; Verg.; Tac.; Stat.; Amm.; Aur. Vict.).

protelare, *to defer, delay, postpone* (Tert.; Hier.; Rufin.; Digest.;
Cod. Iust.), 1, 43, 5: ut mors protelaretur; — *to drive forth
or away* (Sisenn. fr.; Turpil. fr.; Ter.; Fronto; Apul.).

protestari, *to protest, say publicly* (Ulp.; Ambros.; Hier.; Rufin.),
1, 40, 7: ut . . . instare sibi Alexandrum cum gladio pater
. . . protestaretur; 5, 41; 5, 53, 1; — *to testify, bear witness*
(Quint.; Fronto; Hier.; Macr.; et al).

recludere, *to shut up, imprison* (Itala; Iust.; Commod.; Lucif.;
Calar.; Vulg.; Palad.; Gloss. Mai), 1, 13, 2: uxorem Aristo-
boli in castrum reclusit; — *to lay open, disclose, reveal*
(Plaut.; Verg.; Ov.; Tac.).

*refluere (= confluere),[26] *to come together* (of men) (Heg.), 1,
20: plerisque refluentibus ad eum; — *to flow or run back* (of
water) (Verg.; Ov.; Mela; Lucan.; Val. Fl.; Plin. mai.).

*relaxare, *to loosen, free* (of persons) (Heg.), 4, 12: relaxabantur
divites, pauperes interficiebantur (Cf. Joseph. B. I. 4, 6, 3:
ἐξηφίετο) ; — *to loosen* (of things) (Varr.; Verg.; Ov.; Cels.;
Colum.; Sen. poet.).

resumere, *to revive, restore* (Cael. Aur.; Musc.), 1, 45, 9: excitatus
strepitu conclamantium resumsit; — *to recover, receive again*
(Ov.; Suet.).

se resumere, *to revive one's self* (Commodian.), 1, 43, 6: illa ubi
se resumsit paululum; — resumere, *to recover, receive again*
(as above).

*sidere, *to founder, sink* (Heg.), 3, 20, 2: plerique cum ipsis in
profundo sidebant myoparonibus; — *to stick fast* (Nep.;
Prop.; Liv.).

stringere, *to hold in check, govern* (Claud. apud Gild.), 5, 41:
stringuntur liquentia; — *to draw tight, press together* (Liv.;
Ov.; Stat.; Plin. mai.; Plin. min.; Gell.; and Late).

[25] Cf. Ambros; Avien.; Rutil. Nam.: praeludere, *to prelude* (trans.).
[26] Cf. Cic.; Caes.; Nep.; Suet.: confluere, *to come together* (of men).

succidere, *to overthrow, destroy* (Lact.), 4, 22, 3: se . . . succi-
dendos putarunt; 5, 1, 5; — *to cut down* (Enn.; Varr.; Caes.;
Verg.; Liv.; et al).

suggerere, *to state, explain, make a report* (to a king, emperor, etc.)
(Vict. Vit.; Paul. Petr.), 1, 41, 11: suggerit quod impulsus
ab Alexandro pater necem regi parasset; — *to suggest, advise*
(Curt.; Ulp.; Aur. Vict.; and Late).

*suspendere, *to hang up and expose to* (Heg.), 3, 26, 1: ut aestivis
suspensam (aquam) ad auras noctibus more incolarum potui
paret (Cf. Joseph. B. I. 3, 10, 7: ἐξαιθριασθέν = to expose to
sun and air); — *to hang up* (Verg.; Ov.; Liv.; Plin. mai.;
et al).

*tumescere, *to fill up* (Heg.), 5, 1, 3: in circuitu omnia cruore
tumescere; — *to swell up* (Cic.; Verg.; Ov.; Sen. phil.; Tac.).

*uti, *to do, act* (Heg.), 1, 45, 11: permissa sibi utendi ut vellet
potestate; — *to employ, use* (Plaut.; Cic.; Silver and Late).

d) Adverbs.

difficile (= vix, aegre), *hardly* (Fronto; Herm.; Tert.; Ps. Cypr.),
2, 11, 2: difficile quisquam populus . . . Iudaeos non perse-
cutus est; — *with difficulty* (Cato; Cels.; Plin. mai.; Apul.;
Vulg.; et al).

nihilominus, *in the same manner, likewise* (Itala; Rufin.; Vict.
Vit.; Ruric.; et al), 4, 19: nihilominus etiam Lucio Annio
Gerasam destinato insidiis urbem cepit; — *nevertheless, not-
withstanding* (Plaut.; Acc.; Cic.; Caes.; Sen. phil.; et al).

publice, *publicly, openly, before the people* (Gell.; Apul.; Eutr.),
1, 38, 4: ita ut publice condito testamento solus imperii suc-
cessor designaretur; — *on account or in behalf of the state*
(Cic.; Caes.; Sall.; Tac.; Silver and Late).

Hegesippus, in common with other Late writers, extends meanings to sixty-three nouns, six adjectives, forty-six verbs, and three
adverbs.

I note for Hegesippus alone twenty-seven nouns, three adjectives
and thirty-three verbs whose meanings have been extended.

PART II

RARE CLASSICAL, EARLY, POETIC, AND SILVER
WORDS AND MEANINGS

As the Late words and meanings have received special treatment in earlier chapters, the present section will be limited to an investigation of the Rare Classical, Early, Poetic, and Silver words and meanings. In order to facilitate the handling of these words they have been separated into four categories.

In the first category—Rare Classical—will be placed those words which occur for the first time either in form or in meaning in the classical prose writers and then, but rarely.

The second group—Early—will contain the words found first in the ante-classical writers and only rarely, if at all, in classical authors.

The third group—Poetic—will include the words that have been used for the first time in form or in meaning by the classical poets.

The fourth group—Silver—will be made up of words occurring for the first time in form or in meaning in the prose or poetry from Livy to Suetonius.

The words in these four categories will be grouped under each suffix in the morphological divisions as follows: a) Rare Classical; b) Early; c) Poetic; d) Silver.

In each category will be given the Latin word, its English equivalent, the authors who use it in this meaning, and the places where this word and meaning are found in Hegesippus.

In the Rare Classical and Early groups the number of times such a meaning is found in Cicero will be indicated, as nearly as can be estimated from the T. L. L. and Merguet's Lexica to Cicero.

A. Nouns

1. Nouns in -tor, -sor.

a) *conciliator*, a promoter, patron (Varr.; Nep.; Liv.; Tac.; Suet.; Apul.; Auson.), 1, 29, 2; 5, 22. — *concitator*, one who rouses (Cic. (3); Hirt.; Sen. phil.; Tac.; Liv.; Eutr.; Paul.; and Late), 2, 10, 1. — *conditor*, administrator, steward (Cic. (2); Ps. Agenn.; Frontin.; C. I. L.), 5, 18, 1; — the founder of a city (Varr.; Sall.;

59

Nep.; Verg.; Hor.; Ov.; Liv.; Silver and Late), 3, 5, 2; 3, 19. — *confirmator,* one who confirms a thing (Cic. (1); Tert.; Lact.; Dict.; Ps. Rufin.; Novell.; Iulian.), 2, 1, 3. — *contemptor,* a contemner (Sall.; Verg.; Ov.; Liv.; Silver and Late), 1, 41, 2; 5, 18, 3; 5, 53, 1. — *creator,* one who produces or makes (Cic. (1); Ulp.; Filastr.; Aug.; and Late), 2, 12, 1. — *decessor,* predecessor, a retiring officer (Cic. (1); Tac.; Ulp.; C. I. L.; Spart.; Symm.; Amm.; and Late), 1, 43, 3; 1, 44, 7. — *desertor,* one who deserts or abandons a thing (Cic. (3); Caes.; Verg.; Ov.; Silver and Late), 1, 33; 3, 17; 4, 4, 1. — *dispensator,*[1] an overseer, steward (Varr.; Cic. (2); Silver and Late), 1, 44, 7; 1, 44, 8. — *eversor,* a destroyer, a subverter (Cic. (4); Verg.; Sen. rhet.; Quint.; Stat.), 5, 31. — *expugnator,* a conqueror, a stormer (Cic. (2); Liv.; Sen. rhet.; Plin. mai.; Silver and Late), 1, 16, 3; 5, 20, 2. — *habitator,* an inhabitant (Cic. (1); Amm.; Veget.; Macr.), 5, 53, 1. — *litigator,* a litigant (Cic. ep. (1); Plin. min.; Quint.; Tac.; Suet.; Amm.), 2, 1, 2. — *percussor,* a murderer, assassin (Cic. (4); Curt.; Sen. phil.; Suet.; Ambros.), 1, 8; 2, 6, 3; 3, 13; 3, 17 (bis); 5, 2; 5, 16; 5, 18, 2; 5, 19; 5, 22 (bis); 5, 29; 5, 40 (bis); 5, 47, 1. — *repressor,* a represser, a restrainer (Cic. (1); Eutr.; Ambros.; Aug.), 5, 40.

b) *consultor,* an adviser, counsellor (Afran.; Annal. Max.; Sall.; Ps. Sall.; Tac.; Gell.; and Late), 2, 10, 3; 2, 13, 5; 3, 1, 2. — *cultor,* an inhabitant (Plaut.; Catull.; Sall.; Verg.; Ov.; Liv.; Silver and Late), 3, 3, 4. — *ductor,* a leader (Acc.; Varr.; Cic. (2); Lucr.; Verg.; Ov.; Liv.; Stat.), 1, 14, 1; 4, 23, 1; 5, 10, 3; 5, 12. — *precator,* an intercessor (Plaut.; Ter.; Stat.; Iul. Val.; Ambros.; Hier.; and Late), 1, 5.

c) *assertor,* a defender, advocate (Ov.; Sen. phil.; Lucan.; Stat.; Silver and Late), 5, 27; 5, 31; 5, 53, 1. — *auctor,* the Creator and Giver (Verg.; Sen. phil.; Lucan.; Apul.; and Late), 3, 17; 5, 2. — *iaculator,* a javelin-thrower (Ov.; Liv.; Sen. rhet.; C. I. L.), 5, 10, 3; 5, 13. — *monitor,* an instructor, a guide (Hor.; Stat.), 1, 39. — *pugnator,* a fighter (Verg.; Liv.; Suet.), 5, 10, 3. — *violator,*

---

[1] T.L.L. IV, 1401, 28 ff. incorrectly cites Heg. 1, 44, 7 under the ecclesiastical meaning of " priest," " minister," etc.

a profaner, violator (Ov.; Liv.; Vell.; Tac.; Ambros.; Aug.; Hyg.; Macr.; Oros.), 5, 21, 3.

d) *arcessitor* (*accersitor*), one who calls (Plin. ep.; Apul.), 5, 22, 1. — *auxiliator*, a helper (Petron.; Quint.; Tac.; Stat.; Apul.; and Late), 1, 32, 7. — *conturbator*, one who brings ruin (Mart.; Ps. Quint.; Facund.; Epist. pontif.), 4, 4, 1. — *defector*, a rebel, revolter (Pomp. Trog.; Tac.; Suet.; Iust.; Serv.; Oros.; C. I. L.), 4, 30. — *delator*, an accuser, informer (Liv.; Mart.; Quint.; Tac.; Silver and Late), 1, 40, 4; 1, 40, 9. — *exsecutor*, an executor (Vell.; Ict.; Amm.; Apul.; Ambros.; and Late), 1, 29, 3; 1, 38, 3; 1, 40, 9 (bis); 1, 43, 3; 2, 5, 3 (bis); 2, 9, 3; 3, 17 (bis); 4, 10, 2; 4, 33; 5, 46. — *insectator*, a persecutor (Liv.; Quint.; Amm.; Eutr.; Aug.; Paulin.), 1, 41, 4. — *negotiator*, a trader (Quint.; Suet.; Lampr.; Iust.; Ict.; Vulg.; and Late), 4, 30. — *proeliator*, a fighter (Val. Max.; Tac.; Iust.), 2, 10, 4; 3, 3, 6; 4, 7; 4, 23, 2. — *reconciliator*, conciliator, reconciler (Liv.; Apul.; Dionys. Exig.), 1, 38, 6. — *scrutator*, an investigator (Suet.; Iust.; Stat.; Lucan.; Serv.), 2, 9. — *sollicitator*, a seducer, tempter (Sen. rhet.; Ict.), 1, 44, 8.

2. Nouns in *-tas*.

a) *asperitas*, roughness, severity (Varr.; Cic. (5); Sall.; Poetical, Silver and Late), 4, 2; 4, 33. — *celebritas*, a solemnity, festal celebration (Cic. (2); Liv.; Sen. rhet.; Gell.; and Late), 1, 46, 2; 2, 1, 2; 4, 7; 5, 5 (bis); 5, 9, 3; 5, 22; 5, 44, 1 (ter). — *civitas*, city (Rhet. Her.; Dolab. in Cic. ep.; Cic. (4); Ps. Cic.; Caes.; Nep.; Liv.; Silver and Late), 1, 10, 3; 1, 12, 4; 2, 14, 2; 3, 6, 5; 3, 9, 5 (bis); 3, 15, 3; 3, 17; 3, 19 (bis); 3, 20, 1; 3, 20, 2; 4, 1, 2; 4, 3, 2; 4, 4, 5; 4, 8; 4, 9, 1; 4, 16, 1; 4, 19; 5, 53, 1 (bis). — *deformitas*, disgrace (Cic. ep. (2); Bell. Alex.; Liv.; Silver and Late (Ambros.)), 5, 16. — *ebrietas*, intoxication (Cic. (1); Hor.; Ov.; Sen. phil.; Colum.; Ambros.; Aug.), 4, 7. — *fecunditas*, fertility (transf. sense) (Cic. (1); Plin. mai.; Apul.; Tert.; Ambros.; and Late), 3, 6, 4. — *germanitas*, relationship between brothers and sisters (Cic. (2); Liv.; Apul.; Ambros.; and Late), 1, 1, 4; 1, 7, 2; 1, 29, 9; 1, 37, 2; 1, 38, 6; 1, 43, 6. — *hospitalitas*, hospitality (Cic. (1); Mart.; Ambros.; Oros.; Cassiod.), 1, 28, 7; 1, 37, 2; 1, 38, 6; 4, 17. — *ignobilitas*, low birth (Cic. (4); Ov.;

Liv.), 1, 40, 2. — *placiditas*, gentleness of nature or disposition
(Varr.; Gell.; Lact.; Ambros.; Amm.; Cassian.), 1, 10, 1. —
qualitas, nature, quality (Cic. (6); Vitr.; Colum.; Silver and
Late), 1, 6, 2; 3, 6, 4; 3, 26, 1. — *rivalitas*, rivalry in love (Cic.
Tusc. 4, 56; Apul.), 1, 37, 4. — *viriditas*, greenness (Cic. (2);
Plin. mai.; Ambros.), 5, 18, 2.

b) *edacitas*, gluttony (Plaut.; Cic. ep. (2); Ambros.), 4, 32. —
facilitas, ease, facility (Ter.; Rhet. Her.; Cic. (1); Caes.; Vitr.;
Liv.; Silver and Late), 5, 27. — *vilitas*, baseness, worthlessness
(Plaut.; Petron.; Plin. mai.; Apul.; and Late), 2, 9.

c) *fertilitas*, fertility (transf. sense) (Ov.; Plin. mai.; Greg.
M.), 3, 6, 4. — *simplicitas*, simplicity (Ov.; Liv.; Vell.; Mart.;
Quint.; Ambros.; Sidon.), 5, 16.

d) *captivitas*, captivity (Sen. rhet.; Petron.; Quint.; Frontin.;
Tac.; Flor.; Apul.; and Late), 1, 29, 9; 1, 30, 9; 2, 1, 1; 2, 13, 1;
5, 53, 1. — *diversitas*, distance, extent (Sen. phil.; Plin. ep.; Sol.;
Hier.; and Late), 3, 6, 4; — difference, diversity (Sen. rhet.; Sen.
phil.; Colum.; Plin. mai.; Tac.; Silver and Late), 2, 11, 1; 3, 26,
2 (bis); 5, 9, 2. — *enormitas*, vastness (Sen. phil.; Spart.; Veget.;
Capit.; Salv.; Ambros.; Cod. Th.), 2, 15, 5. — *immaturitas*, im-
maturity (Suet. Aug. 34, 2), 5, 22. — *liberalitates* [2] (plur.), gifts
(Suet.; Apul.; Cassiod.; Inscr.), 1, 35, 2. — *necessitas*, need, want
(Tac.; Suet.; Itala; Tert.; Arnob.; Ambros.), 1, 25, 4; 1, 32, 4;
1, 33. — *securitas*, safety, security (Plin. mai.; Plin. min.; Tac.;
C. I. L.), 1, 10, 3; 1, 12, 3; 1, 12, 4; 1, 18; 1, 32, 1; 1, 44, 7;
1, 44, 8; 3, 5, 3; 3, 15, 2; 4, 30; 5, 33, 1; 5, 39, 1; — carelessness,
negligence (Vell.; Quint.; Tac.; Gell.), 2, 17. — *sublimitas*, gran-
deur, loftiness (Plin. mai.; Porphyr.), 1, 15, 1. — *vastitas*, the
vastness (Plin. mai.; Colum.), 1, 35, 4.

3. Nouns in *-io, -tio, -sio*.

a) *acclamatio*, a shout of approbation (Cic. (1); Liv.; Curt.;
Quint.; Plin. ep.; Symm.; and Late), 1, 46, 2. — *adhortatio*, encouragement (Cic. (1); Liv.; Sen. phil.; Silver and Late), 5, 27;
5, 40. — *adsumptio*, an assumption, receiving (Rhet. Her.; Cic.

---

[2] This word is found in Tacitus in the singular in the sense of " gift."

(2); Marcian.; Ulp.; and Late), 1, 1, 7. — *adulatio*, adulation of men (Cic. (1); Caes.; Liv.; and frequent in Tac.; Silver and Late Latin), 1, 39; 1, 41, 9; 1, 42, 6. — *aemulatio*, emulation (in a good sense) (Nep.; Liv.; Colum.; Silver and Late), 1, 26, 1; 5, 2. — *amissio*, death (Cic. (3); Sen. phil.; Val. Max.; Plin. ep.; Itala; Ambros.; and Late), 2, 9; 4, 2, 1; 5, 22. — *appellatio*, name, signification (Cic. (3); Caes. apud Gell.; Vell.; Silver and Late), 1, 6, 3. — *coartatio*, a crowding together (Bell. Alex.; Liv.; Aug.), 3, 15, 1. — *cognitio*, religious knowledge (Cic. (4); Tert.; Cypr.; and Late), 5, 9, 4. — *complexio*, a combination (Cic. (1); Mar. Victorin.; Ps. Mar. Victorin.; Rufin.; Aug.; et al), 2, 9, 1. — *congregatio*, a gathering together (Cic. (4); Sen. phil.; Quint.; Hier.; Aug.; Ambros.), 1, 30, 9; 1, 35, 3; 1, 46, 1; 2, 14, 3; 3, 14.— *coniunctio*, marriage (Cic. (3); Varr.; Nep.; Plin. mai.; Apul.; Tert.; Ambros.; et al), 1, 23; 1, 31, 1; 1, 38, 3; 1, 41, 7. — *conventio*, an agreement (Sall. fr.; Liv.; Fest.; Silver and Late), 1, 15, 2; 1, 21, 1; 1, 22, 2; 5, 35, 1. — *conversio*, a physical change (Cic. (2); Colum.; Flor.; Apul.; and Late), 4, 18; — a mental change (Cic. (5); Plin. mai.; Plin. ep.; and Late), 1, 9, 4; 1, 41, 1; 2, 18; 5, 1, 5. — *correctio*, an improvement (Rhet. Her.; Cic. (6); Quint.; and Late), 1, 40, 4; 2, 9; 4, 4, 5. — *corruptio*, a corrupt condition (Cic. (2); Arnob.; and Late especially), 5, 22. — *creatio*, a choosing of officers (Cic. (1); Papin.; Mod.; Leo M.; Novell.; Hyd.), 5, 16. — *defectio*, sickness, weakness (Cic. (2); Cels.; Plin. mai.; Silver and Late), 1, 32, 5; 5, 24, 2. — *dilatio*, a delaying (Cic. (3); Cael. in Cic. ep.; Liv.; Vell.; Silver and Late), 4, 4, 3; 4, 4, 5. — *dispositio*, an arrangement (de ordine locali) (Rhet. Her.; Cic. (1); Colum.; Vitr.; Silver and Late), 1, 16, 1; 3, 23, 1; 5, 7, 1. — *electio*, a choice, selection (Cic. (1); Liv.; Plin. min.; Vell.; Silver and Late), 1, 25, 3; 2, 13, 1; 3, 7. — *eruptio*, a sally (Cic. ep. (1); Caes. (saepe); Liv.), 5, 8, 1. — *expeditio*, campaign, expedition (Cic. (2); Caes.; Sall. fr.; Hirt.; Liv.; Curt.; Vell.; Tac.; Suet.; Eutr.), 1, 21, 1. — *expulsio*, expulsion (Cic. (3); Liv.; Lact.; Aug.; Rufin.), 1, 44, 3; 4, 31.— *exsultatio*, exultation (Cic. (1); Liv.; Vell.; Sen. rhet.; Suet.), 2, 16, 1; 4, 4, 5; 5, 27. — *factio*, stratagem, snare (Cic. ep. (1); Sall.; Sen. phil.; Tac.; Suet.; Ulp.; Iust.; and Late), 1, 29, 4; 1, 41, 1; 1, 41, 2; 1, 42, 2; 1, 42, 9; 1, 44, 1; 2, 10, 7; 4, 4, 2;

4, 22, 1 (bis). — *functio,* performance of a public office (Cic. (1),
Frg. Vat.; Sulp. Sev.; Aug.; Itala; and Late), 4, 6, 5. — *immoderatio,* want of moderation (Cic. (1); Ambros.; Aug.; Firm.;
Hier.; Fulg.; and Late), 5, 7, 1. — *indignatio,* displeasure, indig-
nation (Hirt.; Liv.; Sen. rhet.; Arnob.; Firm.), 1, 8; 1, 16, 1;
1, 34, 2; 1, 37, 3; 1, 37, 6; 1, 40, 11; 1, 40, 13; 1, 41, 10 (ter);
1, 43, 4; 1, 44, 3; 1, 44, 8; 1, 45, 8; 2, 10, 4; 2, 12, 2; 3, 20, 2;
4, 6, 6; 4, 7; 4, 33; 5, 18, 3; 5, 22; 5, 37, 2; 5, 46; 5, 53, 1. —
intentio, an effort, exertion (Cic. (4); Plin. min.; Liv.; Quint.;
Tac.), 5, 53, 1; — design, purpose (Cic. (1); Plin. min.; Tert.;
Ambros.; Hier.; et al), Praef.; 1, 35, 1; 1, 40, 10; 1, 42, 9; 2, 12,
1; 3, 18, 1. — *interrogatio,* a judicial investigation (Cic. ep. (1);
Quint.; Tac.; Plin. ep.; Marcian.; Ambros.), 4, 33. — *irruptio,* an
invasion, incursion (Cic. (1); Tac.; Suet.; Flor.; Hier.; Aug.;
Oros.), 1, 16, 2; 1, 16, 4; 2, 7, 1; 4, 9, 3; 5, 11, 1; 5, 14, 3. —
multatio, a punishment, penalty (Cic. (1); Plin. mai.; Amm.; C.
I. L.), 1, 43, 7. — *observatio,* a rule, precept (Sall.; Plin. mai.;
Quint.; Gell.; Suet.; et al), 1, 16, 4. — *opinio,* report, rumor
(Caes.; Liv.; Suet.; Iust.), 1, 22, 2. — *prolapsio,* a falling or
tumbling down (Cic. (1); Suet.; Chalcid.), 5, 26, 2. — *prolusio,*
a prelude (Cic. (2)), 3, 8, 1. — *properatio,* haste, quickness (Cic.
ep. (1); Sall. fr.(?); Amm.; Ambros.; Dict.; Ennod.), 3, 24. —
putatio, pruning (Varr.; Cic. (1); Plin. mai.; Colum.; Arnob.),
5, 27. — *rebellio,* renewal of war, revolt (Cic. (1); Caes.; Liv.;
Tac.; Suet.; Treb. Poll.; Capit.), 1, 19, 4; 1, 22, 3; 1, 25, 2; 1,
29, 1; 1, 30, 4; 5, 42, 3; 5, 49, 4; 5, 51, 2; 5, 52, 1. — *reconciliatio,*
a reconciliation (Cic. (1); Sen. rhet.; Suet.; Iust.; Ambros.;
Vulg.), 1, 38, 5; 1, 38, 6; 1, 41, 1. — *redemptio,* bribing (Cic. (2)),
1, 15, 1. — *retractatio,* hesitation, doubt (Cic. (3); Liv.; Arnob.),
3, 5, 2; 3, 13. — *statio,* an anchorage, roadstead (Lentul. apud
Cic.; Caes.; Verg.; Liv.), 4, 27. — *successio,* succession in office
(Brut. in Cic. ep.; Cael. in Cic. ep.; Plin. mai.; Suet.; Flor.;
Iust.; Apul.; Ambros.), Praef.; 1, 39; 1, 40, 10; 1, 41, 3; 1, 42, 3;
1, 43, 3 (bis); 1, 43, 7; 1, 44, 2; 1, 44, 7 (bis); 1, 44, 8; 1, 45, 12;
2, 9; 2, 12, 3; 2, 13, 1 (quater); 4, 6, 5; 4, 17. — *trepidatio,* confusion, trepidation (Cic. (1); Liv.; Quint.; Tac.; Suet.), 1, 32, 6.—
tuitio, a defence, preservation (Cic. (1); Ulp.; Salv.; Hier.; Oros.;
Firm.; Macr.; Cod. Iust.), 3, 6, 5. — *veneratio,* veneration, respect

(Cic. (1); Curt.; Plin. mai.; Plin. min.; Val. Max.; Tac.; Ambros.), 5, 2.

b) *ascensio*, an ascent, ascending (Plaut.; Itin. Alex.; Serv.; Dict.; Vulg.; and Late Latin), 5, 28.—*congressio*, a fight, battle (Quadrig.; Apul.; Cypr.; and Late), 1, 13, 3; 1, 14, 1; 1, 21, 1; 1, 30, 2; 1, 32, 7; 5, 31.— *conquestio*, an accusation (Met. Num.; Cic. (2); Plin. mai.; Quint.; Capit.; and Late), 1, 43, 3. — *contagio*, contamination, corruption (Enn.; Cic. (4); Val. Max.; Lampr.; Firm.; Hier.; Vulg.; et al), 2, 2, 4; 5, 53, 1. — *excidio*, destruction (Plaut.; Paul. ex Fest.), 2, 15, 8. — *habitatio*, a dwelling, habitation (Plaut.; Cic. (2); Caes.), 5, 53, 1 (bis). — *legio*, a large number (Plaut.; Verg.; Val. Fl.; Vulg.), 1, 32, 6. — *potatio*, a drinking bout, potation (Plaut.; Cic. fr. apud Quint.; Apul.; Aquila Rom.; Treb. Poll.; Ambros.; Vulg.; et al), 1, 43, 2. — *receptio*, a reception, receiving (Plaut.; Avit.), 5, 22. — *unctio*, an anointing (Plaut.; Cic. (1); Colum.; Cels.; Sen. phil.), 2, 12, 3.

d) *accessio*, an attack, paroxysm of a disease (Cels.; Sen. phil.; Plin. min.; Suet.; Scrib.; Garg. Mart.; and Late), 5, 8, 2. — *adiectio*, an addition (Liv.; Val. Max.; Vitr.; Sen. rhet.; Sen. phil.; Quint.; Tac.; Suet.; and Late), 4, 17. — *aestimatio*, estimate, opinion (Liv.; Vell.; Val. Max.; Cels.; Curt.; Sen. phil.; Plin. mai.; Tac.; and Late), 1, 35, 3. — *congestio*, a heaping up (Vitr.; Iavol.; Pallad.; Zeno; Ps. Apul.; Mart. Cap.; Ambros.; et al), 1, 16, 4; 5, 21, 3. — *consternatio*, consternation (Liv.; Val. Max.; Sen. phil.; Curt.; Plin. mai.; Suet.; Tac.; Amm.; and Late), 2, 15, 5. — *constitutio*, creation, construction (Vitr.; Itala; Ambros.; and Late especially), 4, 23, 2; — a right, precept, law, decree (Edict. Ved. Poll.; Liv.; Val. Max.; Sen. phil.; Silver and Late), Praef. — *constructio*, erecting, construction (Traian.; Ps. Apul.; Arnob.; Filastr.; and Late), 3, 3, 5; 5, 26, 3. — *consummatio*, a completing, consummation (Sen. phil.; Plin. min.; Quint.; Apul.; Ambros.; and Late), 5, 27; — administration (Sen. rhet.; Plin. mai.; Ulp.; Schol. Pers.; Fulg. Rusp.), 3, 26, 2. — *contagio*, contagion from sickness (Liv.; Colum.; Plin. mai.; Apul.; and Late), 5, 2. — *contradictio*, contradiction (Sen. rhet.; Sen. phil.; Quint.; Tac.; Marcell.; Ulp.; and Late), 5, 2. — *conversatio*, intercourse (Paul. ex Fest.; Sen. rhet.; Sen. phil.; Vell.; Plin. mai.;

5

Quint.; Apul.; and Late), 2, 9, 1. — *deploratio*, a lamenting (Sen. phil.; Tert.; Donat.; Querol.; Symm.; Ambros.; et al), 5, 2. — *dignatio*, respect, esteem (Sen. rhet.; Plin. mai.; Sen. phil.; Suet.; and Late), 1, 34, 2. — *discessio*, departure (Tac.; Donat.; Auson.; Schol. Verg.; Vulg.; et al), 2, 15, 6; 5, 16. — *dispositio*, plan, purpose (Sen. phil.; Colum.; Apul.; Tert.; and Late), 1, 32, 4; 1, 40, 6; 1, 46, 1. — *exsecutio*, performance, execution (Sen. rhet.; Plin. mai.; Tac.; Frontin.; Ambros.), 1, 12, 4; 1, 22, 3; 1, 37, 5; 1, 43, 5; 1, 45, 10 (bis); 1, 45, 12; 2, 17. — *fatigatio*, weariness (Liv.; Cels.; Sen. phil.; Curt.; Silver and Late), 4, 9, 2. — *infestatio*, a disturbing (Frontin.; Tert.; Cypr.; Th. Prisc.; Ambros.; et al), 5, 2. — *infusio*, an infusion (Plin. mai.; Scrib.; Ambros.; Hier.; Aug.), 3, 26, 2 (bis); 4, 17; 5, 53, 1. — *insultatio*, derision, mockery (Val. Max.; Flor.; Hier.; Aug.; Arnob. iun.; Ennod.; Oros.), 5, 22; 5, 37, 2. — *interpolatio*, a modification, alteration (Plin. mai.; Intepr. Iren.), 5, 44, 1. — *mansio*, a stopping-place (Plin. mai.; Suet.; Hier.), 4, 33 (bis). — *minutio*, a diminishing (Quint.; Gell.; Gaius; Tert.; Paul.; Veget.), 3, 26, 1. — *observatio*, reverence, esteem (Val. Max.; Ambros.; Cod. Th.), 1, 12, 2; 2, 9; 2, 13, 1; 2, 14, 5; 5, 2; 5, 5. — *operatio*, a working, a work (Vitr.; Plin. mai.; Firm.; Donat.; Ambros.; Vulg.; Aug.), 5, 53, 1. — *ordinatio*, an appointing of magistrates to office (Suet. Dom. 4, 2), 2, 13, 7. — *persuasio*, an opinion, conviction (Quint.; Tac.; Plin. min.; Suet.), 2, 6, 1. — *petitio*, a petition, request (Liv.; Plin. mai.; Traian. in Plin. ep.; Donat.; Ambros.), 1, 29, 10; 4, 7. — *portio*, a share, part (Cels.; Plin. mai.; Iust.; Ambros.), 1, 39; 2, 6, 3; 2, 9 (ter); 2, 10, 4; 2, 17; 3, 6, 2; 3, 6, 3; 3, 18, 3; 3, 25, 4; 4, 1, 2 (bis); 5, 14, 3; 5, 21, 2; 5, 40; 5, 42, 4; 5, 46. — *praedatio*, a plundering (Vell.; Tac.; Lact.; Vulg.), 3, 20, 1. — *praelatio*, preference (Val. Max.; Tert.; Ambros.; Hier.; Rufin.; et al), 1, 39; 1, 44, 8; 2, 1, 3. — *praesumptio*, anticipation (Plin. ep.; Apul.), 1, 31, 1; 1, 40, 13. — *probatio*, proof, evidence (Sen. phil.; Quint.; Tac.; Plin. min.; Suet.; Lact.), 1, 41, 9; 2, 9. — *purificatio*, a purification (Plin. mai.; Mart.; Cypr.; Ambros.; Hier.; Vulg.), 1, 16, 6; 2, 12, 2; 5, 31; 5, 53, 1. — *redemptio*, redemption, ransoming (Bell. Alex.; Liv.; Sen. phil.; Quint.), 1, 29, 9; 4, 12; 5, 31. — *refectio*, refreshment, collation (Cels.; Plin. min.; Cass. Fel.; Sulp. Sev.), 1, 45, 11; — refreshment from labor or exertion (Cels.; Sen. phil.; Quint.; Plin. min.; Amm.), 4, 33. —

relatio, a reply, answer (Sen. phil.), 4, 4, 3. — *suspectio*, a suspicion (Frontin.; Apul.; Cael. Aur.; Fulg.), 1, 42, 5; 2, 17. — *traditio*, a teaching, instruction (Quint.; Gell.; Lact.; Cael. Aur.; Vulg.), 2, 10, 2. — *ultio*, revenge, vengeance (Liv.; Curt.; Vell.; Sen. rhet.; Val. Max.; Quint.; Tac.; Iust.; Lact.; Ambros.; et al), 1, 1, 7 (bis); 1, 12, 4; 1, 14, 1; 1, 28, 2; 1, 28, 3; 1, 29, 8; 1, 38, 3; 1, 40, 9; 1, 40, 10; 1, 43, 5; 1, 44, 8; 1, 45, 1; 1, 45, 6; 2, 18; 3, 16; 3, 17; 4, 31; 5, 15; 5, 21, 3 (bis); 5, 22.

4. Nouns in *-tus, -sus*.

a) *accessus*, access, approach (Cic. ep. (1); Varr.; Bell. Alex.; Bell. Hisp.; Bell. Afr.; Verg.; Liv.; Silver and Late), 1, 30, 9; 3, 9, 5; 4, 1, 1. — *affectus*, feeling, state of mind (Cic. (1); Ov.; Gratt.; Manil.; Silver and Late, especially Ambros.), 1, 1, 7. — *ambitus*, a circuit, circumference (idea of motion is left out) (Varr.; Hor.; Liv.; Silver and Late), 1, 35, 1 (bis); 3, 26, 1; 4, 4, 3; 5, 10, 1. — *attactus*, a touch (Varr.; Verg.; Ov.; Sil.; Ps. Quint.; Paul.; Apul.; Ambros.; and Late), 4, 18. — *circuitus*, circumference, compass (Caes.; Hirt.; Verg.; Liv.; Silver and Late), 3, 9, 5; 5, 1, 2; 5, 3, 2; 5, 5; 5, 21, 2; 5, 25, 2; 5, 36, 2; 5, 44, 2; 5, 45. — *concentus*, harmony, concord (Cic. (3); Hor.; Sen. phil.; Plin. mai.; Tac.; Gell.; Tert.; Ambros.; et al), 1, 40, 7; 4, 7. — *contactus*, touch, contagion (Sall.; Verg.; Ov.; Manil.; Val. Max.; Colum.; Liv.; Silver and Late), 1, 44, 5. — *contemptus*, contempt (active sense) (Bell. Alex.; Liv.; Val. Max.; Sen. phil.; Silver and Late), 1, 45, 5; 3, 16; 3, 24; 5, 12; 5, 13; 5, 27. — *cursus*, the course or flow of a stream (Cic. (1); Verg.; Ov.; Liv.; Sen. phil.; Plin. mai.; Silver and Late), 5, 46. — *descensus*, a descent (Varr.; Sall.; Liv.; Manil.; Vitr.; Cels.; Plin. mai.; Firm.; and Late), 5, 13. — *despectus*, contempt, low esteem (Rhet. Her.; Tac.; Suet.; Ambros.; Hier.; Aug.; Arnob.; et al), 4, 26, 1; 5, 37, 2. — *excursus*, a sally, charge (Caes.; Tac.), 3, 9, 4; 3, 20, 1; 4, 22, 1; 4, 22, 3; 5, 4, 1; 5, 21, 2; 5, 36, 2 (bis); — an invasion of boats (Bell. Alex.), 3, 26, 3. — *exortus*, a rising (Rhet. Her.; Varr.; Liv.; Curt.; Plin. mai.; Suet.), 5, 46. — *habitus*, dress, attire (Cic. (2); Liv.; Curt.; Sen. rhet.; Silver and Late), 1, 33. — *hiatus*, an opening, aperture (Cic. (3); Verg.; Ov.; Sen. rhet.; Plin. mai.; Suet.; Calp.; Amm.; and Late), 5, 41. — *hortatus*, encouragement (Cic. (2) ; Caes.; Nep.; Ov.; Tac.; Val. Fl.; Sil.; Macr.), 1, 39. — *obiectus*, opposition, interference (Caes.; Lucr.; Verg.; Plin. mai.; Tac.; Apul.), 1, 1, 7; 3, 5, 3; 3, 6, 1; 4, 6, 7; 4, 27; 5, 2; 5, 42, 1; 5, 52, 2. — *obtentus*, a concealing, veiling (Sall. fr.; Aur. Vict.), 1, 40, 2. — *ostentus*,[3] a sign, proof (Sall.; Tac.; Gracch. apud Gell.), 1, 6, 1; 3, 2. — *processus*, advance, progress, course (Cic. (3) ; Verg.; Sulp. Sev.), 1, 10, 3; 1, 32, 6. — *procinctus*, readiness for action (military) (Cic. (2) ; Ov.; Plin. mai.; Tac.), 5, 1, 4. — *profectus*, advantage, success (Varr.; Vell.; Sen. phil.; Quint.; Ambros.; Hier.), 2, 9; 3, 7; 3, 17; 4, 17; 5, 10, 1. — *reditus*, revenue, income (Nep.; Verg.; Liv.; Vell.; Plin. min.; Flor.; Iust.), 1, 40, 5. — *saltus*, a leap, bound (Cic. (1) ; Verg.; Ov.; Sen. phil.; Ambros.), 5, 13; 5, 19. — *spiritus*, a breath, breeze (Varr.; Verg.; Cels.; Plin. min.; Quint.; Frontin.), 4, 18. — *successus*, happy issue, success (Varr.; Verg.; Ov.; Liv.; Tac.; Suet.; Iust.; Hier.), 1, 1, 3; 1, 9, 3; 1, 12, 1; 1, 21, 3; 1, 32, 4; 1, 32, 6; 1, 35, 1; 1, 36, 1; 1, 45, 12; 3, 14; 4, 2; 5, 19; 5, 20, 2; 5, 26, 2; 5, 37, 2. — *suggestus*, seat, throne, tribune (Caes.; Liv.; Plin. min.; Suet.; Flor.), 5, 53, 1. — *ululatus*, a wailing, shout, yell (Caes.; Catull.; Verg.; Ov.; Liv.; Stat.; Lact.; Apul.; Amm.; Ambros.), 1, 44, 8; 3, 15, 1; 5, 44, 1. — *venatus*, hunting, the chase (Cic. (1) ; Verg.; Ov.; Colum.; Plin. mai.; Gell.; Ps. Quint.; Amm.), 1, 37, 7. — *visus*, sight, vision (Cic. fr. apud Plin. mai.; Lucr.; Verg.; Ov.; Quint.; Tac.; Apul.; Ps. Apul.; Ambros.; et al), 3, 9, 5; 5, 49, 1.

b) *amictus*, clothing, a garment (Laev. fr.; Cic. (1) ; Catull.; Verg.; Hor.; Ov.; Tibull.; Prop.; Liv.; Silver and Late), 1, 25, 2 ; 1, 36, 2; 4, 6, 5; 4, 25, 2; 5, 23; 5, 39, 2; 5, 53, 1. — *anhelitus*, breath (Plaut.; Ov.; Val. Max.; Sen. phil.; Plin. mai.; Stat.; Apul.; and Late), 5, 23; 5, 27. — *auditus*, report, rumor (Plaut.; Cic. (2) ; Curt.; Lucan.; Tac.; Suet.; Tert.; and Late), 2, 9. — *congressus*, a fight (Quadrig.; Cic. (1) ; Caes.; Sall.; Liv.; Silver and Late), 1, 1, 7; 1, 9, 2; 4, 23, 1; 4, 32. — *hinnitus*, a neighing (Lucil.; Cic. (1) ; Hor.; Ov.; Liv.; Val. Max.; Suet.; Sil.; Amm.; et al), 5, 16. — *prospectus*, a view, sight (Enn.; Caes.; Bell. Afr.; Verg.; Liv.; Plin. mai.; Amm.), 5, 11, 1. — *sortitus*, a casting or

---

[3] This word is found only in the dative and ablative singular.

drawing of lots (Plaut.; Cic. (1); Verg.), 5, 53, 1. — *suspiritus,*
deep breathing (Plaut.; Cic. ep. (1); Liv.; Apul.), 1, 45, 9. —
vomitus, vomiting (Plaut.; Curt.; Cels.; Sen. rhet.; Sen. phil.;
Plin. mai.; Suet.; Ambros.; et al), 1, 8.

    c) *affatus,* an address (Verg.; Sen. poet.; Val. Fl.; Stat.; Ps.
Quint.; Fronto; Apul.; and Late especially), 5, 33, 1. — *affectus,*
love, devotion (Ov.; Val. Max.; Sen. phil.; Lucan.; Silver and
Late), 1, 25, 4; 1, 37, 7; 1, 38, 3; 1, 40, 12; 2, 12, 2; 3, 15, 1;
4, 4, 1; 5, 16; 5, 18, 2 (bis); 5, 18, 3; 5, 21, 3; 5, 22; 5, 24, 2;
5, 24, 3; 5, 40 (bis); 5, 41 (bis); 5, 44, 1; 5, 45; 5, 46; 5, 53, 1
(bis); 5, 53, 2. — *amplexus,*[4] an embrace (of men) (Verg.; Ov.;
Prop.; Sen. phil.; Lucan.; Cael. Ruf. apud Quint.; Silver and
Late), 1, 44, 4; 1, 44, 5; 2, 4; 5, 53, 1; 5, 53, 2. — *defectus,* ceas-
ing, intermission (Aetna; Plin. mai.; Apul.; Ps. Apul.; Amm.;
Ambros.; et al), 3, 26, 2. — *fastus,* scornful contempt, arrogance
(Catull.; Verg.; Hor.; Tibull.; Prop.; Sen. phil.; Silver and Late
(Ambros.)), 1, 40, 2. — *haustus,* a drink, draught (Hor.; Ov.;
Liv.; Curt.; Phaedr.; Suet. fr.; and Late), 3, 26, 1. — *monitus,* an
admonition, warning (Verg.; Ov.; Val. Fl.), 1, 41, 1; 2, 9; 4, 4,
2. — *nisus,* effort, labor (Verg.; Ov.; Curt.; Sen. phil.; Fest.;
Tac.), 5, 4, 4; 5, 20, 3. — *recursus,* a return (Verg.; Ov.; Liv.;
Silver and Late), 5, 51, 1. — *secessus,* retirement, solitude (Ov.;
Sen. phil.; Plin. min.; Suet.), 2, 3, 4. — *tinnitus,* a ringing, ting-
ling (Catull.; Verg.; Ov.; Sen. phil.; Plin. mai.; Apul.; Solin.;
Amm.), 5, 19. — *vagitus,* crying, squalling of children (Lucr.; Ov.;
Liv.; Plin. mai.; Quint.; Arnob.; Solin.; et al), 5, 18, 2; 5, 40.

    d) *accessus,* increase, addition (Sen. phil.; Mela; Plin. mai.;
Apul.; Amm.; Ambros.; and frequent in Late Latin), 1, 45, 5. —
actus, a deed, work (Gratt.; Manil.; Val. Max.; Silver and very
frequent in Late Latin), 1, 1, 2. — *ambitus,* parade, pomp (Stat.;
Serv.; Prud.; Paul. Nol.; Comment. Lucan.; Sulp. Sev.), 1, 15,
1; 1, 46, 2 (bis). — *appulsus,* a landing, bringing to land (of boats)
(Liv.; Val. Max.; Plin. mai.; Tac.; Iust.), 3, 26, 3. — *ausus,* a
bold deed, attempt (Petron.; Opt. Porf.; and very frequent from
the fourth century on), 1, 8; 3, 20, 3; 4, 7. — *contuitus,* view, sight

---

[4] This word is found in Cic. Div. 1, 79, referring to the "embrace of a
serpent."

(Curt.; Plin. mai.; Symm.; Amm.; Ambros.; Aug.; et al), 2, 9, 1. — *defectus,* lack, failure, scarcity (Liv.; Plin. mai.; Sen. phil.; Eustath.; et al), 4, 27; — end (Plin. mai.; Chalcid.; Mar. Victorin.; Ambros.; et al), 1, 37, 5. — *fotus,* a warming, fomenting (Plin. mai.; Lact.; Amm.; Ambros.; et al), 3, 26, 2. — *ingressus,* a going into, an entering (Vell.; Plin. min.; Spart.; Auson.), 3, 20, 1; 4, 3, 3; 4, 9, 3; 4, 25, 3; 5, 17; 5, 27; 5, 53, 1. — *meatus,* current, ebb and flow (Mela; Plin. mai.; Auson.), 3, 6, 3; 4, 17; 4, 27; 5, 16; — a channel, passage, course (Plin. mai.; Lucan.; Tac.; Claud.), 3, 26, 1 (bis). — *obtentus,* a pretext, excuse (Liv.; Gell.; Val. Max.; Tac.; Iust.; Lact.), Praef.; 1, 25, 1. — *planctus,* lamentation (Curt.; Sen. poet.; Petron.; Lucan.; Tac.; Hier.; Vulg.), 1, 45, 11. — *procinctus,* readiness for action (non-military) (Sen. phil.; Quint.; Cassian.), 5, 27. — *promissus,* a promise (Manil.), 2, 4. — *recursus,* a return (transf. sense) (Val. Max.; Cels.), 1, 29, 7. — *relatus,* a narration, recital (Sen. phil.; Tac.; Auson.; Aug.), 3, 21, 1. — *vomitus,* vomit (Cels.; Plin. mai.), 5, 18, 2 (bis).

5. Nouns in *-us.*

a) *manus,* personal valor, bravery (Caes.; Nep.; Sall.; Verg.; Ov.; Liv.), 1, 1, 5. — *sinus,* the interior part of anything (Sall.; Sil.; Tac.; Plin. min.), 3, 5, 2; 4, 9, 3; 4, 21. — *specus,* a cave, cavern (Varr.; Verg.; Hor.; Liv.; Gell.), 1, 30, 9; 3, 15, 3; 5, 21, 4; 5, 49, 1; 5, 49, 3; 5, 53, 1.

b) *aestus,* heat of fire (Plaut.; Verg.; Aetna; Ov.; Liv.; Silver and Late), 5, 45. — *gelus* (*gelu*), cold, coldness (Cato; Afran.; Q. Cic.; Lucr.; Verg.; Hor.; Prop.; Liv.; Silver and Late), 1, 30, 7; 5, 15. — *nurus,* a daughter-in-law (Ter.; Cic.(1); Ov.; Ict.; Ambros.), 1, 40, 13.

c) *gradus,* ground or position taken by a combatant (Ov.; Liv.; Sen. phil.), 5, 20, 3. — *sinus,* the belly of a sail swollen by the wind (Verg.; Prop.; Ov.; Solin.), 3, 11, 1; 5, 27.

6. Nouns in *-tura, -sura.*

c) *mensura,* power, extent, measure (Ov.; Lucan.; Quint.; Tac.; Plin. ep.), 5, 9, 4.

d) *fultura,* a support, foundation (Vitr.; Colum.; Plin. mai.; Ambros.; Aug.; et al), 5, 20, 1.

7. Nouns in *-ia.*

a) *absentia,* absence (Cic.(3) ; Sen. rhet.; Val. Max.; and here and there in Silver and Late Latin), 1, 9, 2; 1, 44, 3. — *appetentia,* a desire, longing (Cic.(2) ; Plin. mai.; Apul.; Ambros.; and frequent in Late Latin), 1, 37, 5; 5, 24, 2. — *distantia,* difference, diversity (Cic.(1) ; Lucr.; Quint.; Gell.; Apul.; Tert.; Ambros.; and especially in Late Latin), 5, 15. — *munificentia,* munificence, liberality (Sall.; Vell.; Plin. mai.; Tac.; Iust.), 3, 26, 1. — *pluvia,* the rain (Cic. ep.(1) ; Verg.; Colum.; Liv.; Sen. phil.), 5, 2. — *prosapia,*[5] race, family, lineage (Cic.(1) ; Sall.; Quint.; Suet.; Iust.; Apul.; Tert.; Ambros.; and frequent in Late writers), 1, 40, 1; 1, 40, 2; 1, 41, 3; 1, 42, 2; 2, 1, 2; 2, 13, 7; 3, 16; 5, 15 (bis) ; 5, 22, 1; 5, 22, 2; 5, 27. — *reverentia,* reverence, respect (Cic.(1) ; Ov.; Curt.; Mart.; Quint.; Tac.; Silver and Late (Ambros.)), Praef.; 1, 5; 1, 41, 3; 2, 1, 2; 2, 1, 3; 2, 3, 4; 2, 10, 2; 2, 11, 4; 3, 24; 4, 7; 4, 21; 5, 45. — *tolerantia,* tolerance, endurance (Cic.(1) ; Sen. phil.; Quint.; Tac.; Lact.; Ambros.; Vulg.), 2, 9 ; 5, 1, 4.

b) *audientia,* a judicial hearing (Plaut.; Rhet. Her.; Cic.(3) ; Liv.; and frequent from Apul. on among Christian writers and Jurists), 1, 44, 5; 1, 44, 6. — *copia,* an opportunity (Plaut. (saepe) ; Ter.(saepe) ; Cic.(3) ; Sall.(saepe) ; Liv.; Silver and Late), 1, 30, 1. — *exuviae* (plur.), clothing of men (Plaut.; Verg.; Suet.; Mart. Cap.), 4, 17; 5, 5. — *facundia,* eloquence (Ter.; Sall.; Ov.; Cels.; Quint.; Fronto; Gell.; Apul.; and Late), 5, 27. — *fraudulentia,* deceitfulness (Plaut.; Iren.; Hil.; Ambros.; Hier.; Vulg.; et al), 1, 41, 6; 1, 42, 3; 3, 16. — *pervicacia,* stubbornness, steadfastness (Acc.; Cic.(1) ; Liv.; Plin. mai.; Tac.; Treb. Poll.), 5, 36, 2. —*vicinia,* vicinity (Plaut.; Ter.; Cic.(1) ; Verg.; Colum.; Curt.), 4, 18.

c) *exuviae* (plur.), the skin of an animal (Verg.; Lucan.; Suet.; Hyg.; Amm.), 5, 18, 2. — *gratia,* charm, loveliness, beauty (Prop.;

[5] Cic. Tim. 39 considers this word archaic.

Ov.; Quint.; Plin. min.), 1, 35, 1; 1, 35, 4; 1, 35, 6; 1, 36, 2; 1, 37, 2; 1, 37, 3; 1, 40, 7; 1, 41, 8; 5, 43, 1. — *militia*, soldiery (Ov.; Liv.; Val. Max.; Iust.), 1, 25, 4; 1, 29, 10; 1, 30, 1; 1, 30, 3; 1, 41, 7; 2, 4; 5, 27; 5, 52, 1. — *primitiae* (plur.), the beginnings (Verg.; Colum.; Stat.), 1, 1, 8. — *vesania*, madness (Hor.; Val. Max.; Plin. mai.; Flor.; Amm.), 3, 3, 7; 5, 18, 1.

d) *affluentia*, an overflowing (Plin. mai.; Ambros.; Aug.; Isid.; Th. Prisc.; et al), 1, 34, 2. — *eminentia*, preeminence, superiority, excellence (Vell.; Gell.; Ulp.; Vulg.; Cl. Mam.), 5, 15. — *impatientia*, impatience (Val. Max.; Plin. mai.; Tac.; Suet.; Gell.; Apul.), 4, 1, 4; 5, 40. — *infantia*, childhood (Quint.; Tac.; Plin. min.; Macr.; Vulg.; et al), 1, 31, 2; 3, 13; — children, the young (Plin. mai.; Quint.; Tert.; Macr.), 5, 18, 2. — *paenitentia*, repentance (Liv.; Phaedr.; Sen. phil.; Plin. mai.; Quint,; Tac.; Suet.), 1, 9, 4; 1, 37, 7; 1, 42, 2; 4, 30. — *substantia*, existence, essence, reality (Sen. phil.; Quint.; Frontin.; Ambros.; Hier.), 5, 9, 3; 5, 21, 3. — *temulentia*, drunkenness, intoxication (Val. Max.; Plin. mai.; Ambros.; Hier.), 1, 43, 2. — *verecundia*, a disgrace, shame (Liv.; Val. Max.), 2, 9. — *versutia*, cunning (Liv.; Apul.; Min. Fel.; Ambros.), 1, 15, 2; 1, 40, 1; 1, 40, 10; 1, 40, 11; 1, 42, 2; 1, 42, 8; 1, 44, 2; 1, 45, 1 (bis); 5, 24, 3 (bis).

8. Nouns in -*a*.

a) *aerumna*,[6] sorrow, misery, distress (Cic.(20); Sall.; Liv.; Sen. phil.; and very frequent from Apuleius on), Praef.; 1, 9, 4; 1, 25, 1; 1, 29, 10; 1, 32, 5; 1, 32, 6 (bis); 1, 38, 5; 1, 42, 3; 1, 44, 7; 2, 6, 3; 2, 13, 5; 2, 16, 1; 3, 1, 1; 5, 2; 5, 16; 5, 22; 5, 24, 2; 5, 53, 1 (bis). — *alea*, a chance, risk (Varr.; Cic.(1); Hor.; Ov.; Liv.; Silver and Late (Ambros.)), 3, 17; 5, 30. — *cera*, a waxen image (Sall.; Ov.; Plin. mai.; Mart.; Iuv.; et al), 5, 22. — *fenestra*, a breach or opening in a wall (Caes.; Verg.; Colum.; Vitr.; Pallad.; Veg.; Vulg.), 3, 11, 1. — *fibula*, a clasp, pin, buckle (Varr.; Verg.; Ov.; Liv.; Silver and Late), 1, 46, 2. — *gleba*, a lump, mass (Caes.; Lucr.; Plin. mai.; Iust.), 4, 18. — *harena*, the place of combat in the amphitheatre (Cic.(1); Iuv.; Tac.; Suet.; Ict.), 5, 51, 2; 5, 53, 1. — *offensa*, displeasure, hatred, disfavor

---

[6] Cic. Fin. 2, 118 hints that the word was already archaic.

(Cic. ep.(1) ; Ov.; Vell.; Quint.; Tac.; Plin. ep.; Ict.; Vopisc.),
5, 53, 1. — *palea,* chaff (Cic.(1) ; Varr.; Colum.), 5, 39, 2 ; 5, 40. —
tuba, an instigator, inciter (Cic. ep.(1) ; Iuv.), 2, 10, 1. — *vena,* a
water-course (Hirt.; Ov.; Mart.), 3, 26, 2 ; 4, 17 ; 5, 16 (bis). —
vitula, a heifer (Varr.; Verg.; Hier.; Vulg.), 5, 44, 1.

b) *adorea,* martial glory (Plaut.; Hor.; Fronto; Apul.; Ambros.;
et al), 3, 24 ; 4, 29, 2 ; 5, 46. — *animae* (plur.), spirits (Trag. inc.;
Cic.(1) ; Lucr.; Verg.; Hor.; Tibull.; Ov.; Silver and Late), 1, 45,
1. — *carina,* a ship (Enn.; Catull.; Verg.; Hor.; Ov.; Prop.;
Lucan.; Sil.; Stat.), 4, 27. — *concubina,* a concubine (Plaut.;
Cael.; Cic.(1) ; Sall.; Silver and Late (Ambros.)), 1, 11, 1 ;
1, 41, 1 ; 5, 50. — *foveae* (plur.), snares, dangers (Plaut.; Cic.(1) ;
Liv.; Curt.; Hil.; Optat.; Amm.; Ps. Ambros.; et al), 1, 44, 8. —
fulica, a kind of water fowl (Fur. Ant.; Ov.; Plin. mai.; Serv.;
Ambros.; and Late), 5, 36, 2. — *locusta,* a locust (Naev.; Plaut.;
Enn.; Liv.; Plin. mai.; Tac.), 4, 23, 2.

c) *caprea,* a wild she-goat (Verg.; Hor.; Plin. mai.; Val. Max.;
Mart.; Vulg.; Ambros.; and Late), 5, 15. — *fabula,* a by-word
(Hor.; Tibull.; Prop.; Ov.; Sen. phil.), 5, 40. — *fovea,* a ditch
(Lucr.; Verg.; Hor.; Liv.; Paul. ex Fest.; Stat.; Apul.; Tert.;
Ambros.; et al), 4, 22, 1. — *harena,* sand (Verg.; Ov.; Liv.; Vitr.;
Colum.; Silver and Late), 3, 11, 2 (bis). — *iuventa,* youth, age of
youth (Verg.; Hor.; Ov.; Catull.; Liv.; Cels.; Silver and Late),
1, 40, 7 ; 4, 22, 1 ; 5, 19 ; 5, 20, 3. — *lacerta,* a lizard (Hor.; Ov.;
Plin. mai.; Sen. phil.; Mart.), 5, 18, 2. — *plaga,* a region, tract,
quarter (Cic. poet.; Verg.; Liv.; Sen. phil.; Hier.; Vulg.), 4, 16, 2
(bis) ; 4, 27. — *ruina,* a rushing or tumbling down (Lucr.; Hor.;
Prop.; Liv.; Amm.; Cael. Aur.); 4, 27. — *sarcina,* a burden (fig.)
(Ov.; Prop.; Val. Max.; Hier.; Aug.), 1, 26, 4. — *spina,* a thorn
(Verg.; Ov.; Sen. rhet.; Tac.; Ambros.; Vulg.; and Eccl.),
Praef. — *umbra,* a tree, i. e., something that gives shade (Verg.),
5, 41. — *unda,* water (Verg.; Ov.; Hor.; Colum.; Val. Max.; Sen.
phil.; Mart.; Apul.), 2, 9. — *vindicta,* vengeance (Ov.; Phaedr.;
Iuv.; Petron.; Tac.; Ambros.; Aug.), 1, 1, 7 ; 1, 26, 4 ; 1, 30, 13 ;
1, 32, 6 (ter) ; 1, 40, 12 ; 1, 41, 7 ; 1, 41, 10 ; 1, 44, 8 ; 2, 11, 3 ;
2, 12, 2 (bis) ; 2, 14, 2 ; 2, 18 ; 3, 15, 1 ; 3, 16 ; 4, 2 ; 4, 9, 3 ; 4, 11 ;

5, 2; 5, 23; 5, 24, 4; 5, 37, 1; 5, 37, 2; 5, 42, 6. — *vita,* the world (βίος) (Tıbull.; Plin. mai.; Mart.), 5, 40.

d) *arbitra,* a judge (Sen. ep.; Amm.; Diom.; Edict. Diocl.; Possıd.), 2, 13, 2. — *favillae* [7] (plur.), ruins, remains (Stat.; Itin. Alex.; Hier.; Prud.), 3, 15, 4; 4, 18; 5, 16; 5, 53, 1. — *harenae* [8] (plur.), the sands, a sandy plain (Liv.; Sen. rhet.; Mela; Tac.; Suet. fr.), 2, 9. — *manubiae* (plur.), plunder, pillage (Suet.), Praef. — *noxa,* punishment (Liv.), 1, 32, 6. — *piscina,* a pond for bathing (Sen. phil.; Plin. mai.; Suet.; Iren.; Aug.), 1, 37, 1.

9. Nouns in *-men.*

b) *bitumen,* pitch (Cato; Lucr.; Verg.; Aetna; Hor.; Ov.; Gratt.; Silver and Late (Ambros.)), 4, 18 (bıs); 5, 38 (bıs). — *carmen,* a magical incantation (Lex XII tab.; Verg.; Hor.; Ov.; Tıbull.; Prop.; Silver and Late), 3, 2 (bis). — *flamen,* a blast of wind (Enn.; Lucil.; Cic. poet.(1); Catull.; Lucr.; Poetical, Sılver and Late (Ambros.)), 5, 27; 5, 53, 1.

c) *culmen,* roof, gable (Verg.; Ov.; Liv.; Vıtr.; Manil.; Sılver and Late), 5, 1, 4; 5, 27; 5, 31 (bis); 5, 38; 5, 53, 1 (bıs). — *examen,* an examination (Ov.; Pers.; Stat.; Sol.; Lact.), 1, 38, 5; 1, 44, 6; 2, 1, 3; 4, 7; 5, 22. — *germen,* progeny, offspring (Ov.; Iust.; Claud.; Nemes.), 1, 42, 3. — *limen,* a house, dwelling (Verg.; Liv.), 5, 53, 1. — *lumen,* life, light of lıfe (Verg.; Ov.), 3, 16. — *moderamen,* management (Ov.; Ambros.; Hier.; Aug.; Ennod.; Avit.; et al), 3, 23, 1; 3, 25, 3; 5, 24, 2. — *munimen,* a defence, enclosure (Verg.; Ov.; Veget.; Amm.; Pallad.; Ambros.; Vulg.; Aug.), 1, 30, 9; 4, 16, 2; 5, 2; 5, 5; 5, 16; 5, 42, 5; 5, 52, 1. — *semen,* progeny, offsprıng (Ov.; Vulg.), 2, 5, 3. — *solamen,* relief, comfort, consolatıon (Verg.; Sen. phıl.; Val. Fl.; Lucan.; Rufin.), 5, 18, 2. — *velamen,* a cloak, veil, covering (fig.) (Verg.; Ov.; Sen. phil.; Iuv.; Tac.; Ambros.), 2, 13, 6.

d) *culmen,* culmınating point, zenith (Liv.; Lucan.; Sil.;

---

[7] The singular of this word in the meaning of "ruins" is found in Heg. 3, 16; 5, 41.

[8] The singular in the sense of "a sandy plain" is found in Cic. Agr. 2, 71.

Amm.; and Late especially), 4, 26, 1. — *spiramen*, a breeze (Stat.;
Veget.; Amm.; Arnob.; Hier.; Rufin.), 1, 35, 4; 5, 39, 2; 5, 41;
5, 42, 5; 5, 52, 2 (bis).

10. Nouns in -*mentum.*

a) *allevamentum*, alleviation (Cic. (1); Ambros.), 2, 1, 2. — *ex-
perimentum*, a proof, test, trial (Cic. (1); Liv.; Vell.; Tac.; Plin.
min.), 2, 1, 2. — *munimentum*,[9] a fortification (Caes.; Liv.; Curt.;
Tac.), 1, 20; 1, 30, 7; 1, 35, 6; 1, 42, 8; 3, 4, 3; 3, 7; 3, 8, 2;
4, 19; 4, 26, 3; 5, 3, 1; 5, 16 (bis); 5, 19; 5, 20, 2; 5, 31; 5, 36, 1;
5, 36, 2; 5, 53, 1. — a defence (transf. sense) (Sall.; Liv.; Val.
Max.), 1, 44, 7. — *pavimentum*, a pavement (Varr.; Cic.(2);
Caes.; Bell. Alex.; Hor.; Plin. mai.), 5, 53, 1. — *temperamentum*,
control, moderation (Cic.(1); Sen. phil.; Plin. mai.; Tac.; Plin.
min.), 2, 13, 2.

b) *atramentum*, ink (Plaut.; Cato; Lex repetund.; Cic. ep.(1);
Hor.; Vitr.; Cels.; Petron.; Silver and Late), 5, 39, 1. — *calcea-
mentum*, a shoe (Cato; Varr.; Cic.(1); Cels.; Colum.; Silver and
Late especially), 5, 30; 5, 39, 2. — *cognomentum*, a surname
(Plaut.; Varr.; Cic.(1); Sall.; Tac.; Gell.; Apul.; and especially
frequent in Hier.), 1, 29, 1; 4, 27; 4, 30. — *delenimentum*, an
allurement, enticement (Afran.; Laber.; Sall.; Liv.; Silver and
Late (Ambros.)), 3, 2. — *deliramentum*, nonsense, absurdity
(Plaut.; Plin. mai.; Fronto; Apul.; and frequent in Late Latin
(Ambros.)), 5, 22. — *machinamentum*, a military engine (Sisenna
fr.; Liv.; Tac.), 3, 11, 3 (ter); 3, 11, 4; 5, 20, 1; 5, 20, 2; 5, 21, 1;
5, 22, 2. — *operimentum*, a covering (Cato; Cic.(1); Sall. fr.; Plin.
mai.; Ambros.), 5, 9, 3.

c) *alimenta* (plur.), food for fire, fuel (Aetna; Ov.; Liv.; Silver
and Late), 5, 20, 1. — *momentum*, a moment, a short time (Hor.;
Liv.; Cels.; Curt.; Sen. phil.; Suet.; Firm.), 1, 24, 2; 1, 32, 6;
3, 5, 2; 3, 18, 3; 4, 2; 5, 1, 3; 5, 1, 4; 5, 21, 2; 5, 21, 3. — *nutrimenta* [10] (plur.), nourishment, sustenance (Verg.; Val. Max.;
Iust.), 4, 1, 2; 5, 38. — *sacramentum*, an oath (Hor.; Plin. min.;

---

[9] Cf. Enn. fr. var. 7 apud Cic de fin. 2, 106 B and M: *moenimenta.*

[10] Singular in this meaning is found in Plin. mai.; Sen. phil.; Apul.;
Cael. Aur.

Eutr.; Iust.), 1, 41, 6; 4, 6, 8; 5, 46 (bis). — *temptamentum,*[11] an attempt (Verg.; Ov.; Tac.; Gell.; Ambros.; and Late), 1, 6, 2; 1, 19, 1; 1, 22, 2; 1, 40, 10; 1, 41, 6; 1, 41, 9; 1, 42, 6; 1, 43, 3; 2, 1, 4; 2, 8, 5; 3, 6, 2; 3, 9, 3; 3, 20, 2; 4, 4, 2; 4, 22, 1.

d) *delenimentum,* charm, allurement (in a good sense) (Liv.; Sen. phil.; Plin. mai.; Tac.; Fronto; Gell.; Apul.; Ambros.; et al), 1, 44, 7; 2, 9, 1. — *indumentum,* clothing, covering (Sen. phil.; Lact.; Macr.; Hier.; Prud.; Vulg.), 1, 25, 2; 2, 10, 6; 4, 17; 5, 9, 3; 5, 48. — *inquinamentum,*[12] filth (Vitr.; Gell.; Tert.; Paul. ex Fest.; Macr.; Hier.), 5, 24, 3. — *integumentum,* a covering (Liv.; Ambros.; Aur. Vict.), 3, 24. — *munimentum,* a covering for the body, clothing (Iuv.; Iust.), 2, 11, 1. — *purgamentum,* filth, refuse (Liv.; Curt.; Colum.; Sen. phil.; Tac.; Dict.; Arnob.; Th. Prisc.), 5, 18, 1; 5, 24, 3. — *supplementum,* completion (Vell.; Colum.; Apul.; Iust.), 5, 27; 5, 53, 2. — *tutamentum,* a defence, protection (Liv.; Apul.; Itala; Cypr.; Vulg.), 5, 46.

11. Nouns in *-ium.*

a) *confinium,* limit, border (Varr.; Cic.(1); Caes.; Ov.; Liv.; Silver and Late), 2, 9; 2, 12, 2; 3, 6, 1; 3, 6, 2; 3, 14. — *effugium,* a means of escape (Cic.(2); Liv.; Phaedr.; Tac.), 1, 24, 2; 1, 44, 8; 4, 4, 3; 5, 13; 5, 16. — *excidium,* destruction, overthrow (Sall. fr.; Verg.; Liv.; Curt.; Sen. rhet.; Tac.; Lact.; Serv.; Solin.; Iust.; Ambros.), Praef.; 1, 17, 2; 1, 38, 1; 1, 40, 10; 2, 5, 2; 2, 6, 2; 2, 9 (ter); 2, 12, 1; 2, 13, 8; 2, 15, 5; 3, 1, 2; 3, 1, 3; 3, 11, 3; 3, 20, 2; 3, 21, 1; 4, 6, 1; 4, 9, 2; 4, 14; 5, 2; 5, 4, 1; 5, 13; 5, 14, 4 (ter); 5, 15; 5, 16; 5, 18, 3; 5, 22 (bis); 5, 26, 1; 5, 26, 2; 5, 29; 5, 31 (ter); 5, 32; 5, 33, 2; 5, 34, 2; 5, 37, 1; 5, 37, 2; 5, 42, 6; 5, 43, 1; 5, 43, 2; 5, 44, 1; 5, 45; 5, 53, 1. — *fastigium,* exalted rank, dignity (Nep.; Liv.(saepe); Manil.; Vell.; Silver and Late), 1, 36, 1; 5, 22, 1; 5, 22, 2; 5, 46; 5, 49, 1. — *opprobrium,* a disgrace, dishonor (Cic. fr.(1); Nep.; Hor.; Quint.), 5, 27; 5, 53, 1. — *pomerium,* the open space left free from buildings within and without the walls of a town (Cic.(3); Varr.; Liv.;

---

[11] Usually plural. Singular is found in Gell.; Amm.; Heg. 1, 6, 2; 1, 40, 10; 1, 43, 3.

[12] This word is used in a figurative sense three times by Ambrose.

Tac.; C.I.L.), 5, 25, 2. — *refugium,* a place of refuge (Cic.(1); Liv.; Iust.), 1, 32, 4; 3, 25, 1; 4, 4, 6; 4, 9, 1; 5, 17. — *sacrilegium,* profanation of sacred things, sacrilege (Nep.; Sen. phil.; Flor.; Ps. Apul.; Ambros.; Aug.; et al), Praef.; 1, 16, 4; 1, 17, 1; 2, 1, 1; 2, 6, 2; 4, 7; 5, 2; 5, 15. — *stillicidium,* a drop, dripping (Varr.; Lucr.; Sen. phil.; Plin. mai.; Apul.; Tert.), 5, 18, 2. — *suffragium,* help, favor, support (Cic.(1); Hor.; Plin. min.; Ict.; Salv.; Hier.; Spart.; et al), 1, 15, 1; 1, 36, 2; 1, 42, 4; 1, 42, 7; 4, 31; 5, 4, 3; 5, 27. — *supercilium,* a brow, ridge, summit (Bell. Afr.; Verg.; Liv.), 1, 30, 9; 3, 9, 5. — *taedium,* tiresomeness, irksomeness, disgust (Sall.; Verg.; Ov.; Liv.; Plin. mai.; Quint.; Tac.; C.I.L.), 1, 36, 1; 2, 5, 5; 5, 20, 1. — *territorium,* a district, territory (Cic.(1); Varr.; Plin. mai.; Amm.; Pallad.; Pompon.; Eutr.), 4, 23, 2. — *vestigium,* the sole of the foot (Cic.(3); Catull.; Verg.; Ov.; Plin. mai.; Lact.), 3, 12, 3.

b) *compendium,* a short cut, shortening (Plaut.; Cic.(1); Colum.; Plin. mai.; Sil.; and Late especially (Ambros.)), 1, 43, 5; 2, 15, 6; 3, 6, 5; 3, 9, 1; 5, 18, 1. — *coniugium,* a wife (Acc.; Verg.; Prop.; Sen. poet.; Lucan.; Val. Fl.; Iuv.; Itala; and Late), 1, 32, 6. — *dispendium,* loss, detriment (Enn.; Varr.; Lucr.; Ov.; Colum.; Silver and Late), 1, 1, 9; 1, 9, 4; 1, 32, 6; 3, 3, 4; 3, 12, 3; 3, 17; 4, 29, 2; 5, 12; 5, 18, 2; 5, 24, 3; 5, 36, 1. — cost, expense (Plaut.; Ter.; Prop.; Sen. phil.; Stat.; Tert.; and Late especially), 2, 2, 2. — *magisterium,* teaching, instruction (Plaut.; Tibull.; Cels.; Ambros., and Late Latin), 3, 2. — *occipitium,* poll, occiput, back part of the head (Plaut.; Varr.; Cels.; Plin. mai.; Quint.; Scrib.; Amm.), 3, 12, 2. — *pretium,* a penalty (Liv. Andr. fr.; Plaut.; Ter.; Hor.), 1, 41, 6; 1, 43, 7.

c) *adloquium,* an address, discourse (Hor.; Ov.; Liv.; Vell.; Lucan.; Petron.; Silver and Late (Ambros.)), 1, 29, 5; 3, 23, 2; 5, 14, 4; 5, 22. — *contagium,* contagion, infection (transf. sense) (Ov.; Lucan.; Flor.; Gell.; Tert.; and Late), 1, 37, 6; 1, 39; 2, 16, 2; 3, 16; 4, 5; 5, 16; 5, 41 (bis). — *contubernium,* concubinage (Verg.; Sen. phil.; Curt.; Colum.; Petron.; Suet.; Ulp.; and Late, especially Ict.), 1, 40, 3. — *ieiunium,* hunger (Ov.; Lucan.), 5, 18, 2; 5, 18, 3; 5, 21, 3; 5, 24, 2 (bis); 5, 49, 2. — *incendium,* heat (Lucr.; Hor.; Plin. mai.), 4, 27. — *mancipium,* a slave (fig.)

(Ov.; Petron.; Val. Max.), 2, 8, 2. — *ministerium,* ministry, office, service (Verg.; Ov.; Liv.; Plin. mai.; Tac.; Iust.; Serv.; Ambros.; Hier.; et al), 1, 8; 1, 12, 3; 1, 16, 4; 1, 16, 6; 1, 40, 9 (bis); 1, 45, 10; 3, 16; 3, 17 (quater); 3, 26, 2; 4, 5; 5, 1, 3; 5, 21, 3 (bis); 5, 24, 2; 5, 40; 5, 41 (bis); 5, 45; 5, 48; 5, 53, 1 (bis). — *palatium,* a palace (Ov.; Amm.; Lact.; Capit.; Claud.; Hier.; Vulg.; et al), 1, 35, 1. — *praesagium,* a presentiment (Ov.; Sen. rhet.; Flor.; Tac.), 2, 3, 4. — *profluvium,* a flow, flowing (Lucr.; Colum.; Cels.; Plin. mai.; Arnob.; Ambros.; Aur. Vict.; Eutr.), 5, 1, 3. — *remigium,* an oarsman, rower (Verg.; Hor.; Liv.; Tac.), 3, 3, 6; — oarage (Lucr.; Verg.; Ov.; Apul.; Avien.), 3, 2; 4, 15, 2.

d) *commercium,* traffic, trade (Liv.; Sen. phil.; Plin. mai.; Tac.; Prud.; et al), 1, 37, 2; 2, 9; — a place of trade, market-place (Sen. phil.; Lucan.; Plin. mai.; Claud.; Avit.; et al), 3, 20, 1. — *consortium,* fellowship, society (Liv.; Sen. phil.; Colum.; Petron.; Stat.; Plin. min.; Tac.; Apul.; and very frequent in Late writers, especially Christian ones (Ambros.)), 1, 12, 2; 1, 36, 1; 1, 40, 9; 1, 41, 3; 1, 44, 3; 1, 44, 7; 2, 16, 2; 3, 17; 3, 21, 1; 4, 7; 4, 22, 1; 5, 16 (quinquies); 5, 20, 2; 5, 46; 5, 53, 1 (ter). — *contubernium,* intimacy, social intercourse (Sen. phil.; Petron.; Tac.; Suet.; Fronto; Apul.; Spart.; Hier.), 2, 6, 4; — association, relationship (Sen. phil.; Tac.; Ps. Quint.; Lact.; Chalc.; Ambros.; Vulg.; et al), 3, 17 (bis); 5, 53, 1. — *effugium,* a flight (Liv.; Sen. phil.; Tac.), 1, 40, 8; 3, 9, 2; 3, 26, 3. — *exercitium,* military exercise (Vell.; Tac.; Spart.; Vulc. Gall.; Veget.; Capit.), 3, 24. — *ingenium,* a clever device, artifice (Plin. min.), 5, 39, 1. — *mancipium,* a female slave (Liv.), 1, 43, 4. — *ministeria* (plur.), attendants, assistants (Tac.; Suet.; Apul.; Lampr.; Aur. Vict.; Cypr.; Sid.), 1, 12, 2; 1, 28, 1; 1, 41, 11; 1, 44, 8; 5, 2; 5, 31; 5, 48. — *obsequium,* servility, servile condition (Tac.; Suet.; Iust.), 3, 26, 4; 5, 15. — *praecipitium,* precipice, steep place (Sen. rhet.; Suet.; Vulg.), 1, 35, 3; 2, 15, 7 (bis); 3, 9, 5; 3, 17; 4, 3, 3; 4, 27; 5, 8, 1 (ter); 5, 18, 2; 5, 21, 3; 5, 38. — *suffugium,* a refuge (fig.) (Quint.; Tac.; Apul.), 3, 17. — *transfugium,* a desertion (Liv.; Tac.), 1, 14, 1; 1, 30, 2; 4, 19; 5, 18, 3.

12. Nouns in -*or.*

a) *calor,* ardor, zeal (Cic.(1); Ov.; Sen. phil.; Cels.; Val. Max.;

Silver and Late), 5, 2. — *foetor,* stench, offensive smell (Cic. (1) ;
Cels.; Colum.; Plin. mai.; Apul.; Itala; Ambros.; and frequent
among Eccl. writers), 3, 26, 3; 5, 2; 5, 21, 3 (bis). — *fragor,* a
crash, din, noise (Cic.(1) ; Lucr.; Verg.; Ov.; Liv.; Silver and
Late), 2, 9; 3, 20, 2; 4, 9, 2; 5, 2 (bis) ; 5, 16; 5, 19; 5, 26, 2;
5, 29; 5, 52, 2. — *nidor,* smell from something burned (Cic.(1) ;
Hor.; Liv.; Mart.; Apul.), 5, 2; 5, 40; 5, 53, 1. — *nitor,* bright-
ness, splendor (Rhet. Her.; Lucr.; Ov.; Plin. min.; Gell.; Min.
Fel.; Lact.; Aug.), 5, 43, 1.

b) *fervor,* a violent heat (Enn.?; Varr.; Cic.(1) ; Lucr.; Verg.;
Hor.; Ov.; Liv.; Silver and Late), 2, 9. — *rigor,* coldness, cold
(Lucil. fr.; Lucr.; Ov.; Liv.; Plin. mai.; Val. Max.; Plin. min.;
Lact.; and Late), 3, 26, 1.

c) *aequor,* the calm surface of waters other than the sea (Verg.;
Ov.; Sen. phil.; Sil.; Stat.; Iul. Val.; Avien.; and rare in Late
Latin), 3, 26, 1. — *fulgor,* splendor, glory, renown (Hor.; Ov.;
Liv.; Vell.; Val. Max.; Sen. phil.; Silver and Late (Ambros.)),
5, 46. — *marmor,* the sea (Catull.; Verg.; Sil.), 3, 11, 2. — *rigor,*
hardness (Lucr.; Verg.; Ov.; Plin. mai.; Vitr.; Colum.; Cels.),
5, 16; 5, 42, 5. — *sudor,* a liquid moisture (Lucr.; Ov.; Sen. phil.;
Plin. mai.; Ulp.), 3, 12, 3. — *tumor,* pride (Ov.; Quint.; Iust.),
1, 15, 1. — *vigor,* vigor, force, activity (Verg.; Hor.; Ov.; Vitr.;
Liv.; Curt.; Silver and Late (Ambros.)), 1, 1, 2; 1, 12, 1; 1, 12, 2;
1, 28, 3; 1, 28, 5; 1, 37, 7; 1, 43, 3; 5, 21, 3; 5, 46; 5, 53, 1.

13. Nouns in -*culum,* -*cula.*

a) *novacula,* a razor (Cic.(1) ; Cels.; Phaedr.; Petron.; Mart.),
1, 41, 11. — *spiculum,* a dart, arrow (Cic.(2) ; Verg.; Hor.; Ov.;
Liv.), 1, 8; 5, 19; 5, 20, 2. — *vehiculum,* a conveyance, carriage
(Nep.; Liv.; Sen. phil.; Plin. min.; Fronto; Arnob.; Amm.; et
al), 2, 15, 7.

b) *diluculum,* dawn, daybreak (Plaut.; Afran.; Cic.(2) ; Suet.;
Fronto; and Late), 5, 53, 2. — *poculum,* a drink, potion (Plaut.;
Verg.; Hor.; Flor.; Apul.), 1, 43, 1.

c) *retinaculum,* a rope, cable (Verg.; Hor.; Ov.; Vitr.), 1, 30, 9;
3, 11, 1.

d) *ferculum,* a course at a meal (Sen. phil.; Suet.; Mart.; Macr.; Calp.; Auson.; Lampr.; Cypr. Gall.), 1, 40, 7. — *gubernaculum,*[13] guidance, direction (Vell.; Lact.), 2, 13, 2; 4, 26, 2. — *miraculum,* admiration (Plin. mai.; Itala; Cypr.; Rufin.), 1, 37, 2 (bis) ; 1, 38, 1; 4, 7; 4, 18; — wonderfulness, marvellousness (Liv.), Praef.— *obstaculum,* an obstacle, hindrance (Sen. phil.; Amm.; Apul.; Arnob.; Prud.; Aug.), 1, 24, 1; 3, 17; 5, 35, 1.

14. Nouns in *-bulum.*

a) *latibulum,* a hiding-place for men (Cic.(1) ; Apul.), 1, 30, 15; 3, 5, 2.

b) *conciliabulum,* an assembly-place (Plaut.; Fronto; Tert.; Paneg.; Lucif.; et al), 2, 5, 1; 4, 7.

c) *pabulum,* food for men (Lucr.; Ov.; Val. Fl.; Stat.), 5, 46.

15. Nouns in *-um.*

a) *bustum,* ruins (Cic.(4) ; Lucr.; Ov.; Prop.; Lucan.; Plin. mai.; Sil.; Val. Fl.; Quint.; Amm.; and passim in Late Latin), 5, 22. — *canticum,* a song (Cic.(1) ; Prop.; Phaedr.; Sen. phil.; Petron.; Mart.; Quint.; Apul.; and Late especially), 5, 44, 1. — *castrum,* a fortress (Nep.; Paul. ex Fest.; Itin. Silv.; Eutr.; Callistr.; Capit.; Hier.; Vulg.; et al), 1, 6, 3; 1, 13, 2; 2, 9, 2; 2, 13, 3; 4, 6, 7; 4, 9, 4. — *claustra* (plur.), a bulwark (Cic.(1) ; Tac.; Anth.), 2, 9, 1. — *furtum,* trick, stratagem (Sall. fr.; Verg.; Ov.; Liv.; Sen. phil.; Curt.; Silver and Late), 1, 30, 10; 1, 32, 6; 5, 15; 5, 21, 3. — *legatum,* a legacy, testament (Cic.(3) ; Petron.; Quint.; Plin. min.; Suet.; Ulp.; Apul.), 1, 45, 10. — *salum,* the open sea (Cic. (1) ; Nep.; Bell. Afr.; Bell. Hisp.; Liv.; Hier.), 1, 35, 4.

b) *aevum,* the whole age of a man (Plaut.; Enn.; Pacuv.; Sall.; Lucr.; Poetical, Silver and Late), 3, 6, 1; 5, 27. — *calamistrum,* a curling iron (Plaut.; Varr.; Cic. (1) ; Paul. ex Fest.; Petron.; Arnob.; Hier.; et al), 4, 25, 2. — *pomum,* a fruit tree (Cato; Verg.; Plin. min.), 3, 6, 3; 3, 6, 4; 4, 18. — *vadum,* security,

---

[13] This word is classical only in the plural.

guarantee, safety (Plaut.; Ter.), 5, 7, 1; 5, 53, 1. — *venum* [14] (*venus*), a selling (Pacuv. fr.; Sall.; Liv.; Tac.; Gell.; Apul.; Claud.; Porphyr.), 5, 24, 3.

c) *aevum,* a part of a man's life, i. e., childhood, youth, etc. (Lucr.; Verg.; Ov.; Sen. phil.; Sil.; Stat.; Silver and Late), 1, 17, 3; 5, 24, 1. — *claustra* [15] (plur.), an enclosed place, a safe place (Hor.; Val. Max.; Sen. phil.; Tac.; Sol.; Eutr.; Lucif.; et al), 5, 31. — *fluentum,* [16] a river, stream (Lucr.; Verg.; Homer.; Sil.; Apul.; Ser. Samm.; and very frequent in Late Latin), 1, 30, 9; 3, 6, 1; 4, 15, 2 (bis); 5, 16; 5, 41. — *stagnum,* a pool, pond (Cic. poet.; Phaedr.; Verg.; Ov.; Bell. Afr.; Liv.; Cels.), 1, 39; 3, 26, 1.

16. Nouns in *-tudo.*

a) *adsuetudo,* [17] a custom, habit (Varr.; Ov.; Liv.; Mela; Plin. mai.; Tac.; Gell.; Apul.; Amm.; Ambros.; et al), 1, 10, 3; 2, 13, 2; 3, 24. — *altitudo,* depth, extent (transf. sense) (Sall.; Tac.; Ambros.; and Late), 5, 22, 2. — *amaritudo,* bitterness (Varr.; Cels.; Sen. phil.; Colum.; Plin. mai.; Tert.; and Late), 4, 17. — *beatitudo,* happiness (Cic. (1); Petron.; Quint.; Apul.; and Late), 1, 1, 10; 1, 35, 1; 5, 53, 1.

b) *claritudo,* fame, reputation (Cato; Sisenna; Sall.; Vell.; Tac.; Apul.; Vopisc.; Amm.; and Late), 1, 40, 2; 5, 53, 1. — *lenitudo,* mildness, gentleness (Pacuv.; Turpil.; Cic.(2); Aur. Vict.), 1, 25, 4. — *maestitudo,* sadness (Plaut.; Acc.; Ambros.; Sulp. Sev.; Aug.; Pallad.; Cael. Aur.; Leo M.), 1, 8.

d) *aegritudo,* illness of the body (Plin. mai.; Tac.; Silver and Late), 1, 12, 1; 1, 37, 7; 1, 42, 9; 1, 45, 4; 1, 45, 5 (bis); 1, 45, 8; 1, 45, 9; 2, 13, 2; 4, 16, 2; 5, 27; — a sickness (of plants and other things) (Plin. mai.; Cassian.; Chalc.; Macr.), 1, 38, 1. — *amaritudo,* bitterness, sorrow, sadness (Pomp. Trog.; Sen. phil.; Plin.

[14] Found only in the dative and accusative singular. *veno* (as here): Tac.; *venui:* Apul.

[15] The singular is rare. Found in Heg. 5, 11, 2.

[16] Used mostly in the plural. Singular in Heg. 2, 9; 3, 26, 1 (bis).

[17] Usually found in the ablative singular (as here).

6

mai.; Val. Max.; Quint.; Silver and Late), 1, 4. — *necessitudines* [18]
(plur.), relatives, friends (Tac.; Tibull.; Plin. ep.; Suet.; Eutr.;
Amm.), 1, 30, 9; 1, 40, 3; 1, 41, 10; 5, 16; 5, 53, 1 (bis); 5, 53,
2. — *plenitudo,* fullness, plenitude (Colum.; Plin. mai.; Tert.;
Lact.; Sol.; Ambros.), 5, 9, 4.

17. Nouns in *-go.*

a) *caligo,* mental blindness (Cic.(2); Catull.; Manil.; Sen
phil.; Sil.; Iuv.; Apul.; and Late), 5, 46. — *indago,* an investigation, minute searching (Hirt.; Verg.; Liv.; Plin. min.; Frontin.;
Gell.; Amm.; Cod. Iust.; Gloss. Philox.), Praef. — *uligo,* marshy
quality of the earth (Varr.; Verg.; Colum.; Tac.), 3, 26, 1.

d) *prurigo,* the itch (Cels.; Plin. mai.; Mart.; Suet.; Marc.
Emp.), 1, 45, 9. — *scaturigo,* a bubbling source (Liv.; Colum.;
Plin. mai.; Frontin.; Apul.; Sol.; Mart. Cap.; et al), 4, 17.

18. Nouns in *-es* (*ei*).

b) *acies,* a sharp edge or point (Plaut.; Cic.(2); Verg.; Ov.;
Colum.; Cels.; Plin. mai.; Silver and Late), 5, 21, 3. — *sanies,*
bloody matter (Cato; Cels.; Sen. phil.; Plin. mai.), 5, 21, 4.

c) *canities,* gray hair (Catull.; Verg.; Ov.; Curt.; Plin. mai.;
Silver and Late), 5, 53, 1; — old age (Verg.; Hor.; Prop.; Iuv.;
Apul.; Paneg.; Maximin.; Prud.; Eustath.), 5, 53, 1. — *congeries,*
a heap, pile, mass (Aetna; Ov.; Liv.; Colum.; Val. Max.; Silver
and Late), 5, 25, 2; 5, 31. — *rabies,* madness of animals (Ov.;
Colum.; Plin. mai.), 5, 41. — *species,* a picture, likeness (Cic.
poet.), 1, 37, 5. — *temperies,* temperature (Ov.; Plin. mai.;
Fronto; Mart. Cap.), 3, 26, 2 (ter); 5, 27.

19. Nouns in *-monia.*

a) *alimonia,* food, nourishment (Varr.; Gell.; Apul.; Ambros.;
and Late writers in general), 1, 18, 1; 2, 7, 2; 3, 20, 1; 3, 26, 4;
4, 3, 1; 4, 26, 3; 5, 15; 5, 18, 2; 5, 24, 2.

[18] The singular in this sense is found in Heg. 1, 1, 6. Cf. Ambros. De
Exc. Sat. 1, 58.

20. Nouns in -*ile*.

a) *sedile,* a chair, seat (Varr.; Verg.; Ov.; Hor.; Sen. phil.; Plin. min.; Suet.; Fronto; Gell.; Apul.; et al), 1, 41, 1, 5, 18, 1.

b) *cubile,* marriage couch (Trag. inc.; Cic.(1); Catull.; Hor.; Ov.; Prop.; Lucan.; Val. Fl.; Sil.; Stat.; Itala), 2, 5, 3.

21. Diminutives.

a) *fasciola,* a bandage (Cic.(1); Varr.; Hor.; Apul.; Scrib.; Veget.; Amm.; Chiron.; et al), 5, 47, 1. — *oppidulum* (= oppidum), town (Cic. ep.(1); Hor.; Hier.), 3, 20, 3. — *virgula,* a twig (Nep.; Paul. ex Fest.), 4, 17.

b) *adolescentula,* a young maiden (Plaut.; Ter.; Varr.; Apul.; Ambros.; Hier.; Vulg.; et al), 2, 2, 4. — *ancillula,* a young female slave (Plaut.; Ter.; Ov.; Liv.; Silver and Late), 1, 40, 5; 1, 43, 2. — *apicula,* a little bee (Plaut.; Plin. mai.; Fronto; Pallad.; Ambros.; Aug.), 5, 27. — *barbula,* a small beard (Lucil.; Cic.(1); Carm. Epigr.; Hist. Apoll.), 4, 25, 2.

d) *fidicula,* a cord or line used as an instrument of torture (Val. Max.; Sen. phil.; Mart.; Suet.; Ps. Quint.; Amm.; Hier.; Prud.; et al), 1, 44, 8. — *loculus,* a coffin (Plin. mai.; Iust.; Vulg.; Fulg.; Eugipp.), 5, 21, 3.— *mamilla,* the breast, pap (Vell.; Iuv.; Vulg.; Aug.), 5, 18, 2. — *sportula,* a gift, present (Plin. ep.; Ulp.; Cod. Iust.; Iulian. epit. novell.), 2, 1, 2.

22. Compound Nouns.

a) *anfractus,* a winding, bending (Cic.(2); Caes.; Nep.; Lucr.; Verg.; Liv.; Silver and Late), 4, 1, 1; 4, 27. — *antesignanus,* a leader (Cic.(1); Liv.; Ascon.; and passim in Late Latin), 4, 23, 1. — *commilito,* a fellow-soldier (Varr.; Cic. (2); Caes.; Liv.; Silver and Late), 3, 25, 2; 4, 2; 4, 29, 2; 5, 27 (quinquies). — *praecordia* (plur.), entrails, stomach (Cic.(2); Verg.; Hor.; Plin. mai.), 1, 7, 2. — *praeiudicium,* precedent, example (Caes.; Plin. ep.), 4, 29, 2. — *septentrio,*[19] the North (Varr.; Liv.; Vitr.; Curt.; Mela; Tac.), 3, 6, 3; 5, 12. — *triumvir,* a member of the triumvirate, i. e., Antony, Octavian, Lepidus (Nep.; Vell.; Plin. mai.;

[19] The plural in this sense is found in Cic.; Caes. (saepe); Plaut.; Varr.

Suet.; Gell.), 1, 6, 3. — *tubicen,* a war trumpeter (Cic.(1); Bell.
Afr.; Ov.; Liv.; Sen. phil.), 5, 29. — *vindemia,* grape-gathering,
vintage (Varr.; Colum.; Plin. min.; Suet.; Arnob.; Ulp.), 5, 27.

23. Greek Nouns.

a) *Boreas* (βορέας), the north wind (Nep.; Catull.; Verg.;
Aetna; Ov.; Sen. phil.; Silver and Late), 3, 20, 2; 5, 52, 2. —
charta (χάρτης), writing material, paper (Rhet. Her.; Cic.(2);
Hor.; Ov.; Silver and Late), 5, 39, 1. — *chiliarchus* (χιλίαρχος), a
chiliarch, i. e., a commander of a thousand soldiers (Nep.; Itala;
Ps. Rufin.), 4, 30. — *cithara* (κιθάρα), a lute, cithara (Rhet. Her.;
Varr.; Lucr.; Verg.; Hor.; Tibull.; Ov.; Prop.; Silver and Late),
5, 2. — *conchylium* (κογχύλιον), a kind of purple shell-fish (Varr.;
Cic.(2); Cels.; Sen. phil.; Silver and Late), 5, 9, 2. — *contus*
(κοντός), a very long spear, a lance (Varr. fr.; Verg.; Gratt.; Plin.
mai.; Val. Fl.; Silver and Late), 3, 25, 1. — *hydra* (ὕδρα), the
Hydra (Varr.; Cic.(1); Lucr.; Hor.; Prop.), 1, 43, 3. — *hydria*
(ὑδρία), a jug, ewer, pitcher (Cic. (4); Vitr.; C.I.L.; Vulg.), 5,
16. — *machina* (μηχανή), a military machine (Sall.; Verg.; Liv.;
Vitr.; Plin. mai.), 1, 16, 4; 4, 1, 4; 5, 1, 3; 5, 8, 1; 5, 10, 2;
5, 10, 3; 5, 11, 2; 5, 13; 5, 14, 4; 5, 19; 5, 20, 2; 5, 25, 2; 5, 26, 1;
5, 47, 3. — *palma* (παλάμη), a palm tree (Caes.; Verg.; Plin. mai.;
Suet.; Itin. Alex.; Vulg.; and Eccl.), 3, 6, 3 (bis); 4, 16, 2;
4, 17. — *pelagus* (πέλαγος), the sea (Cic. fr.(1); Bell. Hisp.;
Verg.; Ov.; Vitr.; Sen. rhet.; Val. Max.; Tac.), 2, 9. — *peripetasma* (περιπέτασμα), a tapestry, hanging (Cic.(1); Ambros.),
5, 9, 2; 5, 48. — *pyra* (πυρά), a funeral pyre (Bell. Afr.; Verg.;
Ov.; Vulg.), 5, 53, 1. — *radix* (ῥάδιξ), an edible root (Caes.; Hor.;
Ov.; Sen. phil.; Cels.; Colum.), 5, 18, 2 (bis); 5, 36, 2. — *satrapes*
(σατράπης), a satrap, governor of a province (Nep.; Curt.; Iul.
Val.), 1, 29, 1 (bis); 1, 29, 3. — *scaena* (σκηνή), a pretext, intrigue,
fraud (Cael. apud Cic.; Tac.; Apul.; Tert.), 1, 37, 2; 1, 38, 6;
1, 40, 7; 1, 40, 11; 1, 41, 9; 1, 44, 3; 1, 44, 6. — *scopulus* (σκόπε-
λος), a rock, cliff (Cic.(1); Caes.; Verg.; Hor.; Ov.; Sen. phil.;
Val. Fl.), 3, 11, 2; 3, 20, 2 (bis); 4, 27 (bis); 5, 16. — *statera*
(στατήρ), the balance of a scale (Cic.(1); Varr.; Vitr.; Suet.;
Aug.), 3, 11, 1.

b) *catapulta* (καταπέλτης), a catapult (Plaut.; Titin.; Lucil.; Sisenn.; Varr.; Caes.; Bell. Afr.; Liv.; Vitr.; Tac.; et al), 5, 20, 2. — *cetus* (κῆτος), a sea-monster (Plaut.; Varr.; Verg.; Colum.; Plin. mai.; and Late), 3, 20, 2. — *crapula* (κραιπάλη), intoxication (Plaut.; Cic.(2); Sen. phil.; Val. Max.; Liv.; Silver and Late (Ambros.)), 4, 7; 4, 32. — *cratera* (κρατήρ), a vessel in which wine was mingled with water (Naev.; Enn.; Cic. (2); Verg.; Prop.; Ov.; Liv.; Silver and Late), 5, 48. — *cubitum* (*cubitus*) (κύβιτον), an elbow (Enn.; Plaut.; Rhet. Her.; Nep.; Verg.; Hor.; Prop.; Ov.; Silver and Late), 1, 45, 11; — a cubit (Plaut.; Lucil.; Cic.(2); Varr.; Silver and Late), 5, 20, 1. — *cupressus* (κυπάρισσος), a cypress tree (Enn.; Cato; Varr.; Catull.; Verg.; Hor.; Ov.; Vitr.; Silver and Late), 3, 5, 2. — *diplois* (διπλοίς), a cloak, mantle (Novius; Itala; Vulg.; Ps. Aug.; Ven. Fort.; Ps. Thom.), 1, 46, 2. — *ephebus* (ἔφηβος), a male youth from sixteen to twenty years of age (Plaut.; Ter.; Varr. fr.; Cic.(4); Nep.; Petron.; Stat.), 1, 36, 2. — *eunuchus* (εὐνοῦχος), a eunuch (Ter.; Cic.(3) : Caes.), 1, 40, 7. — *hippodromus* (ἱππόδρομος), a hippodrome, a race-course for horses (Plaut.; Mart.; Plin. ep.; Sidon.), 1, 45, 10. — *hymenaeus* (ὑμέναιος), a nuptial song (Plaut.; Ter.; Pacuv.; Turpil.; Lucr.; Verg.; Ov.), 1, 31, 1. — *petra* (πέτρα), a rock (Enn.; Laev. fr.; Sen. phil.; Ambros.; Vulg.; Aug.), 1, 30, 9; 3, 11, 2; 3, 20, 2; 5, 41. — *platea* (πλατεῖα), a city street (Ter.; Caes.), 2, 11, 4; 5, 19.

c) *antrum* (ἄντρον), a cave (Verg.; Hor.; Prop.; Ov.; Sen. phil.; Silver and Late), 1, 30, 9; 1, 35, 3. — *aula* (αὐλή), a palace (Verg.; Hor.; Ov.; Silver and Late (Ambros.)), 1, 13, 3; 1, 16, 3; 1, 37, 5; 1, 37, 6; 1, 38, 4; 1, 40, 2; 1, 40, 7; 1, 40, 9; 1, 41, 11; 1, 44, 7; 2, 13, 4; 4, 25, 3; 5, 47, 1. — *balsamum* (βάλσαμον), a balsam tree (Verg.; Eleg. in Maecen.; Colum.; Mart.; Plin. mai.; Cels.; and Late), 1, 15, 3; 1, 32, 2; 4, 17. — *casia* (κασία), a spice (Ov.; Eleg. in Maecen.; Colum.; Pers.; Plin. mai.; Mart.; Apul.; and Late), 5, 48. — *coccum* (κόκκος), scarlet color (Ciris; Hor.; Lucan.; Plin. mai.; Mart.; Quint.; Suet.; Hil.; Ambros.; and Late), 5, 9, 2 (bis). — *contus* (κοντός), a pole or pike to propel a boat (Verg.; Prop.; Liv.; Sen. phil.; Curt.; Silver and Late), 3, 20, 2. — *corona* (κορώνη), a crown, diadem, as a symbol of office (Verg.; Curt.;

Plin. mai.; Suet.; Fronto; Apul.; et al), 1, 46, 2. — *cyparissus* (κυπάρισσος), a cypress tree (Verg.; Val. Fl.; Itala; Hier.; Serv.; et al), 4, 1, 2. — *hydrops* (ὕδρωψ), dropsy (Hor.; Cels.; Cael. Aur.), 1, 45, 9; 5, 24, 2. — *metallum* (μέταλλον), metal (Verg.; Hor.; Sen. phil.; Plin. mai.), 4, 18; 5, 43, 1. — *murex* (μύαξ), purple dye, purple (Verg.; Ov.; Ambros.), 1, 46, 2. — *Notus* (νότος), the south wind (Verg.; Hor.; Ov.; Lucan.; Gell.), 5, 52, 2.— *phalanx* (φάλαγξ), a band of soldiers, a host (Verg.), 3, 24. — *scaena* (σκηνή), a theatre or field of action (Ov.), 1, 40, 1. — *spado* (σπάδων), a eunuch (Hor.; Liv.; Quint.; Suet.; Ambros.), 1, 23; 1, 40, 7; 1, 40, 8. — *spelaeum (speleum)* (σπήλαιον), a cave (Verg.; Claud.; Prud.; Tert.; C.I.L.), 1, 30, 9; 3, 4, 3; 3, 15, 2; 3, 26, 1; 5, 2. — *terebinthus* (τερέβινθος), a turpentine tree (Verg.; Plin. mai.; Hier.; Vulg.), 4, 23, 2. — *tessera* (τέσσαρες), a watchword (Verg.; Liv.; Sil.; Stat.; Suet.; Amm.), 3, 17. — *ulcus* (ἕλκος), a sore (Lucr.; Verg.; Hor.; Cels.; Plin. mai.), 4, 6, 7. — *zephyrus* (ζέφυρος), a wind (Verg.), 3, 5, 2.

d) *amphitheatrum* (ἀμφιθέατρον), the amphitheatre (Mon. Ancyr.; Vitr.; Sen. phil.; Plin. mai.; Silver and Late), 1, 46, 1; 2, 11, 3. — *aroma* (ἄρωμα), spice, condiment (Cels.; Colum.; and Late), 1, 46, 2. — *cataracta* (καταράκτης), a waterfall, cataract (Vitr.; Sen. phil.; Lucan.; Plin. mai.; Amm.; Ambros.; et al), 4, 27 (bis). — *cinnamomum* (κιννάμωνον), cinnamon (Cels.; Scrib.; Plin. mai.; Marcian.; Itala; Iren.; Ambros.; et al), 5, 48. — *coccum* (κόκκος), things tinted with scarlet (Mart.; Fronto; Ulp.; Paul.; Itala; Vulg.; et al), 5, 48. — *colon (colum)* (κῶλον), a disease of the colon (Scrib.; Plin. mai.; Ser. Samm.; Veget.; Rufin.; Marcell.), 1, 45, 9. — *colossus* (κολοσσός), a large statue (Sen. ep.; Plin. mai.; Stat.; Mart.; Silver and Late), 1, 35, 6 (bis). — *contus* (κοντός), a pole or stick of any kind (Petron.; Plin. mai.; Val. Fl.; Schol. Hor.; Veget.; Aug.; Oros.), 3, 11, 2. — *coracinus* (κοράκινος), a species of river fish (Plin. mai.; Mart.; Pol. Silv.), 3, 26, 2. — *cypros (cyprus)* (κύπρος), a cypress tree (Plin. mai.; Iul. Val.; Vulg.; et al), 4, 17. — *dactylus* (δάκτυλος), a species of palm tree (Plin. mai.; Pelagon.; Veg.; Ambros.; Ps. Ambros.; et al), 3, 6, 3; 3, 26, 2; 4, 17. — *hymnus* (ὕμνος), a song of praise, hymn (Sen. phil. fr.; Lact.; Prud.; Ambros.; Aug.;

Vulg.; and Eccl.), 2, 15, 8. — *hypogeum* (*hypogaeum*) (ὑπόγειον), a vault (Vitr.; Petron.; C.I.L.), 1, 6, 2; 1, 7, 1; 3, 15, 3; 5, 49, 1; 5, 49, 3. — *lepra* (λέπρα), leprosy (Scrib.; Plin. mai.; Vulg.; et al), 2, 12, 3. — *myrobalanum* (μυροβάλανον), the fruit of the Arabian behen-nut from which balsam was made; the balsam itself (Plin. mai.; Mart.), 4, 17. — *opobalsamum* (ὀποβάλσαμον), balsam, the juice of the balsam tree (Cels.; Scrib.; Plin. mai.; Stat.; Mart.; Iuv.; Iust.), 4, 17. — *phiala* (φιάλη), a broad, shallow drinking vessel (Plin. mai.; Mart.; Iuv.; Vulg.; Aug.), 5, 48. — *phantasma* (φάντασμα), an apparition (Plin. ep.; Tert.; Hier.; Aug.), 3, 2. — *spasmus* (σπασμός), a convulsion, spasm, cramp (Scrib.; Plin. mai.; Cael. Aur.; Isid.), 1, 45, 9. — *thronus* (θρόνος), a throne (Plin. mai.; Poet. apud Suet.; Ambros.; Pervig. Ven.; Prud.), 2, 1, 2; 5, 22. — *thymiama* (θυμίαμα), incense (Cels.; Pelagon.; Ambros.; Vulg.; et al), 5, 48.

24. Hybrids.

b) *ballista*, the ballista, a war engine (Plaut.; Caecil.; Sisenn.; Cic. (1); Caes.; Bell. Afr.; Ov.; Liv.; Tac.; Amm.), 3, 12, 2.

25. Miscellaneous Nouns.

a) *alveus*, a ship (Sall.; Verg.; Prop.; Ov.; Liv.; Vell.; Silver and Late), 3, 20, 2 (bis). — *apex*, the highest honor, dignity (Cic. (1); Tert.; and frequent in Late Latin), 1, 40, 2. — *caput*, capital, chief city (Cic. ep. (1); Nep.; Bell. Hisp.; Liv. (saepe); Curt.; Silver and Late), 3, 5, 2. — *cutis*, skin (Planc. Cic. ep. (1); Hor.; Ov.; Colum.; Cels.; Silver and Late), 5, 21, 3. — *fornix*, an arch by which a burden is supported (Rhet. Her.; Varr.; Cic. (1); Sall.; Bell. Alex.; Verg.; Sen. phil.; Plin. mai.; Auson.; and Late), 5, 38 (bis). — *funus*, a corpse (Varr.; Catull.; Verg.; Ov.; and frequent in Silver and Late Latin), 2, 6, 3; 5, 21, 3; 5, 22 (bis); 5, 23; 5, 25, 1; 5, 53, 1. — *gentes* (plur.), strangers, foreigners (Cic. (1); Mon. Ancyr.; Curt.; Lucan. (saepe); Silver and Late), 1, 17, 2. — *hircus*, a he-goat (Varr.; Verg.; Hor.; Sen. rhet.), 5, 15. — *later*,[20] a brick (Varr.; Cic. (1); Caes.; Vitr.; Curt.; Plin. mai.), 4, 27. — *messis*, the harvest, the ingathering of

---

[20] Singular is used in Heg. 4, 27, with collective force, as in Caes. B. C. 2, 8, 1.

the fruits (Varr.; Verg.; Plin. min.; Stat.; Iust.), 5, 27. — *moles,* greatness, force, power (Cic. (3); Liv.; Vell.; Tac.; Sil.; Apul.), 1, 25, 4; 1, 39; 1, 40, 9; 3, 17. — *naevus,* a blemish on the body (Cic. (2); Sen. rhet.; Hor.; Ov.; Sen. phil.), 5, 46. — *rupes,* a rock (Caes.; Verg.; Hor.; Liv.; Plin. mai.; Stat.; Salv.; Claud.), 1, 30, 9; 1, 35, 4; 2, 15, 7; 3, 6, 4; 3, 9, 5; 3, 11, 2; 3, 20, 2 (bis); 4, 1, 1; 4, 27 (bis); 5, 16; 5, 41. — *tabes,* a wasting disease, consumption (Cic. (1); Sall.; Liv.; Val. Max.; Tac.; Lact.; Aur. Vict.), 5, 21, 3. — *triumphus,* a victory (Cic.(2); Plin. mai.; Iust.; Amm.), Praef.; 1, 28, 5; 1, 30, 12. — *uber,* an udder, breast (Cic. (2); Verg.; Ov.; Hor.; Plin. mai.; Val. Max.), 3, 6, 4; 5, 23. — *vertex,* summit, peak, top (Cic. (1); Catull.; Verg.; Hor.; Ov.; Curt.; Mart.), 4, 4, 6. — *vicis,* office, duty (Cic. (1); Sall. fr.; Hor.; Liv.; Phaedr.; Quint.; Tac.; Plin. min.), 1, 16, 6; — a return, recompense, remuneration (Cic. (1); Prop.; Hor.; Ov.; Tac.; Plin. min.; Treb. Poll.), 2, 13, 7.

b) *accipiter,* a bird of prey (Ter.; Lucr.; Varr.; Cic. (1); Verg.; Ov.; Hor.; Silver and Late), 5, 15 (bis); 5, 36, 2. — *ales,* a bird (Pacuv.; Catull.; Lucr.; Cic. (5); Poetical (especially), Silver and Late), 5, 40. — *alveus,* the channel of a river (Pacuv.; Verg.; Hor.; Ov.; Liv.; Silver and Late), 2, 9. — *ars,* cunning, fraud (Ter.; Sall.; Verg.; Tibull.; Prop.; Ov.; Liv.; Silver and Late), 1, 1, 2; 1, 9, 4; 1, 13, 2; 1, 14, 1; 1, 15, 1; 1, 37, 3; 1, 40, 1; 1, 40, 9 (ter); 1, 40, 13; 1, 41, 2; 1, 41, 3; 1, 44, 1; 1, 44, 2; 1, 44, 7; 1, 45, 4; 2, 6, 1. — *callis,* a mountain path (Acc.; Lex agr.; Varr.; Cic. (2); Verg.; Ov.; Liv. (saepe); Silver and Late), 1, 30, 9. — *caput,* the tip, top of trees, etc. (Enn.; Laber.; Cic. (1); Verg.; Silver and Late), 3, 11, 1. — *carpentum* (probably a Celtic word), a vehicle (Liv. Andr.; Naev.; Varr.; Ov.; Liv. (18); Silver and Late), 4, 27. — *cautes,* a rough, pointed rock (Enn.; Cic. (1); Caes.; Verg.; Silver and Late), 3, 20, 2; 4, 27. — *cervus,* a stag (Plaut.; Varr.; Cic. (1); Lucr.; Poetical, Silver and Late), 5, 27. — *clavus,* a nail (Plaut.; Cato; Caes.; Liv.; Vitr.; Silver and Late), 5, 30. — *coniux,* a husband (Plaut.; Pacuv.; Acc.; Cic. (1); Catull.; Verg.; Tibull.; Prop.; Ov.; and other poets), 5, 53, 1. — *cortex,* the bark of trees (Cato; Varr.; Cic. (2); Caes.; Poetical, Silver and Late), 4, 17; 5, 18, 2. — *cuneus,* a wedge-shaped line of battle (Cato; Caes.; Hirt.; Verg.; Ov.; Liv. (saepe); Silver

and Late), 3, 13; 4, 15, 2; 5, 27; 5, 43, 2. — *cupido*, a desire
(Plaut.; Enn.; Sall. (20); Hor.; Verg.; Liv.; Tac. (79); Silver
and Late), 1, 18; 5, 50. — *funis*, a rope or cord used in machines
(Cato; Vitr.; Liv.; Plin. mai.; Tac.; Veget.), 3, 11, 1. — *funus*,
a death (Ps. Liv. Andr.; Lucr.; Verg.; Hor.; Ov.; Liv.; Silver
and Late), 5, 22. — *lues*, a plague, pestilence (Carm. fratr. arv.;
Verg.; Lucan.; Aur. Vict.), 1, 32, 6; 1, 38, 1; 4, 4, 1; 5, 2. — *lux*,
a life (Plaut.; Cic. (1); Verg.; Ov.), 1, 41, 3. — *munia* (plur.),
duties (Plaut.; Cic. (2); Hor.; Liv.; Tac.; Tert.; Amm.; and
Late), 3, 3, 4 (bis). — *nepos*, a grandson (Plaut.; Cic. (2); Sall.;
Hor.; Liv.; Vell.; Tac.; Suet.; Gell.; et al), 1, 42, 2; 1, 42, 3
(quinquies); 2, 18. — *neptis*, a granddaughter (Afran.; Cic. (2);
Sall.; Cels.; Suet.), 1, 36, 1. — *olus*, any vegetable (Afran. fr.;
Hor.; Hier.), 5, 18, 1. — *pix*, pitch (Plaut.; Caes.; Sall.; Lucr.;
Verg.; Liv.; Scrib.; Vitr.; Aug.), 5, 20, 1; 5, 38 (bis). — *satias*,
a sufficiency, an abundance (Acc. fr.; Varr. fr.; Sall. fr.; Lucr.),
1, 18. — *sentis*, a thorn, bramble (Plaut.; Caes.; Verg.; Ps. Verg.;
Ps. Ov.; Colum.), 4, 20. — *sulphur*, sulphur, brimstone (Cato;
Sall.; Prop.; Verg.; Hor.; Poetical, Silver and Late), 5, 20, 1.

c) *agger*, a public or military road (Verg.; Stat.; Tac.; Amm.;
and Late), 5, 3, 1. — *caper*, a he-goat (Verg.; Hor.; Ov.; Colum.;
Plin. mai.; Mart.; Silver and Late), 5, 15. — *caudex*, the trunk of
a tree (Verg.; Ov.; Plin. mai.; Suet. fr.; Apul.; Gell.; and Late),
4, 15, 2. — *compages*, a calking (Verg.; Liv.; Sen. rhet.; Sen.
phil.; Lucan.; Paul. Nol.), 4, 18. — *cornu*, a promontory, a point
of land (Ov.; Mela; Plin. mai.; Liv.; Curt.; Sol.; Flor.), 3, 20,
2. — *fascis*, a burden, load (Verg.; Cels.; Petron.; Quint.; Prud.;
Paul. Nol.), 2, 15, 8. — *fel*, spite, ill-will, malice (Ov.; Mart.;
Plin. min.; Fronto; Tert.; Auson.; Ambros.; et al), 1, 5. — *globus*,
a spherical mass (Verg.; Sen. rhet.; Plin. mai.; Tac.; Amm.;
Apul.; et al), 5, 42, 5; — a crowd, throng, mass of people (Verg.;
Liv.; Tac.), 4, 15, 2. — *gurges*, waters, stream (Cic. poet.; Lucr.;
Verg.; Ov.; Stat.; Amm.), 4, 15, 2; 4, 27. — *lapis*, a precious stone
(Catull.; Hor.; Ov.; Sen. phil.; Tac.), 5, 48. — *limes*, a channel
of a river (Prop.; Ov.), 4, 27; 5, 27. — *mephitis*, a noxious ex-
halation from the ground (Verg.; Pers.), 1, 35, 3. — *messis*, the
standing crops (Tibull.; Ov.), 2, 9. — *miles*, the soldiery, army
(Verg.; Liv.; Vell.; Iuv.; Tac.; et al), 1, 31, 3; 2, 9, 1; 2, 9, 2;

5, 14, 3; 5, 25, 2; 5, 46. — *moenia*, walls, sides (Lucr.; Ov.), 4, 27. — *moles*, great bulk, mass (Verg.; Ov.), 3, 20, 2; 5, 42, 1. — *nux*, a walnut tree, a nut tree (Verg.; Liv.), 3, 26, 2. — *pectus*, the breast (Verg.; Ov.; Liv.; Cels.; Plin. mai.; Quint.; Tac.; Aug.), 5, 4, 4; 5, 5. — *pignus*,[21] a child (Ov.; Liv.; Prop.; Stat.; Ambros.; Hier.), 1, 40, 9; 1, 41, 3; 1, 41, 10; 1, 41, 11; 2, 9; 5, 18, 2; 5, 22 (ter); 5, 41 (ter); 5, 53, 2. — *pondus*, gravity, seriousness (Prop.; Val. Max.; Stat.), 5, 7, 2. — *postes* (plur.), a door (Verg.; Ov.; Sen. poet.; Amm.), 5, 15. — *prosocer*, a wife's grandfather (Ov.; Plin. ep.; et al), 1, 36, 2. — *racemus*, a cluster of grapes (Copa; Plin. mai.), 4, 18. — *seges*, a large quantity (Catull.; Verg.; Ov.; Claud.), 5, 1, 3; 5, 18, 3. — *sors*, fortune, fate (Verg.; Hor.; Ov.; Liv.; Suet.), 1, 32, 6; 1, 38, 1; 1, 38, 5; 1, 40, 5; 1, 41, 9; 5, 22; 5, 53, 1. — *strages*, confusion, downfall (Verg.; Liv.; Sil.; Tac.; Obseq.), 5, 11, 1; 5, 30. — *sucus*, a drug, potion (Tibull.; Ov.), 1, 43, 1. — *torus*, a bed (Ov.; Sen. phil.; Ambros.), 1, 40, 7; — an elevation, a bank of earth (Verg.; Stat.; Plin. mai.), 4, 15, 2. — *ursus*, a bear (Verg.; Hor.; Ov.; Liv.; Sen. phil.), 5, 15. — *vermis*, a worm (Lucr.; Plin. mai.; Serv.; Eustath.; Marc. Emp.; Lampr.), 1, 45, 9. — *vertex*, head (Catull.; Verg.; Ov.; Stat.; Val. Fl), 1, 43, 3; 1, 46, 2; 3, 12, 3; 5, 1, 2. — *vicis*, change, succession (Verg.; Hor.; Ov.; Colum.; Liv.; Sen. phil.; Plin. mai.; Quint.; Iust.; Ambros.), 2, 9; 5, 20, 3; 5, 21, 2. — *viscera* (plur.), the viscera (Lucr.; Ov.; Cels.; Sen. phil.), 1, 8; 5, 18, 2.

d) *arbiter*, lord, ruler, master (of God) (Sen. ep.; Paneg.; Tert.; Claud.; Auson.; Cypr. Gall.; Lact.; Sidon.; and Late), 1, 39; 2, 12, 1; 3, 17; 5, 2; — a judge (in non-controversial matters) (Sen. phil.; Sil.; Stat.; Plin. mai.; Tert.; Claud.), 1, 25, 3; 1, 41, 2. — *canalis*, a canal, channel (Mela; Plin. mai.; Stat.; Sol.), 4, 27. — *fel*, melancholy (a disease) (Plin. mai.; Rut. Nam.; Cael. Aur.), 1, 45, 10. — *instar*, an image, likeness (Liv.; Gell.), 5, 53, 1. — *latus*, relationship (Plin. ep.; Stat.; Paul. dig.), 1, 38, 4. — *limes*, a frontier boundary wall (Vell.; Tac.), 2, 9. —

---

[21] Cited in the plural in the Lexica for " dear ones," i. e., parents, children, for Ov.; Liv.; Stat.; Prop. The specific meaning of " child " for the singular is found in Heg.; Ambros.; Hier. Cf. Hagendahl, Studia Ammianea, 32-33; Funck, Archiv VII, 101; McGuire, 105.

numeri [22] (plur.), a troop, band (Tac.; Plin. ep.; Ulp.; Capit.; Amm.), 4, 26, 1; 5, 3, 1; 5, 20, 1; 5, 21, 2; 5, 30. — *palus*, a lake (Mela; Plin. mai.), 5, 50. — *parentes* (plur.), kinsfolk, relations (Curt.; Flor.; Capit.), 1, 39. — *pedes*, infantry, foot-soldiers (Liv., Tac.; and the historians), 2, 14, 3; 4, 33. — *praeses*, a governor (Tac.; Plin. min.; Suet.; Gell.; Lact.; Eutr.; Spart.), 1, 28, 8; 2, 3, 3; 2, 9 (quater); 5, 15.

SUMMARY

Six hundred and forty-two nouns, including those with the suffixes *-tor* (*-sor*), *-tas, -io* (*-tio, -sio*), *-tus* (*-sus*), *-us, -tura* (*-sura*), *-ia, -a, -men, -mentum, -ium, -or, -culum, -bulum, -um, -tudo, -go, -es, -monia, -ile,* diminutives, compounds, Greek nouns, hybrids, and miscellaneous nouns, have been collected from Hegesippus for this section.

This large number of nouns is divided among the four categories as follows: Rare Classical, 220; Early, 120; Poetic, 139; Silver, 163.

Of the thirty-seven nouns in *-tor* (*-sor*) fifteen are Rare Classical, four Early, six Poetic, and twelve Silver. Of the fifteen Rare Classical nouns four, *confirmator, creator, habitator, repressor,* are found in Cicero and then in Late Latin. In the Early group one noun, *precator,* is cited for Plautus, Terence, Statius, and then for Late Latin.

Twenty-seven nouns in *-tas* have been noted, of which thirteen are Rare Classical, four Early, two Poetic, and nine Silver. In the Rare Classical category the following are worthy of note: *fecunditas,* cited for Cicero, Pliny the Elder, and Late Latin; *germanitas,* in Cicero, Livy, and Late Latin; *hospitalitas,* found in Cicero, Martial and Late Latin; *placiditas,* seen only in Varro and Late Latin; *rivalitas,* in Cicero and Apuleius; *viriditas,* used by Cicero, Pliny the Elder, and Ambrose. Of the four Early words in *-tas* the noun *edacitas* is cited for Plautus, Cicero's Epistles, and Ambrose. In the Silver group in *-tas, immaturitas* is found only in Suetonius; *liberalitates* (plur.), in Suetonius and Late Latin; *necessitas,* in Tacitus, Suetonius and Late Latin; *sublimitas,* in Pliny the Elder and Porphyrio.

The largest group of nouns, which totals ninety-eight, has the

---

[22] The singular in this meaning is found in Heg. 5, 4, 4; 5, 20, 1.

suffix -*io* (-*tio*, -*sio*). Of these, forty-eight are Rare Classical, ten Early, and forty Silver. No Poetical nouns have been found with the suffixes -*io* (-*tio*, -*sio*). In the Rare Classical group the following are cited for classical authors and then for Late Latin: *adsumptio* (an assumption, receiving), *cognitio* (religious knowledge), *complexio* (a combination), *corruptio* (a corrupt condition), *creatio, functio, immoderatio, prolusio, properatio, redemptio* (bribing), *tuitio*. In the Early group several words are found in ante-classical writers and then in Late Latin: *ascensio, congressio, excidio, potatio* (in Cicero's fragments also), *receptio*. In the Silver category the following are found rarely in Silver writers and then in Late Latin: *congestio, constitutio* (creation, construction), *constructio, deploratio, discessio, dispositio* (plan, purpose), *infestatio, infusio, insultatio, interpolatio, mansio, minutio, observatio, operatio, ordinatio, portio, praedatio, praelatio, praesumptio, purificatio, refectio, relatio, suspectio, traditio.*

The third largest group of nouns in Hegesippus has the suffix -*tus* (-*sus*). Thirty nouns in this group are listed as Rare Classical, nine as Early, twelve as Poetic, and seventeen as Silver. In the Rare Classical list the following are noteworthy: *excursus* (a sally, charge), cited for Caesar and Tacitus, and *excursus* (an invasion of boats), found in the Bellum Alexandrinum; *obtentus,* quoted for Sallust and Aurelius Victor; *ostentus,* found in Sallust, Tacitus, and Gellius. Interesting words in the Early group are *sortitus,* used by Plautus, Cicero (1), and Vergil; *suspiritus,* found in Plautus, Cicero Ep. (1), Livy, and Apuleius. Nouns which are found rarely in Silver writers and then in Late Latin are *ambitus* (parade, pomp), *ausus* (a bold deed), *contuitus, defectus* (end), *fotus, ingressus, promissus.*

A rather small group of eight nouns has the suffix -*us*, of which three are Rare Classical, three Early, and two Poetic. No Silver words with this suffix have been noted. All these words seem to be popular with the poets, especially with Vergil and Ovid.

One Poetic word, *mensura,* is cited with the suffix -*sura.*

One Silver word, *fultura,* has the suffix -*tura.*

Twenty-nine nouns ending in -*ia* are nearly evenly divided among the four categories: eight Rare Classical, seven Early, five Poetic, and nine Silver nouns. In the Rare Classical group *distantia* (difference, diversity) is cited once for Cicero, also for Lucretius and Quintilian, and then for Late Latin; *prosapia*, an archaic word, is cited once each for Cicero, Sallust, Quintilian, and Suetonius, and frequently for Late Latin. In the Early list *fraudulentia* is noted only for Plautus and then often in Late Latin. Of the Silver words *affluentia, eminentia,* and *versutia* are rare in Silver Latin, but are found also in Late Latin.

Thirty-nine nouns appear with the suffix *-a*. The Rare Classical group lays claim to twelve, the Early to seven, the Poetic to fourteen, and the Silver to six. In the Rare Classical list *aerumna,* considered archaic by Cicero, is used by Cicero (20), Sallust, Livy, and Seneca the philosopher, and is very frequent from Apuleius on, especially in our author. In the Early list *adorea* is cited for Plautus, Horace, Fronto, and Late Latin. Among the Poetic words *umbra* (a tree) is found only in Vergil and our author. Interesting words in the Silver group are *arbitra* (a female judge), found in Seneca's Epistles and in Late Latin; *favillae* (plur.), quoted for Statius and Late Latin; *manubiae* (plur.), cited only for Suetonius; and *noxa,* found only in Livy.

Nouns with the suffix *-men* number fifteen. No noun with this suffix appears in the Rare Classical group, while three for the Early, ten for the Poetic, and two for the Silver are recorded. In the Early group one noun, *flamen,* is quoted for Cicero's poetry. Of the Poetic words *germen, moderamen,* and *semen* are cited for Ovid and Late Latin, while *munimen* is cited for both Vergil and Ovid and then Late Latin. Of the two Silver nouns *spiramen* is quoted for Statius and Late Latin.

The later suffix *-mentum* is more frequent than the earlier suffix *-men.* Twenty-five nouns have the ending *-mentum,* of which five are Rare Classical, seven Early, five Poetic, and eight Silver. In the Rare Classical group *allevamentum* is most interesting. It is found once in Cicero and then in Ambrose. Two words in the Early group attract attention—*deliramentum,* quoted for Plautus, Pliny the Elder, Fronto, and Late Latin; *operimentum,* found in Cato, Cicero (1), Sallust's fragments, Pliny the Elder, and Ambrose. One of the Poetic words, *temptamentum,* is found in Vergil, Ovid, Tacitus, and Late Latin. Five of the Silver words, while rare in Silver Latin, are found also in Late Latin —

indumentum, inquinamentum, integumentum, munimentum, and *tutamentum.*

An apparently frequent suffix in Latin is *-ium.* Forty-three nouns have been noted with this suffix, of which number fourteen are Rare Classical, six Early, eleven Poetic, and twelve Silver. Of the Rare Classical words *excidium* is very popular with our author, being used forty-seven times. Among the Early words *magisterium* is cited for Plautus, Tibullus, Celsus, and Late Latin; *pretium* (a penalty), for Livius Andronicus, Plautus, Terence, Horace, and our author. Of the Poetic words *ministerium* (ministry, office) is most popular with Hegesippus, appearing at least twenty-five times. The word *palatium* is cited only for Ovid and then for Late Latin. A very popular Silver word with our author is *consortium,* being cited twenty-one times. Two rare Silver words are *ingenium* (an artifice) found in Pliny the Younger, and *mancipium* (a female slave) found in Livy.

The suffix *-or* contributes fourteen nouns to this section. Five of these are Rare Classical, two Early, and seven Poetic. No Silver words with this suffix have been recorded. This is evidently an early suffix which maintained its place during the classical period, but gradually lost its influence, for no new formations have been noted in Hegesippus for Silver and Late Latin.

The suffix *-culum* is found in all periods of Latin. For this section it has been noted ten times—three times for Rare Classical, twice for Early, once for Poetic, and four times for Silver. Among the Rare Classical words *novacula* with the feminine suffix must be noted. Especially interesting are two Silver words which are found rarely in Silver Latin, but more often in Late Latin — *miraculum* (admiration) and *obstaculum.* The word *miraculum* in the sense of " wonderfulness " is cited for Livy only and then our author.

A suffix which was popular in Early Latin, but which lost its influence in Silver and Late Latin, is *-bulum.* Only three instances of its use in our author have been noted — *latibulum* used by Cicero (1) and Apuleius; *conciliabulum* found in Plautus, Fronto, and Late Latin; and *pabulum* (food for men) cited for Lucretius, Ovid, Valerius Flaccus, and Statius.

Sixteen nouns with the suffix *-um* have been listed, of which seven are Rare Classical, five Early, and four Poetic. No Silver nouns with this suffix have been noted. In the Rare Classical category *castrum* (a fortress) is cited for Nepos and then for Late Latin. Of the Early words *vadum* (security, guarantee, safety) is found only in Plautus and Terence.

Of the eleven nouns ending in the archaic suffix *-tudo* four are listed as Rare Classical, three as Early, and four as Silver. None have been noted as Poetic. Of the four Rare Classical words *beatitudo* is cited first by Cicero, Nat. deor. 1, 95. Of the Early nouns with this suffix *lenitudo* is found in Pacuvius, Turpilius, twice in Cicero, and then in Late Latin, while *maestitudo* is used by Plautus and Accius and then in Late Latin.

An archaic suffix which found its way into classical Latin is *-go*. Only five instances have been noted in Hegesippus, three of which are Rare Classical and two Silver. Peculiarly enough, no word with this archaic suffix has been found in our author for any Latin writer earlier than Varro. Of the three Rare Classical words *caligo* alone is used by Cicero (2).

Seven nouns appear with the suffix *-es*, of which two are Early and five Poetic. Of the Early words *acies* (a sharp point) is found first in Plautus, in Cicero (2), and then in poetry and Silver and Late Latin. Of the Poetic words *canities* is used in the sense both of " gray hair " and " old age " by the poets and other later writers.

A rather rare suffix and one that is considered colloquial is *-monia*. Only one Rare Classical instance, *alimonia*, is cited and that for Varro, Gellius, and Late Latin in general.

Another very rare suffix is *-ile*. Only two nouns have been noted with this suffix—*sedile* found in Varro, in the poets and Silver and Late Latin; and *cubile* cited in the fragments of some unknown tragedy, once by Cicero, then in the poets and Silver and Late Latin.

Eleven diminutives have been collected from Hegesippus for this section. Three of these are Rare Classical, four Early, and four Silver. The suffix *-ulus* is cited once, the corresponding feminine *-ula* (*-ola*) eight times, and the neuter *-ulum* once. One reduplicated diminutive, *mamilla*, has been noted with the feminine suffix *-illa*. Six of the eleven diminutives have lost their diminutive force—*fasciola, oppidulum, fidicula, loculus, mamilla, sportula.*

Nine Rare Classical compound nouns have been noted and none for any of the other categories. Of these nine, four—*antesignanus, commilito, praecordia, praeiudicium* — are compounded from a preposition and a noun; one—*anfractus*—from a prefix and a verb; two — *septentrio, triumvir*—from an adjective and a noun; two— *tubicen, vindemia*—from a noun and a verb.

Hegesippus displays a fondness for Greek nouns. They form the second largest category in the treatment of nouns and total seventy-two. Of this large number eighteen are Rare Classical, thirteen Early, twenty Poetic, and twenty-one Silver. In the Rare Classical list the following are interesting: *chiliarchus* found in Nepos and Late Latin; *hydria* cited for Cicero (4), Vitruvius, and Late Latin; *machina* cited for Sallust and others, and appearing in Hegesippus fourteen times; *peripetasma* found only in Cicero and Ambrose; *scaena* (a pretext) cited for Caelius in Cicero, Tacitus, and Late Latin. Noteworthy words in the Early group are *diplois, hippodromus, petra,* and *platea,* which occur rarely in the language. Among the Poetic words *cyparissus, hydrops, murex, phalanx, scaena* (field of action), *spelaeum, terebinthus,* and *zephyrus* are rather rare words. Silver Greek words which appear infrequently in the Silver writers, but commonly enough in Late writers, are *aroma* (spice, condiment), *cinnamomum, coccum, colon* (a disease of the colon), *cypros, dactylus, hymnus, lepra, phantasma, thronus, thymiama.* In the Silver group *hypogeum,* which is cited rarely for Vitruvius, Petronius, and the C. I. L., is found in Hegesippus five times.

In this long list of nouns only one hybrid, *ballista* (from βάλλω), has been noted. It is found in Plautus, Cicero (1), Ovid, Caesar, and frequently in the other historians.

Eighty-eight nouns which could not be classified according to any of the preceding categories have been collected into a miscellaneous list. Eighteen of these miscellaneous nouns are Rare Classical, twenty-six Early, thirty-three Poetic, and eleven Silver. Of the Rare Classical words *apex* (the highest honor, dignity) is cited once for Cicero and then for Tertullian and Late Latin. Among the miscellaneous Poetic words *limes* (the channel of a river), *mephitis, moenia, moles* (great bulk), *sucus* (a drug), *torus* (a bed, in general) appear to be rare words. An interesting point in this group is the singular use of *pignus* in the meaning of "a child," which occurs in Hegesippus at least thirteen times and which has been noted also for Ambrose and Jerome. Among the interesting Silver words are the indeclinable noun *instar* found in Livy and Gellius; *limes* (a frontier boundary wall) cited for Velleius and Tacitus; *palus* (a lake) found in Mela and Pliny the Elder.

B. ADJECTIVES

1. Adjectives in -*bilis*.[1]

a) *exitiabilis*, destructive, fatal (Cic. ep. (1); Verg.; Ov.; Liv.; Vell.; Tac.), 5, 15.

c) *formidabilis*, formidable, terrible (Ov.; Sen. phil.; Stat.; Gell.; Apul.; Tert.; Amm.; Ambros.; et al), 1, 12, 3; 1, 32, 6; 2, 18; 5, 46. — *lacrimabilis*, lamentable (Verg.; Ov.; Arnob.; Ambros.; Salv.; Eutr.; Aur. Vict.), 5, 18, 2; 5, 24, 2. — *venerabilis*, venerable, worthy of respect (Verg.; Liv.; Val. Max.; Quint.; Tac.; Apul.; Eutr.; Ambros.), 2, 1, 2; 5, 53, 1.

d) *exsecrabilis*, detestable (Liv.; Plin. mai.; Eutr.), 1, 44, 8; 5, 24, 4; 5, 41. — *medicabilis*, medicinal, curative (Colum.; Val. Fl.; Pallad.), 1, 45, 9. — *navigabilis*, navigable (Liv.; Sen. phil.; Colum.; Mela; Tac.), 4, 27.

2. Adjectives in -*ilis*.

a) *sterilis*, unproductive, unfruitful (Varr.; Verg.; Ov.; Catull.; Sen. rhet.; Plin. mai.; Iuv.; Tac.; Apic.; Aug.), 4, 16, 2; 4, 17. — *utensilis*, useful (Varr.; Aug.), 2, 15, 8. — *virilis*, male, masculine (Varr.; Sall. fr.; Nep.; Lucr.; Ov.; Liv.; Colum.; Vitr.; Sen. phil.; Fronto), 1, 22, 1; 3, 13.

b) *herilis*, belonging to a master or mistress (Plaut.; Ter.; Afran. fr.; Varr. fr.; Verg.; Hor.; Ov.; Val. Fl.; Ambros.), 1, 15, 2; 3, 17.

---

[1] For further examples of adjectives in -*bilis*, cf. the list under "Compound Adjectives."

7

3. Adjectives in -*alis*.

a) *coniugalis*, coniugal, pertaining to marriage (Varr.; Val. Max.; Tac.; Carm. Epigr.; Tert.; Pervig. Ven.; Iul. Val.; Arnob.; and Late), 5, 53, 1. — *dotalis*, belonging to a dowry (Cic. ep. (1); Hor.; Liv.; Ict.; Schol. Iuv.), 5, 53, 1. — *genitalis*, generative, genital (Varr. fr. apud Gell.; Lucr.; Verg.; Ov.; Colum.; Tert.; Apul.; Ambros.; et al), 3, 12, 2. — *muralis*, belonging to a wall, mural (Caes.; Verg.; Liv.; Cels.; Lucr.; Gell.), 3, 3, 4; 5, 20, 2 (bis); 5, 21, 1; 5, 26, 2; 5, 26, 3; 5, 29; 5, 52, 2 (bis); 5, 53, 1. — *quinquennalis*, quinquennial, every five years (Cic. (1); Plin. min.; Suet.; Vulg.), 1, 35, 2. — *septentrionalis*, northern (Varr.; Vitr.; Sen. phil.; Colum.; Lact.; Isid.), 2, 9; 2, 15, 4; 3, 5, 2; 4, 16, 2 (bis); 4, 27 (bis); 5, 12 (bis); 5, 38; 5, 39, 1.

c) *feralis*, deadly, dangerous, cruel (Verg.; Ov.; Sen. rhet.; Lucan.; Stat.; Plin. mai.; Sen. phil.; Silver and Late (Ambros.)), 1, 43, 5; 1, 45, 2; 1, 45, 10; 3, 2; 3, 15, 1; 5, 18, 2. — *fluvialis*, pertaining to a river (Verg.; Ov.; Sen. phil.; Colum.; Sil.; Tac.; Apul.; Amm.; Ambros.; et al), 3, 26, 1. — *genitalis*, productive, prolific (of things) (Lucr.; Verg.; Ov.; Colum.; Plin. mai.; Sil.; Tert.; et al), 3, 26, 2; 4, 16, 2; 4, 17. — *glacialis*, icy (Verg.; Ov.; Val. Max.; Colum.; Plin. mai.; Iuv.; Aug.), 1, 30, 6. — *letalis*, mortal, fatal (Lucr.; Verg.; Scrib.; Plin. mai.; Suet.; Iul. Val.; Amm.; et al), 1, 27; 5, 19; 5, 53, 1.

d) *aequalis*, drawn, equal (of a battle) (Sil.; Mart.; Iord.), 4, 23, 1. — *coniugalis*, pertaining to a wife or husband (Val. Max.; Colum.; Apul.; Firm.; Serv.; Ambros.; Aug.), 1, 37, 5; 1, 37, 7; 2, 4; 5, 16. — *corporalis*, corporeal, bodily (Sen. phil.; Ps. Quint.; Char.; Papin.; Iavol.; Ulp.; Apul.; and especially in Late Latin), 5, 53, 1. — *genitalis*, native, pertaining to place of birth or origin (Vell.; Iuvenc.; Vopisc.; Iul. Val.; Ambros.; and Late), 5, 25, 2. — *novercalis*, belonging to a step-mother (Stat.; Iuv.; Tac.), 1, 36, 1. — *obsidialis*, belonging to a siege (Liv.; Itin. Alex.), 5, 20, 2. — *parricidalis*,[2] parricidal, murderous (Petron.; Flor.; Ps. Quint.; Iust.; Lampr.; Sol.), 1, 2; 1, 6, 2; 1, 8; 1, 40, 9 (bis);

---

[2] The form *parricidialis* is cited for Ambros. Off. 3, 118; Ambros. Cain et Abel, 1, 2, 5; C.I.L. 3, 427.

1, 40, 10; 1, 41, 3; 1, 43, 3; 1, 44, 3; 1, 44, 5; 1, 44, 7; 1, 45, 1;
2, 12, 1; 3, 1, 1; 4, 7; 5, 18, 1; 5, 22, 1; 5, 22, 2; 5, 41 (bis);
5, 53, 1. — *principalis*, imperial (Plin. min.; Suet.; Hier.), 4, 21.
— *sacerdotalis*, sacerdotal, of priestly rank (Vell.; Plin. min.;
Tert.; Ambros.; Hier.; Rufin.; et al), 1, 17, 1; 1, 36, 2; 4, 6, 4;
4, 6, 5 (ter); 5, 2 (bis); 5, 9, 4; 5, 16; 5, 33, 1; 5, 48.

4. Adjectives in *-aris*.

b) *proeliaris*, belonging to a battle (Plaut.; Apul.; Ambros.;
Paul. ex Fest.; Macr.), 1, 14, 2; 3, 6, 2; 5, 5; 5, 7, 2.

d) *familiaris*, customary, familiar, habitual (Vell.; Curt.; Sen.
rhet.; Colum.; Plin. mai.; Mart.; Plin. min.; Fronto; Tert.;
Arnob.; et al), 1, 9, 3; 1, 41, 2; 5, 50.

5. Adjectives in *-arius*.

a) *compendiarius*, short, compendious (Varr.; Cic. (1); Sen.
phil.; Petron.; Paul. ex Fest.; Ambros.), 1, 22, 2.— *transversarius*, cross-, lying across (Caes.; Vitr.), 1, 30, 9. — *tributarius*,
belonging to tribute (Cic. (1); Plin. mai.; Suet.; Iust.; Gaius;
Vulg.; Aug.), 2, 9, 3. — *vicarius*, vicarious (Cic. (1); Sen. rhet.;
Ps. Quint.; Hyg.), 3, 17.

6. Adjectives in *-orius*.

b) *piscatorius*, belonging to a fisherman, fishing- (Afran. fr.;
Caes.; Liv.; Petron.; Plin. mai.; Plin. min.; Iust.; Fest.; Liv.
epit.; Porphyr.), 3, 3, 6. — *praedatorius*, plundering, predatory
(Plaut.; Sall.; Liv.; Amm.), 1, 26, 1; 3, 22, 1; 4, 4, 3.

d) *bellatorius*, warlike, martial (Plin. ep.; Amm.), 3, 3, 4.

7. Adjectives in *-ius*.

a) *noxius*, harmful, injurious (Cic. (1); Verg.; Ov.; Sen.
phil.; Colum.; Plin. mai.; Hier.), 1, 39; 1, 44, 5; 5, 25, 2; —
guilty, culpable (Sall.; Ov.; Liv.; Sen. phil.; Tac.; Ulp.), 1, 44,
8; 4, 29, 2.

c) *ebrius*, intoxicated, sated, filled (Catull.; Lucr.; Hor.; Plin.
mai.; Vulg.), 1, 32, 2. — *nescius*, incapable, not able (Verg.;
Hor.; Ov.; Quint.; Tac.), 3, 26, 2.

8. Adjectives in *-ivus*.

a) *adoptivus*, adoptive (Cic. (1); Scip. min.; Vell.; Ov.; Sen. phil.; Tac.; Suet.; Ict.; and Late), 1, 27; 1, 33, 1.

c) *insitivus*, ingrafted (Hor. epod. 2, 19), 3, 6, 3; 3, 6, 4. — *recidivus*, renewed (Verg.; Cels.; Mela; Plin. mai.; Sil.), 1, 22, 3; 3, 26, 4.

9. Adjectives in *-osus*.

a) *nemorosus*, full of woods, woody (Sall. fr.; Verg.; Plin. mai.), 3, 6, 4. — *tenebrosus*, dark, gloomy (Cic. fr. (1); Verg.; Ov.; Tert.; Ambros.; Hier.; Vulg.; Aug.; Pelagon.), 5, 29. — *vadosus*, shallow (Caes.; Verg.; Liv.; Sen. rhet.; Lucan.; Sol.), 2, 9; 4, 15, 2.

b) *famosus*, infamous, notorious (Plaut.; Cato; Lucil.; Cic. (2); Sall.; Hor.; Ov.; Liv.; Val. Max.; Tac.; Gell.; Apul.; and Late), 2, 4. — *harenosus*, sandy, full of sand (Cato; Sall.; Verg.; Colum.; Sen. rhet.; Mela; Plin. mai.; Ambros.), 3, 26, 1; 4, 15, 2. — *herbosus*, grassy (Cato; Verg.; Hor.; Ov.), 3, 6, 2. — *meticulosus*, fearful, timid (Plaut.; Apul.; Ulp.; Lact.; Ambros.; Aug.), 3, 8, 3; 5, 53, 1.

c) *clivosus*, hilly, steep (Verg.; Ov.; Colum.; Iuv.; Pallad.; Veget.; Amm.; Prud.; Avit.), 4, 1, 1. — *fragosus*, crashing, roaring, rushing (Verg.; Ov.; Val. Fl.; Iuvenc.; Auson.; Ambros.; Prud.; Aug.; et al), 1, 30, 9. — *lucrosus*, gainful, profitable (Ov.; Plin. mai.; Tac.; Hier.; Ennod.; Isid.), 5, 24, 3. — *nodosus*, knotty (Hor.; Ov.; Sen. phil.; Curt.), 3, 11, 1. — *saxosus*, rocky, stony (Verg.; Colum.), 1, 32, 4; 3, 9, 1; 3, 20, 2.

d) *incuriosus*, careless, indifferent (Tac.; Plin. min.; Suet.; Apul.), 4, 2; 5, 26, 2. — *numerosus*, numerous (Colum.; Plin. mai.; Quint.; Tac.; Plin. min.; Eutr.), 1, 36, 2. — *otiosus*, useless, purposeless (Quint.; Gell.; Min. Fel.; Lact.), 5, 9, 2. — *speciosus*, important, imposing (Liv.; Vell.; Val. Max.; Tac.), 5, 2.

10. Adjectives in *-eus*.

a) *femineus*, feminine, belonging to a woman (Cic. (1); Verg.;

Ov.; Sen. phil.; Manil.; Lucan.; Plin. mai.; Silver and Late), .
1, 12, 2; 1, 17, 3; 1, 32, 1; — unmanly, womanish (Varr.; Ov.;
Manil.; Plin. mai.; Sil.; Stat.; Mart.; Quint.; Plin. min.; Gell.;
Apul.; et al), 3, 17. — *lineus*, linen, made of linen (Cic. ep. (1);
Verg.; Colum.; Cels.; Plin. mai.; Curt.; Tac.; and Eccl.), 4, 17;
5, 9, 3.

b) *ferreus*, made of iron (Plaut.; Enn.; Cato; Varr.; Caes.;
Sall.; Lucr.; Ov.; Verg.; Liv.; Silver and Late), 4, 16, 2; 5, 50.
—*scrupeus*, sharp, rough, steep, rugged (Enn. fr.; Verg.; Val.
Fl.; Ambros.), 1, 30, 9; 4, 27.

c) *aequoreus*, pertaining to the sea (Verg.; Culex; Ciris;
Priap.; Prop.; Ov.; Silver Poetry; used in fourth century by
prose writers: Auson.; Amm.; Paul. Nol.; Ambros.; et al), 5,
41; 5, 46. — *funereus*, funereal (Verg.; Ov.; Sen. poet.; Lucan.;
Val. Fl.; Sil.; Auson.; Serv.; and Late), 5, 44, 1. — *lacteus*, full
of milk (Verg.), 4, 1, 2.

d) *niveus*, clear (of water), limpid (Sen. poet.; Mart.), 3, 6, 3.

11. Adjectives in *-icus*.

a) *immodicus*, immoderate, unrestrained (Sall. fr.; Ov.; Liv.;
Vell.; Colum.; Sen. rhet.; Sen. phil.; Sil.; Quint.; Tac.; Plin.
min.; et al (Ambros.)), 1, 15, 2; 3, 3, 2; 4, 16, 2; 4, 22, 1; 5,
19. — *pacificus*, peaceable, pacific (Cic. ep. (1); Mart.; Claud.;
Ambros.; Hier.; Vulg.), 2, 11, 3.

b) *barbaricus*, foreign, i. e., non-Greek, non-Roman (Enn.;
Cic. (2); Lucr.; Verg.; Ov.; Liv.; Val. Fl.; Sen. phil.; Plin.
mai.; Sil.; Lucan.; Gell.; Apul.; et al), 1, 29, 9; 5, 24, 3; 5, 24,
4; 5, 31. — *hosticus*, hostile, belonging to an enemy (Plaut.;
Varr. fr.; Hor.; Ov.; Liv.; Hyg.), 5, 18, 3.

c) *classicus*, pertaining to a fleet of ships (Prop.; Liv.; Vell.;
Val. Max.; Tac.; Claud.; Beda), 3, 23, 1. — *magicus*, magic,
magical (Verg.; Hor.; Tibull.; Ov.; Colum.; Plin. mai.; Lucan.;
Tac.; Apul.; Lact.; Vulg.; Aug.), 1, 38, 5; 2, 7, 1.

d) *aulicus*, pertaining to a royal palace (Suet.; Tert.; Paneg.;
Spart.; Itin. Alex.; Ambros.; and Late), 1, 8; 1, 23, 3; 1, 35, 4;
1, 44, 2.

12. Adjectives in *-idus*.

a) *madidus*, drenched, wet (Cic. ep. (1); Ov.; Plin. mai.; Mart.; Apul.), 5, 34. — *rigidus*, inflexible, hard (fig.) (Cic. (1); Hor.; Ov.; Liv.; Sen. phil.; Plin. min.; Arnob.), 5, 16.

b) *candidus*, white, dazzling white (Plaut.; Enn.; Acc.; Cato; Varr.; Lucr.; Poetical, Silver and Late), 5, 49, 3. — *validus*, strong, powerful, vigorous (Plaut.; Ter.; Cic. (3); Lucr.; Verg.; Ov.; Liv.; Silver and Late), 1, 1, 9; 1, 13, 1; 1, 16, 2; 1, 16, 3; 1, 24, 1; 1, 24, 2; 1, 32, 4; 2, 9 (ter); 2, 15, 4; 3, 1, 3; 3, 4, 1 (bis); 3, 4, 3; 3, 8, 2; 3, 11, 1 (bis); 3, 12, 3; 3, 22, 1; 3, 23, 1; 3, 24; 3, 26, 4; 4, 9, 5; 4, 17; 4, 23, 1; 4, 25, 2; 4, 26, 1; 4, 29, 2 (bis); 4, 31; 5, 15; 5, 16 (ter); 5, 18, 2; 5, 26, 3; 5, 27; 5, 42, 1; 5, 49, 1; 5, 49, 4; — strong, mighty, effective (transf. sense) (Plaut.; Cic. fr. (1); Sall.; Ov.; Liv.; Quint.; Tac.; Plin. min.; Ambros.), 1, 38, 5; 1, 42, 4; 1, 44, 8; 2, 1, 2; 2, 1, 3; 3, 17; 4, 1, 5; 5, 7, 1.

c) *luridus*, ghastly, wan (Hor.; Ov.; Sen. phil.; Colum.; Plin. ep.), 5, 21, 3. — *pavidus*, fearful, alarmed (Verg.; Hor.; Ov.; Liv.; Sen. phil.; Plin. mai.; Sil.; Aur. Vict.), 1, 40, 8; 3, 17. — *rabidus*, mad, savage (of animals) (Lucr.; Verg.; Hor.; Ov.; Sen. phil.; Plin. mai.; Iust.; Amm.), 5, 39, 2. — *rigidus*, rocky, hard, rough (Ov.), 3, 6, 3. — *vividus*, vigorous, full of life (Lucr.; Verg.; Liv.; Val. Max.; Sen. rhet.; Mart.; Tac.; Ambros.), 1, 43, 3.

d) *tabidus*, wasting away (Liv.; Sen. poet.; Suet.; Aug.), 5, 18, 2; 5, 49, 2.

13. Adjectives in *-inus*.

a) *genuinus*, innate, native, natural (Cic. (1); Flor.; Ulp.; Gell.; Apul.; Chalc.; Amm.), 3, 1, 2.

b) *crastinus*, of or belonging to tomorrow (Plaut.; Cic. ep. (1); Verg.; Hor.; Liv.; Silver and Late), 1, 44, 5. — *peregrinus*, foreign (Plaut.; Cic. (4); Hor.; Ov.; Liv.; Phaedr.; Colum.; Val. Max.; Plin. mai.; Iuv.), 1, 9, 3; 1, 12, 3; 5, 16.

c) *vicinus*, neighboring (Verg.; Hor.; Tibull.; Ov.; Liv.; Lucan.; Macr.), 1, 1, 6.

d) *trinus*, threefold, triple (Stat.; Auson.; Prud.; Sulp. Sev.; Aug.; Chalc.; Th. Prisc.; Venant.; Avit.), 4, 1, 4; 4, 32; 5, 1, 3.

14. Adjectives in -*anus*.

a) *vicanus*, of or belonging to a village (Cic. (2)), 4, 6, 5.

d) *meridianus*, southern (Liv.; Sen. phil.; Vitr.; Plin. mai.; Lact.; Amm.), 2, 9; 4, 16, 2. — *praetorianus*, praetorian, belonging to the imperial guard (Tac.; Suet.; Ict.), 4, 26, 1. — *pridianus*, of the day before (Plin. mai.; Suet.; Apul.; Aug.), 4, 29, 2.

15. Adjectives in -*us*.

a) *caecus*, hidden, concealed (Cic. (1); Lucr. (saepe); Verg. (saepe); Prop.; Ov.; Manil.; Colum.; Silver and Late), 2, 6, 3; 4, 27. — *cruentus*, cruel (Cic. (2); Sall.; Verg.; Ov.; Manil.; Silver and Late), 1, 44, 7. — *decorus*, beautiful (Cic. (1); Sall.; Verg.; Hor.; Ov.; Silver and Late), 5, 53, 1. — *internus*, internal (Sall. fr.; Ov.; Sen. phil.; Plin. mai.; Tac.; Ambros.), 1, 25, 2; 4, 6, 7. — *mundus*, fine, genteel, nice (Cic. (2); Prop.; Liv.), 5, 22. — *nefastus*, forbidden, contrary to religion (Cic. (1); Plin. min.), 2, 5, 3. — *prodigus*, profuse, prodigal (Cic. ep. (1); Hor.; Vell.; Gell.), 1, 40, 1; 5, 42, 6. — *securus*, sure, unconcerned, untroubled (Cic. (2); Verg.; Hor.; Ov.; Plin. mai.; Quint.; Tac.; Plin. min.; Itin. Alex.; Apul.; and Late), 1, 21, 3, 1, 38, 2; 3, 4, 3; 3, 15, 2; 5, 17; 5, 28; 5, 52, 2. — *sedulus*, solicitous (Cic. (1); Hor.; Ov.; Sen. phil.), 1, 5.

b) *amarus*, bitter (Plaut.; Enn.; Cato; Varr.; Lucr.; Verg.; Ov.; Plin. mai. (saepe); Silver and Late), 4, 17. — *densus*, crowded together, set close (Cato; Cic. poet. (2); Caes.; Catull.; Verg.; Ov.; Vitr.; Silver and Late), 5, 35, 1. — *funestus*, filled with misfortune or grief (Acc.; Cic. (1); Varr.; Catull.; Prop.; Ov.; Liv.; Silver and Late), 1, 37, 2. — *largus*, abounding in (Plaut.; Verg.; Lucan.; Sil.), 2, 13, 5. — *mundus*, clean (Ter.; Hor.; Colum.; Gell.), 5, 41. — *properus*, hasty, speedy (Cato fr.; Verg.; Ov.; Tac.), 2, 5, 4; 2, 9; 5, 7, 1; 5, 7, 2. — *supernus*, celestial, supernal (Sisenn. fr.; Hor.; Ov.; Mela; Lucan.; Plin. mai.; Gell.; Ambros.), 3, 2; 5, 22; 5, 27.

c) *anhelus*, panting, puffing, attended with short breath (Lucr.;

Verg.; Ov.; Lucan.; Plin. mai.; Val. Fl.; Sil.; Stat.; Ambros.; et al), 5, 27; 5, 53, 1. — *conspicuus*, visible (Hor.; Ov.; Cels.; Phaedr.; Sen. phil.; Curt.; Plin. mai.; Frontin.; Tac.; Amm.), 3, 3, 6; 3, 11, 3; 5, 29. — *indigus*, needing, in want (Lucr.; Verg.; Ov.; Lucan.; Stat.; Tac.), 3, 4, 1; 4, 27. — *inquietus*, restless (Hor.; Liv.; Sen. phil.; Plin. min.; Suet.; Iust.; Amm.; Vopisc.; Aug.), 2, 1, 3; 2, 9; 3, 20, 2; 4, 16, 1; 4, 27. — *laevus*, awkward, stupid, foolish (Verg.; Hor.; Pers.), 5, 42, 5. — *laxus*, loose, yielding, relaxed (Verg.; Hor.; Ov.; Vitr.; Tibull.; Sen. poet.; Hier.), 3, 11, 2. — *lentus*, lasting or continuing long (Tibull.; Ov.; Cels.; Sen. phil.; Val. Fl.; Amm.), 1, 1, 9. — *obscurus*, turbid (of water) (Ov.), 4, 18. — *quotus*, how great, i. e., how very small (Ov.), 5, 46. — *siccus*, dry (Verg.; Prop.; Hor.; Ov.; Tibull.; Sen. phil.; Lucan.; Plin. mai.; Colum.; Mart.; Sil.), 5, 41.

d) *profluus*, flowing, flowing forth (Colum.; Sid.; Ven. Fort.), 2, 9; 3, 12, 3. — *refugus*, fleeing away (Tac.), 2, 2, 4.

16. Adjectives in -*ax*.

a) *efficax*, effectual, efficacious (Cael. in Cic. ep. (1); Hor.; Liv.; Cels.; Curt.; Vell.; Mela; Tac.; Plin. min.; Apul.; Treb. Poll.), 2, 3, 4; 3, 26, 3; 4, 10, 1.

b) *capax*, capacious, large (Trag. inc.; Varr.; Cic. (1); Ov. (saepe); Lucan.; Plin. mai. (saepe); Colum.; Sil.; Stat.; Tac.; and Late), 4, 27. — *ferax*, fertile, abounding in, productive of (Plaut.; Cato; Varr.; Cic. (3); Caes.; Lucr.; Hor.; Ov.; Colum.; Silver and Late), 3, 6, 3; 4, 18. — *perspicax*, sharp-sighted, perspicacious (Ter.; Trag. inc. apud Cic.; Cic. (1); Apul.; Aug.), 5, 30. — *tenax*, niggardly, stingy, close-fisted (Plaut.; Cic. (1); Ov.; Liv.; Sen. phil.; Suet.; Lact.), 1, 29, 9.

17. Adjectives in -*is*.

c) *pinguis*, fertile, productive (Verg.; Hor.; Colum.; Sen. phil.), 3, 6, 2; 4, 17.

18. Adjectives in -*ensis*.

d) *forensis*, foreign (Plin. mai.; Apul.; Ambros.; Ps. Aug.; Greg. M.), 5, 5.

19. Diminutives.

b) *adulescentulus*, quite young (Plaut.; Ambros.), 1, 36, 2. — *parvulus*, young (Ter.; Cic. (1); Caes.; Nep.; Verg.; Val. Max.; Iust.; Aug.), 5, 53, 1.

c) *novellus*, new (Ov.; Liv.; Veget.; Arnob.; Ps. Cypr.; Hier.; Rufin.), 5, 22.

20. Greek Adjectives.

b) *aerius* (ἀέριος), pertaining to the air (Varr. At.; Cic. (2); Lucr.; Catull.; Hor.; Ov.; Poetical, Silver and Late), 5, 46. — *aetherius* (αἰθέριος), pertaining to the air (Varr. At.; Cic. (8); Lucr.; Poetical, Silver and Late), 5, 27; 5, 41.

c) *mysticus* (μυστικός), mystic, mystical (Verg.; Tibull.; Stat.; Mart.; Lact.; Amm.; Ambros.; Aug.; Vulg.), 1, 6, 4.

d) *arctous* (ἀρκτῷος), northern (Sen. poet.; Lucan.; Mart.; Mart. Cap.; Amm. (saepe); et al), 3, 26, 2.

21. Participles as Adjectives.

i. Present Participles.

a) *ardens*, burning (Cic. (1); Tubero; Ov.; Sen. phil.; Val. Max.; Plin. mai.; Tert.; Amm.), 5, 53, 1 (bis). — *candens*, glowing hot (Rhet. Her.; Cic. (2); Varr.; Lucr.; Verg.; Hor.; Ov.; Colum.; Cels.; Silver and Late), 3, 12, 3. — *furens*, angry (Cic.(2); Verg.; Hor.; Tibull.; Sen. phil.; Silver and Late), 1, 38, 5; 1, 40, 9; 4, 33; 5, 40. — *sequens*, following, next (Nep.; Hirt.; Bell. Hisp.; Liv.; Curt.; Plin. mai.; Tac.; Suet.; Eutr.; Ambros.), 1, 17, 2; 1, 22, 1; 1, 44, 6; 2, 15, 6; 3, 9, 4; 3, 15, 3; 4, 20; 4, 33; 5, 11, 1; 5, 16 (bis); 5, 39, 1; 5, 42, 5; 5, 52, 2.

b) *fervens*, hot, burning (Plaut.; Cato; Caecil.; Lucil.; Cic. (3); Varr.; Caes.; Lucr.; Ov.; Silver and Late), 2, 9; 3, 26, 2; 5, 27. — *fugitans*, fleeing, shunning (Ter.; Ambros. (11); Symm.), 2, 5, 3; 3, 6, 2. — *olens*, stinking, foul, rank (Plaut.; Verg.; Hor.; Ov.; Lucan.), 1, 35, 3. — *viridans*, green, verdant (Acc.; Lucr.; Catull.; Verg.; Plin. mai.; Apul.), 4, 16, 2; 4, 18; 5, 25, 2.

c) *indignans*, indignant (Ov.; Colum.), 1, 37, 2; 2, 18. — *nitens*, flourishing, blooming (Catull.; Verg.; Ov.; Gell.), 3, 6, 2. — *olens*, fragrant, sweet-smelling (Verg.; Ov.; Stat.), 5, 2. — *tepens*, warm (Verg.; Ov.; Plin. mai.), 4, 17. — *virens*, green, verdant (Hor.; Gell.; Itin. Alex.), 3, 19; 5, 18, 2; 5, 41.

ii. Past Participles.

a) *adiunctus*, close, neighboring (Cic. (3); Manil.; Cels.; Curt.; Plin. mai.; Sil.; Stat.; Ulp.; Dict.), 1, 41, 3. — *assuetus*, customary, accustomed (Cic. (3); Verg. (saepe); Ov. (saepe); Liv. (saepe); Silver and Late), 1, 17, 2; 1, 46, 2; 2, 13, 1; 4, 18; 5, 40; 5, 44, 1. — *attonitus*, astonished, terrified (Sall. fr.; Verg.; Tibull.; Hor.; Ov.; Liv.; Curt.; Tac.; Plin. min.; Silver and Late), 1, 41, 9. — *circumcisus*, steep, precipitous (Cic. (2); Caes.), 4, 1, 1. — *commotus*, angered, angry (Cic. ep. (1); Sen. phil.; Suet.; Gell.; Apul.; Itala; Amm.; Vulg.; et al), 5, 7, 1; 5, 18, 3; 5, 46. — *conspiratus*, agreeing, concordant, harmonious (Caes.; Sen. ep.; Suet.; Tert.; Amm.), 5, 6; 5, 10, 2. — *corruptus*, bad, corrupted (Sall.; Bell. Alex.; Hor.; Cels.; rare in Silver Latin; mostly used from Apul. on), 1, 37, 7; 4, 16, 2; 4, 17. — *cumulatus*, rich, ample (Cic. (2); Liv.; Silver and Late), 1, 36, 2. — *diffusus*, wide, spread out (Cic. (1); Dirae; Manil.; Val. Max.; Vell.; Colum.; Silver and Late (Ambros.)), 2, 15, 7; 3, 6, 3; 3, 26, 1; 4, 16, 2. — *directus*, steep (Cic. (1); Caes.; Hirt.), 3, 20, 2; — straight (of a ship's course) (Bell. Alex.; Veget.; Cael. Aur.), 4, 27. — *elatus*, proud, elated (Caes.; Nep.; Amm.), 1, 21, 3. — *feriatus*, keeping holiday, festal (Varr.; Cic. (2); Fast.; Hor.; Sen. rhet.; Sen. phil.; Silver and Late (Ambros.)), 1, 1, 7; 4, 4, 3; 5, 53, 1. — *intentus*, intent on, attentive to (Sall.; Liv.; Sen. phil.; Tac.; Flor.; Liv. epit.), 1, 30, 1; 1, 40, 8; 1, 43, 3; 2, 9; 3, 2; 4, 6, 11; 5, 24, 4. — *placitus*, pleasing, agreeable (Sall.; Verg.; Stat.; Iust.), 3, 17. — *praeruptus*, hasty, rash, precipitate (Cic. (1); Tac.), 1, 2; 1, 13, 2; 1, 36, 2; 1, 37, 5; 2, 10, 1; 2, 10, 2. — *provectus*, advanced (of time) (Cic. (3); Nep.; Liv.; Sen. phil.; Iul. Val.; Arnob.; Auson.; Pallad.), 1, 17, 3. — *situs*, situated, living (of persons) (Sall. fr.; Vell.; Curt.; Plin. mai.; Tac.; Apul.), 2, 10, 4; 2, 15, 1; 3, 1, 1; 4, 6, 7; 4, 9, 1; 4, 16, 2; 5, 4, 4; 5, 35, 2; 5, 38; 5, 53, 1.

b) *abstrusus*, hidden, concealed (Pacuv.; Acc.; Varr.; Cic. (6); Ov.; Lucan.; Vell.; Manil.; Stat.; Tert.; and Late), 5, 50. —

acceptus, pleasing, agreeable, acceptable (Plaut.; Cic. (5); Varr.;
Nep.; Sall.; Verg.; Ov.; Liv.; Silver and Late), 1, 12, 2; 1, 41,
4. — *concitus,* swift, rapid, speedy (Trag. inc.; Ov.; Sen. phil.;
Sil.; Apul.; Don.; Dict.; Paneg.; et al), 5, 28. — *consultus,* ex-
perienced, skillful (Cato; Cic. (2); Sall.; Hor.; Liv.; Silver and
Late), 1, 13, 1; 2, 9, 1; 5, 44, 1. — *depositus,* weak, infirm, worn-
out (Caecil.; Acc.; Lucil.; Verg.; Ov.; Sen. phil.; Homer.; Apul.;
Ambros.; Hier.; et al), 5, 24, 1; 5, 27. — *exercitus,* disciplined,
trained (Plaut.; Tac.; Claud.; Tert.), 2, 13, 2; 3, 6, 2; 4, 29, 2. —
feriatus, unoccupied, idle, free, disengaged (Plaut.; Novius; Varr.;
Cic. (2); Trebon.; Verg.; Sen. phil.; Stat.; Mart.; Plin. min.;
Gell.; Fronto; and Late especially), 4, 19; 5, 22; 5, 27. — *salsus,*
salty (Ter.; Bell. Alex.; Verg.; Cels.; Sen. phil.; Plin. mai.;
Mart.; Amm.), 4, 16, 2. — *suspectus,* suspicious, distrustful (Cato;
Tert.; Itala; Amm.; Ambros.; Rufin.; et al), 1, 41, 3; 1, 44, 3;
5, 6; 5, 21, 3; 5, 38.

c) *desuetus,* unaccustomed (Verg.; Liv.; Sen. phil.; Lucan.;
Stat.; Veget.; Claud.), 5, 24, 2 (bis). — *devotus,* devoted (Ov.;
Gratt.; Sen. phil.; Lucan.; Stat.; Suet.; Apul.; Ps. Quint.; Tert.;
and Late), 3, 16. — *expertus,* tried, proved (Verg.; Liv.; Vell.;
Tac.; Suet.; Iust.), 3, 3, 1. — *sacratus,* holy, sacred (Verg.; Ov.;
Val. Max.; Sen. phil.; Plin. mai.; Mart.; Ambros.), 1, 36, 2; 2,
5, 1; 2, 9; 5, 48. — *secretus,* secret, solitary, retired (Hor.; Sen.
phil.; Mart.; Tac.), 3, 17; — hidden, concealed (Verg.; Hor.; Ov.;
Liv.; Pers.; Lucan.; Petron.; Mart.; Tac.; Iul. Vict.), 5, 44, 1. —
solitus, wonted, accustomed, usual (Verg.; Ov.; Tibull.; Sen. rhet.;
Curt.; Sen. phil.; Val. Max.; Tac.; Plin. min.; Arnob.; Capit.),
1, 16, 6. — *succinctus,* prepared, equipped (Ov.; Quint.; Amm.;
Claud.), 5, 19.

d) *celebratus,* brilliant, pompous (Liv.; Suet.), 1, 6, 1. — *cir-
cumspectus,* wary, cautious (Sen. rhet.; Sen. phil.; Colum.; Quint.;
Suet.; Ps. Quint.; Fronto; Lact.; Zeno), 1, 44, 8. — *defunctus,*
dead (Curt.; Sen. phil.; Lucan.; Plin. mai.; Mart.; Stat.; Sil.;
Suet.; Gaius; Itala; and Late), 2, 9. — *deiectus,* humble, low (Sen.
phil.; Apul.; Ambros.; and Late), 1, 40, 3. — *eviratus,* unmanly,
effeminate (Mart.; Arnob.; Ambros.), 3, 1, 2. — *memoratus,* aforesaid, before-mentioned (Liv.; Plin. mai.; Gell.; Apul.; Amm.;
Aug.), 1, 13, 1; 1, 15, 3; 1, 29, 1; 1, 30, 1; 2, 13, 1; 2, 15, 3;

3, 3, 6; 3, 5, 2; 3, 19 (bis) ; 3, 26, 2; 4, 4, 2; 4, 15, 3; 4, 27;
5, 16 (bis) ; 5, 47, 1; 5, 50. — *praedictus*, before-mentioned, pre-
viously named (Liv.; Vell.; Plin. mai.; Quint.; Tac.), 1, 22, 1;
3, 20, 2; 4, 15, 2; 5, 51, 3. — *praeruptus*, extreme, critical (Vell.
2, 2, 3), 1, 24, 2; 2, 9; 3, 9, 2.

iii. Gerundives.

a) *miserandus*, worthy of pity (Cic. (3) ; Sall.; Verg.; Ov.;
Liv.), 1, 44, 7.

b) *pudendus*, disgraceful, shameful (Trag. inc. fr.; Cic. (1) ;
Verg.; Ov.; Quint.; Tac.; Suet.; Cl. Mam.; Lampr.), 5, 53, 1.

c) *reverendus*, awe-inspiring, venerable (Ov.; Iuv.; Gell.;
Spart.; Ambros.; Oros.), 4, 9, 5.

22. Compound Adjectives.

i. Adjectives compounded with a Preposition or Particle.

a) *devius*, erroneous, inconstant, inconsistent (Cic. (3) ; Sil.;
Apul.; Lact.; Arnob.; Ambros.; and Late), 2, 12, 1. — *immutilatus*,
not maimed, not mutilated (Sall. fr.), 1, 29, 7. — *importuosus*,
without a harbor (Sall.; Liv.; Plin. mai.; Tac.; Plin. min.), 1,
35, 4; 3, 20, 2 ; 4, 27. — *incautus*, dangerous, unguarded (Sall. fr.;
Lucr.; Liv.; Tac.), 1, 32, 6. — *incruentus*, bloodless, without blood-
shed (Sall.; Liv.; Curt.; Tac.), 4, 30; 5, 4, 3. — *infecundus*,
sterile, unfruitful (Sall.; Verg.; Ov.; Mela; Colum.; Ambros.;
Prud.), 3, 6, 3; 5, 16. — *infensus*, hostile, inimical (Cic. (4) ;
Verg.; Liv.; Tac.; Suet.; Aug.), 5, 53, 1. — *informis*, unformed
(Rhet. Her.; Liv.; Plin. mai.), 5, 50. — *inquies*, restless (Sall.;
Vell.; Tac.; Apul.), 4, 4, 1. — *intactus*, untouched, intact (Sall.;
Verg.; Hor.; Liv.; Quint.), 1, 17, 2; 1, 21, 2. — *intectus*, uncovered
(Sall. fr.; Sen. phil.; Tac.; Apul.; Amm.), 5, 4, 1; 5, 42, 5. —
intutus, defenceless, unguarded (Sall. fr.; Liv.; Tac.; Nazar.),
1, 14, 1; 1, 26, 3; 4, 16, 2. — *inviolatus*, inviolable (Caes.; Liv.),
1, 38, 5. — *invius*, impassable, without a road (Sall. fr.; Verg.;
Ov.; Liv.; Curt.; Sen. phil.; Eutr.), 1, 30, 9; 1, 32, 4; 2, 9; 3, 9, 1;
3, 23, 1; 4, 1, 1; 5, 15 (bis). — *nefandus*, abominable, execrable
(Cic. (3) ; Verg.; Liv.; Quint.; Ps. Quint.; Iust.), 5, 2; 5, 16. —
peridoneus, very well adapted, very fit (Sall. fr.; Caes.; Tac.;

Suet.; Apul.), 1, 30, 10. — *praeacutus*, sharpened, pointed (Sall.; Caes.; Ov.), 4, 18; 5, 21, 3; 5, 50. — *praeceps*, inclined, disposed (Sall.; Liv.; Tac.), 4, 6, 10; 5, 24, 3. — *praevius*, going before, leading the way (Cic. fr. (1); Ov.; Stat.; Auson.; Lact.; Amm.; Ambros.; et al), 4, 2. — *semirutus*, half-destroyed (Sall. fr.; Liv.; Tac.; Flor.; Amm.; Claud.), 5, 16; 5, 24, 1. — *semiustus*, half-burned (Cic. (1); Verg.; Ov.; Liv.; Vell.; Tac.; Suet.), 5, 42, 5. — *sublimis*, distinguished, eminent, noble (Varr.; Hor.; Ov.), 3, 2; 5, 38. — *suppar*, nearly equal (Cic. (1); Vell.; Auson.; Amm.; Ambros.; Serv.), 3, 26, 2; 5, 16.

b) *concavus*, hollow (Enn.?; Cato; Cic. (1); Lucr.; Verg.; Ov.; Sen. phil.; Mela; Val. Fl.; Apul.; Avien.), 5, 53, 1. — *congruus*, suitable (Plaut.; Apul.; Cypr. Gall.; Iren.; Itala; Veget.; Amm.; Ambros.; Hier.; et al), 1, 8; 1, 39. — *decrepitus*, very old, decrepit (Plaut.; Ter.; Val. Max.; Sen. phil.; Petron.; Apul.; Itala; Tert.; Lact.; Hier.; Aug.; et al), 1, 40, 7. — *impos*, not master of, without power over (Plaut.; Sen. phil.; Suet.; Fronto; Apul.; Lact.), 1, 37, 6; 5, 41. — *incanus*, quite gray, hoary (Plaut.; Verg.; Colum.; Suet.), 1, 43, 3. — *inclutus*, renowned, famous (Enn.; Cato; Cic. fr. (1); Sall. fr.; Lucr.; Verg.; Hor.; Liv.; Sen. poet.; Colum.; Sil.), 1, 38, 5; 1, 41, 9. — *incoctus*, uncooked, raw (Plaut.; Fab. Pict. apud Gell.; Marc. Emp.; Th. Prisc.), 5, 18, 1. — *innoxius*, innocent, blameless (Cato; Sall.; Liv.; Curt.; Tac.; Ambros.), 1, 41, 10; 2, 6, 4; 2, 8, 2; 3, 24; 4, 6, 2; 4, 7; 5, 22; 5, 45. — *innumerus*, countless, numberless (Plaut.; Lucr.; Verg.; Ov.; Plin. mai.; Tac.; Gell.; Auson.; Eutr.; Ambros.), 1, 1, 3; 1, 12, 2; 1, 31, 2; 2, 9; 5, 4, 4; 5, 22. — *insons*, guiltless, innocent (Plaut.; Sall. fr.; Verg.; Hor.; Liv.), 1, 45, 1; 2, 6, 4. —*obnoxius*, liable to punishment (Plaut.; Cic. ep.; Sall.; Ov.; Tibull.; Liv.; Ict.; Cod. Iust.), 3, 17; — servile, submissive (Plaut.; Sall.; Liv.; Tac.), 4, 20. — *pervius*, passable (Ter.; Cic. (1); Verg.; Ov.; Liv.; Plin. mai.; Mart.; Tac.; Sol.; Macr.), 4, 27. — *sublimis*, high, lofty (Plaut.; Ter.; Varr.; Catull.; Verg.; Hor.; Ov.; Liv.; Colum.; Tert.; Ambros.; Mart. Cap.), 2, 1, 2; 4, 1, 1; 5, 1, 4; 5, 15.

c) *accommodus*, suitable (Verg.; Stat.; Tert.; Cypr. Gall.; Sol.; Lampr.; Ambros.; Vopisc.), 1, 28, 7; 3, 20, 1; 4, 11. — *consors*, common, sharing (de rebus) (Lucr.; Verg.; Prop.; Manil.; Lucan.;

Tert.; Ter. Maur.; Chalc.; Ambros.; et al), 4, 2. — *conterminus,* neighboring, bordering on (Ov. (saepe); Lucan.; Plin. mai. (saepe); Mela; Stat.; Sil.; Tac.; Apul.; and Late), 4, 16, 2. — *degener,* ignoble, base (Verg.; Liv.; Lucan.; Sen. phil.; Stat.; Sil.; Tac.; and Late), 1, 31, 3; 5, 16; 5, 45; — unlike, different from (Ov.; Curt.; Sil.; Stat.; Plin. mai.; Tert.; and Late), 3, 17. — *efferus,* very wild, fierce (Lucr.; Verg.; Mela; Amm.), 1, 35, 4; 1, 41, 9. — *exanimis,* lifeless (Verg.; Hor.; Ov.; Liv.; Quint.; Tac.; Suet.; et al), 5, 2; 5, 21, 3. — *exsors,* deprived of (Verg.; Liv.; Curt.; Sen. phil.; Plin. mai.; Tac.; Ambros.; Vulg.), 1, 2; 1, 13, 3; 1, 15, 1; 1, 19, 4; 1, 41, 1; 2, 6, 1; 3, 12, 3; 3, 18, 2; 3, 26, 4; 5, 8, 1; 5, 24, 4; 5, 34; 5, 40. — *illacrimabilis,* unwept, unlamented (Hor. carm. 4, 9, 26), 1, 45, 10. — *immedicabilis,* incurable (Verg.; Ov.; Sil.; Hil.; Ambros.), 1, 45, 5. — *immitis,* severe, inexorable (Verg.; Ov.; Liv.; Sen. rhet.; Plin. mai.; Tac.; Suet.), 1, 40, 8; 2, 1, 1; 4, 23, 3; 5, 15; 5, 53, 1. — *immobilis,* unmoved, immovable (Verg.; Plin. mai.; Tac.; Lact.), 5, 16; 5, 44, 1. — *immunis,* free from, devoid of (Verg.; Ov.; Hor.; Vell.; Sen. phil.; Plin. mai.; Lact.; Sol.), 2, 14, 3; 3, 7; 3, 14; 5, 18, 3; 5, 28; 5, 50. — *impacatus,* not peaceable (Verg.; Sen. phil.; Stat.; Amm.; Claud.; Aug.), 3, 1, 2. — *impar,* unequal to, not a match for, inferior (Verg.; Hor.; Ov.; Liv.; Tac.; Suet.), Praef.; 1, 40, 3; 3, 8, 3; 5, 26, 2; 5, 28. — *impatiens,* impatient (Verg.; Ov.; Sen. phil.; Curt.; Tac.; Plin. min.; Suet.; Amm.; Hier.; Macr.), 1, 43, 6; 2, 9. — *impavidus,* fearless (Verg.; Hor.; Liv.; Sen. phil.), 3, 9, 3; 5, 27; 5, 53, 2. — *imperterritus,* undaunted (Verg.; Sil.; Ambros.; Greg. M.), 4, 1, 5; 5, 28. — *inaccessus,* inaccessible (Verg.; Plin. min.; Flor.; Tac.; Sol.; Ambros.; Vulg.), 5, 15; 5, 34. — *inassuetus,* unaccustomed (Ov.; Orat. imp. Claud.; Sil.; Sulp. Sev.), 4, 27.—*inconsolabilis,* inconsolable (Ov.; Amm.; Hier.; Ambros.), 2, 9. — *incredulus,*[3] incredulous (Hor.; Quint.; Ambros.; Vulg.), 1, 40, 8; 2, 12, 1. — *indebitus,* not due (Verg.; Ov.; Digest.; Aug.), 2, 1, 2. — *indefessus,* unwearied (Verg.; Ov.; Tac.; Plin. min.; Ambros.), 5, 44, 1. — *inevitabilis,* unavoidable, inevitable (Ov.; Sen. phil.; Tac.), 1, 41, 7. — *inexcusabilis,* inexcusable (Hor.; Ov.; Ict.; Chalc.; Ambros.; Aug.), 2, 1, 3. — *inex-*

[3] Used substantively in Heg. 5, 16.

pertus, unacquainted with (Hor.; Liv.; Tac.; Aug.), 4, 18; —
untried, unproved (Verg.; Curt.; Liv.; Stat.; Tac.; Plin. min.),
2, 9. — *inexpugnabilis,* impregnable (Ov.; Liv.; Curt.; Vell.; Sen.
phil.; Plin. mai.; Iust.), 5, 2; 5, 16. — *infaustus,* unfortunate,
unhappy (Verg.; Plin. mai.; Tac.), 1, 36, 1; 1, 40, 9. — *informis,*
unshapely, hideous, deformed (Verg.; Hor.; Tibull.; Sen. ep.;
Tac.), 3, 17; 4, 9, 4. — *iniussus,* unbidden, of one's own accord
(Verg.; Hor.), 3, 17; 5, 38. — *innocuus,* unharmed (Verg.; Tac.;
Claud.; Ambros.), 1, 32, 6. — *innoxius,* harmless (Verg.; Sen.
phil.; Plin. mai.; Tac.), 5, 27; 5, 46. — *inoffensus,* unharmed,
untouched (Tibull.; Lucan.), 5, 42, 1; — undisturbed, placid
(Verg.; Ov.; Sen. phil.; Mart.; Tac.; Plin. ep.; Gell.; Pallad.;
Ambros.), 1, 25, 4; 1, 38, 5; 4, 16, 2. — *insanus,* tempestuous,
boisterous (of the sea, wind, etc.) (Verg.; Tibull.), 5, 46. —*instabilis,* unsteady, tottering (Verg.; Ov.; Liv.; Curt.), 4, 15, 2; 5, 27. —
insuetus, unusual, to which one is not accustomed (Verg.; Liv.),
2, 9. — *insuperabilis,* insuperable, invincible (transf. sense) (Verg.;
Ov.; Sen. phil.; Frontin.; Plin. min.), 2, 9; 4, 23, 1; 5, 15; 5, 33,
2; 5, 41; 5, 53, 1 (bis). — *intaminatus,* undefiled (Hor.; Tert.;
Ambros.; Sulp. Sev.; Anon.), 5, 16 (bis). — *intemeratus,* undefiled, unviolated (Verg.; Ov.; Tac.; Ambros.; Mart. Cap.), 1, 39. —
intractabilis, unyielding, inflexible (Verg.; Sen. phil.; Gell.; Iust.;
Hier.), 1, 44, 8. — *intrepidus,* undaunted (Ov.; Liv.; Curt.; Sen.
phil.; Lucan.; Val. Fl.; Tac.; Gell.; Claud.), 3, 11, 3. — *invalidus,*
sick, feeble (Ov.; Liv.; ·Plin. mai.; Tac.; Gell.; Dict.; Aug.),
1, 7, 2; 1, 40, 7; 4, 1, 4; 5, 18, 1; 5, 18, 2; 5, 24, 2. — *inviolabilis,*
inviolable (Lucr.; Verg.; Sen. phil.; Sil.; Tac.; Lact.; Cod. Th.),
1, 22, 1; 1, 32, 6 (bis). — *irreparabilis,* irreparable (Verg.; Colum.;
Sen. ep.), 5, 32. — *irritus,* vain, useless, ineffectual (Verg.; Catull.;
Prop.; Ov.; Liv.; Quint.; Tac.; Plin. mai.; Apul.), 1, 16, 1;
1, 16, 4; 1, 24, 1; 4, 3, 3; 5, 19; 5, 20, 2. — *obnoxius,* subject,
exposed to (Ov.; Liv.; Phaedr.; Sen. phil.; Plin. mai.; Plin. ep.;
Tac.), 5, 24, 4; 5, 27. — *pervigil,* ever-watchful (Ov.; Plin. mai.;
Tac.; Plin. min.; Chalc.; Ambros.), 5, 1, 4. — *praecelsus,* very
high (Verg.; Stat.; Ambros.; Aug.; Salv.; Avit.), 3, 20, 2. —
praedulcis, very agreeable (Verg.; Plin. mai.; Val. Fl.; Ps. Cypr.;
Ambros.), 2, 9. — *praevalidus,* very strong, very powerful (transf.
sense) (Verg.; Liv.; Tac.; Gallican.), 1, 14, 1; 4, 29, 2. — *rebellis,*

rebellious, insurgent (Verg.; Ov.; Vell.; Curt.; Tac.; Flor.), 2, 1, 2; 3, 24. — *resupinus,* supine, lying on one's back (Verg.; Ov.; Plin. mai.; Vopisc.), 4, 15, 2. — *seminex,* half-dead (Verg.; Ov.; Liv.; Sil.; Tac.; Spart.; Hier.; Ser. Samm.), 4, 1, 4; 5, 18, 1; 5, 21, 3; 5, 28; 5, 47, 2. — *semivir,* effeminate, womanish, unmanly (Verg.; Liv.; Lucan.; Stat.; Lact.), 5, 53, 1. — *vesanus,* fierce, raging, furious (Verg.; Ov.; Prop.; Liv.; Calp.; Amm.), 1, 32, 6; 3, 17.

d) *degener,* unworthy of (Sil.; Tac.; Ambros.), 2, 18; — unfit for war (Liv.; Lucan.; Sil.; Stat.; Amm.), 3, 16; 3, 24; 5, 27. — *illicitus,* forbidden, unlawful (Sen. phil.; Stat.; Tac.; Traian. in Plin. ep.; Apul.; Lact.; Sulp. Sev.; Claud.; Aug.; Macr.), 2, 5, 3; 4, 4, 3; 4, 25, 2. — *immaculatus,* unstained, unsullied (Lucan.; Lact.; Amm.; Ambros.; Vulg.; Aug.), 5, 16; 5, 31. — *impossibilis,* impossible (Quint.; Apul.; Iust.; Tert.; Ulp.; Lact.; Amm.; Ambros.; et al), 1, 30, 9; 1, 43, 3; 2, 15, 4. — *inaestimabilis,* inestimable (transf. sense) (Liv.; Sen. phil.; Val. Max.; Lact.), 3, 9, 5. — *inconsultus,* unasked, not consulted (Liv.; Suet.; Amm.; Symm.; Ambros.; Aug.; Claud.), 1, 26, 2; 2, 1, 2; 4, 26, 1; 5, 16. — *indubius,* not doubtful, certain (Quint.; Tac.), 1, 37, 6; 1, 42, 2; 3, 20, 1. — *inefficax,* ineffectual, ineffective (Sen. phil.; Plin. mai.; Veget.; Ambros.), 4, 3, 3. — *inenarrabilis,* indescribable (Liv.; Vell.; Sen. phil.; Lact.), 3, 6, 3. — *inexpletus,* unsatisfied, unfilled (Stat.; Val. Fl.; Amm.; Hier.), 5, 21, 3. — *inexploratus,* unexamined (Liv.; Sen. phil.; Plin. mai.; Ambros.; Priscill.; Cassiod.), 4, 21. — *inhonorus,* without honor (Plin. mai.; Iul. Val.; Eutr.; Ambros.), 1, 13, 3. — *innavigabilis,* unnavigable (Liv.; Lact.; Hier.; Iord.), 2, 9; 4, 27. — *insuperabilis,* unsurmountable, cannot be passed over (lit.) (Liv.), 3, 9, 1. — *intutus,* unsafe (Plin mai.; Tac.; Amm.; Ambros.), 5, 17. — *invalidus,* inefficient, powerless (Liv.; Frontin.; Tac.; Iust.), 1, 42, 5; 5, 24, 2. — *irrationabilis,* irrational, without reason (Quint.; Apul.; Itala; Tert.; Iren.; Ambros.; Hier.; et al), 1, 28, 9; 1, 32, 6; 2, 9; 3, 18, 1. — *praeferox,* very fierce (Liv.; Tac.; Suet.), 4, 31.

ii. Adjectives compounded of a Noun and a Verb.

c) *pomifer,* fruit-bearing (Hor.; Ov.; Sen. phil.; Mela; Plin.

mai.; Frontin.; Sol.; Vulg.; Aug.; Isid.), 3, 26, 2. — *ruricola,* rural, rustic, country- (Ov.; Lucan.; Itin. Alex.), 5, 44, 1. — *veneficus,* poisoning (Ov.; Plin. mai.; Sol.), 1, 40, 9.

iii. Miscellaneous Compound Adjectives.

a) *aliquantus,* some, considerable (Sall.; Bell. Afr.; Liv.; Colum.; Frontin.; Apul.; Tert.; Herm.; Chalc.; Aug.; Avit.), 4, 23, 3.

b) *omnipotens,* almighty, all-powerful (Enn.; Catull.; Verg.; Val. Max.; Ambros.; Vulg.; Aug.; Cl. Mam.; et al), 1, 43, 2; 3, 17 (ter); 5, 2; 5, 31. — *unanimus,* of one mind or heart (Plaut.; Catull.; Verg.; Stat.; Auson.; Ambros.; et al), 1, 40, 10.

c) *bicornis,* two-mouthed (of a river) (Verg.; Ov.; Stat.; Rut. Nam.; Auson.; Symm.; Hier.), 2, 9. — *longaevus,* aged, of great age (Verg.; Mart.; Firm.; Ambros.), 1, 43, 3; 5, 53, 1.

23. Miscellaneous Adjectives.

a) *aeger,* poor (Cic.(2); Liv.; Sen. phil.; Sil.; Val. Max.; Stat.; Tac.), 4, 16, 2. — *conchyliatus,* of a purple color (Cic.(1); Petron.; Plin. mai.; Suet.; Sid.), 4, 25, 2. — *dedecor,* shameful, unbecoming (Sall. fr.; Stat.; Itala; Tert.; Auson.; Ambros.; Rufin.), 5, 27; 5, 43, 2. — *lacer,* mangled, lacerated (Sall. fr.; Verg.; Ov.; Val. Fl.; Tac.; Plin. min.; Flor.), 4, 1, 4; 5, 2. — *paluster,* fenny, marshy, swampy (Cic.(1); Caes.; Hor.; Liv.; Colum.; Plin. mai.; Ulp.; Vulg.), 3, 26, 1. — *teres,* smooth (Caes.; Verg.; Ov.; Liv.; Min. Fel.), 4, 15, 2. — *velox,* swift, quick (Caes.; Lucr.; Verg.; Hor.; Ov.; Liv.; Lucan.; Plin. mai.; Stat.; Mart.; Gell.; Claud.; Sid.), 5, 20, 2.

b) *campestris,* level, flat (Cato; Varr.; Cic.(2); Caes.; Nep.; Bell. Afr.; Hor.; Liv.; Silver and Late), 3, 6, 4; 3, 19. — *muliebris,* womanish, effeminate, unmanly (Trag. inc. fr.; Sall. fr.; Cic. (1)), 3, 17. — *quadragensimus* (*quadragesimus*), fortieth (Cato; Varr.; Cic.(3); Colum.; Plin. mai.; Tac.; C.I.L.), 3, 15, 1. — *vehemens,* strong, powerful, forcible (Cato; Lucr.; Hirt.; Bell. Hisp.; Liv.; Cels.; Colum.; Scrib.; Plin. mai.), 5, 1, 3.

c) *celeber,* renowned, distinguished (Hor.; Tibull.; Ov.; Liv.;

8

Vell.; Stat.; Silver and Late), 3, 2. — *lugubris,* mournful, doleful (Lucr.; Ov.), 5, 44, 1. — *silvester* (*silvestris*), wild, uncultivated (Hor.; Ov.; Colum.; Plin. mai.), 3, 6, 4. — *ultrix,* avenging (Verg.; Ov.; Lucan.; Sil.; Stat.; Fronto; Amm.; Ambros.; Hier.; et al), 1, 38, 3; 5, 53, 1.

d) *deses,* inactive, indolent, idle (Liv.; Sen. phil.; Colum.; Tac.; Plin. min.; Amm.; et al), 2, 8, 3. — *infulatus,* adorned with a fillet (Suet.; Prud.; Sid.; C.I.L.), 1, 17, 1. — *liber,* allowable, possible (Quint.; Plin. ep.), 5, 15.

SUMMARY

Three hundred and thirty adjectives, comprising those with the suffixes *-bilis, -ilis, -alis, -aris, -arius, -orius, -ius, -ivus, -osus, -eus, -icus, -idus, -inus, -anus, -us, -ax, -is,* diminutives, Greek adjectives, participles used as adjectives, compound adjectives, miscellaneous adjectives, have been listed for our author.

Of these three hundred and thirty adjectives, ninety are Rare Classical, sixty-four Early, one hundred and eighteen Poetic, and fifty-eight Silver.

Seven adjectives have been listed under the suffix *-bilis,* of which number one is Rare Classical, three Poetic, and three Silver. Besides these seven, seventeen other adjectives, which appear in the Poetic and Silver categories of "Adjectives compounded with a preposition or a particle," have this suffix—*illacrimabilis, immedicabilis, immobilis, impossibilis, inaestimabilis, inconsolabilis, inenarrabilis, inevitabilis, inexcusabilis, inexpugnabilis, innavigabilis, instabilis, insuperabilis, intractabilis, inviolabilis, irrationabilis, irreparabilis.* While this suffix is usually passive in meaning, in archaic and in late Latin the active meaning is frequently found.[4]

Three of the adjectives of this list—*exitiabilis, irrationabilis, medicabilis*—are used with active meanings.

Four adjectives have been noted with the suffix *-ilis,* three of which adjectives are Rare Classical, and one Early. Two of the Rare Classical adjectives, *sterilis* and *virilis* (male, masculine), appear in Varro first and then in the poets, while the other adjec-

---

[4] Cooper, p. 98.

tive, *utensilis,* is found only in Varro and Augustine. The one Early adjective, *herilis,* is cited for Plautus, Terence, Afranius, Varro, the poets, and others.

The suffix -*alis* lays claim to twenty adjectives, six of which are Rare Classical, five Poetic, and nine Silver. No Early adjectives with this suffix have been found. The word *genitalis* is found with three distinct meanings—" generative " or " genital," " productive " or " prolific," and " native " or " pertaining to the place of birth or origin." The adjective *coniugalis* appears with two distinct meanings—" conjugal " or " pertaining to marriage " and " pertaining to a husband and wife." An interesting use of the adjective *aequalis* in the sense of " drawn " in speaking of a battle has been noted for Silius, Martial, Iordanes, and our author. A very frequent word in Hegesippus is *parricidalis,* being used twenty-one times. The other spelling *parricidialis* is found in Ambrose, but not in our author.

A very rare adjectival suffix is -*aris.* Two examples of its use, one Early and one Silver, have been found. The Early adjective, *proeliaris,* is found first in Plautus and then in Apuleius and Late Latin, and is recorded four times in Hegesippus. The one Silver example, *familiaris* (customary, habitual), appears frequently in Silver and Late Latin.

Four Rare Classical adjectives end in -*arius*—*compendarius, transversarius, tributarius,* and *vicarius.* They are all developed from nouns, and are found in Cicero, except *transversarius* which is cited only for Caesar and Vitruvius.

Adjectives in -*orius* are derived from nouns in -*tor* (-*sor*). Three adjectives in -*orius* have been noted, two of which are Early—*piscatorius* and *praedatorius;* and one Silver—*bellatorius.* The word *bellatorius* is cited only for Pliny's Epistles and Ammianus Marcellinus.

Three adjectives ending in -*ius* have been listed for Hegesippus. The one Rare Classical example, *noxius,* is found in our author in the sense of both " harmful " and " guilty." The two Poetic examples are *ebrius* and *nescius.*

Another small group of adjectives has the suffix -*ivus.* The three instances noted here are derived from verbs. The one Rare Classical example is *adoptivus,* while *insitivus* and *recidivus* are cited for the Poetic category. The adjective *insitivus* is used in its literal sense of "ingrafted" and is cited only for Horace, Epod. 2, 19, in this meaning.

One of the most numerous classes of adjectives has the suffix *-osus*. Adjectives with this suffix are regularly derived from nouns. Sixteen adjectives in *-osus* have been discovered in Hegesippus, of which three are Rare Classical, four Early, five Poetic, and four Silver. Of the Rare Classical examples *tenebrosus* is found once in the fragments of Cicero, then in the poets, and finally in Late Latin. Among the Early words *famosus* (infamous) is quoted for Cato, Lucilius, Cicero(2), and others; *meticulosus* is cited for Plautus and Late Latin. Of the Poetic adjectives with this suffix, *saxosus* is noted for Vergil and Columella. A Silver adjective of this group which is found only in Quintilian and Late Latin is *otiosus*.

Eight adjectives have the suffix *-eus*. Two of these are Rare Classical, two Early, three Poetic, and one Silver. They are all denominative. Of the two Rare Classical examples *femineus* appears with two distinct meanings—"feminine" and "unmanly." Of the Poetic words *aequoreus* is not found in prose until the fourth century, and *lacteus* is cited only for Vergil. The one Silver word, *niveus* (limpid), is found in Seneca's poetry and in Martial. It is interesting to note also that seven of these eight adjectives in *-eus* are used by Vergil.

Seven adjectives in our author have the suffix *-icus,* of which number two are Rare Classical, two Early, two Poetic, and one Silver. Of the two Rare Classical adjectives *pacificus* is cited only for Cicero's Epistles (1), Martial, and Late Latin. The one Silver example, *aulicus,* is found in Suetonius and Late Latin.

Hegesippus makes use of ten adjectives ending in *-idus*. Two are Rare Classical, two Early, five Poetic, and one Silver. This suffix was quite popular with the poets, particularly with Ovid, who is acquainted with eight of the ten adjectives in *-idus* noted in our author. Among the Early words *validus* is found in its literal sense of "strong" at least forty times in Hegesippus, and in its transferred sense of "effective" eight times. Of the Poetic words *rigidus* (rocky, rough, hard) is met with only in Ovid.

A suffix used rarely by the writers of the classical period is *-inus.*

Five examples of this suffix have been found in Hegesippus, one of which, *genuinus,* is Rare Classical, being cited once for Cicero and then for Late Latin. Two Early adjectives have this suffix— *crastinus* found in Plautus, Cicero's Epistles(1), the poets, Silver and Late Latin; *peregrinus* in Plautus, Cicero(4), the poets, Silver and Late Latin. The one Poetic instance of this suffix is in *vicinus,* while in *trinus,* which is found in Statius and Late Latin, is seen the sole contribution to the Silver category.

Four examples of the suffix -*anus* have been noted. Only one Rare Classical word, *vicanus,* is listed and' that twice for Cicero. The three other words are in the Silver group—*meridianus* in Livy, Vitruvius, and others; *praetorianus* in Tacitus, Suetonius, and the Jurists; *pridianus* in Pliny the Elder, Suetonius, Apuleius, and Augustine. This last adjective is formed from an adverb, while the other three are denominative.

The largest group of suffixal adjectives, numbering twenty-eight, ends in -*us.* This suffix was popular with the poets, especially with Vergil, Horace and Ovid. Nine of this large group of adjectives are found in the Rare Classical group, seven in the Early, ten in the Poetic, and two in the Silver. Of the Rare Classical words *mundus* (fine, genteel, nice) is used twice by Cicero and is found also in Propertius and Livy; *nefastus* (contrary to religion) in Cicero(1) and Pliny the Younger. Among the Early words *largus* (abounding in) is found in Plautus, Vergil, Lucan, and Silius.; and *mundus* (clean) in Terence, Horace, Columella, and Gellius. Interesting Poetic words are *laevus* (awkward, stupid) used by Vergil, Horace, and Persius; *obscurus* (turbid, in speaking of water) found in Ovid; and *quotus* (how great, i. e., how very small) also found in Ovid. Two Silver adjectives which appear rarely are *profluus* noted for Columella, Sidonius, and Venantius Fortunatus; and *refugus* found in Tacitus.

A suffix which was very active in classical times, but whose influence declined in Silver and Late Latin, is -*ax.* Only five adjectives with this suffix have been noted in Hegesippus, but the five are used by Cicero. The one Rare Classical example, *efficax,* is noted for Caelius in Cicero's Epistles(1), Horace, Livy, Silver writers, Apuleius, and Trebellius Pollio. The other four adjectives with this suffixal ending are in the Early group—*capax, ferax, perspicax,* and *tenax.*

One Poetic adjective, *pinguis* (fertile, productive), with the suffix -*is* is recorded. It is found also in Vergil, Horace, Columella, and Seneca the philosopher.

The suffix -*ensis* contributes one Silver adjective, *forensis* (foreign), which is used by Pliny the Elder, Apuleius, Ambrose, and other Late writers.

The diminutive adjectives are not very numerous—only three being found in Hegesippus. Two of these diminutives are classed as Early—*adulescentulus* found in Plautus and Ambrose; and *parvulus* in Terence, Cicero(1), Caesar, Nepos, Vergil, Valerius Maximus, Iustinus, and Augustine. The one Poetic diminutive, *novellus,* has a reduplicated suffix and is cited for Ovid, Livy, and Late Latin. In Hegesippus *parvulus* alone of the three diminutive adjectives has retained its diminutive force.

Hegesippus employs only four Greek adjectives in this section of his vocabulary. The two Early adjectives—*aerius* and *aetherius*—are cited first for Varro Atacinus, Cicero, the poets, Silver and Late Latin. The one Poetic example, *mysticus,* is found in the Classical and Silver poets and in Late prose, while the single Silver Greek adjective, *arctous,* is quoted for the Silver poets and Late prose.

Thirteen present participles used as adjectives have been found in Hegesippus, four of which are Rare Classical, four Early, and five Poetic. No Silver instances were noted. One of the Rare Classical participial adjectives, *sequens,* is found fourteen times in Hegesippus and is the only one of the thirteen adjectives not found in the poets. A noteworthy Early participial adjective is *fugitans* cited for Terence, Ambrose(11), and Symmachus. All the Poetic participial adjectives—*indignans, nitens, olens* (fragrant), *tepens, virens*—are interesting because they are found rarely outside of the poets.

Forty-one past participles have been used adjectivally in Hegesippus, seventeen of which are Rare Classical, nine Early, seven Poetic, and nine Silver. Twenty-four of these forty-one participial adjectives have been made from verbs of the third conjugation, nine from the first, six from the second, and only two from the fourth conjugation. Uncommon participial adjectives in the Rare Classical group are *circumcisus* (steep, precipitous), *elatus* (proud), and

praeruptus (hasty, rash). Of the Early adjectives interesting ones
are *exercitus* found in Plautus, Tacitus, Claudius Claudianus, and
Tertullian; *suspectus* (suspicious) in Cato, Tertullian, Itala, Ammianus Marcellinus, Ambrose, and others.   Only one Poetic
instance, *succinctus,* is worthy of note, being cited for Ovid, Quintilian, Ammianus Marcellinus, and Claudius Claudianus. Several
of the Silver adjectives deserve special mention—*celebratus* (brilliant, pompous) found in Livy and Suetonius; *deiectus* (humble,
low) in Seneca the philosopher, Apuleius, Ambrose, and Late
Latin; *eviratus* (unmanly) in Martial, Arnobius, and Ambrose;
memoratus (aforesaid) found in Livy, Pliny the Elder, and Late
Latin, and noted eighteen times in Hegesippus; and *praeruptus*
(extreme, critical) cited once for Velleius and three times in our
author.

Three gerundives with adjectival force have been noted. The
one Rare Classical example, *miserandus,* is found in Cicero(3),
Sallust, Vergil, Ovid, and Livy.   The only Early instance,
pudendus, is used by an unknown writer of tragedy, Cicero(1),
Vergil, Ovid, Quintilian, Tacitus, Suetonius, Claudianus Mamertus,
and Lampridius. The single Poetic adjective, *reverendus,* is found
in Ovid, Juvenal, and Late Latin.

Adjectives compounded with a preposition or a particle form the
largest group of adjectives in Hegesippus—one hundred and nine.
Twenty-three of this large number are Rare Classical, thirteen
Early, fifty-five Poetic, and eighteen Silver. The following prepositions or prefixes have been used in the formation of these compound adjectives: *ad, con, de, ex, in, ne, ob, per, prae, re, semi, sub,
ve.* Nearly three-fourths of the total number of adjectives—
seventy-four, to be exact—are compounded with *in-*(negative). It
is interesting to note that fourteen of the twenty-three Rare Classical adjectives are Sallustian, and that one of these fourteen, *immutilatus* (not maimed), is cited only for the fragments of Sallust.
Another Rare Classical word, *suppar,* is found only once in Cicero,
then in Velleius, and in Late Latin.   Noteworthy examples in the
Early category are *congruus* (suitable) and *incoctus* (raw, uncooked) found in Plautus and Late Latin; *decrepitus* and *impos* in
Early Latin, then in Silver and Late Latin; and *incanus* in Plautus,
Vergil, Columella, and Suetonius. Among the Poetic words the

following are found in the poets and Late Latin: *accommodus* (suitable), *illacrimabilis, immedicabilis, imperterritus, inconsolabilis, ·incredulus, indebitus, inexcusabilis, iniussus, inoffensus* (unharmed), *insanus* (tempestuous, of the sea), *intaminatus,* and *praecelsus.* From the Silver category compound adjectives which are found rarely in Silver Latin and then in Late Latin are *immaculatus, impossibilis, inconsultus* (unasked), *indubius, inefficax, inexpletus, inhonorus, innavigabilis, insuperabilis* (in its literal sense of " cannot be passed over "), *intutus,* and *irrationabilis.*

Only three adjectives compounded of a noun and a verb have been listed. All are in the Poetic ˙category—*pomifer* found in Horace, Ovid, Silver and Late Latin; *ruricola* in Ovid, Lucan, and the Itinerarium Alexandri; and *veneficus* cited only for Ovid, Pliny the Elder, and Solinus.

Five miscellaneous compound adjectives are interesting because of their composition. One is Rare Classical, two are Early, and two Poetic. The word *aliquantus* is compounded from two adjectives; *omnipotens* from an adjective and a present participle; *longaevus* and *unanimus* are compounds of adjectives and nouns; and *bicornis* is formed from an adverb and a noun.

Eighteen miscellaneous adjectives which could not be classified according to the preceding categories are grouped together. Seven of these are Rare Classical, four Early, four Poetic, and three Silver. Among the Rare Classical words *dedecor* (shameful) is found in Sallust's fragments, Statius, and Late Latin, and is used twice by Hegesippus. The Early word, *muliebris* (unmanly), is cited only for an unknown writer of tragedy, the fragments of Sallust, and once for Cicero. Interesting Silver words are *infulatus* found only in Suetonius and Late Latin; and *liber* (allowable) in Quintilian and Pliny's Epistles.

C. Verbs

1. Verbs derived from Nouns.

a) *aestimare,* to judge, think (Sall.; Liv.; Plin. mai.; Sen. phil.; Quint.; Tac.; Fronto; Tert.; and Late), 1, 37, 5; 2, 9. — *bacchari,* to rage with anger (Varr.; Cic.(2); Verg.; Stat.; Suet.; Exup.; Hier.; et al), 5, 22, 3. — *comitari,* to go or follow with someone (Varr.; Cic.(2) ; Caes.; Nep.; Lucr.; Verg.; Silver and Late), 1, 13,

3; 1, 46, 2; 5, 1, 2; 5, 22, 1.—*comperendinare*, to put off to the third day (legal term) (Cic. (6); Fronto; Symm.; Amm.; Ambros.), 1, 15, 2. — *conviciari*, to revile, reproach, taunt (Varr.; Liv.; Sen. phil.; Quint.; Suet.; Apul.; Tert.; Arnob.; Amm.; Ambros.; et al), 1, 30, 9; 1, 31, 2; 5, 15; 5, 44, 1. — *ditare*, to enrich (Rhet. Her.; Culex; Hor.; Ov.; Liv.; Stat.; Plin. mai.; Quint.; and Late), 1, 41, 6. — *famulari*, to serve, wait on (Cic.(1); Catull.; Publil.; Val. Max.; Lucan.; Plin. mai.; Val. Fl.; Sil.; Stat.; and frequent from Tert. on), 1, 32, 1; 2, 9, 1.— *fluctuare*, to hesitate, vacillate (Rhet. Her.; Cic.(1); Verg.; Liv.; Curt.; Val. Max.; Sen. phil.; Suet.; Apul.; Amm.; Ambros.; and Late), 1, 31, 3; 3, 2; 4, 15, 2. — *frustrari* (pass.), to deceive one's self (Sall.; Sil.), 4, 2. — *iubilare*, to shout, raise a shout of joy (Varr.; M. Aurel. apud Fronto; Vulg.; Aug.), 5, 16. — *lapidare*, to stone (Bell. Hisp.; Petron.; Flor.; Suet.; Ambros.; Vulg.; Aug.), 3, 2; 5, 2 (bis); 5, 32. — *lenocinari*, to cajole, flatter (Cic.(2); Sen. phil.; Plin. min.; Ambros.), 1, 37, 3. — *lucrari*, to win, acquire (fig.) (Cic.(1); Hor.; Stat.; Amm.; Vulg.), 5, 18, 3. — *metari*, to measure off, lay out (Sall.; Caes.; Verg.; Liv.; Plin. mai.), 3, 5, 2. — *munerari* (trans.), to present with (Cic. ep.(1); Hor.), 1, 41, 1. — *periclitari*, to be in danger (Caes.; Liv.; Petron.; Cels.; Plin. mai.; Mart.; Quint.; Tac.; Plin. min.; Suet.; Apul.; Ambros.), 3, 24. — *rimari*, to investigate, examine (Cic.(1); Tac.; Gell.), 5, 44, 1. — *signare*, to express, signify, indicate (Cic.(1); Verg.; Ov.; Vell.; Sen. phil.; Lucan.; Quint.; Tac.; Amm.; Capit.), 2, 3, 1; 3, 17. — *stagnare*, to be inundated (Sall. fr.; Ov.; Plin. mai.; Sil.), 5, 1, 3. — *tripudiare*, to dance, caper (Cic.(1); Liv.; Sen. phil.; Lact.; Ambros.), 5, 37, 2.

b) *aestimare*, to think (Acc.; Varr.; Sall.; Plin. mai.; Curt.; Sen. phil.; Quint.; and Late especially), 1, 19, 1; 1, 22, 3; 1, 30, 14; 1, 35, 3; 1, 36, 1; 1, 36, 2; 1, 38, 6; 1, 40, 1; 1, 41, 4; 1, 41, 9; 1, 44, 3; 1, 44, 8 (bis); 1, 45, 11; 2, 1, 2 (bis); 2, 4 (bis); 2, 8, 3; 2, 9; 2, 12, 2; 2, 15, 2; 2, 18; 3, 1, 2; 3, 3, 2; 3, 3, 5; 3, 3, 6; 3, 4, 1; 3, 6, 4; 3, 7; 3, 9, 4; 3, 14 (bis); 3, 20, 1; 3, 20, 2; 3, 25, 1; 3, 26, 1; 3, 26, 2; 4, 18; 5, 27; 5, 29; 5, 31; 5, 49, 3. — *arietare*, to disturb, harass (Plaut.; Sen. phil.; Curt.; Nazar.; Chalc.; Plin. mai.; Cypr. Gall.), 4, 15, 2. — *aquari*, to bring or fetch water

(Cato; Caes.; Sall.; Hirt.; Bell. Afr.; Bell. Hisp.; Verg.; Liv.; Colum.; Fronto; and Late), 3, 14. — *auxiliari,* to aid, help (Plaut.; Ter.; Pacuv.; Lucil.; Gracch.; Rhet. Her.; Cic. ep.(1); Sall.; Caes.; Vitr.; Ov.; Plin. mai.(53); Sil.), 5, 31. — *calcare,* to trample upon (Cato; Varr.; Verg.; Ov.; Hor.; Colum.; Silver and Late), 5, 2. — *callere,* to understand (Plaut.; Ter.; Acc.; Afran.; Cic.(3); Hor.; Liv.; Pers.; Plin. mai.; Tac.; Gell.; Apul.; and Late), 5, 13. — *coronare,* to crown (Plaut.; Cato; Cic.(3); Poetical, Silver and Late), 4, 8.— *fabulari,* to speak (Plaut.; Ter.; Titin.; Afran.; Ambrosiast.; Aug.; Mar. Merc.; Ennod.; Caes. Arel.; Greg. M.), 3, 2. — *fastidire,* to disdain, loathe (Plaut.; Titin.; Turpil.; Lucil.; Cato; Varr.; Cic.(2); Verg.; Ov.; Hor.; and very frequent from Livy on), 1, 44, 7; 5, 22, 2; 5, 22, 3; 5, 37, 2. — *fluctuare,* to be restless, uncertain (Plaut.; Catull.; Liv.; Val. Max.; Sen. phil.; Lact.; Ambros.; Rufin.; Hier.; Aug.; et al), 1, 44, 5. — *foedare,* to pollute, defile (Plaut.; Enn.; Cic. poet.(1); Sall.; Rhet. Her.; Catull.; Verg.; Prop.; Ov.; Liv.; Silver and Late), 5, 1, 3. — *foetere,* to have a bad smell (Plaut.; Varr.; Cels.; Colum.; Petron.; Plin. mai.; Mart.; Tert.; Amm.; Ps. Ambros.; Hier.; et al), 5, 2. — *frustrare,* to bring to naught (Sisenn.; Catull.; Verg.; Liv.; Val. Max.; Curt.; Colum.; Tac.; Apul.; and Late), 2, 15, 6. — *generare,* to beget (of a father) (Enn.; Cic.(2); Verg.; Hor.; Ov.; Sen. phil.; Val. Max.; Curt.; Mart.; Quint.; Paul. Fest.; Itala; and Late especially), 1, 39.— *maculare,* to pollute, defile (Plaut.; Verg.; Catull.; Ov.; Liv.; Tac.), 5, 31; 5, 41. — *militare,* to perform military service (Ter.; Cic.(2); Liv.; Vell.; Curt.; Tac.; Suet.), 5, 46. — *pumicare,* to polish, to rub with pumice stone (Lucil.; Catull.; Mart.; Apul.; Hier.; Aug.; Isid.), 4, 25, 2.

c) *calcare,* to despise, scorn, contemn (Ov.; Liv.; Sen. phil.; Lucan.; Sil.; Stat.; Quint.; Apul.; and frequent in Late Latin), 5, 2. — *catenare,*[1] to chain, fetter (Hor.; Sen. rhet.; Val. Max.; Colum.; Calp.; Stat.; Quint.; Flor.; Suet.; Hil.; Avell.; Symm.; et al), 3, 16. — *currere,* to sail (Prop.; Verg.; Ov.; Mart.; Iuv.; Drac.), 5, 27. — *donare,* to forgive, remit (Ov.; Liv.; Sen. poet.;

---

[1] This word is rare except in the perfect, passive participle. Other forms are cited for Colum.(1); Ven. Fort.(2).

Lucan.; Stat.; Flor.; Suet.; Iust.), 5, 7, 2. — *epulari,* to eat, feast upon (Verg.; Iust.; Ps. Cypr.), 5, 40 (ter). — *fluctuare,* to be in a ferment, to be disturbed (Catull.; Verg.; Val. Max.; Sen. phil.; Curt.; Suet.; Apul.; Amm.; Paneg.; Ambros.; Hier.; Aug.; et al), 4, 25, 3. — *iaculari,* to throw, hurl (Verg.; Ov.; Petron.; Colum.; Plin. mai.; Apul.), 5, 1, 4; 5, 10, 2. — *librare,* to brandish, swing, balance (Verg.; Ov.; Liv.; Curt.; Sen. phil.; Lucan.; Quint.; Sulp. Sev.), 5, 19; 5, 22. — *rimari,* to search for, rummage (Verg.; Ov.; Sen. phil.; Colum.; Iuv.; Tac.), 5, 18, 2; 5, 25, 1. — *rorare,* to trickle, drip (Lucr.; Ov.; Plin. mai.; Sil.; Apul.; Pervig. Ven.; Ambros.), 3, 10. — *stagnare,* to form a pool, stagnate (Verg.; Curt.; Sen. phil.; Plin. mai.), 5, 2. — *triumphare,* to triumph over, conquer (Hor.; Ov.; Plin. mai.; Tac.; Gell.; Iust.; Lact.; Aur. Vict.; Treb. Poll.), 3, 1, 2. — *vaporare,* to warm (Hor.; Colum.; Pers.; Petron.; Plin. mai.; Apul.; Lampr.; Ambros.), 3, 19.

d) *acervare,* to heap up (Liv.; Sen. phil.; Plin. mai.; Tert.; Pallad.; Cael. Aur.), 5, 18, 2. — *copulare,* to join in matrimony (Sen. phil.; Quint.; Ulp.; Apul.; Hier.; Rufin.; et al), 1, 28, 5; 1, 40, 2; 2, 2, 4; 5, 16. — *foederare,* to join, unite (Flor.; Min. Fel.; Tert.; Novat.; Iul. Val.; Iul. Vict.; Ambros.; Symm.; Hier.; Aug.; et al), 1, 1, 5; 4, 23, 1. — *fulminare,* to strike with lightning (Sen. phil.; Plin. mai.; Quint.; Min. Fel.; Lact.; Firm.; Serv.; Claud.; Aug.; et al), 1, 44, 8. — *loricare,*[2] to clothe in mail (Liv.; Plin. mai.; Tert.), 5, 5. — *ordinare,* to appoint to office (Suet.; Lampr.; Ict.; Iust.; Eutr.), 1, 28, 7. — *pavimentare,* to trample down (Plin. mai.), 4, 23, 2. — *sinuare,* to extend in a curve (of places) (Plin. ep.; Mela; Tac.; Calp.), 4, 1, 1; 5, 18, 2. — *vallare,* to surround, circumvallate (Liv.; Tac.), 5, 24, 4. — *velare,* to hide, conceal (Tac.; Plin. min.), 1, 37, 3; 1, 40, 1; 4, 6, 2.

2. Verbs derived from Adjectives.

a) *aequare,* to equal, to come up to (Caes.; Verg.; Prop.; Ov.; Liv.; Silver and Late), 3, 26, 2; 4, 11. — *cavare,* to hollow out (Varr.; Lucr.; Verg.(saepe); Ov.; Liv.; Curt.; Silver and Late), 3, 11, 1. — *celebrare,* to solemnize (Cic.(1); Catull.; Verg.; Ov.; Liv.; Plin. mai.; Val. Fl.; Frontin.; Tac.; Suet.; Apul.; and Late),

---

[2] Most frequently used in the perfect, passive participle as here.

1, 17, 2; 5, 44, 1 (bis). — *infestare,* to attack, molest (Bell. Alex.;
Ov.; Vell.; Sen. phil.; Suet.; Iust.; Sol.; Liv. epit.), 1, 14, 1;
1, 22, 2; 1, 26, 1; 2, 15, 6 (bis); 4, 16, 1; 5, 1, 4. —*mollire,* to
overcome, unman (Cic. ep. (1); Tac.), 1, 1, 7.—*nudare,* to expose,
leave defenceless (Caes.; Verg.; Liv.), 5, 4, 4; — to unsheathe,
draw (Nep.; Ov.; Liv.), 1, 16, 6. — *saevire,* to rage (fig.) (Sall.;
Caes.; Lucr.; Verg.; Ov.; Hor.; Val. Fl.; Gell.; Lact.; Aug.),
5, 21, 3. — *vacare,* to devote one's self to (Cic.(1); Vell.; Curt.;
Sen. rhet.; Ov.; Val. Max.; Sen. phil.; Stat.; Quint.; Tac.; Suet.),
5, 5.

b) *artare,* to hem in, confine (Plaut.; Lucr.; Liv.; Manil.; Vell.;
Colum.; Lucan.; Sen. phil.; Sil.; Stat.; Mart.; and Late), 3, 5, 2;
4, 1, 1; 4, 1, 4; 4, 27. — *celerare,* to quicken, hasten (Plaut.;
Turpil.; Lucr.; Verg.; Sil.; Stat.; Tac.; Iuvenc.; Amm.; Ambros.),
3, 9, 1; 3, 18, 2; 3, 25, 4; 5, 22. — *clarere,* to be evident, clear
(Enn.; Turpil.; Lucr.; Quint.; Tert.; Symm.; Ambros.; and Late
especially), Praef.; 3, 20, 2; 5, 16. — *densare,* to crowd together,
set close (Enn.; Liv.; Curt.; Val. Fl.; Calp.; Carm. Epigr.; Vulg.;
and Late), 1, 32, 4; 3, 23, 1. — *interpolare,* to give a new appearance to, change (Plaut.; Cic. ep.(1); Ulp.), 1, 9, 3; 2, 9; 5, 46. —
miserari, to pity, compassionate (Acc. fr.; Verg.; Sil.; Iust.;
Coripp.; Schol. Iuv.), 5, 45. — *rutilare,* to have a reddish glow
(Acc. fr.; Verg.; Min. Fel.; Ambros.; Hier.; Vulg.; Rufin.), 5,
16. — *saevire,* to be angry (Plaut.; Ter.; Sall.; Lucr.; Hor.;
Tibull.; Ov.; Liv.; Mart.; Iust.; Eutr.), 4, 8; 5, 2. — *sauciare,* to
wound, hurt (Plaut.; Cic.(3); Bell. Alex.; Ov.; Plin. mai.; Fulg.),
1, 7, 2. — *trepidare,* to be in a state of trepidation (Plaut.; Ter.;
Sall.; Caes.; Bell. Afr.; Verg.; Hor.; Ov.; Liv.; Sen. phil.; Silver
and Late), 5, 20, 2. — *turpare,* to dishonor, disgrace (Pacuv.; Cic.
fr. apud Hier. ep.; Liv.; Stat.; C.I.L.), 3, 1, 1; 3, 8, 3; 5, 37, 2. —
venustare, to beautify (Naev. apud Fulg.; Firm.; Ambros.; Avit.;
Ennod.; Ps. Cassiod.), 1, 35, 6; 2, 1, 2; 3, 6, 3; 3, 26, 1.

c) *acerbare,* to embitter, to make harsh or bitter (Verg.; Val.
Fl.; Stat.; Tert.; Ambros.; Mart. Cap.; Claud.; Paul. Nol.), 1,
40, 1; 1, 43, 5; 2, 9, 1; 4, 13, 2. — *degenerare,* to dishonor (Prop.;
Ov.; Val. Max.; Stat.; Capit.; Hil.; and Late), 2, 1, 2. — *gemi-
nare,* to augment, increase (Verg.; Tibull.; Ov.; Publil.; Liv.;

Manil.; Silver and Late), 2, 12, 1. — *gravare,* to oppress, weigh down (Verg.; Hor.; Ov.; Liv.; Curt.; Tac.; Iust.), 1, 38, 5; 1, 40, 2; 1, 40, 12; 1, 44, 7; 1, 45, 1; 1, 45, 5; 1, 45, 9; 4, 25, 3; 5, 1, 2; 5, 1, 3; 5, 12; 5, 22; 5, 24, 2; 5, 53, 1. — *insignire,* to adorn, decorate (Verg.; Sen. phil.; Plin. mai.; Tac.; Ambros.), 1, 41, 1; 1, 46, 2; 3, 6, 3. — *lassare,* to weary, fatigue (Tibull.; Ov.; Manil.; Sen. rhet.; Cels.; Lucan.; Sen. phil.; Mart.), 3, 24. — *levare,* to raise, lift up (Verg.; Ov.; Hor.; Liv.; Plin. mai.; Colum.; Flor.), 1, 45, 11; 4, 18; 5, 16 (bis); 5, 53, 1. — *manifestare,* to manifest, make public (Ov.; Stat.; Iust.; Ambros.; Ambrosiast.; Hier.; Vulg.; Claud.; Aug.; Ict.), Praef.; 1, 17, 2; 1, 28, 9; 1, 29, 10; 1, 40, 7; 1, 43, 7; 1, 44, 3; 2, 15, 8; 3, 6, 3; 3, 20, 2; 3, 26, 1; 4, 6, 9; 4, 25, 1; 4, 33; 5, 44, 1. — *mundare,* to clean, cleanse (Ps. Verg.; Colum.; Ambros.; Hier.), 1, 17, 2. — *mutilare,* to mutilate, maim (Ov.; Liv.; Curt.; Spart.), 1, 29, 7. — *obliquare,* to turn, bend aside (Verg.; Ov.; Sen. phil.; Tac.), 5, 27. — *penetrare,* to pierce into, penetrate, enter (Lucr.; Verg.; Vell.; Curt.; Val. Fl.; Plin. mai.; Tac.; Iust.), 1, 35, 4; 3, 13; 5, 16; 5, 37, 2. — *propinquare* (intrans.), to draw near, approach (Verg.; Stat.; Tac.; Aur. Vict.; Amm.), 4, 27. — *sociare,* to unite, associate by marriage (Verg.; Ov.; Liv.; Tac.; Spart.), 1, 37, 3; 1, 42, 5. — *truncare,* to maim, cut off (Ov.; Liv.; Lucan.; Stat.; Tac.; Iust.; Ambros.; Hier.; Claud.), 2, 13, 6; 4, 23, 3 (bis); 5, 53, 1. — *vacuare,* to make empty (Lucr.; Colum.; Stat.; Sil.; Mart.; Ps. Quint.; Ambros.; Sid.; Frontin.; et al), 1, 44, 7; 3, 11, 2; 5, 15.

d) *asperare,* to aggravate, make worse (Sil.; Stat.; Tac.; Hermog.; Cael. Aur.; Porphyr.), 1, 45, 5; — to rouse up, excite (Stat.; Tac.; Symm.; Amm.; Iul. Val.; Cael. Aur.), 1, 38, 3. — *sibi blandiri,* to delude one's self (Sen. phil.; Quint.; Iuv.; Mart.; Plin. ep.; Tert.; Ambros.; and Late especially), 1, 42, 2. — *crispare,* to curl, crisp the hair (Sen. phil.; Plin. mai.; Apul.; Ambros.; Mart. Cap.; Hier.; et al), 4, 25, 2. — *inquietare,* to disturb, disquiet (Sen. rhet.; Sen. phil.; Petron.; Tac.; Plin. min.; Suet.; Tert.; Cypr.; Digest.; Ambros.; Vulg.), 1, 22, 3.— *participare,* to share with (Liv.; Iust.; Spart.; Iren.; Auson.; Ambros.; Vulg.), 1, 40, 5. — *profanare,* to profane, desecrate (Liv.; Ov.; Petron.; Stat.;

Vulg.), 1, 1, 1. — *publicare,* to reveal, disclose, publish (Plin. ep.; Suet.; Iust.), 1, 44, 3.

3. Verbs derived from other Verbs.

b) *oblitterare,* to blot out of remembrance (Acc. fr.; Cic.(2); Catull.; Liv.; Tac.; Suet.), 1, 45, 12; 2, 10, 2; 5, 40. — *statuere,* to stop, cause to stand still (Plaut.; Prop.; Verg.; Liv.; Stat.; Arnob.; Cypr.; Chalc.; Th. Prisc.), 1, 30, 7; 3, 24 (ter); 5, 16; 5, 20, 3; 5, 41.

4. Verbs derived from Adverbs.

c) *temerare,* to violate, profane (Verg.; Ov.; Liv.; Sil.; Tac.; Sid.; Amm.; Ambros.; Claud.), 1, 1, 2; 5, 34, 1; 5, 34, 2; 5, 53, 1.

5. Verbs derived from Diminutives.

a) *pullulare,* to grow, spread, increase (Nep.; Apul.; Amm.; Cypr.; Salv.; Ambros.), 2, 6, 3.

6. Hybrids.

a) *strangulare,* to choke (Cic.(2); Cels.; Plin. min.; Lact.), 5, 24, 2.

7. Frequentative Verbs.

a) *amplexari,* to suffer, endure, receive freely (Cic.(4); Sen. phil.; Iul. Val.; Oros.), 1, 42, 9; 2, 13, 3. — *aversari,* to reject, shun (Sall. fr.; Bell. Hisp.; Ov.; Liv.; Val. Max.; Sen. phil.; Plin. mai.; Stat.; Tac.; Suet.; Apul.; et al), 3, 22, 2; 5, 16; 5, 40. — *eructare,* to vomit forth (Cic.(1); Verg.; Colum.; Sol.; Paneg.; Vulg.; Aug.), 4, 7. — *grassari,* to rage, to proceed with violence (Sall.; Hor.; Liv.; Tac.; Iust.; Amm.; Aur. Vict.), 5, 18, 1. — *iactare,* to boast (Caes.; Hor.; Ov.; Liv.; Sen. rhet.; Phaedr.; Curt.; Tac.), 2, 7, 1; 3, 2; 5, 41. — *increpitare,* to chide, rebuke (Caes.; Verg.; Liv.; Stat.; Oros.), 1, 26, 3; 2, 10, 6. — *intentare,* to threaten (Cic. (2); Verg.; Quint.; Lact.), 1, 41, 7. — *natare,* to overflow with, to swim with (Cic.(1); Verg.; Ov.; Aug.), 5, 29. — *visitare,* to visit, go to see (Cic.(1); Suet.; Aug.), 1, 42, 9; 4, 17.

b) *adventare,* to approach, arrive at (with accessory idea of speed) (Plaut.; Ter.; Varr.; Cic. ep.(21); Caes.; Sall.; Verg.; Liv.; Curt.; Tac.; Amm.), 1, 19, 2; 1, 26, 3; 3, 13. — *circumcursare*, to run about in, at, etc. (Plaut.; Catull.; Iul. Val.; Dict.; Amm.), 3, 24.— *circumspectare*, to look around, behold (Plaut.; Ter.; Cic.(1); Sall.; Hor.; Liv.; Sil.; Stat.; Tac.; Amm.; et al), 1, 44, 4; 1, 44, 7. — *coeptare*, to begin (Plaut.; Ter.; Cic.(2); Sall.; Lucr.; Plin. mai.; Sil.; Tac.; Suet.; Gell.; Apul.; Fronto; Amm.; et al), 3, 8, 1. — *coniectare*, to guess, conjecture (Ter.; Cic.(1); Caes.; Liv.; Curt.; Plin. mai.; Tac.; Fronto; Tert.; Iul. Val.; Auson.; Amm.; et al), 4, 9, 2. — *defensare*, to defend (Plaut.; Sall.; Ov.; Stat.; Tac.; Amm.; and Late), 3, 3, 4; 3, 23, 1; 5, 4, 3; 5, 14, 2; 5, 20, 2; 5, 42, 5; 5, 46. — *ductare*, to lead, conduct (Plaut.; Sall.; Tac.; Quint.; Amm.), 1, 16, 4; 1, 29, 1. — *fugitare*, to flee in haste (Ter.; Plin. mai.; Cypr. Gall.; Amm.; Rufin.; Chron. Gall.), 2, 5, 3; 2, 9, 1. — *imperitare*, to command, govern, rule (Plaut.; Sall.; Lucr.; Hor.; Liv.; Curt.; Plin. mai.; Tac.; Flor.), 1, 12, 1; 1, 13, 1; 1, 15, 1; 1, 19, 4; 1, 32, 1; 1, 36, 1; 1, 45, 12; 2, 1, 1; 2, 4; 2, 5, 1; 2, 5, 5; 2, 9 (bis); 2, 13, 5; 2, 13, 6; 4, 32; 5, 15 (bis); 5, 46. — *incursare*, to assault, attack (Plaut.; Liv.; Tac.; Amm.), 2, 7, 1. — *latitare*, to conceal (Plaut.; Cic.(3); Hirt.; Bell. Afr.; Hor.; Ov.; Val. Max.), 4, 22, 1. — *obiectare*, to charge, accuse of, reproach with (Plaut.; Cic.(2); Caes.; Sall.; Liv.; Ov.), 1, 25, 2; 1, 26, 3; 1, 37, 2; 2, 5, 3; — to expose, abandon, endanger (Pacuv. fr.; Sall.; Verg.; Liv.), 2, 9; 3, 20, 2. — *prospectare*, to view, gaze upon (Plaut.; Cic. ep.(1); Sall.; Catull.; Verg.; Ov.; Liv.; Tac.; Suet.), 3, 5, 2; 5, 4, 2. — *quassare*, to shatter, batter (Naev. fr.; Lucr.; Verg.; Liv.), 5, 26, 1.— *vellicare*, to pluck, pick, nip (Plaut.; Varr.; Quint.; Paul. Fest.; Calp.; Paul. Nol.), 4, 25, 2.

c) *captare*, to sniff (the air) (Verg.; Ciris; Ov.; Sen. phil.; Colum.; Lucan.; Plin. mai.; Ps. Quint.), 5, 39, 2. — *convectare*, to bring together in abundance (Verg.; Sil.; Stat.; Tac.; Amm.; Ps. Ambros.; Cod. Th.; Coripp.), 4, 13, 2; 4, 27. — *crepitare*, to crackle (of fire) (Lucr.; Verg.; Sil.; Ps. Rufin.; Sulp. Sev.; Gild.; Drac.), 2, 11, 4. — *dictare*, to prescribe, recommend (Ov.; Manil.; Sen. phil.; Colum.; Petron.; Plin. mai.; Sil.; Stat.; Plin. min.; Quint.; Apul.; and Late), 2, 1, 2. — *incessere*, to fall upon, attack

(Verg.; Ov.; Liv.; Curt.; Sen. phil.; Suet.), 3, 3, 4; — to assail, accuse (Ov.; Stat.; Quint.; Tac.; Suet.; Gell.), 1, 14, 1; 1, 18; 1, 25, 2 (bis); 1, 40, 3; 1, 40, 6 (bis); 1, 40, 8; 2, 8, 1; 2, 15, 5; 3, 9, 2; 4, 3, 1; 4, 25, 3; 5, 2; 5, 18, 3; 5, 33, 1. — *nutare,* to totter, shake (Verg.; Ov.; Liv.; Tac.; Plin. min.; Calp.), 4, 1, 4. — *pensare,* to purchase, buy (Ov.; Vell.; Val. Max.), 1, 14, 2. —*resultare,* to resound, reverberate (Verg.; Plin. mai.; Mart.; Plin. min.), 5, 6; 5, 19; 5, 26, 2; 5, 44, 1. — *sustentare,* to prop up, support (Verg.; Plin. mai.; Claud.), 3, 11, 1. — *vellicare,* to afflict, vex (through envy) (Prop. 2, 5, 8), 1, 26, 2.

d) *nutare,* to waver, falter (Tac.; Suet.; Eutr.; Aur. Vict.), 5, 4, 3; 5, 42, 4. — *pensare,* to consider, ponder (Liv.; Curt.), 1, 41, 9; 5, 15; 5, 24, 2. — *percursare,* to pass through, traverse (Tac.; Plin. min.; Iul. Vict.), 1, 19, 1; 3, 20, 3; 5, 35, 2; 5, 36, 1; 5, 49, 1; 5, 50. — *pulsare,* to accuse before a tribunal (Stat.; Ict.; Claud.), 4, 4, 5. — *suspectare,* to mistrust, suspect (Tac.; Apul.; Aur. Vict.), 1, 30, 1; 1, 40, 13; 1, 43, 3; 1, 45, 8; 2, 15, 8; 3, 3, 5; 3, 5, 2; 5, 3, 1; 5, 6; 5, 39, 2. — *se volutare,* to wallow (Phaedr.; Plin. mai.; Veget.), 5, 22.

8. Inchoative Verbs.

a) *acquiescere,* to obey, agree to (Bell. Afr.; Sen. ep.; Suet.; otherwise Late Latin in this meaning and found especially in the Jurists and Eccl. writers (Ambros)), 1, 15, 1; 1, 30, 5; 2, 8, 1; 2, 9, 1 (bis); 2, 9, 3; 2, 12, 2; 3, 16; 3, 18, 2; 4, 4, 3; 5, 3, 1; 5, 4, 4; 5, 33, 2. — *consenescere,* to become powerless, lose force (Varr.; Cic.(4); Sall.; Liv.; Val. Max.; Flor.; Symm.; Lact.; Amm.; et al), 1, 26, 4. — *dulcescere,* to become sweet (Cic.(1); Sen. phil.; Plin. mai.; Ambros.; Paul. Nol.; Mart. Cap.), 4, 17; 5, 41. — *effervescere,* to rage vehemently (Cic.(4); Tac), 1, 40, 8.— *ingemiscere,* to sigh or groan over (Cic.(1); Verg.; Stat.; Apul.; Amm.; Ambros.), 1, 17, 2. — *insolescere,* to grow haughty or insolent (Sall.; Tac.; Cato apud Gell.; Iust.; Amm.), 2, 1, 2; 2, 10, 6; 3, 13. — *requiescere,* to rest or repose in the grave (Cic.(1); Ov.; Mart.; Petron.; Orell. inscr.; de Rossi inscr.; C.I.L.), 5, 15.

b) *accrescere,* to be added to, to be joined to (Cato; Ps. Sall.; Hor.; Liv.; Phaedr.; Tac.; Plin. ep.; Val. Fl.; Fronto; Ulp.;

Papin.; and Late), 1, 35, 6. — *adolescere,* to increase, grow (Plaut.;
Varr.; Cic.(4) ; Caes.; Sall.; Poetical, Silver and Late), 5, 20, 1. —
arescere, to become dry (Plaut.; Cato; Varr.; Cic.(3) ; Lucr.; Rhet.
Her.; Silver and Late (Ambros.)), 5, 21, 3; 5, 24, 2. — *assues-
cere,*[3] to accustom one's self to (Plaut.; Varr.; Cic.(8); Caes.;
Sall.; Poetical, Silver and Late), 1, 12, 3. — *calescere,* to become
hot or warm (Cato; Cic.(2) ; Lucr.; Ov.; Vitr.; Cels.; Sen. phil.;
Plin. mai.; Sil.; Apul.; Amm.; et al), 3, 12, 3. — *consenescere,* to
grow old (Plaut.; Cic.(3) ; Varr.; Prop.; Hor.; Ov.; Liv.; Colum.;
Sen. phil.; Plin. mai.; Suet.; and Late), 4, 26, 1; 5, 27. —
desuescere, to become unaccustomed (Titin.; Verg.; Tibull.; Liv.;
Sen. phil.; Stat.; Quint.; Ambros.; et al), 4, 26, 1. — *excrescere,*
to grow up, rise up (Cato; Cels.; Sen. phil.; Colum.; Plin. mai.;
Lucan.; Tac.; Quint.; Suet.; Frontin.; Lact.; Hier.; Aug.), 1, 16,
4; 3, 5, 2. — *turgescere,* to swell up, to swell (Enn. fr.; Varr.; Ov.;
Plin. mai.), 3, 11, 1; 5, 18, 2.

c) *aegrescere,* to become diseased (of the body) (Lucr.; Plin.
mai.; Ser. Samm.; Ambros.; Aug.; Macr.), 4, 16, 2. — *clarescere,*
to become illustrious (Lucr.; Stat.; Quint.; Tac.; Hil.; Cypr.;
Spart.; Capit.; Lact.; Vulg.; et al), 2, 12, 1. — *contremescere*
(*contremiscere*), to tremble at or be afraid of a thing (Hor.; Sen.
phil.; Min. Fel.; Iust.; Lucif.; Ps. Rufin.; Aug.; and Late), 5,
16. — *crebescere* (*crebrescere*), to increase, become frequent (Verg.;
Val. Fl.; Quint.; Tac.; Plin. ep.; Spart.; Lact.; Iuvenc.; Amm.;
Veget.; Aug.; et al), 4, 17. — *crudescere,* to grow worse, increase
(Verg.; Sil.; Stat.; Tac.; Priscill.; Auson.; Symm.; Amm.;
Ambros.; Ps. Rufin.; Oros.; Sid.), 5, 2. — *exhorrescere,* to tremble
at, to be terrified at (Verg.; Val. Max.; Suet.; Vulg.), 1, 44, 8. —
fatiscere, to fall to pieces, to crumble (Lucr.; Verg.; Val. Fl.;
Sil.; Stat.; Gell.; Iul. Val.; Ambros.; Prud.; et al), 3, 11, 1; 4,
18. — *inhorrescere,* to quake, tremble (Hor.; Ov.), 4, 9, 1. —
innotescere, to become known (Ov.; Liv.; Phaedr.; Plin. mai.;
Tac.; Iust.; Ict.), 1, 44, 2; 4, 21. — *inolescere,* to grow in, on, or
to something, implant itself (Verg.; Gell.; Auson.; Ambros.;
Pacat.), 5, 24, 3. — *intumescere,* to rise, swell up (Ov.; Sen. phil.;

---

[3] Heg. 1, 12, 3, is the only reference cited in the T.L.L. II 908, 15-16 for
the reflexive use.

9

Plin. mai.), 4, 15, 2. — *iuvenescere*, to grow young again (Ov.; Plin. mai.), 1, 43, 3. — *marescere*, to become weak or feeble (Ov.; Liv.; Colum.; Plin. mai.; Vulg.; Aug.), 5, 27; 5, 53, 1. —*patescere*, to be opened, to be laid open (Verg.; Sen. phil.; Plin. mai.), 5, 42, 2; — to be disclosed, to become evident (Verg.; Sen. phil.), 1, 40, 13. — *vanescere*, to pass away, disappear (Ov.; Pers.; Sen. phil.; Quint.; Tac.; Plin. min.; Aug.), 5, 2.

d) *coalescere*, to grow strong (fig.) (Liv.; Pomp. Trog.; Tac.; Ps. Quint.; Vell.; Paneg.; and Late), 4, 16, 2. — *obrigescere*, to grow hard, become hardened (fig.) (Sen. ep.; Aug.), 5, 21, 3. — *recrudescere*, to break out again (fig.) (Liv.; Curt.; Sen. phil.; Cypr.; Hier.), 1, 9, 4; 5, 42, 3. — *valescere*, to acquire strength (fig.) (Tac.), 3, 24.

9. Compound Verbs.

   i. Verbs compounded with a Preposition or a Particle.

   a) *abdicare*, to deprive, strip, rob (Cic. (1); Sol.; Lact.; Paneg.; Ambros.; and Late), 5, 31. — *abnuere*, to refuse (Cic. (1); Lucr.; Plin. mai.; Val. Max.; Sil.; Iuv.; Tac.; Fulg.), 3, 17; — to deny (Cic. (3); Sall.; Liv. (saepe); Tac. (saepe); very popular with Ambros.; Hier.; Aug.), 1, 33; 1, 40, 12; 1, 45, 11; 2, 16, 1; 3, 22, 1; 4, 6, 8; 5, 16; 5, 27; 5, 47, 3. — *absorbere*, to swallow, devour (Cic. (1); Hor.; Sen. phil.; Curt.; Mela; Plin. mai.; Lucan.; Sil.; Amm.; Paneg.; Vulg.; et al), 5, 24, 3; 5, 41. — *absumere*, to consume in eating or drinking (Varr.; Verg.; Hor.; Liv.; Colum.; Plin. mai.; Silver and Late), 5, 40. — *adicere*,[4] to give, bestow (persons) (Caes.; Bell. Afr.; Liv.; Poetical, Silver and Late), 1, 40, 9. — *adminiculare*, to support, aid (Varr.; Gell.; Cens.; Iul. Val.; Aug.; et al), 1, 28, 5. — *adulari*, to flatter (Cic. (3); Nep.; Liv.; Tac.; Silver and Late), 1, 41, 2. — *advertere*, to know, perceive, understand (Cic. ep. (1); Varr.; Liv.; Plin. mai.; Tac.; Apul.; Amm.; Ambros.; et al), 1, 9, 1; 1, 39; 1, 40, 10 (bis); 1, 41, 8; 1, 42, 4; 2, 11, 4; 2, 15, 7; 3, 15, 4; 3, 24; 4, 2; 4, 8; 4, 26, 2; 4, 28, 2; 5, 14, 1; 5, 14, 4; 5, 35, 1. — *advolvi* (*se advolvere*), to throw one's self at the feet of (Sall.; Liv.; Vell.; Curt.; Val. Max.; and rare in Silver and Late Latin), 5, 49, 1. —

---

[4] The sense in Heg. 1, 40, 9 is " to give in marriage."

RARE CLASSICAL, EARLY, POETIC, AND SILVER

affluere, to run or flow to (Varr.; Sall.; Cic. (3); Lucr.; Verg.; Hor.; Liv.; Silver and Late), 1, 10, 2; 1, 28, 6; 3, 25, 2. — *allegare*, to bring forward, relate, recount (Cic. (2); Quint.; Tac.; Plin. ep.; Suet.; Ps. Quint.; and Late), 1, 45, 1; 3, 18, 1; 4, 4, 3; 4, 18; 5, 47, 1. — *allevare*, to raise, lift up (Sall.; Bell. Alex.; Ov.; Curt.; Silver and Late), 2, 4. — *ambire*, to encircle, surround, encompass (Varr.; Sall.; Poetical, Silver and Late), 2, 5, 4; 3, 23, 1; 5, 53, 1. — *anniti*, to rest upon, lean upon (Cic. (1); Verg.; Colum.; Val. Max.; Tac.; Mart. Cap.; Apul.), 1, 45, 11. — *applicare* (intrans.), to land, bring to (ships) (Bell. Hisp.; Frontin.; Iust.; Greg. Tur.; Hist. Apoll.; Cassiod.), 1, 38, 6. — *aspirare*, to blow (Varr.; Cic. (2); Catull.; Verg.; Poetical, Silver and Late), 5, 27. — *atterere*,[5] to weaken, impair, exhaust (Sall.; Val. Max.; Curt.; Petron.; Plin. mai.; Silver and Late (Ambros.)), 1, 9, 4 (bis); 1, 30, 7; 3, 19; 5, 15. — *attestari*, to bear witness (Varr.; Phaedr.; Plin. mai.; Gell.; Tert.; Itin. Alex.; Iul. Val.; Ambrosiast.; Aug.; et al), 3, 13. — *attexere*, to add (Varr.; Cic. (2); Caes.; Apul.; Iul. Val.; Ambros.; Aug.), 2, 9; 3, 17; 5, 15; 5, 47, 1. — *circumfundi* (*se circumfundere*), to crowd around, press upon (Caes.; Verg.; Ov.; Liv.; Silver and Late), 1, 31, 1; 3, 20, 2; 4, 1, 5; 4, 15, 1; 5, 6 (bis); 5, 7, 2; 5, 19; 5, 37, 1. — *circumfundere*, to lie around, be adjacent (Cic. (2); Ov.; Liv.; Sen. rhet.; Plin. mai.; Silver and Late), 3, 6, 2; — to surround (Cic. (3); Caes.; Varr.?; Nep.; Poetical, Silver and Late), 1, 32, 6; 3, 26, 3; 4, 19; 5, 15; 5, 16. — *circumsaepire*, to surround (Cic. (2); Liv.; Colum.; and rare in Silver and Late Latin), 4, 20. — *circumsonare*, to make something to echo or resound (Cic. (1); Verg.; Liv.; Ov.; Sen. phil.; Flor.; Salv.; Amm.), 2, 15, 8; 4, 25, 2; 5, 27. — *circumvallare*, to surround, encompass (Cic. ep. (1); Caes.; Bell. Hisp.; Dolab.; Liv.; Silver and Late), 1, 44, 6; 1, 46, 2; 2, 15, 5; 3, 9, 5; 3, 13; 3, 23, 1; 5, 14, 4; 5, 19; 5, 20, 2; 5, 27; 5, 38; 5, 52, 2; 5, 53, 1. — *coartare*, to confine, enclose (Cic. (2); Caes.; Liv.; Cels.; Sen. phil.; Colum.; Plin. mai.; and Late), 2, 15, 7; 3, 26, 3. — *cohonestare*, to honor, grace (Cic. (4); Liv.; Apul.; and Late), 5, 15. — *collidere*, to strike or dash together (Sall.; Manil.; Sen. phil.; Petron.; Curt.; and Late), 3, 20, 2. — *colligere*,

[5] The perfect, passive participle is found in Cic. Verr. 5, 94 used as an adjective.

to deduce, infer, conclude (Cic. (5); Varr.; Ov.; Liv.; Poetical, Silver and Late), 5, 16. — *commaculare*, to pollute (fig.) (Cic. (1); Sall.; Val. Max.; Stat.; Fronto; Tert.; and Late), 5, 32. — *complanare*, to raze (Cic. (1); Bell. Alex.; Dict.; Amm.; Rufin.; Vulg.; Cod. Iust.; Lex Visig.), 5, 2. — *componere*, to build, erect (Cic. ep. (1); Verg.; Prop.; Vitr.; Phaedr.; Colum.; Vopisc.; Amm.; et al), 5, 52, 2; — to pacify, quiet (Cic. (1); Liv.; Vell.; Curt.; Tac.; Suet.; Spart.; Amm.), 3, 1, 2. — *comprehendere*, to take, catch (of fire) (Hirt.; Verg.; Ov.; Liv.; Manil.; Vitr.; Sen. poet.; Curt.; Iren.; Arnob.; Vulg.; et al), 5, 42, 2. — *condere*, to write, compose (Cic. (3); Verg.; Lucr.; Hor.; Prop.; Ov.; Liv.; Val. Max.; Plin. mai.; Quint.; Gell.; Tert.; and Late), 1, 38, 4. — *conducere*, to levy mercenaries, to hire soldiers (Caes.; Nep.; Liv.; Curt.; Sil.; Flor.; Iust.; Veget.; Amm.; Vulg.), 5, 16 (bis). — *confodere*, to pierce, stab (Sall.; Nep.; Poetical, Silver and Late), 1, 28, 3. — *congregare*, to collect, accumulate (Cic. (1); Vitr.; Vell.; Sen. phil.; Plin. mai.; Stat.; Quint.; Tac.; Flor.; and Late especially), 2, 9, 3; 3, 3, 6. — *coniungere*, to join in marriage (Varr.; Lucr.; Verg.; Liv.; Sen. phil.; Val. Fl.; Sil.; Tac.; Suet.; Ulp.; et al), 1, 37, 3. — *consauciare*, to wound severely (Rhet. Her.; Suet.; Veget.; Ambros.), 4, 11. — *conspirare*, to conspire (Caes.; Liv.; Silver and Late), 1, 1, 9; 4, 6, 2; 4, 19; 5, 4, 3; 5, 41. — *constipare*, to crowd closely together (Cic. (1); Caes.; Amm.; Potam.; and Late especially), 5, 25, 1. — *contexere*, to compose, put together, contrive, devise (Cic. (1); Nep.; Sen. phil.; Quint.; and Late), 1, 37, 2; 2, 12, 3. — *contingere*, to obtain, acquire (Cic. (1); Lucr.; Verg.; Manil.; Phaedr.; Val. Fl.; Sil.; Apul.; Tert.; Itala; Arnob.; et al), 2, 1, 2. — *convehere*, to bring together (Varr.; Cic. (1); Caes.; Lucr.; Liv. (saepe); Plin. mai.; Tac.; Silver and Late), 5, 14, 3 (bis). — *convertere*, to turn (in a hostile sense) (Bell. Alex.; Bell. Afr.; Verg.; Liv.; Lucan.; Val. Fl.; Sil.; Suet.; Flor.; Vulg.; Dict.), 5, 21, 4. — *corripere*, to censure, blame (Cael. in Cic. ep. (2); Caes.; Ciris; Hor.; Liv.; Val. Max.; Sen. phil.; Silver and Late), 2, 12, 1. — *decerpere*, to diminish, take away (Cic. (2); Catull.; Quint.; Plin. min.; Apul.; and Late especially), 4, 11. — *decurrere*, to discuss, treat (Cic. (1); Tert.; Cypr.; Lact.; Chalc.; Ambros.; et al), 4, 18. — *deducere*, to change (Cic. (3); Caes.; rare in Poetical, Silver and Late

Latin), 1, 38, 5; 1, 40, 9. — *deerrare*, to stray, deviate (transf. sense) (Rhet. Her.; Lucr.; Vell.; Sen. phil.; Colum.; Quint.; Arnob.; Amm.; et al), 1, 43, 6. — *deficere*, to die (Caes.; Ov.; Tibull.; Sen. phil.; Cels.; Colum.; Mela; Silver and Late especially), 1, 40, 8; 1, 45, 12; 2, 6, 1; 5, 21, 3; 5, 22, 1; 5, 23; 5, 24, 2; — to end, stop (Cic. (2); Aetna; Hor.; Ov.; Manil.; Silver and Late), 3, 6, 4. — *defici* (pass.), to be in need of, destitute of (Cic. (1); Hirt.; Aetna; Ov.; Sen. rhet.; Vell.; Val. Max.; Ulp.; et al), 5, 21, 1. — *deflectere*, to turn aside something (Cic. (2); Catull.; Verg.; Liv.; Sen. phil.; Colum.; Plin. mai.; Ps. Quint.; Min. Fel.), 3, 26, 2. — *defungi*, to die (Cic. ep. (1); Eleg. in Maecen.; Plin. mai.; Quint.; Tac.; Suet.; Itala; Tert.; Vulg.; and Late), 1, 29, 1; 1, 34, 2; 1, 37, 7; 1, 40, 10; 1, 42, 9; 2, 2, 4 (bis); 2, 3, 2; 2, 13, 1; 5, 23. — *deicere*, to deprive (Caes.; Verg.; Liv.; Petron.; Sil.; Tac.; Optat.), 2, 18. — *demergere*, to sink, settle, plunge (Cic. (1); Ov.; Colum.; Mela; Paul. Fest.; Apul.; Tert.; Lact.; and Late), 4, 1, 1; 5, 40; — to overwhelm, oppress (transf. sense) (Nep.; Hor.; Liv.; Sen. phil.; Petron.; Apul.; and Late), 4, 29, 2. — *deonerare*, to unload, unburden (Cic. (1); Arnob.; Schol. Iuv.; Amm.; Schol. Hor.; Ambros.), 1, 20. — *deperire*, to be lost (Varr.; Cic. (2); Caes.; Lucr.; Ov.; Liv.; Sen. phil.; Colum.; Tert.; Hil.; Vulg.; et al), 1, 39.—*derelinquere*, to leave after one's self (transf. sense) (Cic. (1); Plin. mai.; Gaius; Tryph.; Ulp.; Tert.; and Late especially), Praef.; 1, 1, 10; 2, 14, 4; 3, 3, 4; 5, 21, 3. — *derivare*, to divert (fig.) (Cic. (1); Ambros.; Cod. Th.; Petr. Chrys.; Cod. Iust.), 4, 6, 2. — *descendere*, to penetrate deeply (Sall.; Hor.; Liv.; Sen. rhet.; Sen. phil.; Quint.; Hil.; Mar. Victor.; Boeth.; Pallad.), 5, 21, 3. — *deservire*, to be a slave to, to be subject to (Cic. (2); Ov.; Stat.; Sen. phil.; Ps. Quint.; Apul.; and Late especially), 1, 28, 7. — *destillare* (*distillare*), to drip or trickle down (Varr.; Verg.; Fest.; Cels.; Sen. phil.; Colum.; Lucan.; Plin. mai.; Fronto; Tert.; Itala; Vulg.; et al), 1, 15, 3; 4, 17. — *destruere*, to pull down, destroy (Cic. (1); Verg.; Ov.; Sen. phil.; Ps. Quint.; Tac.; Plin. ep.; Suet.; and Late), 1, 19, 1; 1, 25, 4. — *detegere*, to expose, lay bare (Cic. (1); Verg.; Liv.; Ov.; Cels.; Sen. phil.; Silver and Late), 2, 15, 6. — *determinare*, to limit, circumscribe (transf. sense) (Cic. (2); Sen. phil.; Plin. mai.; Suet.; and Late especially), 2,

9, 1. — *detrectare,* to refuse (Cic. fr. (1); Caes.; Sall.; Verg.;
Tibull.; Prop.; Liv.; Silver and Late), 1, 1, 2; 1, 28, 7; 1, 32, 2;
4, 13, 1. — *deurere,* to burn up, consume (Caes.; Bell. Hisp.; Liv.;
Obseq.; Val. Max.; Colum.; Frontin.; Tac.; Suet.; Digest.; Gell.;
Min. Fel.; et al), 5, 43, 1; 5, 53, 1. — *digladiari,*[6] to fight with
swords (Cic. (1); Inscr.; Oros.), 3, 25, 2. — *dilabi,* to flee, escape
(Sall.; Nep.; Liv. (saepissime); Sen. phil.; Curt.; Plin. mai.;
Frontin.; Tac.; Suet.; Amm.; Sulp. Sev.; et al), 1, 19, 2; 1, 20;
2, 15, 7; 4, 3, 1; 5, 53, 1. — *diloricare,* to tear open one's dress
(Cic. (1); Apul.; Ambros.), 1, 6, 2; 1, 25, 2. — *dirigere,* to draw
up troops in battle array (Caes.; Bell. Alex.; Bell. Hisp.; Bell.
Afr.; Verg.; Liv.; Vell.; Silver and Late), 3, 3, 4; — to straighten
something bent (Cic. (2); Lucan.; Plin. mai.; Manil.; Sen. phil.;
Cels.; Sil.; Tert.; Greg. Tur.; Oros.), 5, 46; — to direct a journey,
attack, etc. (Cic. (3); Caes.; Nep.; Verg.; Liv.; Vell.; Sen. phil.;
Curt.; Apul.; and Late), 1, 9, 3; 4, 15, 3; 4, 29, 1; — to direct a
speech, accusation, etc. (Cic. (3); Culex; Val. Max.; Sen. phil.;
Curt.; Quint.; and mostly Late), 1, 41, 9; 2, 8, 4. — *discernere,*
to separate, divide (Varr.; Lucr.; Verg.; Hor.; Gratt.; Liv.; Silver
and Late), 3, 4, 1. — *disicere,* to rout, scatter (Varr.; Cic. (1);
Lentul.; Caes.; Sall.; Nep.; Verg.; Liv.; Val. Fl.; Tac.; Suet.;
Amm.), 4, 15, 2. — *disponere,* to manage (Q. Cic.; Sen. rhet.; Sen.
phil. (saepe); Curt.; Silver and Late), 1, 12, 3. — *se dissociare*
(*dissociari*), to separate one's self (Nep.; Stat.; Modest.; Lact.;
Aug.; et al), 5, 44, 1. — *dissolvere,* to dissolve (an assembly)
(Cic. (1); Sen. phil.; Tac.; Suet.; Iust.; Serv.; Auson.; Macr.;
et al), 4, 10; — to destroy (Cic. (2); Nep.; Lucr.; Vitr.; Colum.;
Val. Fl.; Paul.; Tert.; and Late), 5, 2; 5, 52; — to make effemi-
nate (Bell. Alex.; Liv.; Sen. rhet.; Val. Max.; Phaedr.; Tac.;
Firm.; Eutr.; Aug.; et al), 4, 25, 2. — *disterminare,* to separate,
divide (Cic. (1); Lucr.; Sen. phil.; Plin. mai.; Mela; Tac.; Apul.;
Paul.; Avien.; Amm.; et al), 3, 6, 1; 4, 27. — *edere,* to beget (of
men) (Cic. (1); Verg.; Hor.; Ov.; Liv.; Tac.; Suet.), 4, 31. —
egredi, to leave, pass out of (Caes.; Sall.; Liv.; Plin. mai.; Val.
Max.; Quint.), 3, 26, 1. — *elevare,* to lift up, raise (Caes.; Apul.;
Vulg.; Claud.; Capit.), 1, 44, 8; 2, 3, 4; 2, 18; 3, 5, 2; 3, 11, 3;

---

[6] The T. L. L. V 1131, 54-55 incorrectly cites Heg. 3, 25, 2 as a passive
use.

3, 14; 3, 20, 2; 5, 21, 4; 5, 22, 2; 5, 29; 5, 41. — *eludere*, to parry, avoid (a blow) (Cic. (1); Sen. rhet.; Mart.), 3, 11, 2; 5, 14, 1; 5, 19. — *enatare*, to swim away (Rhet. Her.; Bell. Alex.; Vitr.; Hor.; Sen. rhet.; Phaedr.), 2, 16, 1. — *enavigare*, to sail away, to sail out (Cic. (1); Curt.; Suet.; Apul.; Ict.), 1, 29, 10. — *epotare*,[7] to quaff, swallow (Cic. (2); Liv.; Cels.; Quint.; Suet.), 1, 28, 1; 1, 45, 2. — *evirare*, to weaken, deprive of strength (Varr.; Catull.; Mart.; Arnob.; Veget.; Ambros.; Cael. Aur.), 3, 11, 2. — *exaedificare*, to build up, erect (Cic. (4); Caes.; Sall.; Curt.), 1, 25, 3; 1, 35, 2; 5, 39, 1. — *exciere*, to rouse, excite, disturb (transf. sense) (Sall.; Verg.; Liv.; Tac.), 1, 8; 1, 20; 1, 21, 1; 1, 26, 3; 1, 26, 4; 1, 36, 2; 3, 25, 2; 4, 3, 3; 4, 11; 5, 12; 5, 20, 3; 5, 40; 5, 53, 2. — *excolere*, to cultivate, tend (Varr.; Ov.; Plin. mai.; Prop.; Mart.; Plin. min.; Eumen.; Cl. Mam.), 4, 27. — *exsaturare*, to satiate (fig.) (Cic. (1); Verg.; Stat.; Amm.), 1, 8; 2, 8, 4; 5, 21, 4; 5, 51, 3. — *se extendere*, to exert one's self (Caes.; Liv.), 5, 28. — *exuere*, to deprive, despoil (Caes.; Liv.; Tac.), 2, 15, 5; 5, 52, 2; — to forget, to put off in a mental way (Cic. N. D. 3, 3, 7), 1, 39. — *exulcerare*, to make sore, wound (Varr.; Sen. rhet.; Cels.; Colum.; Plin. mai.; Ambros.), 1, 40, 8; 5, 44, 1. — *illacrimare*, to bewail, lament (Cic. (3); Nep.; Verg.; Hor.; Ov.; Liv.; Cels.; Curt.; Sil.; Tac.; Suet.; Apul.), 1, 36, 2 (bis); 1, 42, 4; 2, 9, 2; 5, 53, 2. — *illaqueare*, to entrap, entangle (Cic. (1); Hor.; Ambros.), 4, 9, 4. — *illidere*, to dash against (Cic. (1); Verg.; Vell.; Cels.; Sen. phil.; Curt.; Plin. mai.; Quint.; Tac.; Suet.; Amm.; Ambros.), 1, 29, 8; 1, 35, 4; 3, 11, 2; 3, 17; 3, 20, 2 (bis); 4, 1, 4; 4, 18; 4, 27 (bis). — *illuminare*, to illuminate (Cic. (1); Colum.; Stat.; Apul.; Cassiod.), 5, 41. — *implere*, to execute, carry out, fulfil (Cic. (2); Ov.; Liv.; Plin. ep.; Tac.; Vulg.; and Eccl.), 1, 17, 1; 4, 3, 2; 5, 16; 5, 53, 2. — *inficere*, to dye (Caes.; Verg.; Hor.; Prop.; Sen. rhet.; Val. Max.; Sen. phil.; Silver and Late), 1, 40, 7; 3, 20, 2; 5, 9, 2. — *inflare*, to inflate, make flatulent (Cic. (1); Ov.; Cels.; Scrib.; Pers.), 5, 24, 2. — *inflectere*, to influence, prevail upon (Cic. (1); Ps. Sall.; Verg.; Ambros.), 1, 14, 1; 1, 30, 9; 1, 40, 9; 1, 40, 11; 1, 40, 13; 1, 43, 6; 1, 44, 8; 1, 45, 1; 2, 4; 2, 9, 2; 2, 11, 4; 3, 16; 5, 14, 4; 5, 17; 5, 33, 1; 5, 35, 1; 5, 43, 2. —

[7] This word is found mostly in the perfect, passive participle. Other forms are rare.

infundi (middle), to mingle with anything, to mix itself (in a bad sense) (Cic. (2)), 5, 16. — *ingerere,* to force upon (Cic. (1); Tac.; Iust.), 1, 44, 2. — *iniungere,* to enjoin, impose upon (fig.) (Caes.; Bell. Alex.; Liv.; Plin. min.; Sid.), 5, 52, 2. — *inniti,* to rest upon (Caes.; Nep.; Ov.; Liv.; Sen. phil.; Plin. mai.; Tac.; Apul.), 4, 27. — *insilire,* to leap upon (Sall.; Hor.; Ov.; Lucan.; Suet.; Fronto; Apul.), 5, 28; 5, 53, 1. — *intendere,* to increase, enhance (Sall.; Tac.; Plin. ep.), 5, 33, 1. — *intercidere,* to go to ruin, be lost, perish (Cic. poet. (1); Liv.; Tac.; Iust.), 3, 24; 5, 21, 3. — *intermiscere,* to intermix, to mix into (transf. sense) (Bell. Hisp.; Hor.; Liv.; Sen. phil.; Iust.; Schol. Pers.), 1, 16, 4; 1, 31, 1. — *intexere,* to link, connect, entwine (transf. sense) (Cic. (3); Tert.), 1, 35, 5; 2, 9. — *introducere,* to bring into, lead into (Sall.; Caes.; Liv.; Sen. rhet.; Curt.; Suet.), 5, 2; 5, 16. — *involvere,* to involve, obscure, conceal (Cic. (1); Verg.; Hor.), 1, 44, 7. — *irrepere,* to creep in or into (Cic. (1); Plin. mai.; Colum.; Tac.; Suet.; Apul.), 2, 9; 5, 38. — *obruere,* to surfeit, overload (Cic. (3); Nep.), 4, 32. — *obstrepere,* to hinder, stand in the way (Cic. ep. (1); Sen. phil.; Plin. mai.; Flor.), 5, 53, 1. — *obterere,* to destroy (transf. sense) (Cic. (2); Sen. phil.; Tac.; Iust.; Nazar.), 3, 13. — *obtruncare,* to kill, slay (Trag. inc. apud Cic. (1); Sall.; Sisenn.; Verg.; Liv.; Vell.; Curt.; Tac.; Fronto; Iust.), 1, 12, 4; 1, 16, 5; 1, 31, 2; 2, 10, 7; 2, 12, 1; 2, 15, 6; 3, 4, 2; 5, 22. — *percurrere,* to traverse, pass through (Caes.; Lucr.; Verg.; Ov.; Prop.; Plin. mai.; Flor.), 4, 25, 1. — *perferre,* to conduct, manage, carry out (an embassy) (Cic. (1); Verg.; Prop.; Stat.; Tac.; Suet.), 5, 22. — *perimere,* to kill, slay (Cic. poet. (1); Verg.; Ov.; Val. Max.; Plin. mai.; Mart.; Tac.; Plin. min.; Apul.; Aug.), 1, 30, 12; 1, 30, 14; 1, 32, 6; 1, 41, 3; 1, 41, 9; 1, 45, 1 (bis); 2, 5, 5; 2, 17; 2, 18 (ter); 3, 7; 3, 17 (bis); 4, 6, 2; 4, 9, 4; 4, 9, 5; 4, 13, 2; 4, 16, 1; 4, 32; 5, 1, 3; 5, 22; 5, 30; 5, 31; 5, 32; 5, 47, 1; 5, 49, 4; 5, 51, 2; 5, 53, 1. — *perstringere,* to narrate briefly (Cic. (4); Vulg.; Hier.), 1, 38, 5. — *pertendere,* to proceed, go on (Bell. Alex.; Liv.; Suet.), 4, 21. — *porrigi* (passive), to extend, stretch itself (Caes.; Verg.; Hor.; Liv.; Plin. min.; Fronto), 1, 35, 3. — *praeeminere,* to overtop (Sall. fr.; Aug.), 3, 5, 2. — *praeoccupare,* to preoccupy, seize upon (Caes.; Nep.; Liv.), 1, 26, 3; 3, 26, 4; 5, 22, 3. — *praeponderare,* to outweigh (fig.) (Cic. (1)), 5, 4, 4.

—*praeripere*, to forestall, anticipate (Cic. (1) ; Sen. phil.; Tac.), 4, 4, 3. — *praetendere*, to hold out as an excuse, to simulate, pretend (Cic. (1) ; Liv.; Quint.; Tac.; Plin. min.; Suet.; Flor.; Paul.; Apul.), 1, 22, 1; 1, 22, 3; 1, 42, 2; 1, 44, 4; 2, 1, 2; 2, 4; 2, 9; 2, 17; 3, 14; 4, 4, 2; 4, 6, 4; 5, 6. — *praetergredi*, to pass by (Cic. ep. (1) ; Bell. Afr.; Sall.; Ambros.), 2, 15, 8. — *praeterire*, to surpass, excel (Varr.; Verg.; Ov.; Vell.), 2, 8, 3. — *praetexere*, to adorn, furnish, provide (Cic. (2)), 3, 11, 1; — to pretend, to allege as an excuse (Cic. (1) ; Liv.; Val. Max.; Vell.; Tac.; Iust.), 1, 28, 7; 3, 1, 1. — *praevenire*,[8] to anticipate (Sall.; Ov.; Liv.; Tac.; Plin. min.; Suet.; Eutr.), 1, 1, 6; 1, 17, 2; 1, 30, 7; 1, 40, 8; 1, 43, 5; 1, 45, 11; 2, 18; 3, 1, 3; 3, 3, 4; 3, 17; 4, 7; 4, 19; 4, 29, 1; 4, 29, 2 (bis) ; 4, 30; 4, 31; 5, 16; 5, 18, 1; 5, 21, 3 (bis) ; 5, 22, 1 (bis); 5, 22, 2; 5, 40; 5, 42, 1; 5, 47, 3; 5, 53, 2; — to hinder, prevent (Sall.; Ov.; Liv.; Tac.; Plin. min.; Suet.; Eutr.), 1, 21, 3; 1, 29, 9; 1, 43, 6; 1, 44, 3; 1, 44, 7; 2, 5, 1; 2, 5, 4; 2, 6, 3; 2, 10, 2; 2, 11, 1; 2, 17; 3, 14; 4, 16, 1; 4, 20; 4, 33; 5, 8, 1; 5, 16; 5, 19; 5, 29; 5, 35, 2; 5, 38; 5, 53, 1 (bis). — *praevertere*, to prevent, make useless (Sall. fr.; Caes.; Ov.; Liv.; Lucan.; Gell.; Ser. Samm.), 1, 29, 8; 1, 29, 10; 1, 33; 3, 25, 1. — *proruere* (intrans.), to fall upon, rush upon (Caes.; Curt.; Gell.), 3, 24; 5, 20, 2; — *proruere* (trans.), to demolish (Caes.; Liv.; Curt.; Tac.), 5, 19. — *prosequi*, to speak about, describe (Rhet. Her.; Verg.; Sen. phil.; Quint.; Plin. min.; Hier.), 2, 1, 2. — *proturbare*, to drive forth, repel (Caes.; Liv.; Colum.; Val. Fl.; Tac.; Plin. min.; Ps. Quint.; Apul.; Iust.), 4, 10, 1; 5, 1, 4; 5, 4, 3; 5, 4, 4; 5, 34. — *rebellare*, to revolt, rebel (Hirt.; Liv.; Suet.; Eutr.; Iul. apud Aug.), 1, 10, 3; 1, 19, 2; 2, 9, 1; 2, 9, 2; 4, 1, 3; 4, 4, 2; 4, 26, 1; 5, 35, 2; 5, 46 (bis). — *recensere*, to count, reckon, survey (Caes.; Ov.; Liv.; Colum.), 2, 9; 5, 24, 3. — *refulgere*, to glitter, glisten (Cic. poet.; Verg.; Hor.; Liv.; Curt.; Plin. mai.; Pallad.), 1, 46, 2; 4, 18; 5, 27; 5, 44, 1. — *refundere*,[9] to pour back, flow back (Cic. (1) ; Verg.; Ov.; Cels.; Lucan.), 5, 16 (bis). — *reparare*, to rebuild, repair (Bell. Alex.; Plin. min.; Eutr.), 1, 19, 1 (bis) ; 1, 20; 3, 1, 4; 3, 20, 1; 4, 3, 1; 5, 2; 5, 14, 2;

---

[8] No distinction is made for this word in any of the Lexica between the meaning " to anticipate " and the meaning " to hinder," " to prevent."

[9] Heg. 5, 16 (bis) uses this word reflexively.

5, 16; 5, 21, 1; 5, 26, 1; 5, 31 (bis); 5, 32; — to renew, restore (fig.) (Cic. (1); Hor.; Ov.; Liv.; Vell.; Lucan.; Plin. mai.; Tac.; Plin. min.; Eutr.), 1, 30, 7; 2, 9; 3, 11, 3; 4, 2; 5, 16; 5, 26, 1. — *reservare*, to save, preserve, keep from perishing (Cic. (1); Caes.; Cels.), 1, 36, 2; 1, 43, 3; 2, 9; 2, 10, 7; 5, 4, 1. — *retorquere*,[10] to turn back (Cic. (1); Caes.; Verg.; Ov.; Hor.; Val. Max.; Sen. phil.; Sil.; Mart.; Plin. min.; Claud.), 5, 4, 4; 5, 42, 6; 5, 52, 2; 5, 53, 1. — *revincire*, to bind, fasten (Caes.; Lucr.; Verg.; Ov.; Prop.; Claud.), 4, 7; 4, 18; 5, 53, 1. — *subtexere*, to add, append, subjoin (Nep.; Tibull.; Liv.; Sen. phil.; Val. Max.; Colum.; Plin. mai.; Suet.; Ambros.), 1, 40, 13; 4, 6, 9; — to contrive, compose, prepare (Nep.; Tibull.; Amm.), 2, 9; 5, 20, 2. — *subvertere*, to overthrow (Sall.; Hor.; Suet.), 5, 14, 1; 5, 14, 3. — *succedere*, to march up, approach (Caes.; Liv.; Tac.), 3, 12, 3 (bis); 5, 19. — *succingere*, to gird, surround (transf. sense) (Cic. (2); Liv.; Plin. mai.; Petron.; Sil.; Quint.; Stat.; Plin. min.), 5, 9, 3. — *suffigere*, to fasten or fix on (Cic. (1); Bell. Afr.; Catull.; Hor.; Vell.; Val. Max.; Phaedr.; Suet.; Apul.; Iust.; Paul.; Hil.; Prud.; Oros.), 1, 12, 4. — *suffodere*, to dig under, undermine (Cic. (1); Sall.; Bell. Alex.; Vell.; Curt.; Plin. mai.; Tac.; Vulg.), 2, 15, 4. — *suffundere*, to suffuse, fill (Cic. (1); Verg.; Ov.; Tibull.; Lucr.; Sen. phil.; Plin. mai.), 1, 42, 3. — *supplantare*, to supplant, upset (Cic. (1); Sen. ep.; Ambros.), 4, 2. — *suspendere*, to hold up, support, raise up (Caes.; Verg.; Sen. phil.; Colum.; Mela; Sil.; Stat.; Pallad.), 4, 15, 2; 5, 36, 2. — *transmittere*, to despatch, send off (Caes.; Liv.; Vell.; Colum.; Tac.), 5, 49, 3. — *transverberare*, to pierce through, transfix (Cic. (2); Verg.; Liv.; Sen. phil.; Val. Max.; Tac.; Lact.), 1, 1, 2.

b) *abligurrire*, to waste or spend in luxurious indulgence (Ter.; Apul.; Sid.), 4, 7; 4, 32. — *abscidere*, to cut off (Plaut.; Varr.; Cic. (1); Lucr.; Caes.; Verg.; Hor.; Ov.; Liv.; Silver and Late), 1, 29, 7; 4, 1, 1. — *absorbere*, to devour (transf. sense) (Plaut.; Cic. (3); Catull.; Itala; and Late), 2, 3, 1; 5, 40. — *absumere*, to waste, consume, destroy (transf. sense) (Plaut.; Ter.; Acc.; Cic. (1); Lucr.; Verg.; Ov.; Liv.; Silver and Late), 1, 12, 1. —

---

[10] This word is used reflexively in Heg. 5, 4, 4; 5, 52, 2. There are no citations for the reflexive use in any of the Lexica.

accelerare (trans.), to hasten (Acc.; Caes.; Nep.; Lucr.; Liv.; Quint.; Plin. mai.; Tac.; Apul.; and Late), 1, 37, 3; 1, 40, 7; 1, 45, 6; 2, 3, 3; 2, 5, 3; 3, 17; 5, 2; 5, 22. — *accendere*, to incite, rouse up (Acc.; Sall. (17); Verg.; Ov.; Liv.; Curt.; Plin. mai.; Quint.; Tac.), 1, 1, 7; 1, 24, 1; 1, 32, 7; 1, 42, 8; 2, 13, 2; 2, 13, 8; 3, 4, 3; 3, 9, 4; 3, 11, 1; 3, 12, 1; 4, 1, 3; 4, 1, 5; 4, 3, 1; 4, 6, 10; 5, 8, 2; 5, 10, 1; 5, 18, 3; 5, 26, 3; 5, 29; 5, 34; 5, 42, 5; 5, 53, 1; 5, 53, 2. — *accingere*, to gird, arm (Varr. Atac.; very frequent among the poets; Liv.; Quint.; Tac.; Plin. min.; Apul.; Hier.; and Late), 1, 6, 2; 5, 5. — *accire*, to summon, call (Acc.; Varr.; Cic. (4); Sall.; Poetical, Silver and Late), 3, 22, 1. — *adigere*, to compel, force (Plaut.; Cic. (1); Quint.; Tac.; Carm. Epigr.; Amm.; Oros.; et al), 5, 16; 5, 24, 3. — *adorare*, to venerate, worship (Laev. fr.; Verg.; Prop.; Ov.; Liv.; Sen. phil.; Colum.; Lucan.; Silver and Late), 3, 2; 3, 14 (bis). — *adornare*, to prepare, get ready (Plaut.; Ter.; Cic. (3); Caes.; Liv.; Gell.; Amm.; Apul.; Ambros.; et al), 5, 24, 3. — *adurere*, to burn, scorch (Ter.; Cato; Laber.; Varr.; Cic. (3); Poetical, Silver and Late), 4, 18. — *advertere*, to turn, direct (Ter.; Cic. (1); Verg.; Ov.; Liv.; Colum.; Curt.; Stat.; and rare in Silver and Late Latin), 2, 13, 4. — *affari*, to speak to, address, accost (Acc.; Cic. (5); Poetical especially, Silver and Late), 5, 22. — *affectare*, to desire, aspire to, seek after (Plaut.?; Sall.; Nep.; Ov.; Liv.; Silver and Late), 1, 23; 1, 36, 1; 1, 40, 10; 1, 41, 9; 1, 42, 8; 1, 44, 7; 4, 23, 1; 5, 22, 2. — *aggerere*, to bear, carry, convey (Plaut.; Varr.; Cic.(1); Caes.; Verg.; Sen. phil.; Curt.; Silver and Late), 1, 16, 4. — *ambire*, to solicit (Plaut.; Ter.; Varr.; Cic. (4); Sall.; Verg.; Hor.; Ov.; Liv.; Silver and Late), 1, 44, 8; 2, 10, 3; 4, 25, 3; 5, 16. — *amburere*, to burn wholly up (Plaut.; Acc.; Cic. (4); Sall.; Verg.; Hor.; Liv.; Silver and Late), 5, 2. — *amplecti*, to hold firmly, grasp (Plaut.; Ter.; Liv. Andr.; Poetical, Silver and Late), 3, 20, 2. — *anniti*, to serve, to do a service to (Plaut.; Cic. ep. (1); Sall.; Liv.; Plin. mai.; Sil.; Silver and Late), 1, 17, 2; 2, 10, 3; 5, 16, 1; 5, 30. — *approperare*, to hasten (Plaut.; Ter.; Cic. (4); Bell. Afr.; Ov.; Liv.; Sil.; Tac.; Auson.), 5, 22, 1. — *arridere*, to be favorable (Plaut.; Lucr.; Sen. phil.; Petron.; Plin. mai.; Calp.; Lact.; Avien.; Amm.; Ambros.; et al), 1, 44, 3. — *aspergere* (*aspargere*), to scatter, bespatter (Plaut.; Rhet. Her.;

Varr.; Cic. (2); Lucr.; Verg.; Hor.; Liv.; Silver and Late),
1, 46, 2; 3, 20, 2. — *assistere*, to be present (Plaut.; Ter.; Prop.;
Liv.; Val. Max.; Sen. phil.; Plin. mai.; Stat.; Quint.; Tac.; Suet.;
Apul.; Itala; Tert.; et al), 2, 1, 2. — *attinere* (trans.), to hold
fast, keep, detain (Plaut.; Trag. inc.; Cic. (1); Tac. (saepissime);
Fronto; Amm.; Apul.; et al), 1, 1, 7. — *attollere*, to lift up, raise
(Plaut.; Pacuv.; Ter.; Sall. fr.; Poetical, Silver and Late), 5, 21,
3; 5, 28. — *aufugere*, to flee or run away (Plaut.; Ter.; Cato;
Cic. (7); Nep.; Liv.; Tac.; Suet.; Apul.; and Late), 1, 19, 2;
1, 21, 1. — *circumvehi*, to sail around (Plaut.; Caes.; Bell. Alex.;
Nep.; Liv. (saepe); Curt.; Mela; Plin. mai.; Tac.), 4, 27. —
cognoscere, to copulate (Turpil.; Ov.; Colum.; Tac.; Papin.; Itala;
Hil.; Ambros.; Hier.; Vulg.; Aug.), 1, 22, 1. — *coire*, to assemble
(Ter.; Trag. inc.; Varr.; Cic. ep. (1); Caes.; Catull.; Poetical;
Liv.; Silver and Late), 5, 8, 2. — *comminuere*, to break (Plaut.;
Enn.; Cato; Sisenn.; Varr.; Cic. (2); Poetical, Silver and Late),
2, 15, 7; 3, 11, 3; 3, 12, 2. — *commori*, to die at the same time
with (Plaut.; Sall. fr.; Liv.; Sen. phil.; Plin. mai.; Quint.; and
Late mostly), 1, 17, 1; 5, 12; 5, 53, 1. — *complacere*, to be pleasing
(Plaut.; Ter.; Gell.; Apul.; Tert.; Nemes.; Sol.; Ambros.; and
Late), 1, 42, 5; 5, 16. — *componere* (= ponere), to place (Varr.
Atac.; Cato; Varr.; Cic. (2); Poetical, Silver and Late), 1, 40, 7;
2, 4; — to perform, finish (Plaut.; Ter.; Pollio; Cic. (1); Sall.;
Caes.; Nep.; Liv.; Poetical, Silver and Late), 4, 28, 1; — to devise,
contrive (Plaut.; Tibull.; Prop.; Liv.; Tac.; Ps. Quint.; Amm.;
Avien.; et al), 1, 37, 2; 1, 41, 4; 1, 41, 11 (bis); 2, 10, 1; 4, 6, 9
(bis); 4, 7 (bis); 5, 33, 1; — to make an agreement, to plan
(Plaut.; Ter.; Cic. (1); Sall.; Verg.; Hor.; Ov.; Liv.; Stat.;
Mart.; Tac.; and Late), 1, 13, 2; 1, 30, 2; 1, 43, 3; — to feign,
invent, simulate (Plaut.; Cic. (2); Sall.; Liv.; Val. Max.; Quint.;
Tac.; Apul.; Tert.; and Late), 1, 40, 4; 1, 41, 3; 1, 44, 7. —
concelebrare, to celebrate, solemnize (Plaut.; Afran.; Cic. (1);
Liv.; Poetical, Silver and Late), 1, 36, 1. — *conciere*, to rouse up
(Plaut.; Ter.; Pacuv.; Acc.; Afran.; Verg.; Lucr.; Ov.; Liv.;
Silver and Late), 5, 6; 5, 36, 2. — *confabulari*, to converse together
(Plaut.; Ter.; Varr.; Paul. Fest.; Iren.; Firm.; Mar. Vict.; et al),
5, 53, 1. — *configere*, to fasten (Enn.; Vitr.; Colum.; Lucan.;
Petron.; Paul. Fest.; Apul.; Vulg.; Aug.), 5, 30. — *confluere*, to

come together in multitudes (Plaut.; Varr.; Cic. (4); Caes.; Nep.;
Liv.; Poetical, Silver and Late), 4, 1, 2. — *confundere*, to shed
(Cato; Cic. (1); Hor.; Vitr.; Colum.; Lucan.; Plin. mai.; Gell.;
Cypr.; et al), 5, 1, 3. — *conglobare*, to crowd together, collect
(Sisenn.; Sall.; Ps. Sall.; Liv.; Tac.; Apul.; Veget.; Amm.; et
al), 2, 18. — *conscendere*, to ascend, mount (Lucil.; Caes.; Bell.
Hisp.; Catull.; Lucr.; Liv.; Poetical, Silver and Late), 3, 2. —
conserere, to join or engage in (battle) (Plaut.; Caes.; Sall.;
Verg.; Ov.; Liv.; Silver and Late), 1, 13, 3; 1, 16, 4; 1, 19, 2;
1, 24, 2; 2, 10, 4; 2, 14, 4; 5, 22; 5, 35, 2; 5, 36, 2. — *consternare*,
to terrify, alarm (Pacuv.; Caes.; Sall.; Hirt.; Ov.; Liv. (saepe);
Silver and Late), 1, 28, 3; 5, 23; 5, 30. — *conterere*, to wear out,
exhaust (of men) (Naev.; Plaut.; Cic. (1); Lucr.; Sen. phil.;
Mart.; Itala; Amm.; Lact.; Vulg.; et al), 2, 15, 6. — *convenire*,
to be fit, suitable (Plaut.; Cato; Cic. (1); Hor.; Ov.; Vitr.;
Colum.; Lucan.; Stat.; Herm.; Amm.; et al), 1, 35, 5; 1, 36, 1. —
convertere, to set out for, to seek (Plaut.; Cic. (2); Sall.; Nep.;
Caes.; Sen. phil.; Liv.; Flor.; Amm.), 3, 25, 1. — *decumbere*, to
lie down on a bed or couch (Plaut.; Ter.; Cato; Copa; Sen. ep.;
Suet.; Ps. Quint.; Ulp.; and Late), 1, 6, 3. — *decurrere*, to pass
through a space of time (Plaut.; Ter.; Cic. (1); Lucr.; Prop.;
Phaedr.; Tert.; and Late especially), 1, 29, 1. — *deficere*, to be
weak, faint (Ter.; Cic. (2); Verg.; Ov.; Liv.; Sen. phil.; Curt.;
Silver and Late), 5, 18, 2. — *defraudare*, to cheat, deprive (Plaut.;
Ter.; Lucil.; Cato; Varr.; Cic. (2); Plin. mai.; Petron.; Fronto;
Apul.; and Late), 1, 41, 3; 2, 4; 5, 18, 2; 5, 21, 3; 5, 27. — *demere*,
to cut off (Plaut.; Varr.; Q. Cic.; Ov.; Sen. rhet.; Sen. phil.;
Plin. mai.; Suet.; Ulp.; Auson.; et al), 3, 3, 8. — *demorari*, to
dwell, live abide (Plaut.; Vitr.; Ulp.; Fronto; Gell.; Apul.; Tert.;
Ambros.; and Late), 1, 44, 3; 5, 16; 5, 46. — *deperire* (trans.),
to be desperately in love with (Plaut.; Ter.; Catull.; Quint.;
Fronto; Gell.; Ps. Cypr.; Lact.; Hier.; Vulg.), 2, 2, 4. — *derelinquere*, to leave after one's self (proper sense) (Plaut.; Cic. (3);
Sall.; Catull.; Sen. phil.; Curt.; Plin. mai.; and Late especially),
1, 42, 2; 1, 42, 3; 1, 45, 10; 2, 3, 2; 2, 8, 3; 2, 13, 8; 2, 15, 8;
3, 16; 4, 2; 4, 30; 5, 5; 5, 11, 2; 5, 49, 3; 5, 51, 1; 5, 53, 1. —
derivare, to lead, draw off (of waters) (Plaut.; Titin.; Caes.;
Hirt.; Bell. Alex.; Sen. phil.; Plin. mai.; Iust.; Amm.; Ambros.;

et al), 3, 26, 1 (bis). — *desilire,* to dismount (Plaut.; Cic. (1);
Caes.; Verg.; Ov.; Hor.; Prop.; Silver and Late), 3, 22, 1; 3, 25,
2; 5, 12. — *despoliare,* to rob, plunder, despoil (Plaut.; Ter.;
Turpil.; Cic. (2); Sen. phil.; Petron.; Mart.; Quint.; Pompon.;
Tert.), 3, 3, 4; 5, 30. — *despuere,* to spit out, to throw up (Naev.;
Varr.; Ciris; Liv.; Plin. mai.; Pers.; Petron.; Ps. Ambros.; Hymn.
Ambros.; Prud.; Claud.; Cael. Aur.; Mart. Cap.), 3, 20, 2. —
determinare, to enclose with boundaries (Plaut.; Lucr.; Liv.;
Germ.; Plin. mai.; Frontin.; Tert.; Ulp.; Iren.; Amm.; et al),
1, 17, 2; 3, 6, 1. — *devehere,* to carry away, convey (Plaut.; Enn.;
Rhet. Her.; Cic. (2); Caes.; Nep.; Liv.; Ov.; Silver and Late),
5, 40. — *dirumpere,* to break, burst asunder (Plaut.; Varr.;
Cic. (1); Sen. phil.; Tac.; Apul.; and Late especially), 1, 24, 1. —
disperdere, to destroy (Plaut.; Pacuv.; Cato; Com. inc.; Titin.;
Cic. (1); Sen. phil.; Calp.; Gell.; Lact.; Amm.; Vulg.; et al),
5, 43, 1. — *dissociare,* to separate, deprive (Lucil.; Varr.; Cic. (3);
Nep.; Hor.; Ov.; Manil.; Sen. phil.; Silver and Late), 1, 34, 1;
3, 1, 3; 3, 17. — *dissolvere,* to do away with, get rid of (feelings)
(Volac.; Cic. (2); Liv.; Quint.; Frontin.; Ulp.; Hil.; Min. Fel.;
et al), 1, 9; 3, 19. — *distendere,* to distend, swell out (Plaut.;
Lucil.; Enn.; Lucr.; Verg.; Hor.; Ov.; Colum.; Silver and Late),
3, 6, 4; 5, 24, 2. — *eliminare,* to turn out of doors (Enn.; Acc.;
Quint. poet.; Sid.; Pompon.; Ambros.), 1, 44, 3. — *enare,* to escape
by swimming, swim away (Plaut.; Sall. fr.; Cic. (1); Liv.; Val.
Max.; Sil.), 3, 20, 2; 3, 26, 3. — *excidere,* to lose, forfeit, be de-
prived of (Plaut.; Ter.; Prop.; Ov.; Liv.; Curt.; Sen. rhet.;
Suet.), 1, 39; 3, 7. — *exciere,* to stir up, rouse up (Plaut.; Lucr.;
Verg.; Tac.), 5, 11, 1. — *excutere,* to knock out, force out, expel
(Plaut.; Ter.; Lucil.; Cic. (2); Verg.; Ov.; Plin. mai.; Colum.;
Plin. min.; Suet.), 3, 20, 2; 3, 26, 4. — *exuberare,* to be abundant
(Acc. fr.; Verg.; Mela; Plin. mai.; Frontin.; Lact.; Amm.), 5,
16. — *illicere,* to attract, win over (Ter.; Cic. (3); Sall.; Lucr.;
Liv.; Plin. mai.; Lact.; Amm.; Aur. Vict.), 2, 13, 4. — *se immer-
gere,* to betake one's self, to plunge one's self (Plaut.; Iust.), 1,
41, 2; 2, 9; 3, 8, 2. — *incantare,* to chant a magic formula (Frg.
XII Tabb. tab. VIII, 26 apud Plin. 28, 17), 3, 2. — *increpare,*
to reprove, chide (Plaut.; Sall.; Liv.; Tac.; Plin. min.; Suet.;
Flor.), 5, 2; 5, 24, 4. — *indere,* to give to, to attach to, to confer

(Plaut.; Sall.; Liv.; Vell.; Mela; Tac.), 3, 3, 3; 4, 27. — *infodere,*[11] to bury, inter (Cato; Varr.; Caes.; Nep.; Verg.; Hor.; Colum.; Plin. mai.; Pers.; Sil.; Stat.; Vulg.; Aug.), 1, 30, 8. — *ingerere,* to charge, reproach with (Ter.; Cic. ep. (1); Hor.; Liv.; Tac.; Suet.), 1, 41, 10. — *ingruere,* to attack, assail (Plaut.; Verg.; Plin. mai.; Tac.), 2, 9; 2, 18; 3, 3, 4; 5, 16; 5, 19; 5, 35, 1; 5, 36, 2; 5, 41; 5, 42, 5. — *insilire* (intrans.), to leap upon or into (Plaut.; Caes.; Hor.; Ov.; Liv.; Phaedr.; Lucan.; Plin. min.; Apul.), 3, 26, 3; 4, 30; 5, 34. — *intorquere,* to hurl (fig.) (Lucil.; Cic. (1); Sil.), 5, 16. — *involare,* to attack, seize (Plaut.; Ter.; Lucil.; Bell. Alex.; Plin. mai.; Tac.; Apul.), 3, 4, 1. — *nescire,* not to know, to be unacquainted with (Ter.; Plaut.; Verg.; Lucan.; Iuv.; Flor.; Ambros.; Hier.; Gennad.), 1, 40, 1. — *obiacere,* to lie over against (Enn. fr.; Liv.; Mela; Tac.; Frontin.; Plin. min.), 1, 35, 1; 3, 5, 2. — *obire,* to die (Plaut.; Hor.; Liv.; Vell.; Plin. mai.; Suet.; Eutr.; Ambros.), 1, 37, 7; 5, 41. — *oboriri,* to arise, appear (Ter.; Cic. (1); Nep.; Lucr.; Verg.; Ov.; Liv.; Sen. rhet.; Curt.), 5, 40. — *obserare,* to bolt, bar (Ter.; Liv.; Suet.; Amm.), 1, 16, 3; 5, 18, 2; 5, 44, 1. — *observare,* to guard, watch (Plaut.; Cic. poet. (1); Ov.), 3, 25, 4. — *occipere,* to begin (Plaut.; Ter.; Sall.; Lucr.; Liv.; Tac.; Amm.), 1, 15, 2; 1, 20. — *opperiri* (trans.), to wait for, await (Plaut.; Ter.; Liv.; Tac.; Iust.), 4, 16, 1. — *oppignerare* (*oppignorare*), to pledge, give as a pledge (fig.) (Ter.; Sen. phil.; Ambros.), 1, 29, 9; 1, 42, 2. — *percolere,* to honor (men) (Plaut.; Tac.), 1, 28, 7. — *perpetrare,* to perpetrate, commit, do, accomplish (Plaut.; Varr.; Liv.; Curt.; Tac.; Vulg.; Aug.), 5, 14, 3. — *perstrepere,* to raise a clamor (of persons) (Ter. eun. 600), 1, 28, 8. — *posthabere,* to neglect, to place after (Ter.; Cic. (2); Caes.; Verg.; Tac.), 1, 29, 10; 1, 44, 3; 2, 13, 7; 5, 16. — *praecellere,* to surpass, excel (Plaut.; Sil.; Tac.; Suet.; Ict.; Apul.; Vulg.; Aug.), 5, 7, 1; 5, 9, 2. — *praeferre,* to exhibit, display, show (Sisenn.; Cic. (1); Planc. in Cic. ep.; Caes.; Ov.; Liv.; Curt.; Mart.; Tac.; Apul.), 1, 30, 7; 4, 4, 2. — *praefestinare,* to hasten too much (Plaut.; Afran.; Ps. Ov.; Liv.; Colum.; Donat.), 5, 38. — *praeoptare,* to desire more, to choose or wish rather (Plaut.; Ter.; Caes.; Liv.; Curt.; Quint.; Tac.; Iust.), 1,

---

[11] This word is used reflexively in Heg. 1, 30, 8.

28, 7; 1, 32, 7; 2, 9. — *promovere*, to effect, accomplish (Ter.; Fronto; Gell.; Iust.), 3, 23, 1. — *prostituere*, to prostitute (Plaut.; Catull.; Ov.; Sen. rhet.; Suet.; Lact.), 1, 37, 2. — *proterere*, to tread under foot (Plaut.; Caes.; Verg.; Ov.; Liv.; Val. Max.), 5, 25, 2. — *recidere*, to cut away, cut off (Cato; Verg.; Hor.; Ov.; Lucan.; Quint.; Calp.; Porphyr.), 4, 18; 5, 2. — *referire*, to strike back (Plaut.; Sen. phil.; Ambros.), 2, 15, 6. — *remeare*, to return, to come or go back (Plaut.; Cic. (1); Verg.; Hor.; Liv.; Sen. phil.; Plin. mai.; Tac.; Apul.; Ambros.), 1, 2; 1, 32, 6; 2, 2, 4; 5, 16 (bis); 5, 20, 2. — *resilire*, to spring back, rebound (Quadrig.; Ov.; Liv.; Vitr.; Plin. mai.; Quint.), 4, 18 (bis). — *retrudere*,[12] to thrust back (Plaut.; Cic. (3); Itin. Alex.; Sulp. Sev.; Hier.; Cod. Th.; Not. Tir.), 4, 9, 5. — *revereri*, to revere, reverence (Plaut.; Rhet. Her.; Curt.; Colum.; Plin. min.; Gell.), 1, 39 (bis); 4, 6, 7. — *succenturiare*, to place in reserve (Plaut.; Ter.; Caecil.; Favorin.; Hier.), 5, 4, 2. — *succingere*, to gird about, arm (Enn. fr.; Rhet. Her.; Anton. apud Cic.; Verg.; Liv.), 1, 5. — *succidere*, to cut down, fell, cut off (Enn. fr.; Varr.; Caes.; Verg.; Liv.; Vitr.; Colum.; Sen. poet.; Sil.), 5, 11, 1; 5, 21, 4; 5, 25, 2. — *transfugere*, to desert (Plaut.; Nep.; Liv.; Tac.; Suet.), 5, 18, 3; 5, 25, 1.

   c) *abnegare*, to refuse (Verg.; Ov.; Colum.; Val. Fl.; Lucan.; Quint.; Tert.; Itala; et al), 1, 38, 1. — *abolere*, to take away, destroy (transf. sense) (Verg.; Liv.; Sen. phil.; Plin. mai.; Silver and Late), 1, 41, 10; 3, 18, 1; 4, 5; 5, 2. — *absistere*, to desist from, cease from (Verg.; Hor.; Liv. (saepe); Curt.; Sil.; Val. Fl.; Tac.; et al), 5, 1, 3. — *absumere*, to destroy by fire (Ov.; Liv.; Vell.; Sen. phil.; Plin. mai.; Suet.; Gell.; Papin.; Sol.; Itala; Lact.; Amm.; Hier.; et al), 5, 2. — *accommodare*, to give (Ov.; Curt.; Quint.; Plin. min.; Ict.; Tert.; Sid.; Lact.; Optat.; Hier.; et al), 3, 20, 2. — *accumulare*, to increase (Lucr.; Manil.; Sil.; Stat.; Gell.; Cypr.; Optat.; Iuvenc.; Ambros.; Porphyr.; et al), 2, 9, 1; 3, 22, 2. — *adolere*, to burn, consume by fire (in a non-religious sense) (Moret.; Ov.; Colum.; Gell.; Tert.; Act. Arv.; et al), 4, 27; 5, 20, 2; 5, 38; 5, 42, 5; 5, 42, 6; 5, 52, 2 (bis). — *adoperire*,[13] to cover up or over (Verg.; Ov.; Liv.; Val. Max.;

---

[12] Used by Cicero only in the perfect, passive participle.

[13] Found generally in the perfect, passive participle as in Heg. 1, 46, 2.

Lucan.; Plin. mai.; Iuv.; Stat.; Suet.; Lact.; Hyg.; Mart. Cap.,
Oros.), 1, 46, 2. — *adurere*, to kindle, inflame (transf. sense)
(Hor.; Ov.; Prop.; Sen. phil.; Plin. mai.; Apul.; Ambros.; et al),
5, 24, 3. — *aggerare*, to pile up (Verg.; Moret.; Vitr.; Phaedr.;
Curt.; Colum.; Stat.; Ps. Quint.; Tac.; Apul.; Sid.), 4, 15, 1. —
amicire, to cover, envelope (transf. sense) (Catull.; Verg.; Hor.;
Ov.; Fronto; Vulg.; and Late), 3, 24. — *aspirare*, to favor, be
favorable to (Verg.; Ciris; Tibull.; Ov.; Val. Max.; Sen. phil.;
Curt.; Homer.; Stat.; Macr.; et al), 1, 26, 4; 1, 44, 8; 1, 45, 12;
4, 17; 4, 26, 1. — *assurgere*, to increase in size, to swell (Verg.;
Sen. phil.; Curt.; Colum.; Plin. mai.; Stat.; Novat.; Avien.;
Symm.; Amm.; Ambros.; et al), 4, 16, 2; 4, 27; — to rise (of
mental objects) (Verg.; Val. Max.; Sen. phil.; Homer.; Stat.;
Quint.; Plin. min.; Flor.; Symm.; Amm.; Oros.; et al), 1, 26, 2;
1, 26, 4. — *attollere*, to raise, exalt (transf. sense) (Verg.; Liv.;
Manil.; Val. Fl.; Sil.; Homer.; Stat.; Silver and Late), 1, 32, 6;
1, 42, 5; 2, 9, 1; 3, 24; 5, 37, 2. — *se attollere*, to raise one's self
(Verg. (saepe); Ov.; Liv.; Silver and Late), 5, 42, 5; 5, 53, 1; —
to extend itself (transf. sense) (Verg.; Sen. phil. (saepe); Sil.;
Stat.; Quint.; and Late), 3, 26, 1. — *circumferre*, to cast around
(eyes, glances) (Verg.; Ov.; Liv.; Manil.; Sen. phil.; Silver and
Late), 5, 53, 1. — *coire*, to copulate (Lucr.; Ov.; Sen. phil.; Curt.;
Plin. mai.; Silver and Late), 1, 42, 3. — *colligere*, to receive (Ov.;
Quint.; Frontin.; Itala; Dict.; Lact.; Ambros.; Hier.; Vulg.; and
Late), 1, 44, 7. — *se colligere*, to cover one's self with or conceal
one's self with (Verg.; Liv.; Plin. mai.; Sil.; Quint.; Lact.; and
Late), 4, 1, 5. — *commaculare*, to defile, pollute (Verg.; Tac.; Hos.
Geta), 5, 2; 5, 34, 2. — *conserere*, to join, connect (Aetna; Tibull.;
Ov.; Mat. carm. fr.; Liv.; Cels.; Silver and Late), 5, 42, 4. —
contorquere, to hurl (weapons) (Verg.; Lucr.; Ov.; Sil.; Lucan.;
Quint.; and Late), 1, 8; 5, 23. — *convellere*, to dismember, shatter
(Lucr.; Verg.; Ov.; Colum.; Lucan.; Stat.; Silver and Late), 1,
8. — *debellare*, to conquer, vanquish, subdue (Verg.; Ov.; Liv.;
Val. Max.; Silver and Late), 2, 9; 2, 11, 1; 4, 11; 4, 25, 1; 5,
52, 2. — *dedignari*, to scorn, disdain (Verg.; Ov.; Sen. phil.;
Curt.; Colum.; Silver and Late), 1, 15, 1; 1, 29, 8; 1, 36, 2;
1, 38, 2; 1, 40, 1; 2, 4; 2, 9; 5, 18, 1. — *defodere*, to dig, to dig in
(Verg.; Culex; Vitr.; Curt.; Colum.; Plin. min.; Hier.), 3, 15, 3;

10

5, 29; 5, 49, 3; — to dig out, excavate (Hor.; Colum.; Plin. mai.;
Veget.; Drac.; Herm.; Isid.; et al), 5, 21, 3 (bis). — *degere*, to
live (Hor.; Cels.; Curt.; Plin. mai.; Sil.; Stat.; Tac.; Apul.;
Tert.; and Late especially), 1, 19, 4; 1, 28, 8; 1, 36, 1; 1, 43, 5;
2, 2, 2; 2, 3, 4; 3, 5, 2; 3, 21, 1; 3, 21, 2; 4, 9, 1; 4, 23, 3; 5, 16;
5, 27. — *deicere*, to humble (Verg.; Sen. phil.; Stat.; Mart.;
Quint.; Apul.; Tert.; Lact.; et al), 3, 9, 1. — *depasci*, to consume,
eat (transf. sense) (Verg.; Sen. phil.; Stat.; Sil.; Tert.; Symph.;
Paneg.; Hier.; et al), 1, 45, 9; 2, 11, 4; 3, 16; 5, 1, 4; 5, 2;
5, 21, 3; 5, 38; 5, 43, 1. — *desaevire*, to rave furiously, to rage
(Verg.; Hor.; Colum.; Lucan.; Suet.; Ps. Quint.; Flor.; Tert.;
Ps. Ambros.; Hier.), 2, 8, 4; 3, 1, 1; 3, 20, 2; 5, 1, 3. — *designare*,
to delineate, represent (Ov.; Vitr.; Sen. phil.; Avien.; Mart. Cap.;
Brev. de Hier.; et al), 4, 5. — *detegere*, to disclose, reveal (Ov.;
Liv.; Sen. rhet.; Silver and Late), 1, 44, 7; 1, 44, 8; 3, 2. —
devastare, to lay waste, devastate (Ov.; Liv.; Sen. phil.; Apul.;
Itala; Vulg.; and Late), 1, 18, 1; 5, 51, 1. — *devolvi* (passive with
middle force), to tumble down, fall headlong (Catull.; Ov.; Liv.;
Germ.; Sen. phil.; Silver and Late), 5, 1, 4. — *dilacerare*, to tear
to pieces (Catull.; Ov.; Sen. phil.; Homer.; Tert.; Arnob.; Lact.;
Vulg.; et al), 5, 16; 5, 21, 4; 5, 51, 2. — *diripere*, to tear or snatch
away (Ov.; Hor.; Curt.; Tac.; Amm.), 5, 20, 2. — *dissimulare*,
to neglect, be negligent, omit (Ov.; Sen. ep.; Cels.; Colum.;
Petron.; Silver and Late), 1, 1, 9; 1, 40, 9. — *egerere*, to void,
discharge (from the body) (Ov.; Plin. mai.; Tac.; Sol.; Vulg.),
5, 24, 3. — *eludere*, to elude, evade (Verg.; Liv.; Petron.; Tac.;
Suet.), 1, 40, 8; 5, 14, 4. — *emerere*, to deserve (Prop.; Ov.; Sil.;
Lucan.; Quint.), 4, 6, 3. — *emicare*, to be conspicuous, prominent,
to shine forth (Hor.; Curt.; Flor.; Iust.), 1, 19, 3; 2, 14, 5; 4,
29, 2; — to spring forth, to spring out (Verg.; Ov.; Liv.; Curt.;
Plin. mai.; Quint.), 3, 25, 1. — *emollire*, to mollify, to make mild
or gentle (Ov.; Aur. Vict.), 1, 40, 5; 1, 40, 10. — *eviscerare*, to
disembowel (Enn.; Pacuv.; Cic. poet. (4); Verg.; Sil.; Lact.;
Apul.), 1, 40, 9; 5, 24, 3. — *exaestuare*, to boil, rage (transf. sense)
(Verg.; Ov.), 1, 40, 12; 3, 22, 1; — to boil, foam up (Verg.; Liv.;
Curt.; Iust.), 4, 16, 2. — *exagitare*, to rouse up, stir up (Lucr.;
Ov.; Colum.; Sil.; Aug.), 1, 39. — *exasperare*, to stir up, agitate
(the sea) (Ov.; Liv.; Sen. rhet.), 1, 35, 4; 4, 27 (bis). — *excolere*,

to honor, reverence (Ov.; Phaedr.; Lact.), 1, 39; 2, 3, 4.—*excurrere,*
to project, extend (Ov.; Liv.; Plin. mai.), 3, 20, 2. — *exercere,* to
cultivate, till (Verg.; Hor.; Ov.; Tac.; Plin. min.), 3, 6, 3; 5,
50. — *exhalare,* to breathe forth (spirit, soul) (Verg.; Ov.; Sen.
ep.), 1, 29, 8; 1, 45, 10; 5, 23. — *exhibere,* to show, display (Ov.;
Cels.; Plin. min.; Suet.), Praef. — *exsaturare,* to satiate, sate (Cic.
poet. (1); Ov.), 5, 40. — *illinere,* to smear (Hor.; Cels.; Sen.
phil.), 5, 20, 1. — *immolare,* to kill, slay (Verg.; Phaedr.), 4, 25,
2. — *immori,* to die in or upon (Ov.; Sen. rhet.; Sen. poet.; Plin.
mai.; Lucan.), 5, 21, 3. — *immurmurare,* to whisper (Verg.; Ov.;
Stat.; Amm.; Ambros.; Cod. Th.), 1, 41, 9; 3, 2. — *impingere,*
to force to, drive to (transf. sense) (Verg.; Sen. phil.; Lucan.;
Tac.; Lact.), 1, 8. — *imprecari,* to imprecate, call down upon
(Verg.; Sen. phil.; Mart.; Suet.), 1, 37, 2; 3, 13; 5, 22;
5, 40. — *inaestuare,* to boil or rage in (anything) (Hor.; Prud.),
2, 9. — *inclinare,* to cause to lean, to bend (Ov.; Liv.; Quint.),
1, 35, 4; 5, 53, 1. — *incumbere,* to press upon, threaten (Verg.;
Hor.; Sen. phil.; Plin. mai.; Iuv.; Quint.; Iust.; Sol.), 5, 16;
5, 26, 1; 5, 49, 1. — *se inferre,* to enter, go into (Verg.; Liv.;
Vell.), 5, 29. — *infremere,* to rage, roar (Verg.; Lucan.; Val. Fl.;
Sil.; Iuv.), 1, 40, 13; 3, 15, 1. — *infundere,* to diffuse, spread (of
things not liquid) (Verg.; Ov.; Liv.; Colum.; Curt.; Plin. ep.),
4, 4, 5. — *infundi* (passive), to enter (Verg.; Curt.; Flor.), 5, 4, 4;
5, 42, 4. — *ingemere,* to mourn, lament (Lucr.; Verg.; Hor.; Val.
Fl.; Tac.), 1, 30, 13. — *ingruere,* to attack, assail (fig.) (Verg.;
Liv.; Colum.; Plin. mai.; Tac.), 3, 20, 2; 5, 2; 5, 44, 2. — *inhabi-
tare,* to dwell in, inhabit (Ov.; Petron.; Sen. phil.; Plin. mai.;
Apul.; Dict.; Ambros.; Aur. Vict.), 2, 11, 2; 2, 17; 4, 18; 4, 22, 1;
5, 53, 1 (ter). — *inicere* (manum), to seize, lay hands on (Verg.;
Ov.; Liv.; Sen. phil.; Val. Max.; Plin. min.), 5, 39, 1; 5, 41
(bis). — *innatare,* to float upon or in (Verg.; Hor.; Plin. mai.;
Mela; Tac.; Plin. min.), 5, 21, 4. — *innectere,* to bind or fasten
together (Verg.; Hor.; Ov.; Liv.; Cels.; Sil.; Tac.; Aur. Vict.),
5, 21, 3; 5, 50. — *se inserere,* to join, engage in (Ov.; Tac.),
2, 10, 3; 5, 30. — *inspirare,* to inspire, infuse (i. e., to promise)
(Verg.; Curt.; Stat.; Quint.; Ambros.), 3, 26, 4. — *instaurare,* to
make ready, prepare (Verg.; Plin. mai.; Tac.), 1, 41, 1; 3, 20, 1. —
insurgere, to rise up (of persons) (Verg.; Sil.; Veget.), 3, 15, 1;

5, 2; 5, 28; 5, 46 (bis) ; — to rise (of places) (Verg.; Liv.; Sil.; Tac.), 5, 20, 1; 5, 49, 1; — to rise up against (Ov.; Stat.), 1, 28, 4; 1, 45, 3; 2, 15, 3; 3, 1, 3 ; 3, 2. — *intercipere*, to take away (Ov.; Liv.; Sen. rhet.; Curt.; Tac.; Suet.), 2, 12, 3. — *interfundere*, to flow between (Verg.; Hor.; Plin. min.; Avien.), 2, 9; 5, 15. — *internectere*, to bind together (Verg.; Stat.; Chalc.; Boeth.), 1, 46, 2. — *intexere*, to interweave (Verg.; Ov.; Curt.; Petron.; Plin. mai.; Ps. Cypr.; Hier.; Ambros.), 5, 9, 2; — to cover, surround (Verg.; Ov.; Vitr.), 3, 5, 2; 3, 6, 3; 4, 1, 2; 5, 21, 2. — *intonare*, to thunder (transf. sense) (Hor.; Ov.; Prop.; Liv.; Val. Fl.), 5, 46. — *intorquere*, to hurl (weapons) (Verg.; Sen. phil.; Sil.), 3, 11, 2. — *introgredi*, to enter (Verg.; Chalc.; Hier.; Vulg.; Ennod.), 4, 25, 3. — *invertere*, to plough up (Verg.), 2, 3, 1. — *involvere*, to overwhelm (Verg.; Sil.; Tac.; Vulg.), 3, 11, 3; 3, 20, 2; 5, 13; — to roll up, churn up (the sea) (Lucr.), 3, 20, 2. — *obniti*, to oppose, resist (Verg.; Vell.; Val. Fl.; Tac.; Aug.), 1, 29, 2; 5, 14, 4. — *obserare,* to bolt, fasten (transf. sense) (Catull.; Hor.; Ambros.; Aug.), 1, 40, 9. — *obumbrare,* to conceal (Ov.; Petron.; Ambros.), 1, 44, 1. — *oppetere*, to perish, die (Verg.; Plin. mai.; Tac.; Amm.; Prud.), 1, 45, 1. — *pererrare,* to wander through, roam over (Verg.; Ov.; Hor.; Colum.; Sen. phil.), 2, 9. — *perhorrere*, to shudder or tremble greatly at (Ov.; Amm.; Iul. Val.; Ambros.), 5, 40. — *praecedere,* to go before, precede (Hor.; Liv.; Val. Max.; Plin. mai.; Plin. min.; Suet.), 5, 22 (ter). — *praetendere*,[14] to extend (of land) (Verg.; Liv.; Plin. mai.; Tac.), 3, 6, 5; 3, 26, 2 (bis) ; 4, 16, 2. — *praetermeare*, to go by, pass by (intrans.) (Lucr.; Ambros.), 1, 35, 4; 4, 1, 2 ; 4, 22, 1. — *praetexere*, to conceal, disguise (fig.) (Verg.; Claud. Ruf.), 5, 13; 5, 50; — to border (Verg.; Plin. mai.; Tac.), 3, 6, 3 (bis) ; 3, 6, 5; 3, 20, 2. — *praevidere*, to foresee, to see beforehand (Verg.; Ov.; Tac.), 5, 13. — *procurrere*, to extend, project (of places) (Verg.; Ov.; Curt.; Plin. mai.; Plin. min.), 1, 35, 4. — *proludere*, to rehearse, prelude, practise beforehand (Verg.; Ov.; Flor.; Anthol. Lat.), 5, 37, 2. — *prominere*, to jut out, project (Ov.; Liv.; Mela; Curt.; Tac.; Plin. min.), 1, 30, 9; 3, 11, 1. — *proterere*, to fell,

---

[14] This word is used intransitively in all the citations in Heg. In Verg.; Liv.; Plin. mai.; Tac., either *praetendi* or *se praetendere* is found in this meaning.

lay low (in battle) (Hor.; Tac.), 5, 42, 4. — *recensere*, to survey
(Verg.; Quint.; Mm. Fel.), 2, 1, 2; — to recount, narrate (Ov.;
Curt.; Plin. min.; Apul.; Ambros.), 4, 18 (bis); 5, 16. — *reflectere*, to turn back (Catull.; Ov.; Val. Max.; Sen. poet.; Plin. mai.;
Macr.), 5, 36, 2; 5, 42, 4. — *refulgere*, to shine, rise resplendent
(transf. sense) (Prop.; Vell.; Sen. phil.; Plin. mai.), 1, 41, 2. —
refundi (passive used in a middle sense), to extend itself (Verg.;
Lucan.; Sil.; Val. Fl.; Claud.), 4, 27. — *relabi*, to fall back (Ov.;
Tac.), 5, 4, 4; — to flow back, fall back (of water) (Verg.; Hor.;
Ov.; Curt.; Sil.; Tac.), 3, 20, 2; — to relapse, fall back (transf.
sense) (Hor.; Aug.), 3, 1, 2. — *reluctari*, to struggle against, resist
(Verg.; Hor.; Ov.; Tac.; Plin. min.), 1, 45, 9. — *renidere*, to be
resplendent, glitter (Lucr.; Verg.; Hor.; Claud.), 5, 53, 1. —
reparare, to revive, refresh (Ov.; Liv.; Quint.), 1, 33; 4, 2; 5, 1,
4. — *rependere*, to repay, requite (transf. sense) (Verg.; Prop.;
Ov.; Val. Max.; Sen. phil.; Stat.; Plin. min.; Gell.), 1, 8; 1, 39;
4, 9, 3; 4, 26, 1; 5, 46. — *repercutere*, to cause to rebound, to drive
back (Ov.; Val. Max.; Plin. min.), 1, 35, 4; 3, 11, 1; 3, 26, 3. —
reserare, to open (Verg.; Ov.; Plin. mai.), 2, 15, 4; 3, 3, 6; 5,
44, 1; 5, 50. — *resolvere*, to dissolve (Verg.; Ov.; Colum.; Curt.;
Sen. phil.; Plin. mai.; Sil.; Aug.), 4, 15, 2; 4, 18; 5, 2 (bis);
5, 16; — to enfeeble, enervate (Verg.; Prop.; Ov.; Cels.; Sen.
phil.; Colum.; Plin. mai.; Sil.), 1, 45, 9; 4, 9, 2. — *resplendere*,
to glitter, shine brightly (Verg.; Sen. phil.; Sil.; Manil.; Ambros.;
Hier.; Vulg.; Claud.), 4, 18. — *resumere*, to recover, receive again
(Ov.; Sen. phil.; Suet.; Iust.; Claud.), 5, 53, 1. — *resurgere*, to
appear again, rise again (Verg.; Ov.; Prop.; Liv.; Sen. phil.; Tac.;
Gell.; Iust.), 3, 26, 1 (bis). — *resuscitare*, to revive, resuscitate
(transf. sense) (Ov.; Paul.; Vulg.), 1, 37, 7. — *retegere*, to disclose, reveal (Verg.; Hor.; Tac.), 1, 17, 2. — *revolare*, to fly back
(fig.) (Ov.; Vell.), 3, 16; 5, 53, 1. — *subruere*, to overthrow,
demolish (fig.) (Lucr.; Hor.; Liv.), 3, 16.—*subrigere (surgere)*,
to lift up, raise up (Verg.; Liv.; Sen. phil.; Plin. mai.; Sil.;
Arnob.; Ambros.), 3, 20, 2; 3, 26, 2; — to rise, to be built (Verg.;
Sen. phil.), 5, 21, 2. — *subtexere*, to conceal, hide (Lucr.; Verg.;
Iuv.; Amm.; Lact.; Iul. Val.; Cassian.), 1, 44, 2. — *succendere*,
to inflame (with passion) (Prop.; Ov.; Sen. phil.; Iuv.; Sil.),
1, 43, 4; 4, 6, 8; 5, 53, 1. — *sufficere*, to give, furnish (Verg.),

,5, 30. — *suspendere*, to suspend, stop (Ov.; Plin. mai.; Quint.; Ps. Quint.; Veget.; Diom.), 4, 21; 5, 46.

d) *abdicare*, to expel someone from a magistracy (trans.) (Plin. mai.; Diom.; Schol. Iuv.; Ps. Cypr.; Marc. Com.; Vir. Ill.), 1, 43, 7; — to exclude, cast off (Plin. mai.; Itala; Tert.; Iren.; Ambros.; and Late), 4, 8. — *absolvere*, to free (Plin. mai.; Tac.; Fronto; Apul.; and Late), 3, 17; — to remove, take away (Val. Max.; Liv.; Sen. phil.; Quint.; Gell.; Ter. Maur.; Ambros.; Vulg.; Claud.; et al), 1, 30, 15; 3, 26, 1. — *abundare*, to be abundant (transf. sense) (Liv.; Vitr.; Phaedr.; Colum.; Sen. phil.; Plin. mai.; Quint.; Frontin.; Suet.; Ulp.; and Late), 5, 23. — *adnectere*, to connect (referring to men) (Curt.; Tac.; Tert.; Iul. Val.; Amm.; Cypr. Gall.; et al), 1, 7, 1. — *adnuntiare*, to announce (Sen. phil.; Curt.; Plin. mai.; Suet.; Stat.; Apul.; Tert.; Itala; Vulg.; Prud.; et al), 1, 40, 3; 1, 41, 1; 1, 45, 11; 5, 27. — *adstipulari*, to agree with (Liv.; Plin. mai.; Apul.; Iul. Val.; Ambros.; and often in Late Latin), 1, 15, 1; 1, 30, 1; 5, 8, 2. — *affectare*, to grace with, to honor (Liv.; Ambros.; Hier.; Aug.; Sulp. Sev.), 1, 24, 3; — to affect, feign (Sen. rhet.; Sen. phil.; Plin. mai.; Stat.; Tac.; Quint.; Ps. Quint.; Apul.; Tert.; Amm.; et al), 1, 37, 4; 1, 41, 5. — *arrodere*, to nibble or gnaw at (Liv.; Plin. mai.; Nemes.; Arnob.; Pers.; Ambros.; Sid.), 5, 24, 2. — *assistere*, to aid in defending (Sen. phil.; Stat.; Plin. min.; Quint.; Tac.; Paul.; Apul.; and frequent in Late Latin), 1, 28, 7. — *associare*, to join to, unite with (Stat.; Ser. Samm.; Iuvenc.; Char.; Chalc.; Mar. Victor.; Pallad.; Ambros.; and Late), 1, 9, 2; 1, 10, 1; 1, 17, 2; 2, 2, 3; 2, 7, 1; 2, 12, 2; 2, 13, 7; 2, 13, 8; 3, 6, 1; 4, 13, 1. — *attollere*, to extol, praise (Vell.; Sen. phil.; Lucan.; Sil.; Stat.; Quint.; Tac.; Ambros.; Oros.; et al), 1, 42, 5; 2, 9, 1; 5, 37, 2. — *circumiacere*, to surround, encircle (Liv.; Cael. fr. apud Quint.; Apul.; Paul. Nol.), 4, 17. — *circumspicere*, to see (Liv.; Vulg.; Claud.; Oros.; Eustath.), 3, 24; 5, 26, 2; 5, 44, 1. — *circumvagari*, to wander about (Vitr.; Ps. Aug.), 3, 26, 1. — *collidere*, to bruise, injure (Cels.; Sen. phil.; Plin. mai.; Sil.; Gaius; and Late), 5, 38; — to be set at variance (Sen. phil.; Petron.; Stat.; Arnob.; Ennod.), 5, 27. — *colluctari*, to struggle with (Sen. rhet.; Sen. phil.; Colum.; Suet.; Apul.; Tert.; Amm.; Ambros.; and Late), 4, 2; 5, 16. — *competere* (intrans.), to belong

to, to be due to (Quint.; Ulp.; Ict.; Tert.; and Late), 1, 14, 1;
1, 15, 1; 1, 36, 1; — (trans.), to seek along with someone (Sen.
rhet.; Quint.; Iul. Val.; Iust.; Ennod.; Isid.), 1, 42, 5; 5, 16. —
conclamare, to call upon, invoke (Sen. phil.; Mart.; Damas.;
Prosp.; Avit.; Cod. Iust.), 5, 26, 2. — *concremare*, to burn up,
consume (Liv.; Sen. phil.; Plin. mai.; Quint.; Suet.; Itala; Amm.;
Arnob.; et al), 2, 9, 1; 5, 15; 5, 49, 4. — *conserere*, to engage in
(conversation) (Curt.; Arnob.; Amm.; Sulp. Sev.; Boeth.), 5, 10,
1; 5, 10, 3; 5, 26, 2. — *consummare*, to complete, perfect (Liv.;
Manil.; Vell.; Val. Max.; Sen. phil.; Colum.; Silver and Late),
4, 4, 5; 5, 20, 3; 5, 27. — *consumere*, to devour, consume (by grief)
(Liv; Sen. phil.; Ps. Quint.; Hyg.; Val. Max.; Vulg.; Pomer.),
3, 2. — *convenire*, to summon before a tribunal (Cels. dig.; and
very frequent among Ict.; Apul.; Tert.; Optat.; Symm.; Ambros.;
et al), 1, 8. — *conversari*, to live, abide (Sen. rhet.; Sen. phil.;
Curt.; Colum.; Plin. mai.; Ulp.; Apul.; and Late), 5, 16; 5, 53,
1. — *convulnerare*, to wound severely (fig.) (Sen. rhet.; Sen. phil.;
Symm.; Chron.; Salv.), 1, 45, 5. — *decolorare*, to corrupt, disgrace
(Quint.; Capit.; Lampr.; Priscill.; Symm.; Serv.; Ambros.
(saepe); Rufin.; et al), 1, 41, 3. — *deflectere* (intrans.), to turn
aside (Tac.; Plin. min.; Suet.; Ps. Quint.; Apul.; Ulp.; Paneg.;
Ambros.; Vulg.; et al), 4, 9, 3; — (trans.), to avoid (Stat.; Apul.;
Avian.), 1, 37, 4. — *dehonestare*, to disgrace, dishonor (Liv.; Sen.
phil.; Prud.; Tac.; Suet.; Fronto; and Late), 1, 32, 2; 5, 24, 4;
5, 47, 1; 5, 53, 1. — *se demergere*, to conceal one's self, to betake
one's self (Cels.; Lact.; Hil.; Ambros.; Hier.; Greg. M.), 1, 21, 1.
— *desponsare*, to betroth (Vell.; Suet.; Min. Fel.; Tert.; Itala;
Ambros.; Hier.; Aug.; et al), 1, 40, 5; 1, 42, 3. — *diluere*, to wash
away (Plin. mai.; Tert.; Veget.), 5, 22. — *dirigere*, to send
(Manil.; Ps. Sen. ep.; Paul.; Modest.; Iul. Val.; Cypr.; Ambros.;
Cic. fr. apud Serv.; and very frequent in Late Latin), 1, 13, 1;
1, 20 (bis); 1, 22, 1; 1, 22, 2; 1, 23, 1; 1, 28, 3; 1, 28, 6; 1, 28, 9;
1, 30, 3; 1, 37, 3; 1, 37, 7; 1, 38, 6; 1, 45, 3 (bis); 1, 45, 11;
2, 5, 5; 2, 6, 2; 2, 9, 1 (ter); 2, 9, 3; 2, 12, 2; 2, 13, 5; 2, 16, 1;
3, 1, 3; 3, 9, 1; 3, 13; 3, 14; 3, 22, 1; 3, 22, 2; 3, 23, 1; 3, 24;
3, 26, 4; 4, 1, 5; 4, 4, 2; 4, 4, 5; 4, 14; 4, 23, 3; 4, 29, 2; 4, 30
(bis); 4, 33; 5, 17; 5, 18, 3; 5, 33, 1; — to lead, bring away
(Sil.; Tert.; Iul. Val.; Optat.; Ambros.; Vulg.; et al), 1, 20; —

to direct (a crime, accusation) (Quint.; Ulp.; Tert.; Paul.;
Papin.; Aug.; Cod. Iust.; et al), 1, 41, 9; — to set out, to march
(Sen. ep.; Itala; Itin. Alex.; Paul. Nol.; Oros.; and Late), 4, 9,
3; — (passive), to extend (Manil.; Germ.; Frontin.; Tert.; Amm.;
Oros.; Hyg.; et al), 4, 18; 5, 3, 1. — *disponere*, to determine, decide
(Sen. rhet.; Sen. phil.; Amm.; Vopisc.; Iul. Val.; Arnob.; and
frequent in Late Latin), 5, 42, 5. — *disseminare*, to scatter (of
persons) (Plin. mai.; Itala; Vulg.; Rufin.; Aug.; Ps. Aug.;
Ruric.), 2, 9, 1; 5, 16. — *dissonare*, to differ, disagree (Vitr.;
Colum.; Sol.; Tert.; Arnob.; Lact.; Ambros.; Hier.; et al), 4, 1,
2. — *ebullire*, to produce, give forth (Sen. phil.; Petron.; Pers.;
Vulg.), 3, 26, 1 (bis). — *emercari*, to purchase (Tac.; Amm.),
1, 41, 2. — *emollire*, to soften (Liv.; Colum.; Cels.; Plin. mai.),
5, 40; — to render weak or ineffective (transf. sense) (Liv.; Tac.;
Aur. Vict.), 1, 12, 2; 3, 11, 2. — *erepere*, to clamber up (Sen.
rhet.; Lucan.; Suet.; Amm.; Spart.), 5, 49, 3. — *eviscerare*, to
squander, exhaust (Sen. phil.; Ambros.; Aug.; Cod. Iust.), 5, 16.
— *exacerbare*, to provoke, make angry (Liv.; Plin. min.; Suet.;
Paul.; and Digesta), 1, 25, 4; 1, 44, 3. — *exasperare*, to irritate,
provoke (Liv.; Cels.; Plin. mai.; Val. Max.; Apul.; Capit.), 1, 2;
1, 25, 4; 1, 26, 2; 1, 28, 9; 1, 37, 7; 1, 39; 1, 40, 2; 1, 40, 5;
1, 40, 8; 1, 41, 3; 1, 44, 7; 1, 45, 4; 2, 9, 1 (bis); 2, 9, 3; 4, 7;
4, 18; 5, 2; 5, 24, 2; 5, 40. — *exosculari*, to kiss fondly, eagerly
(Plin. ep.; Tac.; Suet.; Fronto), 5, 40. — *expostulare*, to demand
vehemently (Val. Max.; Tac.; Plin. min.; Suet.; Tert.), 5, 2. —
exsatiare, to satisfy, sate, glut (Liv. 40, 28, 2), 5, 40. — *immorari*,
to tarry in, linger near (Colum.; Plin. mai.; Cels.; Aug.; Cael.
Aur.), 3, 9, 4; 5, 19; 5, 20, 2; 5, 36, 1; — to linger near, tarry
(fig.) (Sen. phil.; Cels.; Plin. mai.; Quint.; Aug.), 3, 5, 2; 5, 16.
— *imponere*, to build (Liv.; Curt.; Tac.; Paul.; Tert.), 1, 11, 2;
5, 36, 1. — *inclinare*, to yield, fall back (military term) (Liv.;
Tac.), 1, 16, 4; — to change, alter, bend (Liv.; Quint.), 1, 29, 9.
— *inebriare*, to make drunk, inebriate (Plin. mai.; Sen. phil.;
Tert.; Ambros.; Hier.; Vopisc.; Aug.), 1, 11, 1; 4, 7 (bis). —
incubare, to threaten, encroach upon (Sen. phil.; Sil.; Flor.),
2, 10, 6; 3, 8, 3; 5, 1, 3; 5, 4, 3. — *inequitare*, to ride upon (Flor.;
Apul.; Arnob.), 5, 46. — *infundere*, to saturate, soak thoroughly
(Colum.; Pallad.; Veget.; Sid.; Macr.), 1, 30, 2; 3, 10; 4, 7; —

to pour in (a force of men) (Sil.; Flor.), 1, 15, 3; — *se infundere*, to pour one's self into, to enter (Amm.; Ambros.), 1, 22, 2; 1, 29, 1; 1, 29, 7; 4, 1, 4; 4, 22, 1; 4, 25, 3; 4, 33; 5, 4, 4; 5, 10, 1; 5, 16; 5, 21, 3; 5, 27; 5, 40; 5, 50. — *se ingerere*, to obtrude, to force one's self upon (Plin. min.; Iuv.), 1, 44, 5. — *ingravare*, to oppress, molest (Plin. mai.; Phaedr.; Spart.), 1, 40, 7. — *inhorrere*, to bristle, project (Liv.), 1, 30, 9. — *innectere*, to entangle, involve, implicate (Sen. poet.; Tac.), 1, 40, 1; 1, 41, 3. — *insurgere*, to grow in power, to rise (Tac.), 1, 26, 4. — *intendere*, to turn one's attention to (Sen. phil.; Val. Fl.; Quint.; Iust.), 5, 28; 5, 53, 2. — *intercipere*, to interrupt, hinder (Liv.; Curt.; Quint.; Tac.), 1, 44, 8; 2, 9; 3, 20, 1. — *interequitare*, to ride between (Liv.; Curt.), 4, 15, 2. — *interiacere*, to lie between (Liv.; Plin. mai.; Colum.; Stat.; Quint.; Plin. min.), 3, 26, 1; 4, 27; 5, 4, 3; 5, 12. — *internasci*, to grow between or among (Liv.; Sen. rhet.; Colum.; Plin. mai.; Tac.), 5, 18, 1. — *intervenire*, to interpose (one's authority) (Suet.; Flor.; Ict.), 1, 40, 13. — *involare*, to steal (Petron.; Itala; Potam.; Optat.; Ambros.; Hyg.; Gloss. Amplon.; et al), 3, 22, 1. — *involvere*, to involve, implicate (Plin. ep.; Tac.), 1, 12, 4; 1, 40, 9; 2, 10, 3; 2, 15, 8; 4, 1, 4; 5, 1, 3; 5, 14, 4; 5, 16. — *oberrare*, to wander about (Sen. poet.; Curt.; Plin. mai.; Tac.; Sol.; Claud.), 5, 15. — *obumbrare*, to obscure, eclipse (Plin. mai.; Quint.; Tac.; Arnob.), 3, 6, 5. — *perfundere*, to cover (Sen. ep.; Mart.), 2, 12, 3. — *pertentare*, to test, try (Petron.; Tac.), 5, 21, 3. — *pertrahere*, to conduct forcibly (Liv.; Val. Max.), 1, 41, 9; 5, 53, 1. — *perurgere*, to press or urge greatly (Suet.; Rufin.), 1, 41, 3; 2, 12, 1. — *praedamnare*, to condemn beforehand (Liv.; Suet.), 1, 44, 6. — *praedestinare*, to determine beforehand (Liv.; Auctor paneg. ad Maxim. et Constant.), 1, 7, 1; 1, 30, 1; 1, 44, 3. — *praeeminere* (*praeminere*), to excel, surpass (Sen. rhet.; Tac.; Auson.), 1, 40, 2; 4, 2. — *praemittere*, to set before (Sen. ep.; Tac.; Suet.; Ambros.; Hier.), 5, 31. — *praeponderare*, to be of more weight or influence (Sen. phil.; Stat.; Ps. Quint.; Gell.; Ambros.), 1, 14, 2; 1, 40, 11; 2, 6, 1; 2, 17; 4, 11; 4, 29, 2; 5, 21, 2; 5, 53, 1. — *praesumere*, to presume, take for granted (Val. Max.; Tac.; Iust.; Aur. Vict.; Aug.), 1, 32, 6; 2, 9; 2, 13, 2; 2, 17; 4, 2; — to take beforehand (Quint.; Tac.; Plin. ep.), 4, 2. — *praetendere*, to watch (Frontin.; Itala; Tert.;

Ambros.; Hyg.), 1, 29, 5; 1, 32, 6; 2, 7, 1; 2, 15, 8; 3, 3, 1; 3, 3, 4; 3, 20, 1; 4, 6, 7; 5, 13; 5, 17; 5, 20, 2; 5, 21, 2; 5, 24, 2; 5, 29; 5, 35, 1; 5, 36, 2. — *praevalere*, to prevail (Liv.; Vell.; Phaedr.; Stat.; Quint.; Tac.; Plin. min.; Suet.; Lact.; Oros.; Cypr.; Lucif.; Iord.), 1, 9, 3; 1, 20; 1, 28, 6; 3, 2. — *praevenire* (intrans.), to come beforehand (Liv.; Ict.), 3, 2; 3, 16; 4, 21. — *prosilire*, to spring forth (fig.) (Liv.; Sen. phil.; Petron.; Suet.; Iust.), 4, 7. — *protrahere*, to defer, put off (Suet.; Eutr.; Vopisc.), 1, 32, 7. — *se recondere*, to conceal one's self (Sen. ep.; Quint.), 5, 49, 3. — *reformare*, to restore, rebuild, reestablish (Val. Max.; Sol.; Capit.; Eutr.; Treb. Poll.; Cod. Th.), 1, 10, 3; 1, 14, 1; 1, 17, 3; 1, 18; 1, 25, 4; 1, 26, 1; 2, 11, 3; 2, 13, 1; 5, 2; 5, 21, 1. — *refundere*, to restore, give back (Plin. min.; Ict.; Veget.; Ambros.; Sid.; Cod. Th.; Drac.; Val. imp. apud Treb. Poll.), 1, 28, 5; 1, 37, 7; 1, 43, 3; 2, 13, 5; 5, 9, 4 (bis); 5, 16; 5, 27; 5, 46; 5, 53, 1. — *regerminare*, to spring forth, sprout again, grow again (Plin. mai.; Calp.), 1, 43, 3. — *reluctari*, to be adverse, to be reluctant (Vell.; Petron.; Mart.; Plin. min.; Claud.), 1, 40, 9; 2, 12, 1; 4, 6, 5; 4, 26, 2. — *reniti*, to resist, struggle against (Cels.; Plin. mai.; Apul.), 1, 11, 2; 1, 16, 2; 1, 16, 4; — to resist, struggle against (fig.) (Liv.; Curt.; Plin. mai.; Spart.), 1, 4; 5, 13. — *renuntiare*, to renounce, break off (Quint.; Plin. min.; Suet.; Tert.; Ambros.; Cypr.; Hier.; Aug.), 2, 10, 3; 2, 15, 2; 3, 18, 2; 4, 6, 12; 4, 29, 2; 5, 14, 4; 5, 16. — *reparare*, to renew (a war) (Liv.; Iust.), 1, 22, 3; 5, 46. — *repraesentare*, to portray, represent (of painters, sculptors, etc.) (Plin. mai.), 3, 1, 1; — *se repraesentare*, to present one's self in person (Colum.; Dig.), 1, 15, 2. — *restringere*, to check, restrain (Sen. phil.; Plin. mai.; Stat.; Plin. min.; Apul.; Paneg. Const.), 5, 26, 2. — *retexere*, to narrate, repeat (Stat.; Apul.; Tert.; Lampr.; Auson.; Amm.; Hier.; Rufin.; Claud.), 1, 40, 7; 2, 9. — *retorquere*, to turn or cast back (fig.) (Sen. phil.; Apul.; Iust.; Ict.), 5, 18, 3; 5, 22. — *suffodere*, to hollow out, excavate (Curt.), 5, 20, 1. — *suggerere*, to advise, suggest (Curt.; Ulp.; Vopisc.; Lampr.; Hier.; Rufin.; Aur. Vict.; Avit.; Cassian.; Ennod.), 5, 19; 5, 21, 1. — *supereminere*, to rise above (Sen. phil.; Colum.; Gell.; Veget.; Ambros.; Prisc.), 3, 20, 2; 4, 16, 2. — *superfluere*, to superabound, to be superabundant (Sen. rhet.; Sen. phil.; Petron.; Plin. mai.; Quint.; Tac.), 1, 38, 2. — *superfundere*, to pour upon (Liv.; Vell.; Colum.; Plin. min.; Quint.; Pallad.), 3, 6, 3; 3, 26, 1. — *supergredi*, to surpass, surmount, exceed (Quint.; Tac.; Suet.; Iust.; Amm.; Ambros.), 1, 27; 2, 8, 3; 2, 10, 6. — *supernatare*, to float (Sen. phil.; Colum.; Plin. mai.; Apul.; Ambros.; Aug.; Paul. Nol.), 4, 18 (bis). — *supervenire*, to arrive, come up (Liv.; Curt.; Cels.; Sen. phil.; Suet.), 3, 25, 1; 3, 25, 2; — to take unawares, to surprise (Liv.; Curt.; Stat.; Iust.; Frontin.), 5, 18, 2; 5, 40. — *supervivere*, to survive, outlive (Plin. min.; Suet.; Apul.; Spart.; Iust.; Amm.; Ambros.; Vulg.; Serv.; Paulin.), 2, 18; 3, 16; 5, 21, 3; 5, 22, 1; 5, 38; 5, 45; 5, 53, 1 (bis). — *traducere*, to dishonor, disgrace, expose to ridicule (Liv.; Sen. phil.), 1, 38, 5; 1, 40, 13. — *transcribere*, to make over, to transfer (Liv.; Ict.), 3, 26, 4. — *transgredi* (intrans.), to cross over (Liv.; Vell.; Plin. mai.; Sil.; Tac.; Eutr.), 3, 4, 3. — *transigere*, to spend, pass (time) (Sen. phil.; Tac.; Suet.), 2, 11, 1; 4, 33; — to stab, to pierce through (Phaedr.; Sil.; Tac.; Gell.), 3, 15, 2.

ii. Verbs compounded from a Noun and a Verb.

a) *usurpare*, to acquire, obtain rightfully (Cic. (1); Plin. mai.; Gell.; Iust.), 4, 2. — *venumdare*, to sell (of captured slaves) (Sall.; Liv.; Tac.; Suet.), 3, 26, 4.

b) *mancipare*, to give up, deliver up (Plaut.; Hor.; Plin. mai.; Tac.), 2, 8, 1. — *morigerari*, to comply with, to endeavor to please (Plaut.; Ter.; Acc.; Cic. (1)), 1, 36, 1.

c) *mansuescere*, to mellow, grow soft (Verg.), 3, 6, 3; — to become mild, gentle (Verg.), 1, 44, 8.

. d) *usurpare*, to usurp, assume unlawfully (Liv.; Plin. mai.; Suet.; Cod. Iust.), 1, 6, 1; 1, 26, 3; 1, 30, 6; 2, 1, 1; 2, 1, 2; 2, 12, 3 (bis); 3, 1, 3; 3, 17 (bis); 3, 22, 1; 5, 51, 3.

iii. Verbs compounded from an Adverb and a Verb.

b) *subterfugere*,[15] to flee secretly or by stealth (Plaut.; Digest.), 5, 27.

---

[15] The word is used here intransitively. It is a favorite word of Cicero in its transitive use.

c) *subterlabi*, to glide or flow under (Verg.; Auson.), 4, 15, 2.

iv. Verbs compounded from two Verbs.

d) *valedicere*,[16] to bid farewell (Sen. ep.; Sulp. Sev.), 5, 53, 1.

v. Compound Verbs in -*facere*.

a) *stupefacere*, to stun, stupefy (Cic. (1); Prop.; Verg.; Ov.; Liv.; Sen. phil.; Val. Fl.; Sil.; Lucan.), 1, 9, 3.

b) *expergefacere*, to arouse, excite (transf. sense) (Plaut.; Cic. (1); Rhet. Her.; Lucr.), 4, 29, 2; 5, 8, 2. — *perterrefacere*, to terrify thoroughly (Ter.; Amm.), 4, 23, 3.

d) *expergefacere*, to awaken (Suet.), 2, 4; 3, 15, 1.

vi. Juxtapositions.

d) *crucifigere*, to crucify, nail to a cross (Sen. rhet.; Val. Max.; Quint.; Plin. mai.; Suet.; Ambros.; Vulg.; Aug.; Hyg.; et al), 1, 10, 3; 2, 5, 2; 2, 12, 1; 3, 2 (bis); 5, 2 (bis); 5, 32.

10. Miscellaneous Verbs.

a) *farcire*, to cram, stuff (Varr.; Cic. (1); Vitr.; Plin. mai.; Colum.; Mart.; Plin. min.; et al), 4, 6, 7. — *fatigare*, to harass, fatigue, vex (Cic. (3); Sall.; Nep.; Lucr.; Verg.; Ov.; Liv.; Vell.; Stat.; Tac.; Apul.; and Late), 2, 13, 7; 4, 7; 5, 30. — *figere*, to wound, pierce (Bell. Alex.; Bell. Hisp.; Catull.; Verg.; Ov.; Sen. phil.; Silver and Late), 2, 6, 3; 3, 11, 3; 4, 15, 2; 5, 11, 1; 5, 14, 1; 5, 23. — *fundere*, to kill, destroy (Cic. (1); Verg.; Prop.; Ov.; Sen. phil.; Lucan.; Silver and Late), 1, 17, 1; 1, 21, 1; 4, 22, 2; 5, 53, 1 (bis); 5, 53, 2. — *furere*, to rage with anger (Cic. ep. (2); Lentul. apud Cic. ep.; Verg.; Ov.; Liv.; Sen. phil.; Val. Fl.; Stat.; Mart.; Tac.; Arnob.; Ps. Rufin.), 5, 21, 4. — *gerere*, to wear, bear (Nep.; Verg.; Ov.; Hor.; Sen. poet.; Plin. mai.), 5, 21, 3; 5, 22. — *iacere*, to construct, build (Caes.; Bell. Afr.; Verg.; Liv.), 5, 21, 4. — *iacēre*, to lie, to be situate (Varr.; Brut. in Cic. ep.; Verg.; Liv.; Sen. rhet.; Plin. mai.; Sil.; Iust.), 4, 27 (bis). — *latere*, to be concealed from, to be unknown to (Varr.; Verg.; Ov.; Iust.; Ambros.; Aug.; Avit.), 3, 15, 1; 4, 18. — *madere*, to be wet, to drip, flow (Cic. (2); Verg.; Sen. rhet.; Plin. mai.; Mart.),

---

[16] Found as two words (*vale dicere*) in Cic. Att. 5, 2, 2; and Ov.

5, 16 (bis). — *manere* (trans.), to await, to be about to befall
(Anton. apud Cic. (1) ; Verg.; Liv.; Curt.; Tac.), 1, 39 ; 5, 27. —
micare, to flash, gleam, be bright (Cic. fr. (1) ; Verg.; Ov.; Liv.;
Sen. phil.; Lact.; Prud.), 5, 53, 1. — *mittere*, to cast, hurl, throw
(Caes. (18) ; Lucr.; Catull.; Ov.; Liv.; Curt.; Sen. phil.; Petron.;
Phaedr.; Hier.), 3, 26, 1. — *operire*, to cover, conceal (Nep.;
Lucr.; Tibull.; Verg.; Ov.; Liv.), 5, 40 ; 5, 41 ; 5, 42, 1. — *palari*,[17]
to wander about, to be dispersed (Sall.; Lucr.; Ov.; Liv.; Plin.
mai.; Tac.), 3, 4, 2 ; 3, 25, 1 ; 4, 15, 2 ; 4, 15, 3. — *patrare*, to
perform, accomplish (Cic. (3) ; Sall.; Lucr.; Liv.; Tac.; Aur.
Vict.), 1, 6, 1 ; 1, 7, 2 ; 1, 12, 4 ; 1, 29, 4 ; 1, 30, 15 ; 1, 40, 9 ;
2, 5, 4 ; 5, 5 ; 5, 26, 2 ; 5, 47, 3. — *polire*, to polish, smooth (Frg.
XII Tabb. apud Cic. (1) ; Catull.; Ov.; Plin. mai.; Mart.; Vulg.),
5, 30. — *radere*, to shave (Cic. (2) ; Liv.; Plin. mai.; Iuv.; Mart.,
Suet.; Cael. Aur.), 1, 41, 11. — *solvere*, to bring to an end (Sall.
fr.; Hor.; Liv.; Curt.; Cels.; Plin. mai.; Quint.; Tac.; Plin. min.),
1, 41, 1 ; 1, 45, 11 ; 5, 22. — *sorbere*, to suck in, draw in, swallow
up (Sall. fr.; Verg.; Sen. phil.; Val. Fl.; Plin. mai.), 4, 15, 2. —
sternere, to pave (a road, etc.) (Cic. ep. (1) ; Liv.; Plin. mai.;
Digest.; Vulg.), 5, 30. — *strepere*, to resound (Cic. poet. (1) ;
Sall.; Verg.; Hor.; Liv.; Sen. phil.; Plin. mai.; Quint.; Tac.;
Amm.), 4, 9, 1. — *stringere*, to draw (a sword) (Caes.; Verg.;
Ov.; Liv.; Sen. phil.; Val. Max.; Iust.), 5, 53, 1 ; 5, 53, 2. —
struere, to build, make (Nep.; Verg.; Hor.; Liv.; Curt.; Sen. phil.;
Plin. mai.; Tac.), 4, 23, 2. — *trahere*, to interpret, understand in
a certain way (Cic. (1) ; Sall.; Rhet. Her.; Liv.; Tac.), 1, 37, 5. —
urgere, to force, drive (Sall.; Verg.; Ov.; Quint.), 5, 4, 4. —
vellere, to pluck, pull, tear up (Varr.; Cic. (1) ; Verg.; Hor.;
Tibull.; Prop.; Colum.; Plin. mai.; Lucan.; Ps. Quint.; Vopisc.;
Aug.), 5, 18, 2. — *venari*, to hunt or seek after, to pursue (fig.)
(Rhet. Her.; Hor.; Phaedr.), 1, 41, 2.

b) *adulari* (passive), to be flattered (Caes. Hem.; Cic. (1) ;
Val. Max.), 1, 39. — *carpere*, to enjoy, use (Ter.; Cic. (4) ; Verg.;
Prop.; Ov.; Liv.; Pers.; Val. Fl.; Sil.; Mart.; Gell.; Apul.; and
Late), 1, 40, 9 ; 3, 16. — *cedere*, to fall to one's lot (Cato; Cic. (1) ;
Sall.; Nep.; Lucr.; Verg.; Hor.; Ov.; Liv. (saepe) ; Silver and

---

[17] Used most frequently, as here, in the present participle.

Late), 1, 32, 3. — *clamare* (trans.), to call to someone (Plaut.; Acc.; Lucil.; Verg.; Moret.; Prop.; Ov.; Germ.; Silver and Late), 5, 39, 1. — *compescere*, to check, restrain (Plaut.; Hor.; Ov., Prop.; Vell.; Sen. phil.; Val. Max.; Silver and Late), 4, 7; 5, 36, ·2. — *condere*, to build, erect (a building) (Plaut.; Verg.; Ov.; Liv.; Colum.; Mela; Plin. mai.; Sil.; Stat.; Amm.; et al), 1, 35, 3. — *coquere*, to vex, harass, torment (Plaut.; Catull.; Verg.; Sen. phil.; Sil.; Quint.; Cypr. Gall.; Firm.; Aug.; et al), 1, 7, 2. — *cremare*, to burn, consume by fire (Enn.; Caes.; Lucr.; Poetical, Silver and Late), 5, 49, 3. — *fatigare*, to tire, weary, fatigue (Pacuv.; Sall.; Caes.; Lucr.; Verg.; Ov.; Hor.; Liv.; Sen. rhet.; Silver and Late), 1, 32, 7. — *fervere*, to be inflamed, to rage (transf. sense) (Ter.; Volcac.; Acc.; Afran.; Cic. (1); Verg.; Ov., Hor.; Sen. phil.; Sil.; Iuv.; Stat.; Flor.; Apul.; and Late), 1, 44, 2; 4, 25, 2; 5, 1, 3; 5, 42, 6; — to roam, wander (Acc.; Lucr.; Ov.; Lucan.; Val. Fl.; Sil.; Stat.; Hier.; Greg. M.; Avit.), 2, 14, 3. — *fovere*, to keep warm, to warm (Plaut.; Varr. fr.; Lucr.; Culex; Priap.; Ov.; Manil.; Vitr.; Silver and Late), 5, 23. — *fremere*, to roar, rage, howl (of things) (Enn.; Lucr.; Verg.; Ov.; Sen. rhet.; Silver and Late), 3, 23, 1; 5, 46. — *fungi*, to experience, enjoy (Plaut.; Cic. (1); Lucr.; Bell. Alex.; Hor.; Ov.; Val. Max.; Quint.; Tac.; Suet.; Apul.; Tert.; Hil.; Ambros.; et al), 1, 1, 10. — *ludere*, to disappoint, to thwart (Ter.; Verg.; Hor.), 1, 22, 2. — *niti*, to climb, press forward, advance (Pacuv. fr.; Cic. (1); Lucr.; Verg.; Ov.; Plin. mai.; Lucan.; Tac.), 4, 31. — *pandere*, to open (Plaut.; Lucr.; Verg.; Liv.; Tac.), 5, 46. — *pavere*, to fear, dread (Ter.; Sall.; Hor.; Ov.; Liv.; Lucan.; Plin. mai.; Tac.; Apul.; Vopisc.; Avian.; Rutil.), 4, 3, 2; 5, 53, 1. — *percire*, to excite, stir up (Plaut.; Ter.; Cic. (1); Lucr.; Fronto), 1, 32, 6; 4, 33; 5, 18, 2. — *quatere*, to beat, strike (Ter.; Cic. poet.; Verg.; Hor.; Aur. Vict.), 3, 20, 2. — *scandere*, to climb, mount, ascend (Plaut.; Cic. (1); Verg.; Hor.; Liv.; Tac.; Pacat.), 5, 27. — *scatere*, to be full of, to abound in (Plaut.; Lucr.; Hor.; Liv.; Mela; Plin. mai.; Gell.), 1, 45, 9; 3, 6, 3; 4, 1, 2. — *solari*, to console (Plaut.; Verg.; Hor.; Quint.), 5, 38. — *splendere*, to gleam, glisten (Plaut.; Poet. apud Cic. (1); Lucr.; Verg.; Hor.; Sen. phil.), 5, 53, 1. — *spondere*, to promise in marriage, betroth (Plaut.; Ter.; Poet. apud Varr.), 1, 40, 6. — *trudere*, to push, shove forward (Plaut.; Verg.;

Hor.; Tac.; Amm.; Serv.), 3, 20, 2. — *vagire*, to cry, squall (of small children) (Ter.; Cic. (2); Sen. rhet.; Hier.), 5, 53, 1. — *vorare*, to devour, eat greedily (Plaut.; Cic. (1); Plin. mai.; Iuv.; Mart.; Ambros.), 5, 41.

c) *claudere*, to finish, end, conclude (of time) (Hor.; Ov.; Manil.; Sen. rhet.; Val. Max.; Silver and Late especially), 1, 1, 10; 2, 1, 1; 2, 5, 4; 3, 24; 5, 27; 5, 28; 5, 37, 2. — *condere*, to conceal (of rivers) (Verg.; Aetna; Prop.; Ov.; Curt.; Lucan.; Plin. mai.; Sol.; Paneg.), 3, 5, 2; 3, 26, 1. — *coruscare*, to glitter, glisten (transf. sense) (Verg.; Gratt.; Plin. mai.; Val. Fl.; Apul.; and Late especially), 1, 46, 2. — *domare*, to make arable (Verg.; Aetna; Sil.; Lucan.; Stat.; Mart.; Iuv.; Tert.; Avien.; Anthol.; et al), 3, 6, 3. — *fatigare*, to weaken, impair (Ov.; Sen. phil.; Curt.; Colum.; Eutr.; Symm.; Avien.; et al), 3, 11, 1. — *fervere*, to be on fire, to burn (Lucr.; Verg.; Ov.; Prop.; Vitr.; Colum.; Plin. mai.; Silver and Late), 1, 40, 12. — *fragrare*, to smell, to emit a smell (Catull.; Ciris; Verg.; Val. Fl.; Mart.; Sil.; Suet.; Apul.; Tert.; Itala; Ambros. (saepe); et al), 1, 46, 2. — *fundere*, to fall, to lie down (Verg.; Ov.; Sen. phil.; Lucan.; Val. Fl.; Mart.; Stat.; Amm.; Paul. Nol.), 5, 37, 2; — to spread, diffuse (Lucr.; Manil.; Curt.; Sen. phil.; Plin. mai.; Sil.; Arator), 3, 6, 3; 4, 17. — *furere*, to rage (of things) (Lucr.; Verg.; Hor.; Ov.; Petron.; Sen. phil.; Lucan.; Sil.; Silver and Late), 1, 40, 7; 5, 43, 1. — *gliscere*, to spread, grow (Lucr.; Verg.; Liv.; Tac.), 1, 19, 1. — *iungere*, to join in marriage (Ov.; Liv.; Curt.; Treb. Poll.), 1, 23, 1. — *lambere*, to lick, play upon (of fire) (Lucr.; Verg.; Hor.), 5, 31. — *ligare*, to bind (Hor.; Ov.; Liv.; Lucan.; Tac.; Plin. min.; Suet.; Lampr.), 3, 11, 2; — to unite (transf. sense) (Ov.; Prop.; Sen. poet.; Quint.), 1, 39. — *luctari*, to struggle, contend (physically) (Verg.; Hor.; Ov.; Liv.; Vell.; Sen. phil.; Stat.), 5, 6. — *mactare*, to immolate, sacrifice (Verg.; Hor.; Liv.; Suet.), 1, 8; 5, 1, 3. — *meare*, to go, pass (Hor.; Curt.; Plin. mai.; Tac.), 4, 1, 1; 5, 16. — *mentiri* (trans.), to feign, counterfeit (of persons) (Ov.; Vell.; Mart.; Quint.; Iust.), 3, 2; — to counterfeit, give the appearance of (of inanimate objects) (Verg.; Plin. mai.), 5, 16. — *miscere*, to throw into confusion (Verg.), 3, 20, 2; — *misceri* (passive with middle force), to mingle with (Verg.), 5, 16. — *mulcere*, to sooth, appease (Lucr.; Verg.; Ov.;

Liv.; Vell.; Tac.; Ambros.), 1, 2; 1, 13, 1; 3, 18, 1. — *nutrire,*
to nourish, feed, suckle (of animals) (Hor.; Ov.; Plin. mai.; Iuv.),
5, 41. — *pandere,* to publish, make known (Verg.; Ov.; Catull.;
Orac. vet. apud Liv.; Lucan.; Hier.), 1, 44, 2; 5, 31. — *pangere,*
to pledge, engage (of marriage) (Catull.; Ov.), 1, 41, 7. — *premere,* to hide, conceal (Verg.; Curt.; Tac.; Plin. min.), 1, 38, 6;
1, 41, 3; 1, 41, 10. — *quatere,* to batter (Verg.; Liv.), 3, 11, 1;
5, 20, 2; — to agitate, shake (Verg.; Hor.; Ov.; Liv.; Sen. phil.;
Plin. min.), 5, 46; — to plague, harass, torment (Verg.), 5, 18, 2.
—*rigare,* to water (Lucr.; Tibull.; Liv.; Colum.; Plin. mai.),
3, 6, 3; 4, 17. — *sedere,* to be fixed, resolved, determined upon
(Verg.; Stat.; Val. Fl.; Flor.), 1, 37, 3. — *solari,* to relieve,
assuage (Verg.; Hor.; Ov.; Quint.; Tac.; Plin. min.; Ps. Quint.;
Pacat.), 5, 2; 5, 18, 1; 5, 21, 4; 5, 24, 2. — *solvere,* to annul (Hor.;
Liv.; Curt.; Iuv.; Quint.; Iust.; Eutr.; Ambros.), 1, 29, 1; 1, 40,
13; 1, 42, 5; 1, 42, 6; — to enervate, debilitate (Verg.; Hor.; Ov.;
Curt.; Petron.; Stat.; Quint.; Flor.), 4, 29, 2. — *spirare,* to blow
(of breezes, winds) (Verg.; Curt.; Sen. phil.; Amm.), 3, 5, 2;
3, 26, 1; — to exhale fragrance (Verg.; Stat.), 5, 2. — *sternere,*
to prostrate, overthrow (Verg.; Hor.; Ov.; Liv.; Sil.), 1, 32, 4;
2, 5, 1; 3, 4, 2; 3, 4, 3; 5, 30; 5, 37, 2. — *stringere,* to press
together, draw together, draw tight (Ov.; Liv.; Sen. phil.; Plin.
mai.; Val. Fl.; Stat.; Plin. min.; Fronto; Gell.), 5, 22; 5, 33, 1.
— *tremere* (trans.), to tremble at (Verg.; Hor.; Ov.; Liv.; Lact.;
Aug.), 5, 15.

d) *destinare,* to aim (of weapons) (Nux; Sen. phil.; Petron.;
Stat.; Tac.; Ulp.; Tert.; Sol.; Paneg.; Iul. Val.; Veget.; Amm.),
3, 11, 1; — to send (Suet.; Itala; Lucif.; Ambros. (saepe); and
Late), 1, 37, 2; 2, 14, 2; 4, 19. — *exuere,* to free from, deliver
(Sen. ep.; Sil.), 5, 4, 4. — *se fundere,* to pour itself out (of rivers,
waters) (Manil.; Plin. mai.; Cosmogr.), 5, 41. — *indulgere*
(trans.), to concede, allow (Liv.; Mart.; Tac.; Plin. ep.; Suet.),
1, 37, 2; 3, 2. — *manducare,*[18] to eat (Aug. apud Suet.; Fronto;
Marc. Emp.; Plin. Val.; Ambros.; Hier.; Vulg. (175); et al),
5, 41. — *meare,* to flow (of water) (Curt.; Plin. mai.; Mart. Cap.),
3, 10. — *se miscere,* to take part in, to share in (Vell.; Ict.), 5, 53,

---

[18] Used by Varro in the sense of " to masticate," " to chew."

1. — *nutrire*, to nurse, care for, tend (Liv.; Cels.; Colum.; Plin. mai.), 5, 24, 2. — *patere*, to be exposed or subject to (Liv.; Cels.; Sen. phil.; Vulg.), 5, 17. — *solvere*, to relax, loose (Cels.; Colum.; Plin. mai.), 4, 18. — *sorbere*, to swallow (Cels.; Plin. mai.; Suet.), 5, 24, 2. — *terere*, to exhaust, fatigue (Liv.; Plin. ep.), 1, 13, 1. — *vergere*, to turn one's activities (fig.) (Sen. phil.; Tac.), 4, 21.

Summary

The section on the verbs is by far the largest in the treatment of this portion of the vocabulary of Hegesippus. Seven hundred and ninety-seven verbs are treated under the following types: 1) verbs derived from nouns; 2) verbs derived from adjectives; 3) verbs derived from other verbs; 4) verbs derived from adverbs; 5) verbs derived from diminutives; 6) hybrids; 7) frequentatives; 8) inchoatives; 9) compound verbs; 10) miscellaneous verbs.

This large list of verbs is grouped under the four categories as follows: Rare Classical, 231; Early, 200; Poetic, 213; and Silver, 153.

The verbs derived from nouns form the second largest list in this collection of verbs, with a total of fifty-nine. Of these, nineteen are Rare Classical, seventeen Early, thirteen Poetic, and ten Silver. All of these verbs are of the first conjugation, except *callere*, *fastidire*, *foetere*, and *currere*. Among the Rare Classical verbs the following are noteworthy: *comperendinare* found in Cicero (6) and then in Fronto, Symmachus, Ammianus Marcellinus, and Ambrose; *frustrari* (pass.) in Sallust and Silius; *iubilare* cited for Varro and Late Latin; *munerari* (trans.) for Cicero's Epistles (1) and Horace; and *rimari* (to investigate, examine) found once in Cicero, then in Tacitus and Gellius. Of the Early words *aestimare* (to think) occurs at least forty-three times in Hegesippus; *fabulari* (to speak) is noted only for Early and Late Latin; and *pumicare*, in its literal sense of "to rub with pumice stone," is used in Lucilius, Catullus, Martial, and Late Latin. An interesting Poetic word is *epulari* (to eat, feast upon) which is found in Vergil, Iustinus, and the pseudo-Cyprian. Nearly all the Silver verbs in this group are worthy of mention because they are found rarely in Silver Latin and then in Late Latin—*copulare* (to join in matri-

11

mony), *foederare, fulminare, loricare, ordinare* (to appoint to office), *pavimentare, vallare,* and *velare* (to hide, conceal).

Verbs derived from adjectives form the third largest group in this section, with a total of forty-three. Eight of these are Rare Classical, twelve Early, sixteen Poetic, and seven Silver. Thirty-seven of the total number of verbs in this group belong to the first conjugation, five to the fourth, and one to the second. An interesting verb in the Rare Classical category is *mollire* (to overcome, unman) found in Cicero's Epistles (1) and in Tacitus. Several of the verbs in the Early group are deserving of special comment because they are found in Early Latin, rarely in the poets and Silver Latin, and more frequently in Late Latin: *clarere* (to be evident), *miserari, rutilare, turpare,* and *venustare*. Another Early word, *interpolare,* is noteworthy because of its rare occurrence in Plautus, Cicero's Epistles (1), and Ulpian. Words which occur first in the poets and rarely in Silver Latin, but frequently in Late Latin, are the following: *acerbare*; *manifestare* (to make public), which appears to be very popular with Hegesippus, being cited at least fifteen times; and *mundare*. Silver words which appear rarely in Silver Latin, but which are found in Late Latin, include *asperare* (to rouse up, excite), *participare,* and *publicare.*

Only two verbs which have been derived from other verbs have been noted, and both of these verbs are in the Early category. The verb *oblitterare,* derived from *oblinere,* is found in the fragments of Accius, twice in Cicero, and then in Catullus, Livy, Tacitus, and Suetonius. The other verb, *statuere* (to stop, to cause to stand still), derived from *statutum,* the supine of *sisto,* is cited for Plautus, Propertius, Vergil, Silver and Late Latin.

A single example of a verb derived from an adverb is found in the Poetic category — *temerare*. This verb is derived from the adverb *temere* and is cited for Vergil, Ovid, Livy, Silver and Late Latin.

The Rare Classical verb, *pullulare,* in its tropical sense of " to increase," furnishes a single instance of a verb derived from a diminutive — *pullulus*. This verb occurs in Nepos and then in Apuleius and Late Latin.

One Rare Classical hybrid, *strangulare,* from the Greek στραγγαλόω, στραγγαλίζω, occurs in Hegesippus. It is found also in Cicero (2), Celsus, Pliny the Younger, and Lactantius.

Frequentative verbs are quite prevalent in Hegesippus, forty having been noted. Nine of these are Rare Classical, fifteen Early, ten Poetic, and six Silver. As far as meaning is concerned, these frequentative verbs in Hegesippus are not to be distinguished from the simple verbs. In this respect they are very similar to the diminutive nouns which have not retained their diminutive meaning. With the exception of the verb *incessere*, which belongs to the third conjugation, all the frequentatives in our author are found in the first 'conjugation. The Rare Classical verb, *visitare* (to visit, to go to see), is cited only once for Cicero, then for Suetonius and Augustine. Nearly all the Early frequentatives are found in Plautus. The verb, *circumcursare* (to run about in), occurs in Plautus, Catullus, and Late Latin; *fugitare* (to flee in haste) in Terence, Pliny the Elder, and Late Latin; *imperitare* (to command), which is used at least nineteen times in Hegesippus, occurs also in Plautus, Sallust, Lucretius, Horace, Livy, Silver and Late Latin; *incursare* is used by Plautus, Livy, Tacitus, and Ammianus Marcellinus; *quassare* found in the fragments of Naevius, in Lucretius, Vergil, and Livy; and *vellicare* (to pluck, nip) in Plautus, Varro, Quintilian, and Late Latin. Interesting Poetic words are *incessere* (to accuse, assail), which is used sixteen times by Hegesippus; *pensare* (to buy) found only in Ovid, Velleius, and Valerius Maximus; *sustentare* (to prop up) in Vergil, Pliny the Elder, and Claudius Claudianus; and *vellicare* in its figurative sense of " to afflict," " to vex " (through envy) noted only for Propertius 2, 5, 8. Two noteworthy Silver words which are cited first for Tacitus and which seem to be popular with Hegesippus are *percursare* (to traverse) and *suspectare* (to mistrust, suspect). The reflexive, *se volutare* (to wallow), occurs also in Phaedrus, Pliny the Elder, and Vegetius.

Thirty-five inchoatives have been employed by Hegesippus in this section of his vocabulary, but approximately one-half of them have lost their inchoative force. With the exception of the verbs *fatiscere* and *ingemiscere* all the inchoatives have the form -*escere*. Seven of the thirty-five are Rare Classical, nine Early, fifteen Poetic, and four Silver. One of the Rare Classical verbs which occurs thirteen times in our author is *acquiescere* in the sense of " to obey," " to agree to." This word is cited first for the Bellum

Africanum, then for Seneca's Epistles, Suetonius, and Late Latin, especially among the jurists and ecclesiastical writers. Other verbs in the Rare Classical group which appear infrequently in Latin are *dulcescere, effervescere, ingemiscere, insolescere,* and *requiescere* (to rest in the grave). Among the Early inchoatives, *se assuescere* is interesting because Hegesippus is the only author noted by the T. L. L. for the reflexive use. Rare Poetic words are *clarescere* (to become illustrious), *contremescere, exhorrescere, inhorrescere, inolescere* (to grow in), *intumescere, iuvenescere,* and *patescere.* The four Silver inchoatives—*coalescere, obrigescere, recrudescere, valescere*—are all used in rare, figurative senses.

Five hundred verbs compounded with a preposition or a particle have been listed for Hegesippus. Of these, one hundred and fifty-five are Rare Classical, one hundred and thirteen Early, one hundred and twenty-three Poetic, and one hundred and nine Silver. The following prepositions or prefixes have been employed in these compound verbs: *ab, ad, ambi, circum, cum (co, col, com, con, cor), de, dis (di, dir), ex(e), in, inter, intro, ne, ob, per (por), post, prae, praeter, pro, re, sub, super,* and *trans.* It is worthy of note that the prefix *super* does not appear until Silver Latin where it is found seven times for Hegesippus — *supereminere, superfluere, superfundere, supergredi, supernatare, supervenire,* and *supervivere.* The most popular prefixes are *in, cum,* and *ad,* respectively. The following Rare Classical compound verbs are worthy of special note because they are found only in Classical Latin and Late Latin: *abdicare* (to deprive, rob, strip), *adminiculare, complanare, constipare, decurrere* (to discuss), *deonerare, derivare* (to divert), *digladiari, diloricare, elevare,* which is used eleven times in Hegesippus, *intexere* in its transferred sense of "to intermix," *perstringere* (to narrate briefly), and *praetexere* (to adorn). Early compound verbs which are found in Late Latin and but rarely, if ever, in Silver Latin are the following: *abligurrire, complacere* (to be pleasing), *demorari, eliminare* (to turn out of doors), *se immergere* (to betake one's self), *perstrepere* (to raise a clamor, in speaking of a person), *promovere* (to effect), and *succenturiare.* Uncommon Poetic compound verbs are: *colligere* (to receive), *commaculare, emollire* (to mollify), *inaestuare* (used figuratively), *introgredi, invertere* (to plough up), *obserare* (used figuratively), *perhorrere, praetermeare* (used intransitively), *praetexere* (to disguise), and *resuscitare* (used figuratively).   There is a long list of Silver compound verbs which are worthy of special comment because of their rare occurrence in the Latin of the Silver period: *abdicare* (in both transitive senses of " to expel someone from a magistracy" and "to exclude"), *adstipulari* (to agree with), *affectare* (to honor), *arrodere* (to gnaw at), *associare* (to join to), *circumspicere* (to see), *competere* (to belong to), *conserere* (to engage in conversation), *decolorare* (to disgrace), *se demergere* (to conceal one's self), *desponsare* (to betroth), *diluere* (to wash away), *dirigere* (used forty-six times by Hegesippus in the sense of " to send " and used by him in several other senses), *emercari, eviscerare* (to squander), *exsatiare, inebriare, inequitare* (to ride upon), *infundere* (to soak thoroughly), *se infundere* (used fourteen times by Hegesippus in the sense of " to enter "), *involare* (to steal), *praetendere* (used sixteen times by Hegesippus in the sense of " to watch "), *protrahere* (to defer), *refundere* (to restore), *retexere* (to narrate), and *suggerere* (to advise, suggest).

Five verbs owe their origin to composition from nouns plus verbs. The verb *usurpare* is found in two senses in our author.   In the sense of " to obtain rightfully," it is cited once for Cicero, then for Pliny the Elder, Gellius, and Iustinus.   In the other meaning of " to usurp," " to acquire unlawfully," it is found first in Livy, then in Pliny the Elder, Suetonius, and the Codex Iustinianus, and is used twelve times by Hegesippus in this meaning.   The Poetic verb, *mansuescere,* is also found in two senses: " to grow soft " and " to grow mild."   Both these meanings seem to be special to Vergil.

Only two verbs are compounded from adverbs and verbs.   In both cases the adverb is *subter.*   The verb *subterfugere* is used intransitively and in this intransitive use is cited only for Plautus and the Digests.   It is, however, a favorite word of Cicero in its transitive use.   The other compound, *subterlabi,* is used by Vergil and Ausonius.

One instance of a verb compounded from two verbs has been listed.   The verb, *valedicere,* used as one word, is found only in Seneca's Epistles and Sulpicius Severus.   As two words (*vale dicere*), the phrase is found in Cicero's Epistles and Ovid.

Three compounds of -*facere* have been noted. The verb *expergefacere* is used in its transferred sense of "to excite" by Plautus, the Rhetor ad Herennium, Cicero (1), and Lucretius. In its literal sense of "to awaken" it is found in Suetonius and twice in our author. The Early verb, *perterrefacere*, is cited only for Terence and Ammianus Marcellinus, while *stupefacere* is found once in Cicero, then in the poets, and in Silver and Late Latin.

A single iuxtaposition, *crucifigere*, is cited first for Seneca the rhetor, and Silver and Late Latin. This word is used eight times by Hegesippus.

One hundred and one verbs are classified as miscellaneous, twenty-eight of which are Rare Classical, twenty-seven Early, thirty-three Poetic, and thirteen Silver. Of the Rare Classical verbs, *patrare* (to perform) is used ten times by Hegesippus. Three of the Early words are interesting because of their infrequency—*ludere* (to disappoint, thwart) found in Terence, Vergil, and Horace; *percire* (to excite) cited for Plautus, Terence, Cicero (1), Lucretius, Fronto, and three times in Hegesippus; and *spondere* (to betroth) quoted for Plautus, Terence, and as poetical in Varro. The Poetic verb *miscere* (to throw into confusion) is cited only for Vergil in this meaning. Three of the Silver miscellaneous verbs are found rarely in Silver Latin, but appear in Late Latin—*destinare* (to send) and *manducare* (to eat) are used by Suetonius and Late Latin; *exuere* (to free from, deliver) cited for Seneca's Epistles and Silius; and the reflexive, *se miscere* (to take part in), found in Velleius and the jurists.

D. ADVERBS

1. Adverbs in -*e*.

a) *dubie*, doubtfully (Cic. (2); Sall. fr.; Ov.; Liv.; Sen. phil.; Curt.; Quint.; Tac.), 1, 39; 2, 10, 2 (bis). — *effuse*, far and wide, without order (Sall.; Liv.), 1, 11, 2; 1, 21, 3. — *intente*, with earnestness (Rhet. Her.; Liv.; Tac.; Plin. min.; Vulg.), 1, 7, 1; 5, 42, 1. — *promisce*, indiscriminately (Cic. (2); Liv.; Rut. Lup.; Gell.; Min. Fel.; Chalc.), 5, 1, 3. — *propense*, willingly, readily (Lentul. apud Cic. (1); Liv.; Apul.), 1, 29, 11; 3, 8, 3. — *sceleste*, wickedly (Cic. (1); Liv.; Aug.), 5, 16.

b) *alte*, deeply (Cato; Lucr.; Varr.; Cic. (2) ; Verg.; Ov.; Liv.; Silver and Late), 5, 21, 4; 5, 22. — *astute*, cunningly, craftily (Plaut.; Ter.; Varr.; Cic. (once in Orations; three times in Epistles) ; Gell.; Porphyr.; Lact.; Amm.; Sedul.; Aug.; et al), 1, 29, 3. — *consulte*, deliberately (Plaut.; Liv.; Sen. phil.; Tac.; Min. Fel.; Papin.; Ulp.; and Late especially), 1, 1, 10; 3, 18, 3; 3, 22, 1; 5, 21, 1. — *difficile*, with difficulty (Cato?; Bibac.?; Vell.; Cels.; Plin. mai.; Apul.; Vulg.; Aug.), 2, 11, 2; 4, 18. — *foede*, cruelly, horribly (Pacuv.; Sall. fr.; Cels.; Sen. phil.; Tac.; Aur. Vict.; et al), 3, 20, 2. — *impense*, exceedingly, very much (Plaut.; Ter.; Cic. ep. (1) ; Verg.; Liv.; Plin. ep.; Gell.), 1, 40, 13. — *impigre*, quickly, readily, actively (Plaut.; Sall. fr.; Liv.; Curt.; Tac.), 1, 30, 11; 3, 3, 4; 5, 30; 5, 35, 2. — *propere*, hastily, speedily (Pacuv. fr.; Plaut.; Sall.; Nep.; Ov.; Liv.), 1, 30, 3; 1, 41, 3; 3, 3, 1; 3, 8, 3; 5, 21, 2; 5, 42, 4. — *sobrie*, prudently, circumspectly, sensibly (Plaut.), 1, 38, 2. — *valide*, stoutly, vehemently (Plaut.; Cael. in Cic. ep.; Phaedr.; Vell.; Quint.; Plin. ep.; Fronto; Apul.; Vulg.; Aur. Vict.), 5, 10, 3.

c) *speciose*, showily (Hor.; Liv.; Val. Max.; Colum.; Plin. mai.; Quint.; Iust.; Ambros.), 5, 3, 1.

d) *intente*, with attention (Quint.; Amm.; Lampr.), 1, 6, 2; 5, 36, 1. — *perfunctorie*,[1] superficially, lightly, slightly (Petron.; Ambros.; Aug.; Rufin.; Prosp.; Chalc.), 1, 17, 2; 1, 37, 5; 1, 44, 8. — *prompte*, quickly (Tac.; Plin. ep.), 3, 15, 4. — *provide*, carefully, prudently (Plin. mai.; Frontin.; Eutr.; Chalc.), 1, 20. — *sollicite*, carefully (Plin. min.; Suet.; Aug.), 1, 16, 3; 1, 43, 1; 3, 9, 5.

2. Adverbs in *-ter*.

a) *dementer,* madly (Cic. (1) ; Ov.; Sen. rhet.; Val. Max.; Sen. phil.; Quint.; Aug.; et al), 5, 6. — *pertinaciter*, obstinately, persistently (Varr.; Sall.; Hirt.; Bell. Alex.; Liv.; Vell.; Sen. phil.; Quint.; Plin. min.; Suet.; Amm.), 1, 16, 4; 4, 1, 3; 4, 3, 1; 5, 15; 5, 19; 5, 41; 5, 53, 1. — *properanter*, speedily, quickly (Sall.; Lucr.; Ov.; Tac.; Cod. Th.), 2, 15, 8. — *viriliter*, manfully,

---

[1] Landgraf, Archiv XII, p. 470, calls attention to the use of a negative with this word by Hegesippus and Ambrose.

courageously (Rhet. Her.; Cic. (2) ; Hor.; Ov.; Sen. rhet.; Val. Max.; Sen. phil.; Gell.), 5, 53, 2.

b) *naviter*, diligently, zealously (Ter.; Liv.; Gell.), 5, 52, 2. — *violenter*, violently (Ter.; Sall.; Liv.; Cels.; Colum.; Suet.), 1, 28, 6; 3, 20, 2; 5, 53, 1.

c) *muliebriter*, like a woman, in the manner of a woman (Hor.; Plin. mai.; Iust.; Amm.; Treb. Poll.), 1, 40, 2.

d) *evidenter*, evidently, manifestly (Liv.; Val. Max.; Cels.; Quint.; Iulian. dig.; Suet.; Iavol.), 1, 40, 11; 4, 6, 4. — *impatienter*, impatiently, unwillingly (Tac.; Plin. min.; Iust.; Amm.; Sol.), 1, 44, 3; 3, 17; 5, 16. — *instanter*, vehemently (Quint.; Tac.; Plin. ep.; Suet.; Gell.; Apul.; Aur. Vict.; Hier.), 4, 6, 7; 5, 41. — *multipliciter*, in various ways (Quint.; Flor.; Gell.; Ambros.; Aug.), 3, 26, 2. — *perseveranter*, perseveringly (Liv.; Val. Max.; Scrib.; Plin. ep.; Aug.), 4, 26, 2. — *pervicaciter*, stubbornly, obstinately (Liv.; Tac.; Ulp.; Sid.; Claud. Mam.; Ict.; Aug.), 5, 14, 4. — *sollemniter*, solemnly, in a religious manner (Liv.; Iust.), 5, 1, 3. — *specialiter*, particularly (Cels.; Colum.; Quint.; Ambros.; Rufin.; Hier.), 4, 6, 9.

3. Adverbs in *-o*.

b) *assiduo*, constantly (Plaut.; Lucil.; Plin. mai.; Gell.; Apul.; Modest.; Ulp.), 3, 5, 2. — *immerito*,[2] unjustly (Ter.; Cic. (1) ; Liv.; Quint.), 2, 13, 8; 5, 43, 1. — *liquido*, clearly, plainly (Ter.; Cic. (4) ; Liv.; Ict.), Praef. — *tertio*, for the third time (Ter.; Cic. (2) ; Liv.; Curt.; Val. Max.; Vell.; Plin. min.; Eutr.; Aur. Vict.; Lampr.), 5, 6.

d) *properato*, speedily (Tac.; Ennod.), 1, 29, 6; 1, 40, 9; 4, 16, 2.

4. Compound Adverbs.

a) *desuper-* down from (with the idea of motion) (Caes.; Verg.; Ov.; Sen. phil.; Colum.; Silver and Late (Ambros.)), 1, 15, 2; 1, 16, 4; 3, 13; 4, 1, 4; 5, 23; 5, 35, 1 (bis).

b) *alibi*, elsewhere (Plaut.; Ter.; Cic. (2) ; Liv.; Silver and

² Used usually with a negative.

Late), 3, 6, 4. — *insuper*, over and above, besides (Plaut.; Ter.; Rhet. Her.; Liv.), 5, 16. — *praepropere*, very quickly, with over-haste (Plaut.; Liv.; Ambros.; Aug.), 4, 7. — *utrobique*, on both sides (Plaut.; Cic. (2); Asin. Poll. in Cic. ep.; Nep.; Hor.; Liv.), 3, 23, 1.

d) *desuper*, over, above (without the idea of motion) (Val. Fl.; Stat.; Flor.; Carm. Epigr.; Iust.; Tert.; Lact.; Ps. Hil.; and Late), 5, 49, 3.

5. Miscellaneous Adverbs and Particles.

a) *eminus*, at a fighting distance (Cic. (1); Caes.; Apul.), 5, 14, 1. — *immane quantum*, extraordinarily, uncommonly (Sall. fr. apud Non.; Hor.; Tac.), 2, 10, 6; 3, 20, 2; 5, 28. — *introrsum*,[3] within, inwardly (Hor.; Liv.; Sulp. Sev.), Praef.; 1, 24, 2; 4, 2; 5, 38; 5, 49, 3; 5, 50. — *scilicet*, namely, to wit, that is to say (Varr.; Suet.; Apul.; Tert.; Capit.; Spart.; Lampr.; Eutr.; Amm.; Veget.; Cael. Aur.), 2, 13, 1; 3, 18, 3.

b) *illi*, in that place, there (Plaut.; Ter.), 3, 9, 5. — *iuxta*, equally, in like manner, like (Plaut.; Sall.; Liv.; Val. Max.), 4, 9, 5; 4, 27. — *papae* (interj.), indeed!, how strange!, really! (Plaut.; Ter.; Pers.; Hier.), 1, 7, 1. — *primitus*, first (Lucil.; Varr.; Lucr.; Priap.; Val. Max.; Suet.; Ter. Maur.; Petron.; Gell.; Tert.; Lact.; Amm.; Aug.; et al), 4, 9, 3. — *satis*, very (Plaut.; Ter.; Cic. (rare); Silver and Late), 1, 25, 3; 1, 28, 7; 1, 29, 3; 1, 30, 13; 1, 40, 2; 1, 42, 3; 1, 44, 7; 4, 26, 3; 4, 29, 2. — *vae* (interj.), alas! (Plaut.; Ter.; Verg.; Catull.; Hor.; Liv.; Sen. phil.; Mart.; Tert.; Aug.; Inscr.), 3, 15, 2; 5, 44, 1 (quater).

c) *longum*, long, a long while (Verg.; Hor.; and the Poets), 1, 21, 2; 1, 42, 2; 2, 2, 4. — *passim*, without order, in a mass, indiscriminately (Hor.; Tibull.; Plin. mai.; Tac.; Iust.; Lact.), 5, 7, 1. — *retrorsum*, back, backwards (Hor.; Plin. mai.; Lucan.; Sil.), 3, 11, 1; 5, 16.

---

[3] The form *introrsus* is found in Caes.; Tac.

SUMMARY

Sixty-one adverbs are included in this section of the vocabulary of Hegesippus under the following types: 1) adverbs in -*e*; 2) adverbs in -*ter*; 3) adverbs in -*o*; 4) compound adverbs; 5) miscellaneous adverbs.

These sixty-one adverbs are divided into the four categories as follows: Rare Classical, fifteen; Early, twenty-six; Poetic, five; and Silver, fifteen.

Twenty-two adverbs in -*e* form the largest group, with six listed as Rare Classical, ten as Early, one as Poetic, and five as Silver. It is interesting to note that every one of the Rare Classical adverbs in -*e* is also found in Livy. The adverb *effuse* (far and wide) is found in Sallust and Livy; *promisce* (indiscriminately) in Cicero (2), Livy, and Late Latin; *propense* (willingly, readily) is cited for Lentulus in Cicero, for Livy, and Apuleius; and *sceleste* for Cicero (1), Livy, and Augustine. A very rare Early adverb which has been cited only for Plautus and Hegesippus is *sobrie* in the sense of "prudently," "circumspectly." All of the Silver adverbs in -*e* occur rarely in Silver Latin and are found in Late Latin—*intente, perfunctorie, prompte, provide, sollicite*.

The second largest group of adverbs ends in -*ter* and totals fifteen. Four of these are Rare Classical, two Early, one Poetic, and eight Silver. These adverbs are developed either from participial forms and have the suffix -*nter*, or from adjectives and have the ending -*ter*. One of the Early adverbs, *naviter* (diligently, zealously), is found only in Terence, Livy, and Gellius. The single Poetic adverb, *muliebriter* (like a woman, in the manner of a woman), is cited for Horace, Pliny the Elder, and Late Latin. Among the Silver adverbs with this suffix the following appear rarely in Silver Latin, but are also found in Late Latin: *impatienter, multipliciter, pervicaciter, solemniter*.

Only five adverbs in -*o* have been found in Hegesippus, four of which belong to the Early category and one to the Silver. Three of the Early adverbs in -*o* originated with Terence and are also found in Cicero — *immerito, liquido, tertio*. The other Early adverb, *assiduo*, is found in Plautus, Lucilius, Pliny the Elder, and Late Latin. The single Silver example, *properato*, appears first in Tacitus, three times in our author, and later in Ennodius.

Six compound adverbs occur in Hegesippus, one of which is Rare Classical, four Early, and one Silver. The adverb, *desuper*, appears in two senses—" down from " and " above." In the first sense it is used seven times by Hegesippus, and only once by him in the second meaning. The four Early compound adverbs originated with Plautus and are used throughout all Latin, except *praepropere* which is cited only for Plautus, Livy, and Ambrose.

Ten miscellaneous adverbs which appear under a variety of forms have been listed together. Four of these are Rare Classical and are worthy of note because of their infrequency—*eminus* (at a fighting distance) found in Cicero (1), Caesar, and Apuleius; *immane quantum* (extraordinarily), which occurs three times in Hegesippus, is cited by Nonius for the fragments of Sallust, and by Horace and Tacitus; *introrsum* (inwardly) is used by Horace, Livy, and Sulpicius Severus, whereas the other form, *introrsus*, is found in Caesar and Tacitus; and *scilicet* (namely, that is to say) cited first for Varro, then for Suetonius and Late Latin. Among the four Early miscellaneous adverbs the most interesting is *illi* (in that place) which is noted only for Plautus, Terence, and once for Hegesippus. The three Poetic adverbs — *longum, passim, retrorsum*—are all used by Horace.

Two Early interjections have been included under this list of miscellaneous adverbs and particles—*papae* found only in Plautus, Terence, Persius, and Jerome; and *vae* originating with Plautus, found also in Terence, and then in the poets, and in Silver and Late Latin.

CONCLUSION

THE VOCABULARY OF HEGESIPPUS AND THE QUESTION OF AUTHORSHIP

Many scholars, among them Ronsch, Landgraf, Weyman, Hey, Schanz, and Ussani, have felt that the solution of the question of authorship of the *De Bello Iudaico* depends in great measure on an investigation of the vocabulary, syntax, and style of the work. Ronsch,[1] however, is the only one so far who has made any serious or extensive study of the vocabulary of Hegesippus. With some few exceptions, he has confined himself to a study of the Late Latin words and meanings, feeling rightly, no doubt, that this restricted area would afford the most conclusive evidence for the solution of the question.

From his study of the vocabulary of Hegesippus Rönsch came to the conclusion that Hegesippus and Ambrose were one and the same person. He based his arguments on evidence obtained by dividing the vocabulary of Hegesippus into four groups: 1) words which Hegesippus has in common with other authors, but not with Ambrose; 2) words which Hegesippus has in common with Ambrose and other authors; 3) words which appear only in Hegesippus and Ambrose; 4) words which Hegesippus alone uses. The words in each of these four groups were treated under the following heads: a) word-formations; b) meanings; c) grammatical forms; d) syntactical peculiarities.

My study of the vocabulary of Hegesippus, particularly of the Late Latin vocabulary and semantics, has yielded much material in the form of additions and corrections to be made in these four groups of Rönsch. I shall say nothing about grammatical forms or syntactical peculiarities, as I have not included them in the present study. The syntax, especially, of Hegesippus would in itself easily constitute the subject of an ample monograph.

In the first group — words which Hegesippus has in common with other authors, but *not* with Ambrose — Rönsch has enumerated the following words:

---

[1] Rönsch, Collectanea Philologia, pp. 32-89.

Nouns: *arcuballista, ascensor, binio, caupulus, circumventio, comminutio, compassio, constipatio, contextio, coracinus, democratia, devoratio, diplois, egressio, epitaphium, exagitatio, excidio, excisor, excitatio, exspectator, gazophylacium, hypogeum, impossibilitas, incentivum* (subst.), *incitator, incursatio, inquietudo, instaurator, interminatio, intuitus, manganum, missibile* (subst.), *monarchia, neocorus, neomenia, opitulatio, penetrabile* (subst.), *praereptor, praescientia, praesumtor, properatio, prosecutor, pusillitas, regressio, scenopegia, sepultor, sequestra, sollicitator, spiramen, stibium, stimulator, stolus, tenon, tutamentum, xenodochium.*

Adjectives: *bellatorius, biduanus, conducibilis* (subst.), *ferentarius, immutilatus, incapax, indubius, inexoratus, inexpressus, infulatus, metropolitanus, obsidialis, oppidanus, paschalis, portuensis, purgatorius, solubilis, spontaneus, tantillus* (subst.), *tetragonus.*

Adverbs: *competenter, de proximo, dubio* (so Rönsch reads Heg. 1, 16, 3; I consider it a subst.), *imperatorie, inrationabiliter, in vacuum, maturo* (Weber-Caesar reads *maturato*), *profecto, rationabiliter, superfluo.*

Verbs: *conterminare, diloricare, evaginare, introgredi, necesse habere, remediare, subintrare, subiugare, supervivere, transfretare.*

In this list of words compiled by Rònsch for his first group, I have found the following in Ambrose:

Nouns.

ascensor, Ambros. Iob. 1, 1, 2; Abr. 2, 7, 43; Nab. 15, 64.
compassio, Ambros. paenit. 1, 1, 2; 1, 15, 81.
constipatio, Ambros. hex. 6, 5, 33.
exagitatio, Ambros. Nab. 14, 62.
inquietudo, Ambros. in psalm. 45, 9; epist. 20, 1; Hel. 8, 23.
instaurator, Ambros. epist. 43, 4.
praescientia, Ambros. spir. 3, 16, 117.
properatio, Ambros. off. 1, 18, 74.
pusillitas,[2] Ambros.
stibium, Ambros. virginit. 79.

---

[2] Benoist-Goelzer cites Ambrose for this word, but does not give the reference to the work.

Adjectives.

ferentarius, Ambros. Hel. 13, 47 (used substantively).
paschalis, Ambros. epist. 23, 1.
spontaneus, Ambros. off. 1, 161; 1, 162; 3, 81; epist. 8, 13; 37, 7.

Adverbs.

competenter, Ambros. hex. 1, 1, 1.
rationabiliter, Ambros. epist. 53, 2.
superfluo, Ambros. epist. 32, 8.

Verbs.

diloricare, Ambros. exc. Sat. 2, 12.
subintrare, Ambros. epist. 74, 10.
supervivere, Ambros. vid. 6.

In this first group Ronsch has also included a list of words with meanings which are found in Hegesippus and other writers, but *not* in Ambrose. They are as follows:

Nouns: *accersitor, alloquium, ambitus, apices, conturbator, correptio, diffusio, dissimulatio, dissolutio, genus, incentor, infidelitas, miraculum, platea, praesumtio, protector, vadum, virtus, vulnus, volentia* (subst.).

Verbs: *adquiescere, dirigere, dissimulare, excludere, foederare, inculcare, inequitare, insinuare, praesumere, protelare, renuntiare, requiescere, sequestrare, vellicare, videri* (pass.).

Miscellaneous Words: *collectus, quisque, satis, sedulo, nihilominus, vel.*

In the above list among the words whose meanings Ronsch did not find in Ambrose I have noted the following in Ambrose:

Nouns.

arcessitor (*accersitor*), an accuser, Ambros. epist. 6, **1.**
apices (plur.), a writing, Ambros. apol. Dav. 2, 12, 66; fid. 2, 1, 16; Noe 13, 45; 13, 46; in psalm. 1, 52.
correptio, a reproof, reproach, Ambros. Abr. 1, 4, 28; 2, 7, 42; 2, 7, 43; hex. 6, 6, 38; off. 3, 22, 127; in Luc. 8, 21; in psalm. 37, 56; in psalm. 118, 9, 10; et al.

dissolutio, licentiousness, Ambros. bon. mort. 8, 35.

infidelitas, unbelief, Ambros. epist. 64, 58.

praesumptio, boldness, audacity, Ambros. off. 1, 70; virg. 2, 3; 2, 4.

Verbs.

acquiescere, to obey, Ambros. Nab. 10, 45.

dirigere, to send, Ambros. hex. 5, 10, 29; off. 3, 17, 100; epist. 24, 6.

dissimulare, to neglect, Ambros. exc. Sat. 1, 26; in psalm. 118, 2, 9.

foederare, to join, unite, Ambros. Abr. 2, 6, 28.

inequitare, to insult, Ambros. off. 1, 48, 242; epist. 10, 10; 71, 21.

insinuare, to make known, Ambros. epist. 5, 21; 19, 11; 24, 1; 36, 1; 43, 1.

renuntiare, to break off, Ambros. epist. 2, 8; 29, 12; 37, 42.

sequestrare, to put aside, Ambros. off. 3, 116; epist. 37, 22; inst. virg. 20; exhort. virg. 62.

As for Rönsch's second group—words which Hegesippus has in common with Ambrose and other authors—I think that nothing can be proved therefrom as far as authorship is concerned, and surely nothing as far as the identification of Hegesippus with Ambrose. Such a group would indicate, at the most, that both Hegesippus and Ambrose had vocabularies which were representative of writers of the fourth century. The list of meanings given by Rönsch for this second group is far from complete. Some idea of the number of these meanings found in Hegesippus and Ambrose in common with other authors may be gained by consulting the section on Semantics in this work.

The most important of the four groups for the problem of authorship is the third one—words which appear only in Hegesippus and Ambrose. Rönsch enumerates eight words which are peculiar to both these writers—*refragium, repulsor, repulsorium* (subst.), *adulescentulus, heptamyxos, ablevare, placidare, redoperire.* However, the T. L. L. I, 799, 79 cites the adjective *adulescentulus* for Plaut. Mil. 634.

In this third group, as regards special meanings for Hegesippus and Ambrose, only two words appear in Rönsch's list—*sedulus* and *propinquare*. The verb *propinquare*, however, in this sense of "to be near" is found also in Aug. quaest. evang. 2, 45, 1 and in Rufin. interpr. Joseph. antiq. 16, 21. Moreover, Rónsch's meagre list of meanings special to Hegesippus and Ambrose can be supplemented by the following:

firmitudo (= firmamentum), a prop, support, Ambros. Isaac 4, 31.

incisio, a cut, incision, Ambros. in psalm. 37, 42.

vestigium (= pes), a foot, Ambros. epist. 41, 11.

commacerare, to weaken terribly, Ambros. in psalm. 47, 12.

inhalare, to breathe the odor or fragrance from something, Ambros. hex. 5, 21, 69; virg. 1, 44; 2, 39.

obtexere, to put forth as an excuse, Ambros. in Luc. 8, 78.

The fourth group which Rönsch presents, consists of words and meanings used by Hegesippus alone. His list of words is as follows:

Nouns: *Abramides* (proper noun), *aristocratia, atelia, charadra, coalitus, excitor, praesuasio, repressio, stipamen.*

Adjectives: *asphaltius* (Weber-Caesar reads *Asphaltites* (proper noun)), *cinerulentus, Conopaeus, excidialis, impinguis, inexcruciatus, inexitiabilis, inexustus, irreconciliabilis, melamborius* (subst.), *proelialis* (Ussani reads *proeliaris*), *seleucensis* (proper noun), *tribulis, triumphabilis.*

Verbs: *adopperiri, defurere, intaminare, recongerere.*

The following corrections are to be made in the above list:

Abramides is used by Ambros. epist. 37, 37.

coalitus in the sense of "union" is special to Hegesippus, but in its proper sense of "a joining together" it is found in Ambros. exc. Sat. 2, 55; hex. 5, 21, 69. This word also appears in a doubtful reading in Arnob. 4, 33, in the meaning of "fellowship."

Conopaeus (*Canopeus*) is found in Ambros. epist. 18, 35; Isid. orig. 19, 5, 5; 14, 3, 28. A doubtful reading for this word appears first in Catull. 66, 58.

irreconciliabilis is cited for Act. Niceph. Mart. n. 6.

defurere is used in Hegesippus in the sense of "to relax one's anger," but it is found in Hier. in Gal. 5, 17, p. 502, with the meaning of "to be mad."

One addition should be made to Ronsch's list of verbs special to Hegesippus, if the reading of Ussani's text for Heg. 1, 1, 9 is correct:

refrigere (= refringere) is used in the sense of "to check."

In the fourth group only seven words with meanings special to Hegesippus are given by Rönsch — *devotatio, ingratia* (Weber-Caesar reads *gratia*), *decemprimus, crudescere, insuere, praeesse, subtexere.*

In these seven words the following changes should be made: *crudescere* is found with the meaning of "to be indigestible" also in Rufin. Clement. 4, 18 and in Macr. sat. 4, 7, 5.

subtexere, to which Rönsch gives the specific meaning of "to offer," "to oppose," is used, in my opinion, in the meaning of "to contrive." This latter meaning is found in Nepos, Tibullus, and Ammianus Marcellinus. In fact, Amm. 16, 20 uses the identical expression of Heg. 5, 20, 2: subtexerent impedimenta Romanis.

The present investigation of the vocabulary of Hegesippus, however, has disclosed a comparatively long list of words with meanings that are peculiar to Hegesippus. It will suffice to mention the words not indicated by Rönsch. Further information in regard to them can be obtained by consulting the section on Semantics in the first part of this work, where the words with meanings special to Hegesippus are marked with an asterisk (*). The list is as follows:

Nouns: *adulter, aestiva* (plur.), *circumscriptio, coalitus, conspirati* (plur.), *decessio, epilogus, epitaphium, excisor, fluentum, fragores* (plur.), *fundibalus, hereditas, Hesperus, hiberna* (plur.), *incommoditas, indulgentia, infideles* (subst.), *interpellatio, interpositio, irrigua* (plur.), *lavacrum, media* (plur.), *mysticus* (subst.), *obsequia* (plur.), *obsequium, pabulum, penetralia* (subst.), *placiditas, posteriora* (subst.; used in three senses), *potestas, retinaculum, ruptura, saeptum, superstitio, susceptio, tetragonum* (subst.), *vates.*

12

Verbs: *alligare, circumvagari, convenire, decurrere, defenerare, demetere, depasci, detegere, diloricare, se effundere, egredi, expectare, fovere, imminere, imprimere, incidere, inhorrescere, inniti, inserere, intexere* (three senses), *involvere, laxare, meare, mutuare, nectere, obtendere* (two senses), *occurrere, perstringere* (two senses), *praeicere, praelibare, procumbere, proludere, refluere, relaxare, sidere, superfluere, suspendere, tumescere, uti, vadari.*

Adjectives: *excitatus, finitimus, inaequalis, invelatus, vilis.*

If the four groups of words presented by Ronsch in relation to the problem of authorship are examined anew in the light of the additions and corrections which the present study has indicated, the following observations may be made:

1) The transferring of so many words and meanings from the first to the second group strengthens Ronsch's evidence for Ambrosian authorship, since the number of words and meanings found in Hegesippus and others, but *not* in Ambrose, is greatly reduced.

2) The words and meanings in the second group furnish very little, if any, evidence for the solution of the problem of authorship, and absolutely none so far as the identification of Hegesippus with Ambrose.

3) The words and meanings listed in the third group, that is, the words and meanings special to Hegesippus and Ambrose alone are, on the other hand, so characteristic and peculiar that it would be difficult for anyone to convince himself that such agreement between Hegesippus and Ambrose was accidental. In fact, when the totally different characters of their works are considered, it appears all the more remarkable that any special agreement, no matter how limited or small, should exist between the two writers.

4) As far as the fourth group is concerned, three of the words listed by Ronsch as special to Hegesippus have been found in Ambrose—*Abramides, coalitus, Conopaeus.* Four other words—*aristocratia, atelia, charadra, melamborium* — which are used by Hegesippus directly under the influence of the Greek text of Josephus, can be accounted for as not likely to appear in the genuine, extant works of Ambrose. However, when the semantic changes in this fourth group are examined, there is considerable difference in size between the list of Rönsch and that based on the

present investigation. Whereas only five out of the seven words mentioned by Ronsch have been found with meanings special to Hegesippus, approximately ninety other words have been discovered with meanings used by Hegesippus alone. Such a large list does not help to strengthen the evidence for Ambrosian authorship. It should be stated, however, that many of these words occur in the vocabulary of Ambrose, but not in the specific senses used by Hegesippus. Moreover, all the writings of Ambrose have not been extensively or thoroughly investigated, particularly from the semantic point of view. Later studies may, perhaps, show that many of these meanings in the fourth group have been used by Ambrose.

In conclusion, as a result of this study it seems certain to me that Hegesippus and Ambrose lived at about the same time and came under the same cultural influences. As to the identity of Hegesippus, I would say that there is some probability of his being Ambrose, and, furthermore, that this identity cannot be convincingly impugned by arguments based on a study of the vocabulary.

INDEX VERBORUM

abdicare, 130, 150, 164, 165.
ablevare, 15, 175.
abligurrire, 138, 164.
abnegare, 144.
abnuere, 130.
abolere, 144.
abominatio, 3.
Abramides, 176 (bis), 178.
abscidere, 138.
absentia, 71.
absistere, 144.
absolutio, 32, 40.
absolvere, 150.
absorbere, 130, 138.
abstrusus, 106.
absumere, 130, 138, 144.
abundare, 150.
accelerare, 139.
accendere, 139.
acceptabilis, 11.
acceptus, 107.
accersitor (arcessitor), 32, 61, 174 (bis).
accessio, 65.
accessus, 67, 69.
accingere, 139.
accipiter, 88.
accire, 139.
acclamatio, 62.
accommodare, 144.
accommodus, 109, 120.
accrescere, 128.
accumulare, 144.
acerbare, 124, 162.
acervare, 26, 123.
acies, 82, 95.
acquiescere, 128, 163, 174, 175.
actus, 69.
adhortatio, 62.
adicere, 130.
adiectio, 65.
adigere, 139.
adiudicare, 39.
adiunctus, 106.
adloquium, 77, 174.
adminiculare, 130, 164.
adnectere, 150.
adnuntiare, 50, 150.
adolere, 26, 144.
adolescentula, 83.
adolescere, 129.

adoperire, 144.
adopperiri, 15, 19, 176.
adoptivus, 100, 115.
adorare, 139.
adorea, 73, 93.
adornare, 139.
adsciscere, 39.
adserere, 50.
adsertio, 40.
adstipulari, 50, 150, 165.
adsuetudo, 81.
adsumptio, 62, 92.
adulari, 130, 157.
adulatio, 63.
adulescentulus, 105, 118, 175 (bis).
adulter, 41, 177.
adurere, 139, 145.
adventare, 126.
advertere, 130, 139.
advocatus, 32.
advolvi, 130.
aeger, 113.
aegrescere, 129.
aegritudo, 81.
aemulatio, 63.
aequalis, 98, 115.
aequanimiter, 18.
aequare, 123.
aequor, 79.
aequoreus, 101, 116.
aerius, 105, 118.
aerumna, 72, 93.
aestimare, 120, 121, 161.
aestimatio, 65.
aestiva, 41, 177.
aestus, 70.
aetherius, 105, 118.
aevum, 80, 81.
affari, 139.
affatus, 69.
affectare, 139, 150, 165.
affectus, 67, 69.
affingere, 26.
affluentia, 72, 93.
affluere, 131.
agger, 89.
aggerare, 145.
aggerere, 139.
aggressio, 41.
alea, 72.
ales, 88.

182 INDEX VERBORUM

alibi, 168.
alimenta, 75.
alimonia, 82, 95.
aliquantus, 113, 120.
allegare, 131.
allegatio, 41.
allevamentum, 75, 93.
allevare, 131.
alligare, 51, 178.
allophylus, 7.
alluvio, 21.
alte, 167.
altitudo, 81.
alveus, 87, 88.
amaritudo, 81 (bis).
amarus, 103.
ambire, 131, 139
ambitus, 67, 69, 92, 174.
amburere, 139.
amicire, 145.
amictus, 68.
amissio, 63.
amphitheatrum, 86.
amplecti, 139.
amplexari, 126.
amplexus, 69.
ancillula, 83.
anfractus, 83, 96.
angelus, 7.
anhelitus, 68.
anhelus, 103.
animae, 73.
anniti, 131, 139.
annuntiatio, 3.
antesignanus, 83, 96.
antrum, 85.
apex, 41, 87, 96, 174 (bis).
apicula, 83.
apostolus, 7.
appellatio, 63.
appetentia, 71.
appetere, 51.
appetitor, 1.
applicare, 131.
approperare, 139.
appulsus, 69.
aquaeductus, 7.
aquari, 121.
arbiter, 90.
arbitra, 41, 74, 93.
arca, 32.
arctous, 105, 118.
arcuballista, 7, 173.
ardens, 105.
arere, 26.
arescere, 129.

arietare, 121.
aristocratia, 7, 19, 176, 178.
aroma, 32, 86, 96.
arridere, 139.
arrodere, 150, 165.
ars, 88.
artare, 26, 124.
ascensio, 65, 92.
ascensor, 1, 173 (bis).
asperare, 125, 162.
aspergere (aspargere), 139.
asperitas, 61.
aspirare, 131, 145.
Asphaltites, 176.
asphaltius, 176.
assertor, 60
assiduo, 168, 170.
assistere, 140, 150.
associare, 150, 165.
assuescere, 129.
se assuescere, 164.
assuetus, 106.
assurgere, 145.
astruere, 26.
astute, 167
atelia, 8, 19, 176, 178.
atramentum, 75.
attactus, 67.
attaminare, 16.
atterere, 131.
attestari, 131.
attexere, 131.
attinere, 140.
attollere, 140, 145, 150.
se attollere, 145.
attonitus, 106.
auctor, 60.
audientia, 71.
auditus, 68.
aufugere, 140.
aula, 85.
aulicus, 101, 116.
ausus, 69, 92.
auxiliari, 122.
auxilator, 32, 61.
aversari, 126.

bacchari, 120.
ballista, 87, 96.
balsamum, 85.
baptismum, 8.
baptista, 8.
barbaricus, 101.
barbula, 83.
beati, 32.

momentaneus, 13.
momentum, 75.
monarchia, 9, 173.
monilia, 46.
monitor, 60.
monitus, 69.
morigerari, 155.
mulcere, 159.
muliebris, 113, 120.
muliebriter, 168, 170.
multatio, 64.
multipliciter, 168, 170.
mundare, 125, 162.
mundus, 103 (bis), 117 (bis).
munerari, 121, 161.
munia, 89.
munificentia, 71.
munimen, 74, 93.
munimentum, 75, 76, 94.
muralis, 98.
murex, 86, 96.
mutilare, 125.
mutuare, 55, 178.
myrobalanum, 87.
mysticus, 35, 105, 118, 177.

naevus, 25, 88.
natare, 126.
nationes, 36.
navigabilis, 97.
naviter, 168, 170.
necesse habere, 173.
necessitas, 62, 91.
necessitudines, 82.
nectere, 55, 178.
nefandus, 108.
nefastus, 103, 117.
negotiator, 61.
nemorosus, 100.
neocorus, 9, 173.
neomenia, 9, 173.
nepos, 46, 89.
neptis, 46, 89.
nescire, 143.
nescius, 99, 115.
nidor, 79.
nihilominus, 58, 174.
nimie, 17.
nisus, 69.
nitens, 105, 118.
niti, 158.
nitor, 79.
niveus, 101, 116.
nodosus, 100.
Notus, 86.
novacula, 79, 94.
novellus, 105, 118.
13

novercalis, 98
noxa, 74, 93.
noxius, 99, 115.
nudare, 124.
numeri, 91.
numerosus, 100.
nurus, 70.
nutare, 128 (bis).
nutrimenta, 75
nutrire, 160, 161.
nux, 90.

oberrare, 153.
obiacere, 143.
obiectare, 127.
obiectio, 5.
obiectus, 68.
obire, 143.
oblatio, 5.
obliquare, 125.
oblitterare, 126, 162.
obniti, 148.
obnoxius, 109, 111.
oboriri, 143.
obrigescere, 130, 164.
obruere, 136.
obscurus, 104, 117.
obsequia, 31, 177.
obsequium, 46, 78, 177.
obserare, 143, 148, 164.
observantia, 36.
observare, 143.
observatio, 64, 66, 92.
obsidialis, 98, 173.
obstaculum, 80, 94.
obstrepere, 136.
obtendere, 28, 55, 178.
obtentus, 68, 70, 92.
obterere, 136.
obtexere, 28, 176.
obtruncare, 136.
obumbrare, 148, 153.
obviare, 16, 20, 28.
occipere, 143.
occipitium, 77.
occurrere, 28, 178.
offensa, 72.
officium, 31.
offuscare, 16.
olens, 105, 106, 118.
olus, 89.
omnipotens, 113, 120.
operari, 55.
operatio, 36, 66, 92.
operimentum, 75, 93.
operire, 157.
opimare, 15.

ERRATA

P. 115: *compendarius*; read: *compendiarius*.
P. 170: *solemniter*; read: *sollemniter*.

VITA

William Francis Dwyer was born in Hartford, Connecticut, August 5, 1895. His elementary training was received in that city at St. Joseph's Cathedral School and at the Immaculate Conception School. He was graduated from the Hartford Public High School in 1912 and from St. Thomas' Preparatory Seminary, Hartford, in 1914. His philosophical training was received at St. Mary's Seminary, Baltimore, Maryland, from which he received the degree of A. B. in 1916. His theological course was made at St. Mary's Seminary, Baltimore, and at the Sulpician Seminary, Washington, D. C. On January 11, 1920, he was ordained to the priesthood at Hartford, Connecticut, by the Rt. Rev. John J. Nilan, D. D. For three years and a half he performed the duties of the ministry in the diocese of Hartford, being attached to St. Rose's Church, New Haven, Connecticut. In September, 1923, he entered the novitiate of the Sulpicians at Catonsville, Maryland, and became a member of the Society the following June. From September, 1924, to June, 1927, he was an instructor in Latin and English at St. Charles' College, Catonsville. In September, 1927, he entered the School of Letters at the Catholic University, from which he received his M. A. degree in 1929. While at the Catholic University he pursued courses in Latin under Professor Roy J. Deferrari and Dr. Martin R. P. McGuire; in Greek under Associate Professor James M. Campbell; and in Comparative Philology under Rev. James Geary.

9 781258 276690